Britain

at its best

BY ROBERT S. KANE

The World at Its Best Travel Series
BRITAIN AT ITS BEST
FRANCE AT ITS BEST
GERMANY AT ITS BEST
HAWAII AT ITS BEST
ITALY AT ITS BEST
MEXICO AT ITS BEST (in preparation)
SPAIN AT ITS BEST

A to Z World Travel Guides
PARIS A TO Z
LONDON A TO Z
GRAND TOUR A TO Z: THE CAPITALS OF EUROPE
EASTERN EUROPE A TO Z
SOUTH PACIFIC A TO Z
CANADA A TO Z
ASIA A TO Z
SOUTH AMERICA A TO Z
AFRICA A TO Z

Robert S. Kane

Britain
at its best

 PASSPORT BOOKS

Trade Imprint of National Textbook Company
Lincolnwood, Illinois U.S.A.

For Bedford Pace

Published by Passport Books, Trade Imprint of National
Textbook Company, 4255 West Touhy Avenue,
Lincolnwood, Illinois 60646-1975.
© 1986 by Robert S. Kane. All rights reserved. No part of
this book may be reproduced, stored in a retrieval system,
or transmitted in any form, or by any means, electronic,
mechanical, photocopying or otherwise, without the prior
written permission of National Textbook Company.
Manufactured in the United States of America. Library of
Congress Catalog Card Number: 86-72189

5 6 7 8 9 0 ML 9 8 7 6 5 4 3 2 1

Contents

Foreword
The Two Britains—London and Beyond

Go along with the premise inherent in the title of this book's longest chapter—London as "Everybody's Favorite City"—and the capital's role as a British touristic stumbling block becomes clear. The effect of the eternal London magnetism is twofold. On the one hand, it is a principal factor in drawing visitors to Britain. On the other, it is so effortlessly likeable a city that it unintentionally deters substantial exploration of the kingdom of which it is the seat.

The point of *Britain at Its Best* is to make apparent—in the selective, nonencyclopedic manner of this writer's companion volumes—valid reasons for considering the capital as but one segment of an extraordinarily complex whole. I give no more than grudging credit for a day-long junket to, say, Canterbury Cathedral (the region surrounding it warrants settling in), willy-nilly inspection of the house in which Will Shakespeare was born (what about the adjacent Cotswold villages?), even an overnight expedition to Edinburgh (what with the rest of Scotland awaiting).

It is no longer enough to fly the Atlantic to be dazzled by the Crown Jewels in the Tower, the Elgin Marbles in the British Museum, the eerily visionary Blake paintings at the Tate—and fly back. The idea, today, is to begin and end in London. With exploration of the provinces in between. It is long since time to appreciate that British trains are comfortable, British highways advanced, British provincial hospitality—hotels and restaurants of the kind I have carefully selected for inclusion between these covers—exemplary, and—certainly for those of us from enormous North America—British distances relatively short.

There is no longer any excuse for touristic timidity in this land, especially when one considers that some 49 million of the 56 million Britons live beyond London.

Who is to say he or she knows art in Britain without having seen the Italian Old Masters in Liverpool's Walker Art Gallery, the exquisite collection of small-in-size Dutch seventeenth-century greats in the Manchester City Art Gallery, the spectacular Impressionists in Glasgow? And what of the rich caches of paintings and sculpture and silver and porcelain at the universities (Cambridge's Fitzwilliam and Oxford's Ashmolean are but the two most stellar of these museums), and in the municipal galleries of unlikely medium-size cities— Aberdeen in Scotland's north, the Midlands' Leicester, and the Channel port of Southampton, to cite but three.

Unknown urban Britain is one dimension of this nation. Another, the country house, is nothing less than a national phenomenon. In no other land are the doors of literally hundreds of mansions open to a public increasingly curious about the peculiarly British genius at melding the fine and decorative arts, in rural settings of surpassing beauty. Your excursion from London to, say, Blenheim Palace or Ham House, is fine. But you've just begun. What about portraits of early McLeods in Dunvegan Castle, on the Isle of Skye? Or paintings of generations of servants, with poetic tributes by their masters appended to each, at Erddig, in Wales? Or the bed in which Elizabeth I slept, with its original coverings, at Burghley House, near Peterborough? Or architect Sir John Vanbrugh's domed eighty-foot-high entrance hall at Yorkshire's Castle Howard?

The lively arts are nothing if not decentralized. Why not a provocative play at the respected Birmingham Repertory's striking contemporary theater, a sonorous *Barber of Seville* by the Welsh National Opera in Cardiff, the Scottish Ballet as part of the summer-long festival at Pitlochry, in the Highlands? And choirs! Daily at five or five-thirty, in charming Cathedral cities kingdom-wide, their voices sing out: choose Durham or Ripon or York in the north; Norwich or Lincoln or Worcester in the center; Winchester or Chichester or Exeter, in the south.

It may—or may not—be true that America and Britain are "divided by a common language," to repeat the old bromide. The fact is that we've no communications barrier, as can be the case in other countries. We can read the signs and the menus and the newspapers and the legends beneath paintings in the museums. A jumble of accents— national, regional, social-class—notwithstanding—and what visitor does not enjoy the way Glaswegians and Liverpudlians, not to mention Oxonians, pronounce the Queen's English over a friendly pint in a pub?—we comprehend the cabbies and the actors and the train conductors. Conversely, when we have a question—on urgent matters like the location of the loo—answers come back to us in the tongue of our hosts. It is the same we adopted centuries back, even as we chose political separation from a people with whose descendants we enjoy a common bond as we get to know them, their problems, and their achievements, in the course of journeying the length and breadth of their island kingdom.

ROBERT S. KANE

Great Britain
A Mini A to Z

ADDRESSES: British Tourist Authority offices in North America are at 40 West 57th Street, New York, NY 10019; 612 South Flower Street, Los Angeles, CA 90017; John Hancock Center, 875 North Michigan Avenue, Chicago, IL 60611; Plaza of the Americas, North Tower, Dallas, TX 75201; 94 Cumberland Street, Toronto, Ontario M5R3N3; and 409 Granville Street, Vancouver, British Columbia V6CIT2. Head office is at Thames Tower, Blacks Road, London W6. In London, take advantage of these sources of information: National Tourist Information Centre (for all of England including London), Victoria Station; London Tourist Board counters in Harrods department store, Brompton Road; Selfridges department store, Oxford Street, and Heathrow Airport; Scottish Tourist Board, 19 Cockspur Street; and Wales Tourist Board, 34 Picadilly.

BATHS—private ones, that is, in hotels—can be a sometime thing in Britain, even as we approach the twenty-first century. Luxury and first-class category hotels have them either in toto, or almost completely. But in lower category hotels, and Bed and Breakfast guest houses, they can be rare. Baths with showers, in all except the newest hotels (outside of London, especially) are even rarer; and that includes the hand-operated "spritz" showers attached to tubs, and a commonplace in hotel bathrooms of continental Europe. I make a point of trying to advise on these matters in my evaluations of selected hotels in later chapters. Note, too, that washbasins with taps that mix hot and cold water are seldom encountered beyond London. *With respect to the hotels in this book, please note that all rooms have bath, unless otherwise noted.*

BED AND BREAKFAST, the British-created practice of lodging with total strangers in their homes has swept the planet; it has not swept me with it. I'll take a hotel any night. For four reasons. First, with Bed and Breakfast, you don't know what you're getting into. Will it be clean and tidy? Will the mattress sag? With how many others will you share the family bathroom? Landlords register their houses with local tourist information offices and Bed and Breakfast rental services; in the case of one of the largest of the services, houses "are subject to random inspection," to quote the brochure. Which means they may or may not ever be looked over by the reservations firms. Second, locations, more often than not, are residential neighborhoods, not necessarily convenient—especially without a rented car—to attractions that lure us across the Atlantic. Third, private homes are equipped by their owners to be just that—residences to suit the needs and tastes of family members. Hotels, on the other hand, are equipped for travelers and must meet certain standards. Fourth, you have to enjoy small talk with hosts—whether you like their company or not, the while taking a chance on culinary competence in the matter of breakfasts they prepare for you. Still game? Tourist information centers in every town have lists, and you may write British Tourist Authority (addresses above) for its free booklet, *Bed & Breakfast in Britain.*

BREAKFAST, traditionally—along with afternoon tea—the best meal of the British day, is no longer always of the quality it used to be, at least in hotels. At its best—fresh-squeezed orange juice, porridge or cold cereal with cream, eggs prepared to your order (scrambled, fried, boiled, poached), crispy bacon (English bacon, unless well done, is not necessarily to North Americans' liking), well-cooked sausages and/or kippered herring, coffee with some character—there is no better breakfast in the world. But hotels occasionally take to scrambling eggs in enormous batches, and in advance: they do likewise even with fried eggs. Soft-boiled eggs upon occasion may arrive hard, jam may come in difficult-to-open plastic packets—that kind of thing. (Toast now, as always, is served cold, in metal racks especially designed for the purpose. But that is a British eccentricity that longtime Anglophiles like me have long since come to accept.) It is worth my mentioning, at this point, that London's *luxury*-category hotels invariably do *not* include breakfast in rates, while *other* hotels—of all categories *in* and *out* of London, may or may not. Even when breakfast is included, inquire as to whether it is a full (a.k.a. English, Scottish, Welsh) breakfast, or a simple fruit juice, rolls or toast, and coffee Continental breakfast. Still another breakfast point: many hotels thoughtfully include coffee/tea-making equipment in rooms, with packets of instant coffee and tea bags and sometimes even a chocolate-wafer bar, as well. (The far-flung Trusthouse Forte chain deserves commendation for pioneering in this respect.) Add a piece of fruit that you've purchased while traveling, and you've the making of your own Continental breakfast.

BRITISH AIRWAYS, the internationally respected national carrier, began in 1924 as Imperial Airways and has evolved into the airline with one of the largest route networks in the world, flying to more than 140 cities in more than 70 countries throughout Britain, Ireland, continental Europe, the Middle East, Asia, the South Pacific, and Africa—not to mention Canada (gateway cities extend from Vancouver to Halifax). And last, but hardly least, for the purposes of this book, the United States. No other airline has anywhere near as many gateways linking the United States with a transatlantic country; BA's 15 gateway cities are New York, Boston, Philadelphia, Washington, Baltimore, Anchorage, Los Angeles, Seattle, San Francisco, Miami, Tampa, Orlando, Detroit, Chicago, and Pittsburgh. Aircraft? Most transatlantic hops are aboard Boeing 747s and Lockheed L-1011s, with services in First, Super Club (Business), and Economy classes, as well as the premium-fare (First Class plus a surcharge) supersonic Concordes linking New York and Washington with London. The beautiful part of the Concorde is the fantastic rapidity of the crossing; cruising at twice the speed of sound, it traverses the Atlantic in three hours and 45 minutes. Departing on a morning flight, you take off before 10:00 A.M., Eastern (U.S.) time, enjoy an impeccably served multicourse lunch aloft, clear Customs at Heathrow, take the bus or a taxi into town, check into your hotel, shower, dine leisurely by, say, 8:00 or 8:30 P.M., London time, enjoy a full night's sleep, and—on the morrow—no jet-lag. (Indeed, it's the elimination of jet-lag that has made the Concorde popular with regular business travelers to and from London and the U.S.; surveys indicate that 80 percent of the supersonic's passengers are in that category, with 70 percent of those repeaters, who appreciate not only the fast journey, but special Concorde services, including deluxe departure lounges in the U.S., separate check-in, and fast baggage pickup.) Which brings us to that all-important aspect of the operation of any airline: service. I have never not known a smiling, superbly professional cabin crew on a British Airways flight, regardless of the class or, for that matter, the type of aircraft. (And I include domestic services in the British Isles—comprising, incidentally, shuttles, with meals and drinks served, linking London with Edinburgh, Glasgow, and Manchester.) And my hat is off, too, to BA ground personnel—invariably as congenial as they are efficient. (More airlines link the United States with Britain than with any other country. They include—to give you an idea—

Air-India, Aer Lingus, Air New Zealand, American Airlines, British Caledonian, Delta, Icelandair, Kuwait, Northwest Orient, Pan American, People Express, Trans World, Virgin Atlantic, and World.)

BRITISH RAIL operates the world's most intensive domestic rail system: 14,000 trains a day serve more than 2,000 stations, with those of its Inter-City Network the fastest, most modern, and best equipped. The Inter-Citys run at speeds up to 125 miles per hour and are worth knowing about in connection with visits to northern cities like York, Edinburgh, and Glasgow. On all trains, there are two classes—first, naturally the more luxurious, and a not-bad second. If you've any amount of luggage, I suggest first, if you can afford it, simply because first-class compartments are invariably less crowded, allowing more space for your gear. Now, then, which trains? For daytime hops between points on major lines—London to such cities as Birmingham, Edinburgh, Glasgow, Liverpool, Newcastle, or Manchester—to name some at random—aim for Inter-City trains with attractive modern coaches (called "carriages" in Britain), restaurants, and snack bars. Consider also overnight travel—from, say, Edinburgh or Glasgow to London—aboard really comfortable, well-equipped sleepers (there are one-berth first-class and two-berth second-class accommodations), which include wakeup coffee upon arrival and—worth bearing in mind—obviate the expense of a hotel. Plan very carefully for Sunday rail travel; schedules generally are abbreviated on that day. And if you've precious little time to spare for out-of-London exploration, remember that British Rail operates a series of Britainshrinkers—day-long excursions to such points as Bath, Brighton, Cambridge, Cardiff, Stratford, and York that include sightseeing. Not to be overlooked, on any account, is the *British Rail Pass:* it allows for *unlimited* train travel throughout Britain at *really* bargain rates, for 7-, 14-, 21-day, and one-month periods. But you *cannot* buy the pass in Britain; it must be purchased through a travel agent in North America or from one of the British Rail offices (630 Third Avenue, New York, NY 10017; 510 West Sixth Street, Los Angeles, CA 90014; 333 North Michigan Avenue, Chicago, IL 60601; Plaza of the Americas, North Tower, Dallas, TX 75201; and in Canada: 94 Cumberland Street, Toronto, Ontario M5R1A3; 409 Granville Street, Vancouver, British Columbia V6C 1T2). *Train Tips:* Do as many Britons do; take a snack—candies, cookies, fruit—with you. Don't look for baggage porters in stations; supermarket-type baggage carts that you propel have taken their place. (Or do as I do and carry a collapsible baggage-cart with you.) In the case of a city of any size—where more than one railway station is often the rule—ascertain from just which station your train will depart.

BUS TRAVEL: The long-distance bus—called a coach in Britain—traverses the kingdom. Under the British Bus umbrella, there are three principal networks. National Express links hundreds of points in England and Wales (its Intercity Rapid runs feature refreshments, hostesses, and on-board lavatories). Scottish Bus covers Scotland, and Green Line operates within a 50-mile radius of London. Major terminal is Victoria Coach Station, Buckingham Palace Road, London. *Tip:* You have been traveling in provincial Britain and want to reach Heathrow Airport—to make a transatlantic flight—and bypass London en route. You may do so by means of a special bus operated by the Thames Valley & Aldershot Omnibus Co., between the railway station in Reading—a Midlands city to the west of the capital—and Heathrow Airport. Additionally, there is train service from Reading to Gatwick Airport.

CLIMATE: Milder than you may think and frequently drier, as well. Summer (June through August) averages in the sixties, with seventies as highs in July and August, and the occasional scorcher of a heat wave—say, maybe eighty—which throws the kingdom into a tizzy. (Because there is no real need for air conditioning, people feel the heat when it comes—especially British men, who do not wear summer-weight suits, which are usually unnecessary during the summer months.) Spring (late April and May) and autumn (late September and October) are generally fiftyish. Winter (November through March) averages in the low forties, although thirties weather is not uncommon in January or February. Northern England and Scotland can register somewhat lower temperatures the year round. Moisture of some sort or other can appear at almost any time, not necessarily with notice; that is why Britons carry umbrellas as habitually as the rest of us do Kleenex. Raincoats—even in summer, which can be cool—are a convenience, too. This is not to say, though, that "bright periods," as the British weathermen call them, are all that infrequent.

CLOTHES: Dress as you would in any temperate-zone country, including your own. Men will want at least a tie or two and a jacket and/or suit for more formal occasions, like the theater, opera, concerts, or better restaurants; and women will want clothes correspondingly dressy for such times. During the day, in the course of exploration, be as casual as you like. The important difference with respect to Britain and North America is summer wear. There can, of course, be days that are scorchers when men will be glad to have a short-sleeved shirt and/or a lightweight golf or sport jacket of the kind we wear spring through fall in the United States and Canada. But gents do well to have along—even in summer—a sport jacket and/or suit and/or blazer of the weight we wear in winter at home. Women will feel comfortable the year round with wool or wool-blend suits, sweaters, and the like, as well, of course, as lighter-weight dresses for hot days that can also be worn under coats. And, if one's visit is any time from autumn through spring, a wool scarf and gloves are suggested for both men and women. Never, *at any time of the year*, should male or female be without a raincoat and a collapsible umbrella.

COUNTRY HOUSES—specific recommendations appear in the chapters following—are an essentially British phenomenon. In no other country of the world are there quite literally hundreds of rural mansions open to visitors—as much art galleries (European Old Masters, the great British portraitists of the eighteenth and early nineteenth centuries, and contemporary work, as well) as repositories of museum-caliber furniture (much of it from Britain's Golden Age of interior design—the eighteenth century), with world-class architects (the Adam family) and landscapists (Capability Brown) their creators, dating through a range of centuries—medieval through Victorian. To tour Britain without giving these houses a fair shake, even though they often are out of the way and keep eccentric open-hours, is to neglect a significant dimension of British life, the British social—i.e., class—system, and British culture. Many of these estates still are inhabited and operated by their owners from, say, northerly Harewood House, seat of a first cousin of the queen, the Earl of Harewood, to southerly—and relatively obscure—Braemore House, where its occupant, Sir Hamilton Westrow, himself often takes visitors about. A large group of English and Welsh houses—some 200, along with historical monuments ranging from Roman ruins to entire villages—are owned by the *National Trust*, a nongovernmental, nonprofit organization. If your British tour will be extensive, it would be worth joining the Trust so as to avoid paying entrance fees; write Royal Oak Foundation (its U.S. affiliate), 41 East 72nd Street, New York, NY 10021; Trust members may also visit the separate *National Trust for Scotland's* properties at no charge. Still other monuments—including the Tower of London, Edinburgh Castle, Caernarvon Castle in Wales, Osborne House on the Isle of Wight—are among the 560 properties of the British Government's *Department of the Environment;* you may get into all of them with its Open to View Ticket: write Department O.V., 630 Third Avenue, New York, NY 10017.

COURT CIRCULAR is the daily bulletin issued by the Royal Household, as published in *The Times* and *Daily Telegraph* of London, the better to keep us posted on what the "royals"—as their subjects refer to them affectionately—are up to: dedicating hospitals, welfare centers, or schools; attending opera or film premieres; ribbon-breaking at new factories; visiting far corners of the planet; hosting (or being guests at) parties; mourning at funerals. Datelines are among the planet's more glamorous: Buckingham Palace, Windsor and Balmoral castles, Sandringham House, the royal yacht *Britannia*, for the Queen, Duke of Edinburgh, and Princes Andrew and Edward; Kensington Palace (and Highgrove, their Gloucestershire house) for the Prince and Princess of Wales and their sons, Princes William and Henry (a.k.a. Harry); Kensington Palace, as well, for Princess Margaret (and her children, Viscount Linley and Lady Sarah Armstrong-Jones), the Duke and Duchess of Gloucester (and their children, the Earl of Ulster, Lady Davina Windsor and Lady Rose Windsor), and Prince and Princess Michael of Kent (and their children, Lord Frederick Windsor and Lady Gabriella Windsor); Gatcombe Park, in Gloucestershire, for Princess Anne and her husband, Captain Mark Phillips and their children, Peter and Zara; Thatched House Lodge, in Surrey, for Princess Alexandra of Kent, her husband, Angus Ogilvy, and their children, James and Marina Ogilvy; York House, in the St. James's Palace complex, for the Duke and Duchess of Kent (and their children, the Earl of St. Andrews, Lady Helen Windsor and Lord Nicholas Windsor); and last, but hardly least, Clarence House (and occasionally the Castle of Mey, way at the northern tip of Scotland), for Queen Elizabeth the Queen Mother. (A member of the Royal Family who does not normally undertake royal engagements and whose name you will not often see in the *Court Circular* is the Earl of Harewood, first member of the Royal Family to be divorced—the present Countess of Harewood is his second wife—and a musicologist, whose seat is Harewood House [Chapter 23]. He is a first cousin of the Queen, as the elder son of the late Princess Royal, a sister of the Queen's father, King George VI.)

CURRENCY: The pound is divided into 100 pence, written "p." There are 1p, 2p, 5p, 10p, 50p, and £1 coins, and there are £5, £10, and £20 notes. You are still likely to come across old £1 notes and coins of the old pounds-shillings-pence currency: a shilling is the equal of 5p, and a florin—the two-shilling coin—equals 10p. As in every country, exchange rates are better in banks than from hotel cashiers. *Always* have your passport along when you want to make a bank transaction, remembering that the bank-opening time is invariably 9:30 A.M. The banks usually close at 3:30 P.M. Some are open on Saturday mornings, as well. Note, too, that cashiers—even in many first-class hotels—unless as payment of a bill, will not cash guests' travelers checks, even in small amounts, as a simple courtesy of the kind extended by hotels of all categories the world over. (*Luxury*-category hotels *do*, however, extend this courtesy.)

CUSTOMS: Entering Great Britain: If you've nothing to declare, as most pleasure visitors don't, walk through the "green" channel. (If you *do* have dutiable goods, walk through the "red" channel.) If you're traveling with no more than a bottle of spirits, carton of cigarettes, film only for your use, a camera or two, and neither narcotic drugs nor live animals, well, of course, you'll be passed right through— and with a smile. British Immigration inspectors are quite the politest I know, in any country. They convey the impression that no visitors they've ever met are more welcome than you.

Returning to the United States: Each individual may bring back $400 worth of purchases, duty-free. That is allowable once every 30 days, provided you've been out of the country at least 48 hours. If you've spent more than $400, you'll be charged a flat 10 percent duty on the next $600 worth of purchases. Remember, too, that antiques, duly certified to be at least 100 years old, are admitted duty-free and do not count as part of your $400 quota. Neither do paintings, sculptures, and other works of art, of any date, if certified as original. It's advisable that certification from the seller or other authority as to their authenticity accompany them. Also exempt from duty, but as a part of the $400 quota, is one quart of liquor. And—this is important— there is no restriction on how much one may bring in beyond the $400 limit, so long as duty is paid.

DRINKS: The British drink large quantities of beer. The kind closest to ours is called lager, although hotel bars carry Danish, Dutch, and German imports. But the most popular beer with the British is "bitter"—either "ordinary" or "best." Another variety of beer is "mild"; when "mild" is combined with "bitter," the resulting concoction is called "mixed." Popular, too, is the rich brown brew called stout, made by Guinness, and not unfamiliar to Americans. *Scotch whisky* is usually just plain whiskey in Britain, the nationality being implicit.

The upper classes have for long been quite serious—and knowledgeable—*wine* drinkers. Britain imports more sherry than any other land, and Britons drink considerably more sweet port after dinner than do the Portuguese, who make the stuff. They are very big on table wines, mostly French. They call red Bordeaux "claret" and German white Rhine wines "hock." Commonwealth wines are imported too; best are the Australian reds. English *gin* is as good as Scottish Scotch. Drambuie, made with a Scotch base, is perhaps the best *liqueur* to come out of Britain.

Drinking is done in licensed restaurants, lounges, and theaters, not to mention hotels, where guests may order in their rooms even during hours when the public bars of the hotel must be closed. Drinking is also done in the British institution known as the public house, or *pub*, and known also—particularly in the case of those in residential neighborhoods—as the "local." These last-mentioned serve as social centers—for both male and female—for their districts. (Women's lib has long been commonplace in the British pub, where the barmaid is as prevalent as the barman.) Most pubs serve beers of but a single brewery (Ind Coope, Bass, Charrington, Courage, Watney, and Worthington are among the leading labels), which doubles as the landlord of these retail outlets for their product. Some pubs, though, sell more than one make of brew and are called "free houses."

Pub hours are worth remembering. Generally, pubs are open from 11:00 A.M. to 3:00 P.M. and then from 6:00 P.M. to 11:00 P.M., Monday through Saturday. In England, on Sunday, they are open from noon to 2:00 P.M. and from 7:30 to 10:30 P.M. Open hours tend to be more liberal in Scotland, if not in all of Wales, some parts of which are dry the week long, on a kind of local-option basis. There is usually a call for the last round of drinks and the traditional "Time, Gentlemen, please" at closing.

DRIVING: Everybody knows that Britain persists in driving on the left side of the road. But this is worth repeating, should you not consider that, as a motorist, this is a habit you'll be able to slip into without difficulty. Yes, your own home driving license is valid in Britain, and so is an International Driving Permit, the kind you may have used on the Continent, which your local auto club can tell you how to obtain. Unless signs otherwise indicate, maximum speed is 70 miles per hour on out-of-city highways, two- and four-lane ("dual carriageway" is the term for the latter), and 60 miles per hour on narrower roads. In addition, British law requires that you wear your seat belt.

ELECTRIC CURRENT: If you bring a shaver, hair-dryer or blower, or iron, you'll need a converter gadget; U.S. department stores sell them. And you will also need a set of plugs with the various-size prongs to match the holes of outlets in British hotel-room walls (keep your fingers crossed!). The store where you buy your converter will be able to help you in this regard.

GEOGRAPHY: It is so complex a land and so densely populated—there are some 56 million Britons, more than 80 percent of them English—that it is difficult for North Americans to appreciate that the United Kingdom's area—just over 94,000 square miles—is smaller than that of Wyoming, some 600 miles, as the crow flies, from John o'Groat's, at the northern tip of Scotland, to Land's End, England's southwest extremity. Of the three contiguous parts of the country, England is by far the biggest, with some 50,000 square miles; Scotland follows with more than 30,000 square miles; and Wales is a small third, at just over 8,000 square miles. Water, of course, surrounds this northern island country—the Irish Sea and Atlantic on the west, the North Sea on the east, and the English Channel on the south. England is mostly rolling hills, with its northern Lakes District its most mountainous—and most beautiful. Wales is at its most dramatic in the mountains of its north, and Scotland works out the same way—Lowlands are southern and rolling, Highlands rugged and lake-dotted. The two principal rivers, Thames and Severn, are both in England. England's centuries-old counties—forty-five all told—were abolished in the 1970s, and replaced by six metropolitan and thirty-nine nonmetropolitan counties, each of which has subdivisions. Scotland's thirty-three ancient counties were abolished too, in favor of a dozen regional authorities. And the 12 centuries-old counties of Wales have been replaced by eight new ones. But tradition dies hard in Britain, and old-county names are used, as well as new ones!

HOTELS: *About the hotels in this book:* I have lived in, dined in, and/or thoroughly inspected the hotels carefully selected for evaluation in these pages; they are divided into three price groups: *Luxury, First Class,* and *Moderate.* Hotels operated by crack American chains like *Hilton International* and *Sheraton* will not be unfamiliar to transatlantic visitors, nor, for that matter, will *Holiday Inns.* But there are other chains, British and international, for which orientation is perhaps warranted. Biggest of the lot—its hotels extend around the world, some 750 strong—is *Trusthouse Forte,* with 200-plus hotels in Britain, ranging from affiliates of its Exclusive Hotels division, like London's Hyde Park, through to centuries-old onetime coaching inns, like Shrewsbury's Lion. *Prestige Hotels* is not actually a chain but an association of privately owned luxury hotels, most but by no means all in the countryside; their numbers include some of the best hostelries in Britain. *Gleneagles Hotels* is a small but superior chain of legendary hotels, which takes the name of its flagship, Gleneagles, in Scotland. For want of a better name, a select group of what I call *Orient Express Hotels* (operated by Sea Containers, the company that runs the luxurious Venice Simplon Orient Express trains between London and Venice) extends from northern Scotland to the Midlands; its most distinguished hotel is the Turnberry, in Burns country. *Rank Hotels* is long on scene, in the luxury and first-class categories, with London's Athenaeum its flagship. *Thistle Hotels* has expanded considerably in recent years and comprises luxury and first-class hotels at points throughout Britain, including London, where its premier hotel is the Selfridge. *Crest Hotels,* also Britain-wide, makes a specialty of good-value, first-class/moderate hotels, as do other chains such as *Ladbrooke* and *Stakis,* the last mentioned particularly strong in Scotland. *Leading Hotels of the World,* international rather than British, and an association of privately owned hotels rather than a chain, has a number of British members, London's legendary Savoy through to the Cotswolds' charming Lygon Arms. And *Relais et Châteaux,* still another international association—French-administered, with the David B. Mitchell Company its U.S. representative—specializes in distinctive smaller spots; Hambleton Hall, in the hunt country near Leicester; and Chewton Glen, edging Hampshire's New Forest, are two such.

HOURS OF OPENING: Talk about individualists! In no country of the world with which I am familiar are hours of opening less consistent than in the United Kingdom. There is no national closing day for museums—as is the case with Tuesday in France and Monday in Germany, for example. Before you set out for a museum, art gallery, or open-to-visitors country house or castle or ruined abbey, check and *double*-check opening times. And bear in mind that, beyond London, Sunday open-hours can be very minimal indeed.

MONARCHS: After that of our own country, we know British history better than that of any other land. Indeed, I will wager that Americans can more easily rattle off the names of Britain's nineteenth-century monarchs than they can the names of American nineteenth-century presidents. As in my other guides, I attempt to paint just enough of a background picture, with respect to history, chapter by chapter, to make contemporary visits meaningful. Not unexpectedly, the chapter on London—by far the longest in this book—is the most history-packed. At this point, let me capsulize—to the bare bones, for quick reference as you travel—the reigns of English (and later British) monarchs, beginning with the sainted Edward the Confessor (who began the rebuilding of London's Westminster Abbey as we see it and whose reign was followed, within a year, by the Norman Conquest). Years given indicate the duration of each sovereign's reign:

Edward the Confessor • 1042–1066
Harold • 1066
William I
    (the Conqueror) • 1066–1087
William II • 1087–1100
Henry I • 1100–1135
Stephen • 1135–1154
Henry II • 1154–1189
Richard I • 1189–1199

John • 1199–1216
Henry III • 1216–1272
Edward I • 1272–1307
Edward III • 1327–1377
Richard II • 1377–1399
Henry IV • 1399–1413
Henry V • 1413–1422
Henry VI • 1422–1461
Edward IV • 1461–1483
Edward V • 1483
Richard III • 1483–1485
Henry VII • 1485–1509
Henry VIII • 1509–1547
Edward VI • 1547–1553
Mary I • 1553–1558
Elizabeth I • 1558–1603
James I
   (of England, and VI of
   Scotland) • 1603–1625

Charles I • 1625–1649
[Commonwealth rule of Oliver
Cromwell and Richard Cromwell]
Charles II • 1660–1685
James II • 1685–1688
William III
   and Mary II • 1689–1702
Anne • 1702–1714
George I • 1714–1727
George II • 1727–1760
George III • 1760–1820
George IV • 1820–1830
William IV • 1830–1837
Victoria • 1837–1901
Edward VII • 1901–1910
George V • 1910–1936
Edward VIII • 1936
George VI • 1936–1952
Elizabeth II • 1952–

PASSPORTS are necessary for admission to Great Britain and must be presented to U.S. Immigration upon your return. Apply at U.S. Department of State Passport Offices in major cities (look under U.S. Government in the telephone directory) or—in smaller towns—at the office of the clerk of a federal court and, as long as the practice obtains, at certain post offices. Allow four weeks, especially for a first passport (valid for ten years), for which you'll need a pair of two-inch-square photos, proof of identity, and birth certificate or other proof of citizenship. There's a $42 fee (subject to change) for first passports; renewals—also valid for ten years—are cheaper. If you're in a hurry when you apply, say so; Uncle Sam will usually try to expedite. Upon receipt of this valuable document, sign your name where indicated, fill in the address of next of kin, and keep it with you—*not packed in a suitcase*—as you travel. In case of loss, contact local police, nearest U.S. Embassy or Consulate, or Passport Office, Department of State, Washington, D.C. 10524.

PERFORMING ARTS: A young child picked off the streets at random is bound to have heard that London—with New York—is the world's greatest theater city. Its Royal Ballet is also internationally acclaimed. But there are other ranking ballet troupes in the capital, not to mention symphonic and other classical music of the highest order; I go into detail in the chapter on London. What I want to emphasize, at this point, is that the performing arts are distinguished throughout the country—repertory theater, touring companies, cities' own world-class orchestras—City of Birmingham Symphony and Royal Liverpool Philharmonic, to name but two. Opera—Welsh National, Scottish Opera, to name a couple of companies—can be exciting, too. And Britain is a land of ranking arts festivals; that at Edinburgh is the most famous, but there are many others. Look under *After Dark*, in the chapters following, for specifics.

RESTAURANTS: Forget much of what you've heard about British food. With respect to restaurants, London is an all-planet leader, with some serving British food at its best and with others serving the great foreign cuisines. You will no more have a problem dining well in London than you would in New York or Amsterdam or Vienna or Toronto. Provincial Britain? Edinburgh, with its large warm-weather-months visitor population, the hotel-dotted Lake District, and Bath and Brighton probably lead, with respect to restaurants. But there are good—sometimes extraordinary—places to eat in most other cities, and—not to be neglected, certainly if you read this book—in a select number of country hotels. As a general guide, British fare is delicious when it's simple—roasts of beef, lamb, and pork; beef steaks and grilled lamb chops (one of Britain's best food buys, incidentally); game (of which the British eat a lot); fresh salmon, trout, and other fish; savory pies—beef and kidney, chicken; accompanying vegetables when they're fresh and—not always the case—not overcooked; breakfasts (see under B in this chapter); baked goods (cakes [called *gâteaux*, the French term, when they're fancy], pies, cookies [called biscuits], and, increasingly rarely, breads); and the makings of afternoon tea (*please* don't call it "high"—that's a synonym for an inelegant evening meal)—finger sandwiches, the aforementioned sweet stuff, and, if it's a cream tea, a caloric blob of thick, Devonshire-type cream served with jam and the biscuits called scones. Cheeses—Cheddar and Stilton, but also lesser-known species like Wensleydale, Caerphilly, Derby, double Gloucester, and Lancashire—are invariably offered as an alternative to dessert, and, also invariably, they are excellent. As a general rule, it's worth asking that sauces and gravies be served on the side; except in top-rung, British-cuisine restaurants (or authentic French and Italian spots), they can be gloopy and floury. Food-serving pubs (I recommend many on the pages following) make for the most economical, swiftest, and—very often—very tasty lunches. Last but not least, be grateful—all over Britain—for restaurants operated by Italians, French, Chinese, Danes, Indians, Spaniards, and Greeks who, since World War II, have added a welcome international dimension to the British cuisine scene. And with all due modesty, we've contributed our bit. When the late King George VI and Queen

Elizabeth visited the late President and Mrs. Franklin Roosevelt at Hyde Park before World War II, the globally publicized hot dogs they were served were considered by them as Yankee exotica. Franks—and the hamburger, as well—are now, for better or for worse, ubiquitous, the length and breadth of the kingdom. *Tips:* Book in advance or have your hotel hall porter do so for you, in all but the simpler places. And—when you come across restaurants posting signs as participants in the British Tourist Authority-sponsored "Taste of England," "Taste of Scotland," and "Taste of Wales" programs—look for traditional and local specialties featured on their menus.

Personal favorites? Glad you asked. In evaluations that follow in succeeding chapters, I note 19 restaurants throughout Britain which are, in my opinion—based on cuisine, service, and ambience—among the best restaurants in the kingdom. My honor list follows, alphabetically:

Buttery, Glasgow
Castle Hotel Restaurant, Taunton
Chester Grosvenor Hotel Restaurant, Chester
Chewton Glen Hotel Restaurant, New Milton
Connaught Hotel Restaurant, London
Dorchester Hotel Grill, London
Eastwell Manor Hotel Restaurant, Ashford
English House, London
Four Seasons, Albany Hotel, Birmingham
Hambleton Hall Hotel Restaurant, Hambleton
Harveys, Bristol
Homewood Park Hotel Restaurant, Freshford
Langan's Brasserie, London
Le Gavroche, London
Le Soufflé, Inter-Continental Hotel, London
Lygon Arms Hotel Restaurant, Broadway
Milano, Edinburgh
Peacock Vane Hotel Restaurant, Ventnor, Isle of Wight
Pompadour, Caledonian Hotel, Edinburgh

STEAMSHIP SERVICE, transatlantic, is almost—but not quite—ancient history. Cunard Line's *Queen Elizabeth 2* valiantly maintains scheduled sailings—about a dozen per year—between New York and Southampton (Chapter 20), with certain of the westbound crossings stopping also at tha French port of Cherbourg (see *France at Its Best*) en route to New York. Cunard, in tandem with British Airways, offers a good-value fly-one-way (via the supersonic Concorde), sail-the-other (via the QE2) package.

TELEPHONES: What is important to remember, in the case of public phones, is that you don't insert the money until you have dialed your number and hear a rapid *peep-peep* signal. With the advent of the peep-peeps, plunge your coin into the slot, and, when your party has answered, you are ready to communicate. The busy signal is not all that different from our own, albeit a little higher pitched. If you have problems, dial 100 for help; dial the same number if you want to call collect, using the term "reverse charge." Information is 192 throughout the country. Be careful about transatlantic calls from hotel rooms; service charges made by the hotel can be outrageous. If you do call home from your hotel room, make it collect; otherwise, call from a public booth or a post office, unless your name is Daddy Warbucks. That said, let me note a fairly priced transatlantic phone scheme. It's called *Teleplan*, and a limited number of hotels offer it; those of Hilton International have pioneered the plan, which is a service of AT&T.

THE TIME: Great Britain is on Greenwich Mean Time, five hours ahead of Eastern Standard Time in the United States. Add an additional hour's difference each for Central, Mountain, and Pacific U.S. zones. Clocks in Britain are advanced one hour from about mid-April to mid-September, when the country goes on "Summer Time."

TIPPING: Generally, restaurants and cafés do not add a service charge; tip 15 percent. Tip bellhops and baggage porters nominally; likewise, doormen, for getting you a cab. Tip hall porters—that's English for concierge—*only* if they've performed special services for you during your stay. (Handing you your key is not a special service.) Tip taxi drivers 10 to 15 percent. Barbers and hairdressers get 10 percent, or more—up to 15 percent—if they've done a super job and the shop is a fancy one. Barmen in pubs are not tipped for the drinks they serve clients at the bar; tip only for service at tables.

TOURS, TOUR OPERATORS, TRAVEL AGENTS: Agents, first: select one who is affiliated with the American Society of Travel Agents (ASTA) and preferably, who knows Britain first hand. For an initial trip, some travelers are happy with the convenience of a package. Operators making a particular specialty of Britain—whose packages may be booked through retail travel agents—include Abercrombie & Kent, Air-India Tours, British Airways Tours, Cosmos Tours, Esplanade Tours, Frames, Great Britain Vacations Division of CIE Tours, Globus Gateway, Maupintour, Pan American Airways' Holidays, Trafalgar Tours, Travcoa, and TWA Getaway Tours.

In studying brochures, note location of city hotels (ideally, you want to be *central*, not out in the boonies); places *actually visited* (not passed by, on the bus); and *free time* at your disposal, especially in cities. An introductory package behind you, you're ready for return visits on your own—to where *you* want to go, at *your* speed.

VAT is the British national sales tax, a 15 percent levy on goods, as well as services, such as hotel rooms and meals, in which cases it must, according to British law, be included—along with service charges—in quoted prices. Note, though, that with fairly substantial purchases in stores—the minimum was £60 at time of writing but is subject to change—you may arrange to have the amount of the VAT refunded to you by mail to your home address by the seller who provides you with a certification of your purchase, which you present to British Customs (showing your purchase) upon leaving the United Kingdom. At that point, the Customs-authenticated form is posted to the seller who, usually in a matter of weeks, dispatches your refund to you in the form of a pounds-sterling check that your bank will convert to dollars, charging a fee in the process.

2

London
Everybody's Favorite City

BACKGROUND BRIEFING

It may well be that London has always tried harder because it is an island city, physically detached from the larger Continent, and anxious to prove that the English Channel and the North and Irish seas were quite the reverse of barriers to its development. Your Londoner today is neither aggressive nor restless nor impatient. But surely his forebears must have been. Else how would such a great and beautiful and, for long, powerful city have evolved on a dampish, northern island?

Not that London was without certain advantages. A head start for one. And a name that stuck, for another. The Celts (poets then, as now) were calling the place *Lyndin*—a name with a nice ring to it that meant waterside fortress—as long ago as the first century of the Christian era, when the Roman legions happened up from France to settle in. Always better at adapting than originating, they simply Latinized Lyndin to *Londinium*.

There was a brief period, not long after their arrival, when it was touch and go whether they could stay. The Celts' own queen, Boadicea by name, tried to oust the rascals from the fort they had built. But to no avail. Roman walls went up, and Roman laws were introduced. The Roman culture and the Latin language—all had been implanted by the time of the Roman exodus four hundred years later.

There followed that confusing, albeit alliterative, run of the "E" kings—Egbert and Ethelwulf and Ethelbald and Ethelbert and Ethelred and Edmund and Edred and Edwy and Edgar. Until Alfred the Great—no one has explained his refreshingly distinctive name—none of the Kings was especially London-oriented. Alfred changed all this. He chose London as his capital, which was an achievement in itself. But he was, as well, a pursuer of peace in an age when war was the norm.

Additionally, he set his people's sights on education and literacy, first setting up a school for his largely illiterate nobles and, second, ordering translated the handful of important books of the time from Latin—still the literary tongue of his realm—into English. After settling in, he gave London its first proper government.

William the Conqueror's London: London then was the easterly sector of what all these subsequent centuries has been called the City—which continues jealously to guard its independence of the rest of London. Its government was such that with the invasion of England by William the Conqueror in 1066 the City of London was treated separately, allowing its citizens to elect their officials democratically, as they had since Alfred's time. The Tower of London—or at least the White Tower, its nucleus—went up during William's time.

But just before then, William's predecessor and boyhood chum, the sainted Edward the Confessor, had begun personally to supervise the building of Westminster Abbey to replace an earlier church that had been on the site. It was Edward, with his attention to the Abbey at Westminster, who succeeded in transferring the Court and government from the tower area of the City to Westminster—where it has remained for almost a millennium, with hardly a break.

All the while, under later kings like Richard I (who gave the City the Lord Mayor and the corporation form of government it has never abandoned) and Henry III (who built still another Westminster Abbey—the one we know today), London continued to expand, economically, as well as architecturally and politically. In medieval centuries craft and trade guilds became important. Lawyers formed their still-extant—and still eminently visitable—Inns of Court.

The Tudors and the Reformation: At midpoint in the mid-fifteenth century, England had spent a hundred fruitless years fighting to retain her French territory, to no avail. The ugly civil strife with the beautiful name—Wars of the Roses, between Yorks and Lancasters—followed, with Henry VII's victory at Bosworth Field and then the eventful reign of his son, Henry VIII. Political turmoil, war, disease—nothing stopped London's growth. Although Holbein and other painters had to be imported from the Continent, there was no dearth of domestic architects or artisans.

Henry VIII's reign saw Hampton Court erected as but one of many Tudor-style forerunners of later Renaissance buildings. It was Henry VIII, of course, whose complex marital situation led to the break with the Roman Catholic Church and the establishment of the Church of England. The religious schism resulting was to trouble England for many successive reigns.

Three of Henry's half-dozen wives bore him children, and each reigned: the bright but sickly youngster, Edward VI, for half a decade; the bitterly unhappy Bloody Mary, for still another half-decade, which was marked by her disastrous marriage to Catholic Spain's Philip II and a wholesale massacre of Protestant subjects thereafter; and then Elizabeth I—the spinster Elizabeth, during whose 45 years on the throne England became a world power to be reckoned with. Elizabeth resumed the Protestantism of her father over the Catholicism of her half-sister. Elizabeth's fleet defeated the great Spanish Armada of her ex-brother-in-law and spurned suitor, Philip II. Elizabeth's knights— Raleigh was, of course, but one—secured the colonial empire of the New World.

Stuarts to the throne: It was Elizabeth's reign that produced Shakespeare, Marlowe, Spenser, Bacon, and Drake. The Renaissance architecture of these years took its name from the Queen: these were the decades of the great Elizabethan country houses like Knole; of sprouting new colleges at both Oxford and Cambridge; of elaborate formal gardens setting off the manors and palaces; and of design that formed the basis of the succeeding reign. Jacobean—named for James I—is best typified by Hatfield House, the manor that went up on the grounds of an earlier, smaller house where Elizabeth succeeded to the throne; it was followed by the Renaissance style of the remarkable Inigo Jones.

The son of the ill-fated Mary Queen of Scots (whom Elizabeth imprisoned and beheaded), already James VI of Scotland, succeeded Elizabeth as James I of England, the first of the Stuart dynasty. We know him best for his still-used version of the Bible. He ushered in a troubled era. Charles I, his successor, was so disliked by Parliament that it tried him for high treason and then chopped his head off. (You may see a statue of him in Whitehall not far from where he was beheaded.) The bleak, stern Commonwealth of the Cromwells, father Oliver and son Richard, followed—but only for a decade. Charles II (in the company of orange-vending Nell Gwynn—perhaps the most celebrated of his mistresses) effected the spirited Restoration—not as lavish, perhaps, as the contemporary France of Louis XIV, but one that put London in high spirits, completely unprepared for the tragedy of the plague that killed off a third of its citizens, only to be cruelly followed by the Great Fire that razed the whole of the City. A young inventor and astronomer—not trained as an architect—named Sir Christopher Wren, designed a new St. Paul's Cathedral as a memorial to the old one claimed by the Great Fire. A prolific, long-lived genius, Wren designed 150-plus churches, inspiring an entire school of followers, who created much of the London of ensuing decades.

map by palacios

Queen Anne and the four Georges: The Catholic-Protestant confusion engendered by Henry VIII continued, even now, to influence the choice of occupants for the throne, to the point where Catholic James II was booted out, and Protestant Dutchman Prince William of Orange was called across the North Sea to reign with his English wife, Mary, one of the two Protestant daughters of the deposed James II. The second daughter, Anne, followed William and Mary to the throne and had more success in giving her name to the handsome Baroque school of furniture and design that sprouted over England than in giving birth to an heir—or even heiress. Poor Anne, who reigned only a dozen years, was pregnant seventeen times by her rather simple, albeit good-natured, Danish husband, but only one child lived, to die a young eleven.

Anne, like her predecessors, William and Mary, lived away from the center of town, mainly in the palace at Kensington, the state rooms of which are today open to the public. She never visited Scotland as Queen, although the important Act of Union between England and Scotland came about during her reign.

German relatives—the easy-to-remember four Georges—succeeded Anne. Of these, only the last two were especially interesting: long-reigning George III, who, because of his repressive policies, lost England its non-Canadian colonies in North America; and George IV, because, while Prince Regent during his father's latterly insane years, he commissioned a genius named John Nash to build what we now term Regency London. What Wren did for Baroque London, Nash did for the capital of the early nineteenth century, with Regent's Park, Regent Street, Waterloo Place, and Carlton House Terrace. (Alas, "Prinny's" Carlton House—his town palace—is no more.)

The city had not, to be sure, stagnated during the eighteenth century, which saw the construction of Grosvenor, Hanover, Bedford, and Soho squares and which was, after all, the great era of Georgian architecture and applied arts ranging from silver to furniture. Inigo Jones (whose Whitehall Banqueting House is a requisite London destination) introduced the neoclassic Palladian into London from Italy, and Robert Adam later became its chief practitioner. Cabinetmakers with immortal names like Chippendale, Sheraton, Hepplewhite, and the multitalented William Kent created furniture for Georgian houses. Slender-spired colonnaded churches—James Gibbs's St. Martin-in-the-Fields in London's Trafalgar Square is a prime example—went up in profusion. And the style found great favor in the American colonies, where we still often refer to Georgian houses and churches—as well as latter-day adaptations like banks and schools—as "colonial."

English painters came into their own—late, if contrasted with the Continent, but great: William Hogarth, Sir Joshua Reynolds, Sir Thomas

Lawrence, and those other painters of beautiful English ladies and beautiful English landscapes, namely, Thomas Gainsborough and George Romney, not to mention Scots Sir Henry Raeburn and Allan Ramsay.

Victorian expansion: Victoria—a niece of the brothers George IV and William IV and a granddaughter of George III—ascended the throne in 1837 and stayed there—much of the time in mourning at Windsor for Albert, her German-born husband who died in 1861—until 1901. Her reign of sixty-four years was the longest in English history and saw England evolve into a democratic nation during a long, mostly peaceful era. Victorian London is to be seen at every turn—the City is full of the heavily proportioned construction of the era, with its penchant for the neo-Gothic.

But so much else bears the name of that long-reigning lady: furniture, interiors, fiction, and, hardly the least, morals. This was the age when Britain consolidated her far-flung empire, and even the late-twentieth century traveler is not allowed to forget it; my atlas lists nearly three-score Victorias around the world, ranging from the capital of British Columbia to a fjord in Greenland.

Victoria reigned for so long that her portly heir, Edward VII, was sixty when he succeeded, along with his breathtakingly beautiful—albeit hard of hearing—Queen, Alexandra, daughter of Denmark's King Christian IX. His reign was short—just under a decade—but still it constituted an era, and not as giddy an era as we have been led to believe. Edward VII rarely gets the credit he deserves for diplomatic talents. He was intelligent, and his tact and brains had a lot to do with development of the cordial Anglo-French relations that were to prove so valuable in World War I.

Britain emerged a victor from that conflict, and the decades before World War II saw—among a lot else—the very proper reign of George V and the formidable Queen Mary, as well as the first Labour government under Ramsay MacDonald and the abdication that the world has never stopped talking about: that of the globally popular, brand-new-to-the-throne Edward VIII, who became Duke of Windsor, and the husband of a twice-divorced American, Wallis Warfield Simpson.

Nazi bombs—and today's Britain: World War II was Britain's darkest, yet bravest, hour. Following Nazi Germany's invasion of Poland in 1939, Britain entered the war. The coalition government of Winston Churchill led it to victory, although after the invasion and occupation of France in 1940 it fought alone, until joined by the United States at the end of 1941. London—and other areas of the country—suffered from repeated World War II bombings. Great portions of it were blitzed, and many of its people were killed or wounded. No people were braver than Londoners during World War II, and at no era in history were the British and American peoples closer than during World War II and the immediate post-World War II years. Chances are that the Underground platform at which you wait for a train was slept upon by countless Londoners in the course of almost nightly air raids.

The well-liked wartime king, George VI, was a postwar casualty. He died in 1952, and his elder daughter, Princess Elizabeth (born 1926), became Queen Elizabeth II, while animal-viewing in the bush lodge called Treetops during an official visit to Kenya. (You read a bronze plaque to that effect on the Treetops terrace.) Elizabeth and her husband, Prince Philip, Duke of Edinburgh—a former Greek prince and nephew of the late Lord Mountbatten, last British viceroy of India—have four children: Princes Edward (born 1964) and Andrew (born 1960), Princess Anne (born 1950), and the eldest and heir apparent, Charles, Prince of Wales (born 1948), married in 1981 to the former Lady Diana Spencer.

Following the Royal Family on the social scale is the hereditary peerage, embracing (along with their families, many of whose members have lesser titles) 26 dukes, 200 earls, nearly 500 barons, 132 viscounts, and large numbers of baronets, who are addressed as "Sir," as also are knights, who are granted their titles only for their own lifetimes in recognition of distinctive services of one sort or another to the nation. Knights are only a part of the nearly 700 Honors Lists recipients given annually by the government and ranging from titled lifetime (nonhereditary) barons to recipients of the Order of the British Empire and Companion of the British Empire, who are identified by initials following their names (O.B.E., C.B.E.) rather than titles preceding them. Additionally, there are honors bestowed by the sovereign acting without the advice of the government. These include the Knights of the Garter, the Thistle (for Scots), and the coveted, rarely bestowed Order of Merit.

Governing Greater London: London's oldest and most historic sector, the earlier-described City area, has been self-governing, with its own Lord Mayor and Corporation, since it was founded in medieval times. The Lord Mayor is aided in governing by a couple of dozen additional aldermen, 159 councilmen, and a pair of sheriffs—all of whom work with the guilds, or livery companies, whose origins go back more than half a millennium. Out of more than eighty guilds, a favored dozen are officially designated "great"; they carry considerable prestige and include the Mercers', Grocers', Drapers', Fishmongers', Goldsmiths', and Haberdashers'.

The City, which continues to run its own police department (its bobbies have distinctive red-and-white sleeve insignia), is not unlike New York's Wall Street area in that it is virtually deserted by night, with but a few thousand residents, in contrast to the half-million-plus who labor in the area by day—many of them eternally dressed in the traditional dark-suit "uniforms," topped by the derby hats that are known as bowlers in England, and never, ever without tightly rolled umbrellas.

The rest of London is something else again. Its oldest sector is Westminster, the area that developed around the Abbey and that took its name because of its position west of the City. By the late nineteenth century, the London area was a confusing complex of political entities, and in 1888 the lot joined forces as the County of London, to be governed by the London County Council.

Much more recently, in 1965, Greater London came into being, with an area of 620 square miles—extending beyond the old County of London into several surrounding counties, with a population close to eight million and under the aegis of the Greater London Council. (In contrast, the City embraces but one square mile, with a resident population of 4,500.)

Included in contemporary Greater London are thirty-two boroughs, each governed at the local level by a mayor and a council, with the Greater London Council's administration in the hands of its Chairman, who is, in effect, the mayor of the world's largest-in-area municipality—and its enterprises correspondingly greater than those of many UN member countries. The Greater London Council operates out of County Hall, a massive 1920s block on the north bank of the Thames. Its governing body is comprised of a hundred councilors and sixteen aldermen.

If Britain has come full circle in this second Elizabethan era, so has its capital. It was during the reign of the first Elizabeth that the Empire became great, with London assuming international dominance, both commercial and political. It has been during the reign of the second Elizabeth that the Empire has been largely dismantled. The overwhelming majority of the colonies around the world—the invincible Empire on which the sun never set—are now mostly sovereign republics voluntarily associated with the Commonwealth of Nations. Commonwealth countries range from more than thirty old-timers like Australia and Canada to relative newcomers like Tonga and the Bahamas. Most are republics; some remain monarchies governed by their own prime ministers but with Queen Elizabeth II doubling as their head of state, as well as head of state of the United Kingdom.

Regardless of the nature of the association of their governments with Whitehall and the Crown, London remains a formidable lure to

substantial segments of the population of every Commonwealth country, just as English remains the *lingua franca* of each—varied nationalist linguistic sentiments notwithstanding. If the Commonwealth helped
make London one of the most cosmopolitan of capitals, then the
Continent will make it even more so. For within decades of the loss
of the Empire came membership in the European Common Market.
Of course, there will always be an England—and a London as its
capital.

ON SCENE

Lay of the Land: The beauty of London comes through from the
window of one's sedate black taxi, from the moment of arrival; the
campanile of Big Ben and the tower of Parliament over the Thames,
Victorian grandeur and Georgian elegance, Regency terraces and Renaissance palaces. A further glance or two reveals the polished brass
of Mayfair and its glossy shops, churches by Wren and Gibbs and the
cathedrals, department stores unsurpassed in style or luxury by those
of any city, pageantry that is positively medieval in its splendor, bus
conductors who are earthily Cockney, warmly Caribbean, sedately
East Indian. What primarily interests most visitors is the West End
and the City, contiguous areas on the north side of the Thames.

Start in Piccadilly Circus, core of the visitor's West End. Almost due
north is Regent Street, with its great stores. Almost east is Shaftesbury
Avenue, worth remembering because it leads to the maze of legitimate theaters that are a prime London lure and to the foreign restaurants of Soho.

Walk south on an extension of Regent Street or on Haymarket,
running parallel, and you are in the ancient St. James's area. First
major cross street is club-lined Pall Mall, and one walks east on it to
Trafalgar Square, continuing east to the Strand. In just a few blocks,
it changes its name to Fleet Street, at once newspaper center of the
country and the beginning of the original, still separately governed
City. The Strand is as good a place as any to cross one of the many
bridges leading over the Thames to South London; Waterloo Bridge
leads one to Royal Festival Hall. Farther east, the crossing could be
made on London Bridge, with Southwark Cathedral just over the
water.

Return now to where we started, Piccadilly Circus. Walk directly
west on Piccadilly. Within a few blocks, just beyond the Royal Academy of Arts, is fashionable Bond Street. You may walk it due north
until you come to the major intersecting artery, Oxford Street—with
department stores, including the giant Selfridges.

Return, now, to Piccadilly, and continue walking west. On your left
is Green Park. Contiguous with it are Buckingham Palace Gardens

and St. James's Park. Most impressive approach to the palace is The Mall, cutting through St. James's and Green parks and passing a cluster of royal or once-royal residences—St. James's Palace, Marlborough House, Clarence House, and Lancaster House.

Return once again to Piccadilly, walking it until it terminates at Park Lane. Turn right onto Park Lane, following it to the north, alongside Hyde Park into Mayfair, whose maze of charming streets provides the stuff of limitless exploration. Still another park, Regent's, is way to the north of Mayfair. Kensington, where many visitors stay, lies southwest of Hyde Park. Knightsbridge, Belgravia, and Chelsea—all fashionable—border the park, stretching to Cheyne Walk and the Chelsea Embankment on the Thames.

If London is not quite as street-sign-compulsive as Paris, it is way, way ahead of New York and of such Continental cities as Rome. And the signs invariably tell you not only the name of the street, but the name of the borough and its directional (W. 1, S.W. 2) designation.

THE ESSENTIAL LONDON: A BAKER'S DOZEN REQUISITES

National Portrait Gallery (St. Martin's Lane): I often wish that my first destination on my first trip to London had been the National Portrait Gallery. Its concept is such a brilliant one that the Scots have adapted it in Edinburgh, and they do not often emulate their English cousins so obviously. The purpose is to give one an idea of what Britain has been all about, these many centuries, by means of portraits of its leading personalities—not only kings, queens, and royal mistresses, as important as they have been, heaven knows, but politicians, writers, poets, scientists, and musicians. You'll find the works of such painters as Sir Peter Lely and Sir Godfrey Kneller—the German-born portraitist who rose to eminence in Charles II's court—and of later English masters like Reynolds, Romney, and Lawrence, and of many foreign painters, too. A museum folder "intended for the visitor with only a limited period of time at his disposal" suggests viewing these "Six Famous Portraits in Fifteen Minutes": Sir Walter Raleigh by Nicholas Hilliard; Queen Elizabeth I by Gheeraerts the Younger; Henry VIII by—of course, you know—Holbein; Shakespeare by an unknown artist; that superbly gossipy Restoration diarist, Samuel Pepys, by John Hayls; and the remarkably talented Brontë sisters—Charlotte, Emily, and Anne—by their brother, Branwell. Gets you in the mood, sets the stage; that's what the National Portrait Gallery does. And very well indeed.

Tower of London (Tower Hill): If the Tower, to use the vernacular, is not quite where it's all at, it surely is where it all began. William the Conqueror founded it a millennium ago, and succeeding sovereigns took up where he left off. The Tower has served as military citadel, royal residence, political prison, mint, observatory, and repository of royal property ranging from precious documents to crown jewels. Even today the Tower remains, nominally at least, a royal palace under the direct control of the sovereign.

Its Governor has the privilege of calling home the Queen's House, a Tudor mansion in the Tower complex. Troops under the Governor's command are the Yeoman Warders. Their usual uniform is of blue and is relatively somber, but they are best known (thanks in modern times to a gin called Beefeater) by brilliant red, black, and gold outfits, with Elizabethan white ruffs round their necks, that date to the sixteenth century. They are all mature men, for to become a yeoman warder one must have been not only a sergeant in one of the military services, but a recipient of the Good Conduct or Long Service medal, as well.

Major building is the White Tower, so called because it was originally whitewashed. It was home to a long line of medieval kings; they lived on the top floor, conducted business in the council chamber just below, and worshiped in the beautiful St. John the Evangelist Chapel.

See the aptly named Bloody Tower—for it was where the ghoulish sixteenth-century royal murders occurred. Either Richard III or Henry VII was the culprit, depending upon which version of history one goes along with; victims were the young princes, Edward V and the Duke of York. The Crown Jewels repose in the contemporary, subsurface Jewel House. They comprise a dazzling assortment of orbs, scepters, swords, and, of course, crowns, with the range from Edward the Confessor to Queen Mother Elizabeth—or, in other words, about a thousand years. There remains the Chapel Royal of St. Peter ad Vincula, a Tudor treasure, at whose Sunday morning services the public is welcome.

Westminster Abbey (Victoria Street)—or the Minster in the west, as contrasted to St. Paul's and the Tower in the City to the east—is the core of the "new" London, the area that the court, government, and church developed at the time of Edward the Confessor, a thousand years ago. The Abbey is peculiar in that it is not actually an abbey (monks have not been resident since the time of the first of the three structures on the site), and it is not a cathedral (for it is not the seat, or *cathedra*, of the bishop of a diocese).

It is, instead, designated a "royal particular," and it has become, over the centuries, a national history book in a Gothic cover. It goes back to the mid-thirteenth century, and its elongated, splendidly high nave—despite the jarring presence of inappropriate crystal chandeliers that illuminate it and an early Victorian choir screen—is among the handsomest in England. So, for that matter, is the choir, even though much of it is surprisingly modern. There are fine tombs— Eleanor of Castile's is a standout—and there are other corners and vistas that are esthetically, as well as spiritually, moving. Monarch after monarch (including Elizabeth I and her adversary, Mary Queen of Scots) is buried within, and so are poets and politicians and war war heroes, there being a chapel dedicated to Royal Air Force men killed in the World War II Battle of Britain. The fan vaulting of Henry VII's chapel is superb. (It would be even more so without the distracting multicolored flags protruding from its walls.)

But withal, the Abbey comes through, to at least one not infrequent visitor, as too scrubby-uppied, too classroomy, too official. (And, in recent years, too commercial. One may visit the nave without charge, but a ticket is required for the other areas.) I prefer Southwark across the River, or a Wren—or pre-Fire—church in the City. But you must make a duty call at the Abbey; after all, every sovereign has been crowned there—on the Coronation Chair enclosing the ancient Stone of Scone—since Edward the Confessor, save two: Edward V, the boy king who was murdered in the Tower in 1483, aged 13, and Edward VIII, who abdicated before his coronation.

Houses of Parliament (Parliament Street) are mostly—there are significant exceptions—Victorian, and aside from their importance as the seat of the national legislature (a legislature that once controlled the destiny of great chunks of the world's territory), they represent, at least to me, Victorian architecture and interior design at their most sublime. Westminster—or, more officially, the Palace of Westminster—is everything that the Parliament of a great nation should be— awesome, elegant, monumentally proportioned, and splendidly sited on the Thames.

Its oldest component part, Westminster Hall, goes back to the eleventh century. With its beamed Gothic ceiling, the hall still sees service as a conference site and as the place where monarchs and national heroes lie in state before burial. St. Stephen's Hall is early Victorian, a replica of the ancient structure that had served as the House of Commons for several event-packed centuries. The adjoining sixteenth-century cloister with its fan vaulting is visit-worthy.

Parliament proper takes its bearings from the elaborate Central Lobby; Commons is in one direction, Lords, the other. There are galleries in both houses for visitors; Britons get tickets through their MPs; foreigners mostly take their chances by waiting in line out in front the day they want to get in.

The House of Lords has less power than its opposite number, but its quarters are infinitely more attractive. This, after all, is where the sovereign addresses both houses at Opening of Parliament; thus, the splendid throne and adjacent Robing Room. Commons is simpler for two reasons. First is that traditionally the sovereign has never been welcome within its precincts. Second is that it was bombed out during World War II and had to be rebuilt. The result is a chamber done on traditional lines but with near barnlike severity. Worth noting: Members' benches in Lords are upholstered in red, those in Commons, green. Colors of benches in the upper and lower houses of Parliaments throughout the Commonwealth are identical in color, almost without exception.

British Museum (Great Russell Street) is the most marvelous of the catchall museums, abounding in treasures from every corner of what had been the world's greatest empire. What you are getting into is a repository with the following departments, each and every one globally outstanding: Coins and Medals, Egyptian Antiquities, Greek and Roman Antiquities, Manuscripts, Medieval Antiquities, Oriental Antiquities, Oriental Printed Books and Manuscripts, Printed Books (including globes and maps), Prints and Drawings, and Western Asiatic Antiquities.

For me, the single most spectacular exhibit is the sculpture from the Parthenon in Athens—the so-called Elgin Marbles—that occupy the entire Duveen Gallery and are arranged in frieze form. They were brought to England in the early nineteenth century by the then-Earl of Elgin, and once inspected (they take time, but it is worthwhile) one understands why the Greeks have never forgiven the English for removing them. I am partial, too, to the King's Library, a sumptuous early nineteenth-century chamber created to house books of bibliophile George III and containing such treasures as the Gutenberg Bible, a Shakespeare first folio, and first editions of English books you remember from school and college. There's so much more: the text of the Magna Carta, exquisite Japanese scrolls and pottery, the Rosetta Stone, Michelangelo drawings, Indian sculpture, mosaics that go back to the Roman occupation of Britain, massive Assyrian sculptures of human-headed animals. And, if you can, take a peek at the circular Reading Room, Britain's counterpart of our Congressional Library. *The Museum of Mankind,* in its own home at 6 Burlington Gardens, is the Ethnography Department of the British Museum. This museum is visit-worthy if only because it has the finest specimens extant of the art of the old Nigerian kingdom of Benin—not only of wood, but in iron, bronze, and ivory. There are other exemplary African exhibits. Other galleries turn up such delights as Indonesian puppets, Eskimo carvings, Mexican turquoise mosaics, Australian aboriginal bark painting—the lot masterfully displayed.

Hampton Court Palace (Middlesex) is one of the two out-of-London excursions I include among these dozen requisites. The other is Windsor Castle, and it is touch and go as to which is the more historically important. A strong case could be made for Windsor, but I prefer Hampton Court architecturally. Begun in the early sixteenth century by Cardinal Wolsey, it became a royal residence when the crafty cardinal—in a vain attempt to remain in Henry VIII's good graces—made a gift of it to his king, whose successors lived in it through the reign of the second George, in the mid-eighteenth century.

The medieval portions, built by Wolsey and Henry VIII, form the bulk of this complex of quadrangles. But there are newer and equally splendid late seventeenth-century additions, which William and Mary had Sir Christopher Wren design. The public has been welcome since Queen Victoria opened the state rooms, but there are a thousand more chambers which make up into a mass of apartments. They are put to good use as "grace and favor" apartments—residences given by the sovereign to the offspring or widows of favored Crown servants.

Memorable interiors are the King's Staircase, with murals by an Italian artist imported by Charles II; the Great Hall, with a Gothic wood ceiling; the also-Gothic Great Watching Chamber; various monarchs' bedrooms, presence chambers, closets, and chapels; the Wren-created Cartoon Gallery, intended for a set of Raphael works but now decorated with tapestries that are copies of the original Raphaels; immense kitchens (it is easy to see how Henry VIII developed his gargantuan appetite); exterior courtyards, both Tudor and Wren; and gardens, most particularly the Maze, which dates to Queen Anne's time.

Windsor Castle (Windsor) is at once the oldest and largest continually inhabited of the royal residences. It has, despite alterations, retained its essentially Norman facade.

Henry II's Round Tower is little changed from the time when it went up in the twelfth century, not long after William the Conqueror founded Windsor as the final link in a chain of fortresses ringing London; Norman walls remain, too. If the castle's interiors are not as consistent in style as its facade, they are hardly without interest. One may inspect the State Apartments daily throughout the year, except when the Royal Family is occupying them, which is usually during April, parts of March, May, June, and December; check before you go.

My favorite rooms are the Queen's Presence Chamber, with its Renaissance painted ceiling, Gobelins tapestries, and Grinling Gibbons carvings; the eighteenth-century Grand Reception Room—very French and very grand, indeed; and St. George's Hall, a Gothic rectangle hung with portraits of sovereigns who have been members of the Windsor-headquartered Order of the Garter. Exemplary also is St. George's Chapel, Perpendicular Gothic. Hardly to be missed are art treasures from the Royal collections at Windsor, most especially drawings by Leonardo da Vinci and Holbein, among others. The two-century-old Castle Hotel (High Street, Windsor) has a pair of dining rooms and makes for an agreeable lunch pause.

The Castle's neighbor is *Eton College*, the kingdom's preeminent boys' school, where not-to-be-missed attractions are the chapel—Perpendicular Gothic masterwork—the five-century-old Lower School, the somewhat newer Upper School (an upstart dated 1690), a library full of treasures, including a copy of the first printed Bible, and some early Shakespeare folios; venerable College Hall and its equally old octagonal kitchen; the multiperiod Cloisters; and the Museum of Eton Life, with exhibits that portray the background of a school that has produced 21 of Britain's prime ministers.

St. Paul's Cathedral (St. Paul's Churchyard): This reputed Wren masterwork is Protestant Britain's answer to Catholic Rome's St. Peter's Basilica. (Wren had visited Rome on his Grand Tour.) St. Paul's is smaller, of course, but this is not to say it even approaches the intimacy of Wren's warm and charming City parish churches, any given half-dozen of which I much prefer. Still, one cannot dismiss St. Paul's crucifix in shape, with its long nave and monumental dome. There is no gainsaying it is a major monument, nor that it means a great deal in Britain, to London, and, for that matter, to the British people. Its restoration after World War II bombings was an event of the first rank, and so was the 1981 state wedding in St. Paul's, of the Prince of Wales and the former Lady Diana Spencer.

Wren's St. Paul's replaced the earlier "Old" St. Paul's, an absolutely enormous Gothic structure that went up in the eleventh century, was surpassed in size only by the cathedrals of Seville and Milan and was, from all accounts, magnificent. The Civil War and a fire in 1561 had taken their toll, and in 1660 Charles II set up a Royal Commission to deal with St. Paul's. Wren came up with a controversial plan to save what remained. But in 1666, the cathedral was totally razed by the Great Fire of London, and Wren produced several brand new designs, one of which was utilized.

By 1697, services were being held in the choir of the new structure. But if St. Paul's was Wren's masterwork, it was also his greatest trial. A faction of MPs determined that work was not progressing rapidly enough and voted to withhold half of Wren's salary until the cathedral was complete. Not until 1711 was he able to petition Queen Anne, then on the throne, to order that he be paid the arrears due him. Wren himself lived to see St. Paul's nearly finished. In 1714, at the age of eighty-six, he was fired as Surveyor General of the kingdom, but he had by then settled into residence in Hampton Court and made occasional visits into London to inspect his cathedral. He died at the ripe old age of ninety-one and was buried, appropriately enough, in St. Paul's. A tablet above his grave directs the reader, in Latin: "If you seek his monument, look around."

Kensington Palace (Palace Avenue) is still another London landmark with Wren associations—and with William and Mary connections, as well. King William III had Wren make additions and alterations to the place when he took it over in 1689. His successor and sister-in-law, Queen Anne, made enlargements during her reign, as did Anne's successor, George I, who commissioned William Kent to decorate the interiors with sumptuous painted walls and ceilings.

The parklike gardens are lovely (they include the Orangery that Queen Anne had built), and there are surprises within, like Queen Victoria's bedroom and nursery; Victoria was born at Kensington, as was Queen Mary, wife of George V, and grandmother of Queen Elizabeth II. (Kensington seemed to spawn strong-willed royal ladies.) Kensington is the only inhabited royal palace in town whose state apartments are visitable, and whenever I have been there it has been a puzzlement as to how few visitors are attracted to a place so rich in historic associations, not to mention historic decorations and furnishings. And a surprising number of royals still are in residence; I indicate specifics in Chapter 1.

Banqueting House (Whitehall) is on this honor list of destinations for three reasons. First, it is so convenient that you can easily pop in, in conjunction with a visit to the Changing of the Horse Guards at the Admiralty. Second, it is a place of visual splendor, for its designer was Inigo Jones, and the immense ceiling is the work of Rubens. And third, because it was a part of a royal palace, in the heart of London, it is absolutely riddled with royal associations. The Banqueting House was completed in 1622, in time to serve as the spot from which Charles I walked to nearby gallows and decapitation. Later, Cromwell moved in, as Lord Protector, remaining until his death in 1658. It was to Whitehall that Charles II returned after he was restored to the throne, and it was here, too, that the Dutchman, Prince William of Orange, and his English wife, Mary, accepted the Crown in 1689. The palace, Banqueting House excepted, burned in 1698, by which time asthmatic William and his Queen had long since moved to Kensington, with its presumed fresher air.

Changing of the Guard: The British sovereign traditionally has two principal guards that parade to musical accompaniment at two locales. The Queen's Guard embraces personnel of the various regiments of a composite body known as the Guards Division, all of whom wear vivid red tunics and towering bearskin caps, but who are members of the Scots, Irish, Welsh, Coldstream, or Grenadier Guards, each with its own uniform variations. They are quartered at Chelsea Barracks and stand duty at Buckingham and St. James's palaces and Clarence House (residence of the Queen Mother). Additionally, until 1973—nocturnally, at least—they guarded the Bank of England (thus the expression "Safe as the Bank of England"). The changing of the Queen's Guard takes place at Buckingham Palace at 11:30 A.M. daily in summer and on alternate days the rest of the year.

The other guard of the sovereign is the Queen's Life Guard, whose personnel come from among the two regiments of the Household Cavalry—the Blues and Royals, who wear blue tunics and whose helmets have red plumes; and the Life Guards, with red tunics and white plumes. Their functions include serving as bodyguards to the sovereign on spectacular al fresco occasions and guarding—while mounted on horseback—the Admiralty at the Horse Guards, Whitehall, where the changing ceremony takes place at 11:00 A.M. (10:00 A.M. on Sundays). The Household Cavalry live at Hyde Park Barracks in Knightsbridge and can be seen each morning marching through the park to the Admiralty. Still another Guard-Changing spectacle: 11:30 A.M. weekdays at the Tower of London.

National Gallery (Trafalgar Square) is the neoclassic building that dominates Trafalgar Square. It is so conveniently located that I marvel more of my countrymen don't go in. It houses one of the superlative collections of Old Masters, but it is strong, as well, on the French Impressionists. The range, in other words, is European painting from the thirteenth century through the nineteenth, both British and Continental. There are more than a score of galleries on the main floor, with a café in the basement. The Italian medieval work—Masolino's *Saints John the Baptist and Jerome,* for example—is a joy. One sees, as well, Bronzino and Titian, Bellini and Botticelli, among the Italians, who are possibly no better represented anywhere else outside of Italy; Vermeer and Rembrandt (represented by a whopping 19 paintings), among the Dutch; Goya, Murillo, and Velásquez, among the Spaniards. The Golden English eighteenth century of Reynolds, Gainsborough, Hogarth, and their contemporaries is strongly represented, along with later British greats like Constable and Turner. The eighteenth-century French—Watteau and Chardin—are present, and there are many galleries of later French work—Degas, Manet, Cézanne, Seurat,

Monet, Renoir. Once hooked on this brilliant collection, I wager you'll find yourself returning to it on every London visit; I do.

Cabinet War Rooms (Clive Steps, beneath a statue of Lord Clive, at the end of King Charles Street) are as good a reason as any to stroll alongside the splendidly detailed Victorian ministries of Whitehall—a part of town too often neglected by visitors. The subterranean complex—relatively recently restored by, and under the aegis of, the also-too-neglected Imperial War Museum (below)—is a suite of 19 chambers wherein His Majesty's Government, under Prime Minister Winston Churchill, conducted the war between late August in 1939 through to the Japanese surrender in 1945, functioning even during Nazi air raids. You see the Cabinet Room in which a hundred meetings took place during the height of the Blitz. The Transatlantic Telephone Room is the place from which Churchill spoke to President Roosevelt in the White House. The Map Room was the war planners' nerve center. Throughout, designers have placed authentic equipment of the era—bulky, old-fashioned British telephones, chairs and desks, file cabinets and memo pads, teacups and lamps, and even cigarette packs, matchboxes, and newspapers. Churchill's bedroom is perhaps the most memorable of the interiors; on view is the PM's chamber pot (there was no modern sanitation), along with a legend explaining that he so disliked using the pot that he slept aboveground whenever possible. World War II constituted Britain's finest hour of the modern era; a self-guided tour of the remarkable rooms helps explain why. (Unless hours change, the rooms are open Sunday mornings—when just about nothing else in London is, churches excepted.)

ARCHITECTURAL LONDON: AN ALPHABETICAL SAMPLER

Of the great cities, none is quite the delightful architectural mix of many eras in quite the same way as London. Gothic, Renaissance, Georgian, Regency, Victorian, Edwardian, and, yes, our own era, as well; London has them all.

Not everything in my alphabetical selection below is open to the public; some places are only partially open, and some are no more than monuments of interest to passersby.

Bank of England (Threadneedle Street) gives its name—simply The Bank—to the busy City area it dominates both structurally and as the unique bank that serves both the British government and the private banking industry. The bank itself, though mostly modern and mostly unvisitable to the public, retains the one-story, wall-like facade that

Sir John Soane (whose house, not far distant, is recommended on another page) designed for it in the early nineteenth century in neo-classic style. Behind is a modern structure. Only the entrance hall is open to the public.

Bridging the Thames are mostly modern structures. The most famous, the one that was falling down in our childhood nursery rhyme—*London Bridge*—did just that. Or at least its early nineteenth-century successor did. Too venerable to cope with modern traffic, it suffered the indignity of being taken apart and transported piece by piece to Arizona, where it has been reerected, to be succeeded by a more functional replacement. *Tower Bridge* is a charming neo-Gothic structure dating only to the turn of the century, with the Tower of London as a backdrop. *Westminster Bridge*, nineteenth century and nondescript, is highly efficient. So, for that matter, is the much newer (pre-World War II, albeit romantically named) *Waterloo Bridge*. The view is nice when you find yourself crossing it, en route to or from Royal Festival Hall. And the vista is equally impressive for pedestrians traversing *Southwark Bridge*, as nice a way as any to approach Southwark Cathedral, on the South Bank.

Buckingham Palace (The Mall) is, of course, the sovereign's London home and a household word throughout the world. It is named for the Duke of Buckingham and Chandos, who erected it in the eighteenth century, selling it to George III in 1761. George IV had his architect, John Nash, remodel it in the early nineteenth century. Queen Victoria—who eventually took it over as her town house—made changes, as did her grandson, George V, as recently as 1913.

The only parts of the palace open to the public are the Queen's Gallery and the Royal Mews (see Museums). The setting—Buckingham Palace Gardens, an extension of Green and St. James's parks—is exceptionally capacious and little short of inspired, considering that the palace is in the heart of a great urban center.

Should you be invited inside, rooms to see are the throne-dominated red and gold State Ballroom, where state banquets are held and where the Queen conducts investitures and other ceremonies; Throne Room, with its frieze of the Wars of the Roses; Nash-designed Music Room, with a circular dome supported by Corinthian columns; and White Drawing Room—with gilded plasterwork, yellow draperies, and French and Regency furnishings. And there is a chance of a Palace invitation; the guest list for each of the royal garden parties totals 9,000.

Chelsea Royal Hospital (Royal Hospital and Ormond West roads) is one of the anachronisms that make London so interesting. Charles II founded it as a veterans' hospital in the seventeenth century— much like the Louis XIV-established Les Invalides in Paris. It is still another Wren work with additions by Robert Adam, among others. Every year, on "the nearest convenient Sunday to the birthday [May 29] of his Gracious Majesty King Charles II, Our Royal Founder" (as the printed program puts it), the Hospital observes Founder's Day in its splendid chapel. Preceding the services, the Governor of the Hospital, in plumed hat, reviews red-coated inmates at a parade on the grounds. At the Chapel service, there is a fanfare by military trumpeters, and prayers include one taken from the 1662 edition of the Book of Common Prayer, that gives thanks "for the Restoration of the Royal Family." Not every Sunday service at the hospital is so elaborate but the hospital is never without interest. Great Hall and Chapel are open to visitors, and so is the Council Chamber, with portraits by Lely, Kneller, and Van Dyck.

Clubs, mostly for gents, but usually with privileges for their ladies, are a tradition that, for better or worse, the British have exported to distant corners of the planet, not excluding nonwhite ex-colonies where dark-skinned locals were rarely, if ever, admitted, except as servants. Surely a case could be made for the role of the club in the dissolution of the Empire; I shall not forget an unavoidable stay at the whites-only English Club, in preindependence Zanzibar. But suffice it, at this point, to make mention of the locale of a few of the clubs and to admire them their architecture, if not necessarily their exclusivity. St. James's Street, leading from Piccadilly down to St. James's Palace, is the site of a choice trio—the late-eighteenth-century *Brooks* and its also venerable across-the-street neighbors, *Boodles* and *Whites.* Pall Mall—the name is believed to have come from a Restoration game, *paille-maille*—which runs perpendicular to St. James's Street, is almost exclusively clubs—the *Reform* and the *Travellers'*, both by the same Sir Charles Barry who designed the great staircase hall of neighboring Lancaster House; the *Oxford and Cambridge*, with its largely academic membership (and super roast beef and Yorkshire pudding in its restaurant, if you're invited), and a number of others, from the *Conservative* at St. James's Street to the *Athenaeum* at Pall Mall's other extremity, Waterloo Place.

Downing Street, a narrow thoroughfare that lies between St. James's Park and Whitehall, with government ministries all about, is most celebrated for the house at No. 10, which has been the home of Prime Ministers since George II offered it to Sir Robert Walpole well over two centuries ago. Within is the street-floor Cabinet Room. Since Walpole's time, there have been a number of renovations, including one by the noted Sir John Soane in 1825. No. 10 is not the only noteworthy house on the street. No. 11 is where Chancellors of the Exchequeur live, and No. 12 is the official digs of the Chief Government Whip, a not unimportant parliamentary political leader. None of this trio of houses is open to the public, but a stroll past can yield glimpses of government brass and their colleagues, or at the very least members of the press *waiting* for government brass and their colleagues.

Lambeth Palace (Lambeth Road) is an absolutely super Middle Ages cluster. It's the London seat of the Archbishops of Canterbury (the top administrators of the Church of England) and has been these many centuries. There's a formidable gatehouse, an imposing Great Hall, and a venerable detached chapel. The problem is open-hours; double check before you go.

Law Courts (Strand) comprise a splendidly sprawling Victorian Gothic cluster (Her Majesty dedicated them in 1882) and are officially the Royal Courts of Justice. Cases tried are civil and are usually open to visitors; Monday through Friday 10:30 A.M.–1:00 P.M. and 2:00 P.M.–6:00 P.M. Pop in to have a look.

Lincoln's Inn and the other Inns of Court: Lincoln's Inn (Chancery Lane) is a sanctuary of tranquility in the midst of the City: half an hour's stroll through it is indeed a London treat. It is one of the so-called Inns of Court, which traditionally control the practice of law in England and which include resident quarters for member-lawyers, as well as other facilities. Lincoln's Inn (named for a medieval Earl of Lincoln) goes back to the fifteenth century. What you want to see are Old Hall, built the year Columbus discovered our shores; New Hall—late nineteenth century; the library, opened by Queen Victoria in 1845; and the much older Chapel, which was consecrated in 1623, with poet-cleric John Donne at the opening service. Few monarchs have not participated in a Lincoln's Inn activity of one sort or other. And no less than nine prime ministers have been Lincoln's Inn-ers, Walpole through to Asquith.

The other Inns of Court are City neighbors of Lincoln's Inn. *Gray's Inn* (Holborn) is an also-medieval complex. The Great Hall, dating to Tudor times, is exemplary, and so are the library, chapel, and gardens. The *Inner and Middle Temples* (Middle Temple Lane) share the same complex, as well as the *Temple Church* (see Ecclesiastical London). The Great Hall of each Temple is its masterwork.

London County Hall (Belvedere Road) is a nine-story, 1,500-room, nineteen-twenties neo-Renaissance pile, distinguished by a curved colonnaded front. Situation is Thames-front. To see are the octagonal Council Chamber (the council's meetings, usually alternate Tuesday afternoons, are open to the public) and the Members' Library.

Mansion House (Mansion House Street) is the Georgian building that for long has served as the official home of the City of London's Lord Mayor. Its most distinctive feature is a Corinthian portico, from which incumbents watch parades and make speeches. Major public room is the misnamed Egyptian Hall (its design is neoclassic). There is, as well, the minuscule Lord Mayor's Court of Justice, still in session daily, with His Worship or an alderman presiding and with cells directly belowstairs.

Marble Arch is a detached segment of Buckingham Palace that George IV's architect, John Nash, intended originally as the principal gateway. It was not broad enough for royal coaches, so it was moved to a less strategic point some years later. Finally, in 1851, it was transplanted to the site where Park Lane and Oxford Street intersect, where it has remained ever since.

The Monument (Fish Street Hill)—and that is its proper name—is a freestanding column, extending from a point on the Thames's north bank, in the City, some 202 feet heavenwards. It is believed to have been originally designed by scientist Robert Hooke, but Sir Christopher Wren was involved in its construction. It went up in 1671, and its function is to commemorate the horrendous Great Fire of 1666, which destroyed much of the city including many medieval churches, some half a hundred of which were replaced by Wren structures. If you have the strength or the youth or both, you may ascend to the summit; there are 311 steps.

Old Bailey (On the street named for it) is not, alas, very old. The building itself, that is. It is mostly turn-of-century with a dome apparently intended to complement that of neighboring St. Paul's. The business at hand is the trial of criminal cases in this most celebrated of the world's criminal courts. Visitors are welcome, usually morning and afternoons, Monday through Friday. Every so often, officers of the court toss dried flowers on the floor—a symbolic carryover from the time when the court was connected with the infamous (and smelly) Newgate Prison, which stood on its site.

Royal Exchange (Cornhill) is no longer an exchange but rather the home of an insurance company. It's the third such structure on the site and is mid-nineteenth century, with a Corinthian portico (from which new sovereigns are traditionally proclaimed) and inner quadrangle that used to be where exchange business was transacted, but is now the site of exhibitions. The exchange is nicely combined with nearby *Guildhall* (Cheapside), the City's City Hall, going back six centuries, with an impressive Great Hall (the site of major City ceremonies), and an art gallery.

St. James's Palace complex: Sovereigns have not lived in *St. James's Palace* for over a century, but tradition dies hard in Britain and foreign ambassadors to the Crown are still accredited to the Court of St. James. The front facade, looking out onto St. James's Street and the men's clubs that line it, is the old Tudor-era gatehouse of the palace and the oldest part of it remaining. The part of the palace called York House is the residence of the Duke of Kent. Another section includes "grace and favor" apartments, awarded by the Crown to the families of loyal servants, and the Chapel Royal (see Ecclesiastical London). The palace is not open to the public, but its courtyard is and makes for a rewarding stroll. The setting is, after all, the onetime home of Henry VIII and his children, Edward VI, Bloody Mary, and Elizabeth I, not to mention other sovereigns through to the last century's William IV and Queen Adelaide. Ever since, oaths of office have been administered to monarchs at St. James's, including Elizabeth II in 1952, and it is from the palace balcony that, on the death of the sovereign, the traditional proclamation is made: "The King is dead! Long live the King!"

Marlborough House is named for the first Duke of Marlborough, although it was the pet project of his Duchess, Sarah, who commissioned Sir Christopher Wren to design it as the couple's town house, while Sir John Vanbrugh, with whom the tempestuous Sarah had fallen out, was putting up the Blenheim Palace (later described) she came to despise. Marlboroughs stayed on until George IV's time, when the Royal Family took title. After William IV died, his widow, Dowager Queen Adelaide, moved in upon the accession of her niece, Victoria, to the throne.

Later, Marlborough House was home to Victoria's oldest son, while he was Prince of Wales. When the Prince of Wales became Edward VII and moved to Buckingham Palace, his younger son, the Duke of York—later, George V—replaced him. When George acceded, his widowed mother, Queen Alexandra, succeeded him at Marlborough House, and upon the death of George V in 1936 George's widow, Queen Mary, returned to the house she had known as the Duchess of York, remaining there—the place furnished with the fine antiques she had collected, but still with no modern plumbing—until she died in 1953. A few years later, Mary's granddaughter, Elizabeth II, signed a Royal Warrant turning the house over to the British Government, so that it could be converted for the use of Commonwealth prime ministers.

Consequently—and rather sadly—the house bears little resemblance to its Wren period or even to more recent royal occupancies. Still, plasterwork, fireplaces, and ceilings of principal main-floor rooms are intact, and so are paintings depicting the Duke of Marlborough's battles, in the main hall (Battle of Blenheim), main staircase (Battle of Ramillies), and east staircase (Battle of Malplaquet). Upstairs, all of the rooms save an Edwardian smoking room have been turned into workaday offices. Queen Mary's sitting room—the historic one in which her son Edward VIII revealed to his mother and sister his plans to abdicate—is now a steel-and-leatherette conference room.

Lancaster House went up in 1825 for the then-Duke of York. In 1827, it became the property of the Marquess of Stafford, who added a Staircase Hall as high as the house itself and illuminated from above by an absolutely enormous lantern. Corinthian columns support the elaborate ceiling from the second-floor level, and the walls are surfaced ingeniously in *faux-marbre* inset with a series of Italian copies of Veronese paintings. Lancaster House, since 1912, has been the property of the British Government, which uses it for luncheons and receptions. The fanciest post-World War II event was Prime Minister Sir Winston Churchill's luncheon in the Great Gallery honoring Queen Elizabeth II on her Coronation.

Clarence House, just beyond St. James's, is the same age as Lancaster House and is named for its first resident, King William IV, who was Duke of Clarence at the time; it has been a royal residence ever since. Current occupant is Queen Elizabeth, the Queen Mother, who replaced her daughter Queen Elizabeth II, and her son-in-law, the Duke of Edinburgh, as residents when they succeeded her at Buckingham Palace, after the death of King George VI. Not open to the public.

Scotland Yard (Broadway): The "New," which became part of Scotland Yard's title when it moved in 1890 from Whitehall, has never been more apt. Scotland Yard, or more accurately the Metropolitan Police, moved from its atmospheric Victorian building on the Victoria Embankment, to its *really* new quarters—in 1967. To a passerby the Yard looks like an ordinary glass and concrete office tower. But I am told that within are the very latest in laboratories, TV and radio communications, and the noted Criminal Records Office.

Stock Exchange (Old Broad Street) is, along with the neighboring Bank of England, the financial core of the Commonwealth. Securities-market buffs will enjoy the view from the balcony of the trading sessions on the floor, Monday through Fridays, traditionally from 10:00 A.M. to 3:15 P.M.

University of London (Bloomsbury): Overshadowed by Oxford and Cambridge, both of which are centuries older, the relatively modern (1836) University of London is bound to be underappreciated. It has some 36,000 students in thirty-five buildings and fourteen specialized institutes, and its principal buildings are in Bloomsbury, near the British Museum. Built with a Rockefeller foundation grant in the nineteen-twenties, they were dedicated by George V in 1933 and include the 210-foot-high Tower, a library of 900,000 volumes, and the Senate House, for administration. There are two first-rank museums, later recommended: Courtauld Institute and Percival David Foundation of Chinese Art. University College, older than the University of London, of which it is now a part, goes back to 1828 and has its own home on Gower Street. It has some 5,000 students in a number of faculties, including the Slade School of Art. Also on Gower Street are the globally renowned London School of Tropical Medicine and Royal Academy of Dramatic Art.

LONDON CHURCHES: AFTER THE ABBEY AND ST. PAUL'S

Next to Rome, London is Europe's greatest church city, surpassing Paris and, indeed, all of the other European capitals. Norman (the British way of saying Romanesque), Gothic, Renaissance, Baroque, even a cathedral in Byzantine style: London has them all.

A Dozen-Plus All-London Standouts

Southwark Cathedral (London Bridge) does not attempt to compete with Westminster Abbey, although perhaps it should. Across the river, in South London, it was antedated by an earlier Norman church, but its more or less present Gothic look dates from the twelfth through the fifteenth centuries, when the elaborate choir and the fine transepts were constructed. The high nave is actually Victorian. Although Southwark has been a cathedral or, in other words, the seat of a bishop in charge of a diocese, only since the turn of the present century, it is not without a rich history. During the unhappy reign of Henry VIII's elder daughter, the Catholic Bloody Mary, Protestant martyrs were tried in Southwark. James VI was married there, and John Harvard, founder of the American university bearing his name, was baptized there (the Harvard Chapel of the Cathedral honors him).

Westminster Cathedral (Ashley Place): There are some six million Roman Catholics in Britain, and enough of them live in and around London for it to constitute an archdiocese headed by an archbishop of cardinal's rank, whose seat is turn-of-the-century Westminster Cathedral. This Byzantine beauty is London's least-known major church, and more's the pity. Although the cathedral opened in 1903, it still is not completed. Only half of the dozen chapels that ring the nave are decorated with the mosaics intended for them. Length is 360 feet. The nave is 117 feet high, and the campanile (to which, please note, there is an elevator to take visitors to an observation tower that affords a smashing view of London) is 273 feet high. Capacity is 2,000, all seated and able to see the sumptuous high altar, over which, suspended from the ceiling, is an immense red and gold cross.

St. Bartholomew the Great (West Smithfield) is essentially Romanesque and, except for St. John the Evangelist Chapel in the Tower of London, the oldest in town. It is a neighbor of both St. Bartholomew's Hospital (the oldest in London) and the smaller St. Bartholomew the Less Church. St. Bartholomew the Great goes back to the early twelfth century, and, although much of it was destroyed at the time of the Reformation, enough remains—the masterful choir, part of the nave, and other architectural treasures—to make the church one of the first rank. An all-Britain standout.

St. Margaret's Westminster (Parliament Square), is, because it is part of the Westminster Abbey complex, overshadowed by the Abbey. But it has been the official church of the House of Commons for four of its ten centuries, and, perhaps even more significant to readers of society pages, it is the venue for fashionable weddings; St. Margaret's bridegrooms have included Samuel Pepys, John Milton, and Sir Winston Churchill.

Brompton Oratory (Brompton Road) is, like Westminster Cathedral, Catholic and is, again like Westminster Cathedral, of a refreshingly uncommon-to-London style. You have the not unpleasant feeling, on an oratory visit, that you're in Rome or Florence. It is a late nineteenth-century variation of Italian Renaissance noted for its music.

Chapel Royal of St. James's Palace (Pall Mall) is the only part of the palace open to the public and then only for Sunday services. Its chef d'oeuvre is the ceiling, which Holbein is believed to have painted and which shows easily discernible royal initials—"H" for Henry VIII and "A" believed to stand for Anne of Cleves, Wife No. 4, to whom Henry was married in 1540, the date appearing on the ceiling. Other queens were married in the chapel, too, not least among them being Victoria, three centuries to the year after Anne and Henry.

Queen's Chapel, Marlborough House (Pall Mall) is a lovely Inigo Jones work named for Queen Henrietta Maria, wife of Charles I, who inaugurated it. Choir boys' gowns are as they have been for centuries and the royal pews are original.

Chapel Royal of St. Peter ad Vincula, in the Tower of London (Tower Hill), is the oldest of England's chapels royal, dating to the twelfth century, and where many sovereigns worshiped, including two—Queen Anne Boleyn and Queen Catherine Howard—just before they were executed. The Gothic look of the place remains. The choir's musical skills are esteemed; visitors are welcome at Sunday services and do not have to pay the usual Tower admission fee.

Chelsea Royal Hospital Chapel (Royal Hospital Road), like the hospital itself, was designed by Wren, with its chief decorative element a massive mural called *The Last Muster.* A Sunday service—with the pensioners in their traditional uniform and the choir in equally old-style vestments—is a treat.

Guards' Chapel, Wellington Barracks (Birdcage Walk), is essentially post-World War II, for the beautiful original was badly bombed. Some of the old remains, though, and there is always music by one of the various Guards' regiment bands at Sunday services to which visitors are welcome.

Temple Church (Temple) is the place of worship shared by the Inner Temple and the Middle Temple, two of the four London Inns of Court. It goes back some eight hundred years, combining Gothic and Romanesque features impressively, with a chancel of the former period appended to the original round church of the latter.

All Souls' (Langham Place at Regent Street) was designed by John Nash, the Regency architect. It was war-damaged but the restoration is commendable, and the interior is quite as handsome as the near-circular exterior is distinctive.

St. Peter's (Eaton Square) is one to have a look at when you are inspecting Belgravia. A landmark of rectangular Eaton Square, it is a late nineteenth-century neoclassic structure, understandably popular for *haute monde* weddings.

St. Mary Abbots (Kensington High Street) is an oasis of quiet and beauty in the heart of Kensington. It is Victorian Gothic, with an unusually tall spire (278 feet) and, among other attributes, an unusual cloistered walkway. Pop in for a rest, while doing the Kensington shops.

Ten by Wren

Aside from the earlier-recommended St. Paul's, Sir Christopher Wren designed more than fifty seventeenth-century London churches, most in the City. By no means all have survived World War II intact; of some, only towers or less remain. Others have been beautifully restored. What follows are ten Wren churches that I especially like; *do take in any others that you pass by;* the City ones all feature weekday lunchtime services and concerts, and every single one is a jewel. Only the first is not in the City.

St. James's (Piccadilly): Devastation during World War II was almost complete. The restoration, with the exception of an unfortunate Victorian stained glass window behind the altar, has been first-rate, with the glorious arched ceiling as it was and the baroque organ rebuilt (Grinling Gibbons carved the gilt cherubs atop it). Visit the worth-knowing-about café, convenient for casual lunches.

St. Bride's (Fleet Street) is a restoration of a Wren church that was the eighth on the site and below which has been found the remains of a Roman house. St. Bride's worshipers have included Chaucer, Shakespeare, Milton, Evelyn, and Pepys. The restoration was made possible by contributions from Fleet Street newspaper neighbors. But the American press has a soft spot for St. Bride's, too. Among the memorial plaques is one given to honor U.S. journalists who lost their lives in the course of their work abroad, by the Overseas Press Club of America, through the efforts of a colleague and friend of mine, the late Madeline Dane Ross.

St. Clement Danes (Strand) is, like later-described St. Mary-le-Strand, on an island in the Strand. It is less harrowing to reach, however. Post-World War II restoration was brilliant, and in the process the Royal Air Force adopted the church as its official place of worship. This is the church of "Oranges and Lemons say the bells of St. Clemens," and the nursery rhyme is commemorated annually at a youngsters' service. Withal, the interior is what makes it most stand out—pulpit, painted reredos, U.S. Air Force-donated organ, and ceiling supported by Corinthian columns.

St. James Garlickhythe (Upper Thames Street) seems dwarfed by its substantial steeple and is a surprise within, for its ceiling is the highest of any in the City. Decor is elegantly simple. Hythe, I learned from the verger, used to mean cove—a place where ships tied up and, in this instance, one assumes, where their chief cargo was garlic.

St. Lawrence Jewry (Gresham Street), so named because of its situation in an ancient ghetto quarter, is extra-substantial Wren, in keeping with its designation as the official church of the Corporation, or Council, of the City of London. Its lengthy rectangular interior is accented by a series of handsome brass chandeliers, splendid plasterwork, and typical dark-wood pews, altar, and organ. The City's landmark, Guildhall, is next door. A dazzler.

St. Mary Abchurch (Abchurch Lane off Cannon Street) is distinguished by a painted dome that dominates the squarish interior, contrast coming from white walls and the dark wood of the superb Grinling Gibbons-carved altar.

St. Benet, Paul's Wharf (Upper Thames Street), has a graceful exterior, with garlands of stone atop each clear-paned window. Within, the feeling is one of great height. Ceiling plasterwork is exceptional. If you don't understand the language being spoken, fear not. Services are conducted in Welsh.

St. Mary-le-Bow (Cheapside) is oddly Italianate Wren—light walls and ceilings are of a piece. A great gold crucifix hangs from the ceiling. Floors are black and white marble. The feeling is of luxuriant space. There is a Norman crypt.

St. Mary Aldermary (Watling Street) is a Wren shocker, the master in a Gothic mood; and it works, if one overlooks a bit of well-meant Victorian gussying up. Wren's ceiling is his version of Gothic fan vaulting. There are side aisles framed by Gothic arches, and the other Wren-Gothic touches are charming, too.

St. Stephen Walbrook (Walbrook) is another Italianate Wren, with a series of sixteen columns lining the inside of the oblong interior and framing an immense coffered dome. Oddly, somewhat heavily handsome—but with style.

A Quartet by James Gibbs

James Gibbs's output in the first half of the eighteenth century embraced ten London churches, not to mention important work at both

Cambridge and Oxford. He was later than Wren and was obviously influenced by that master, with the result handsomely and typically Georgian. Gibbs's work in turn inspired countless designers of the steepled churches that became a commonplace of colonial America.

St. Martin-in-the-Fields (Trafalgar Square) was completed by Gibbs in 1726, and George I was its first church warden. His coat of arms remains in the church above the chancel arch. To this day, St. Martin's is the sovereign's parish church. It is, as well, the official church of the Admiralty. (There are both Royal and Admiralty pews.) There is a sumptuous gilded and cream ceiling, supported by rows of Corinthian columns. The pulpit has Grinling Gibbons carving.

Grosvenor Chapel (South Audley Street) is just off Grosvenor Square, site of the American Embassy and for that reason a gathering place for many Americans during World War II; a plaque within records the special American association.

St. Mary-le-Strand (Strand) is, rather ingeniously, built upon an island in one of London's most horrendously traffic-filled thoroughfares, so that by the time you are able to cross the street to gain admittance, you feel constrained to offer thanks in the church for having arrived safely, at the same time praying that you will be able to make an equally safe exit from the little island to the across-the-street sidewalk. Within, a gilded ceiling shelters a neoclassic interior. En route out, before you step into that traffic, look up at the handsome white steeple.

St. Peter's (Vere Street) is another small Gibbs treasure and still substantially Georgian. St. Peter's, completed in 1724, antedated St. Martin-in-the-Fields and is a kind of St. Martin in miniature.

Additional, Mostly Anglican Churches

St. Etheldreda's (Ely Place) is the first pre-Reformation church to be returned from Anglican to Roman Catholic jurisdiction and stands in a little-visited City cul-de-sac. It is a Gothic treasure, well restored after World War II. The west window, originally fourteenth century, is said to be one of the biggest in all London. There are, as well, a little cloister and a crypt.

St. Olave, Hart Street (off Fenchurch Street), is a beautiful Gothic church entered through its own well-enclosed yard (the benches are nice for a rest on a busy sightseeing day). The building is essentially fifteenth century—with stone walls, Gothic arched windows and aisles, and a beamed ceiling. Mr. and Mrs. Samuel Pepys were members of the parish (there is a bust of Mrs. Pepys erected by her husband).

St. Helen's, Bishopsgate (Bishopsgate), is another basically Gothic church. It is more elaborate than St. Olave, with Renaissance pieces and additions from other eras, even including a Victorian screen. The flattish timbered roof evokes medieval times; so, for that matter, does the church as a whole, its more modern appurtenances notwithstanding.

St. Dunstan-in-the-West (Fleet Street) is early nineteenth-century neo-Gothic, with a winning octagonal shape, a wedding-cake tower, and an interior more comfortable and inviting than distinguished. Agreeable for a pause after, say, Dr. Johnson's House, in nearby Gough Square.

St. Botolph Without Aldgate (Aldgate High Street): Botolph, the patron saint of English travelers, a kind of U.K. St. Christopher, was English-born (seventh century) and so popular that in the City alone are three churches named for him, two with locations so similar-sounding that they can be confusing. (One is at Bishopsgate, but the other two are at Aldersgate and Aldgate.) All three are of interest, but I have selected Aldgate; it's mostly mid-eighteenth century and high-ceilinged, with Doric columns for support.

Other London Places of Worship

Bloomsbury Central Baptist Church, Shaftesbury Avenue; *First Church of Christ Scientist*, Sloane Terrace; *Westminster Congregational Chapel*, Buckingham Gate, Westminster; *West London Synagogue* (Reformed), Upper Berkeley Street; *Central Synagogue* (Orthodox), Great Portland Street; *St. Anne and St. Agnes Lutheran Church* (seventeenth century), Gresham Street; *John Wesley's Chapel* (Methodist, built in 1778), City Road; *Regent Square Presbyterian Church*, Regent Square; *St. Sophia Cathedral* (Greek Orthodox), Moscow Road; *Westminster Friends Meeting House*, St. Martin's Lane; *Salvation Army Regent Hall*, Oxford Street; *Spiritualist Association*, Belgrave Square; *Hindu Center*, Grafton Terrace; *Central Mosque*, Park Road; *Sikh Temple*, Sinclair Road; *Buddhist Society*, Eccleston Square.

MUSEUMGOER'S LONDON: TWO DOZEN FAVORITES

The British Museum, perhaps more than any other, reflects the acquisitions made available to a major imperial power. It, the National Gallery, and the National Portrait Gallery—the last-mentioned because it sets the stage for London—are among my earlier Top Ten London attractions. But they are only a starter, for museums. I have selected an additional 24 museums that I especially like.

Tate Gallery (Millbank) is outstanding for its specialties. British painting from the Renaissance onward and modern work from the Impressionists through to, say, last week. In the superlative English section, there are fine Hogarths, Gainsboroughs, and Reynoldses. But the star of the Tate is J. M. W. Turner, the early nineteenth-century English painter who was a good half-century ahead of his time and who is better represented at this museum than at any other. There are exceptionally strong Constable and Blake sections, too, fine French works, and frequently excellent short-term exhibits. The museum building is attractive and a joy to explore. In a word, one of Europe's most important collections.

Victoria and Albert Museum (Cromwell Road)—the "V and A" to Londoners—is a unit of the group of South Kensington museums devised by Prince Albert, after his Great Exhibition of 1851. Victoria herself laid the cornerstone in 1899, not long before she died; her son, Edward VII, opened the building in 1909—not long before he died. The V and A is a great repository of British *and* Continental decorative and fine arts. Emphasis is on European work from the Middle Ages onward. Not unexpectedly, English furniture and furnishings are particularly strong. But there are treasures ranging from paintings by Raphael to Renaissance ship models of solid gold. Not-to-be-missed exhibits are the room settings—a room from Clifford's Inn, London, of the seventeenth century; a room from Henrietta Place, London, designed by James Gibbs; a room from a house in Hatton Garden, London, of the eighteenth century; the music room from Norfolk House, London, the work of James Wyatt; another chamber by Robert Adam; a Regency room of Thomas Hope; and other settings illustrating the contribution of designers ranging from exuberant William Kent to restrained William Morris.

Courtauld Institute Galleries (Woburn Square) is one of London's—and all Europe's—best-kept museum surprises. A unit of the University of London and with a Bloomsbury location near the British Museum, the Courtauld—one floor up in a nondescript building via an enormous and rather creaky self-service elevator—is an absolute treasure. There are three major collections. Best known is of Impressionists and post-Impressionists—the collection of the late Samuel Courtauld, an industrialist. Manet's *A Bar at the Folies-Bergère* in itself makes a visit worthwhile. But consider also Toulouse-Lautrec's *La*

Chambre Separée, Monet's *Vase de Fleurs,* Renoir's *La Loge,* and Gauguin's *Haymaking.* Old Masters include rich Italian representation— Botticelli, Bellini, Veronese, Tintoretto, for example—but other painters' work, too. I particularly like the Cranach *Adam and Eve* and a lady called Mrs. Malcolm painted by Sir Henry Raeburn.

Buckingham Palace museums (Buckingham Palace Road): British sovereigns can be excused not opening their London home to the public; none in Europe, save the Swedish monarchs, open the town palaces they live in to visitors. Still, if Buckingham proper is not open to the public, two parts of it are. The first and more visited of the two is the *Queen's Gallery,* occupying part of a former chapel and entered from Buckingham Palace Road. Space being relatively small, the exhibition policy is eminently sound. There is no permanent exhibit. Rather, the show changes once or twice a year and consists of groupings of works from Her Majesty's priceless private collections, the range Old Masters to royal portraits. Not to be missed.

The other Palace museum, the *Royal Mews,* is entered by its own impressive gateway, also on Buckingham Palace Road. This is Her Majesty's stables, with which are incorporated a museum of royal coaches. There are other coach museums in Europe—those of Lisbon and Munich's Nymphenburg Palace come to mind. What makes the Mews unique is that the coaches, most of them at least, are still in use when the occasion demands—the Gold State Coach, for example, dates from George III's reign and still is used at coronations. The Irish State Coach goes to work every year when the sovereign opens Parliament. The State Landau is used regularly when Queen Elizabeth fetches visiting foreign heads of state from railway stations. There are a lot more, and there are, as well, the comfortably housed royal horses, the corps of coachmen and grooms who headquarter here, and historic photographs of monarchs or their families atop the backs of their steeds.

Wallace Collection (Manchester Square) occupies Hertford House, eighteenth-century dwelling of the Dukes of Manchester. It has an ambience not unlike that of New York's Frick Collection, except that Hertford House gives the impression of having been considerably more lived in. The Wallace Collection was a gift to the British people from the widow of Sir Richard Wallace who, with his ancestors, had collected it mostly in France. Baroque paintings are the chief lure— the great Dutch and Flemish artists are all present, Rembrandt and Steen, Rubens and Van Dyck. But the French—Boucher, Fragonard, Watteau—are big—eighteenth century mainly. And so are Spaniards like Murillo and Velázquez; and the English—like Gainsborough,

Reynolds, and Romney. Painting is only part of the collection; there is armor, for example, and eighteenth-century French furniture.

Museum of London (The Barbican) is a repository of Londoniana through the ages. You start with the prehistoric era, continue through the Dark Ages, the formative period of Roman London, or Londinium, and continue on through medieval, Tudor, later-Renaissance, Georgian, Regency, Victorian-Edwardian, and contemporary London, the last represented by, among other objects, Queen Elizabeth II's coronation robe. There are ancient coins, precious glass, furniture (including the bed slept in by King James II and his alliteratively named Queen, Mary of Modena), and a Victorian fire engine. Setting is a boldly contemporary pavilion, with access by a series of ramps and walkways from the street.

Sir John Soane's Museum (13 Lincoln's Inn Fields) is where the prolific architect lived the last quarter-century (1813–37) of a long life. The setting is an eighteenth-century City square, and the house was designed by Sir John as both home and museum. Contents include an astonishing variety of art and antiques: Roman relics, Egyptian works, Greek sculpture, Italian art, and other paintings—England's Turner, as well as Venice's Canaletto, not to mention a Lawrence of Sir John himself. Most fascinating are two Hogarth series—*The Election* and *The Rake's Progress*. They are explained in detail by a resident guard, standing before a prominent wall sign directing visitors not to tip their lecturer. There will *indeed* always be an England.

Wellington Museum (Apsley House, Hyde Park Corner) was the first Duke of Wellington's London home. Robert Adam was the original designer. Most remarkable single exhibit is in the dining room—a service of silver plate from the Regent of Portugal, which took well over a hundred silversmiths several years to create. The entrance hall catches one up with its larger-than-life statue of Napoleon clad in a fig leaf. There are other similarly eccentric treasures. Then one moves along to the house's oddly uncelebrated treasures: its paintings. Fact of the matter is that Apsley House shelters a major London collection: Italians, including Correggio, Basaano, and Pannini; Spaniards, including Velásquez, Murillo, and a Goya of the first Duke of Wellington; Flemings, like Rubens and Teniers; Dutchmen, including Steen and de Hooch; and Britons, including Reynolds and still another Ducal portrait by Lawrence.

The Greenwich complex: Greenwich first comes up in history as Placentia Palace, the very same in which Henry VIII lived and where his daughter, Queen Elizabeth I, was born. Later, during the reign of William and Mary, Sir Christopher Wren was commissioned by the Crown to design a naval hospital, now the *Royal Naval College*. Utilizing the position of the earlier Inigo Jones-designed Queen's House—inland from the Thames—as a focal point, Wren created two grand colonnades leading to and framing in the background the Queen's House and doubling as walls of the pair of domed blocks that constitute hospital-cum-college. Because the college remains very much in business, with midshipmen inhabiting it, its two great interiors traditionally may be seen only in the afternoon.

Worth seeing are the college's *Painted Hall* (with murals on walls and ceiling by Sir James Thornhill), which is now the midshipmen's dining room; and the *Chapel*, with a blue-and-gold ceiling and a celebrated painting of St. Paul, by Benjamin West, behind the altar.

Earlier-mentioned *Queen's House* is now but one of the three principal sectors of the *National Maritime Museum:* ships models and plans, navigational instruments, naval weapons and uniforms, and paintings of exceptional caliber. Personal favorites: Elizabeth I, by an unidentified genius; Charles I, by the studio of Daniel Luytens; Queen Henrietta Maria, by Van Dyck; Nelson, by L. F. Abbott; Lady Hamilton, by Romney.

There are other Greenwich attractions: Wren-designed Flamsteed, the original *Royal Observatory* building, outside which is the Greenwich Meridian-Longitude Zero, marked across the observatory's courtyard. Nearby is the venerable sailing vessel, *Cutty Sark* (the Scotch whisky was named for it, not vice versa). In Greenwich is a charmer of a church, *St. Alfege*, the work of Wren's assistant, Nicholas Hawksmoor, built during the reign of Queen Anne, who insisted that the church contain a royal pew. Lunch at the Trafalgar Tavern, whose special lures are mementos of Lord Nelson.

Royal Academy of Arts (Burlington House, Piccadilly) is housed in a mid-nineteenth-century palazzo that has become a Piccadilly landmark. It's been staging annual summer shows for more than two centuries; there are, as well, special exhibits, which can be of extraordinary caliber. Membership is selected through a complicated process. Sir Joshua Reynolds was the first president; Sir Christopher Wren was one of his successors. Not to be missed: the so-called Private Rooms, a suite of opulent galleries retained from earlier eighteenth-century Burlington House, with choice holdings from the Academy's own collection on view, including a sculpted Michelangelo *Madonna* and works by onetime members, including Reynolds, Gainsborough, and Turner. Cafeteria.

Percival David Foundation of Chinese Art (53 Gordon Square) is a unit of the University of London less celebrated than its sister-museum, the Courtauld Institute Galleries. Located in a Bloomsbury town house, this is a superlative display of Chinese treasures—porcelain, enamelware, and scrolls. All told, there are some 1,500 objects surveying Chinese art for the last millennium.

British Theatre Museum (Covent Garden): Drama buffs, in this most theater-rich of capitals, will find Siddons' Sheraton dressing table and letters, manuscripts, photos, and costumes galore—even one of Nijinsky's.

Dulwich College Picture Gallery (College Road) is a hike from central London, make no mistake. Give yourself half a day, and try to select a sunny one so that you can enjoy a stroll through this unlikely South London suburb with a still-bucolic air to its park-and-garden setting and its gem: the Sir John Soane-designed (1814) picture gallery—the first public one in London. On display are a collection of Old Masters—including Rembrandt and Rubens and some fine English works, as well—Lelys, Knellers, Hogarths, Ramsays, and Gainsboroughs among them. Go by train from Victoria Station.

Imperial War Museum (Lambeth Road): The empire is, of course, no more, but the Imperial War Museum stubbornly retains the name it has had since World War I days. You may or may not be attracted because of its associations with an empire that is extinct or because the theme is war or because the setting is the original mental hospital called by a name that has become part of the language: Bedlam. Still, the place may surprise you. What it sets out to do is show how the empire, oops, the Commonwealth cooperated during the course of the two World Wars. The domed building is superb Regency, with a graceful portico. Galleries—navy, air, army—are chock-full of war objects, ranging from an actual German submarine to a French tank and a World War II Spitfire aircraft. Big surprise is the Picture Gallery; all of the works have war-related themes and their creators include Sargent, Wyndham Lewis, Feliks Topolski, and Epstein.

Kenwood (Hampstead Heath) is visitable as a great Robert Adam house (later counseled) and as a repository of paintings, these of the collection of brewer Edward Cecil Guinness, who bequeathed them, with the house, to the public in 1927. Kenwood constitutes a choice collection—both Gainsborough and Reynolds are heavily represented. So are Turner and Landseer, and so are the French, through Boucher and Watteau, and the Dutch, with Rembrandt and Vermeer.

Natural History Museum (Cromwell Road): Its absolute glory of a mock-Romanesque facade—two steeple-like towers over the entrance, a pair of square towers delineating its flanks—makes this the most architecturally distinguished of the South Kensington museums; even the next-door Victoria and Albert Museum pales in contrast. Architect Alfred Waterhouse's building was begun in 1873 and not completed until seven years later. The facade is esthetic reward enough. Go inside, then, to the Central Hall; you might well have entered a Romanesque cathedral on the Italian peninsula, except that this space has an added attraction—a suspended passageway at its extreme end that just has to be modeled on the Bridge of Sighs in Venice's Doges' Palace. Exhibits? Most spectacular is a staggeringly immense blue whale. But this is a world-class museum, with its range of mammals and fossils, birds and fishes, insects and reptiles, rocks and minerals. And I should point out that, if my experience is typical, you and your party will be the only nonteacher adults in attendance; the masses of class groups are overwhelming enough for this place to be known also as the Museum of British Schoolchildren. Cafeteria.

Science Museum (Exhibition Road): Not unlike counterparts in Chicago, Washington, and Munich, London's Science Museum is (a) enormous and (b) child-filled. But the kids can't be faulted, given exhibits like pioneering railway locomotives and equally early autos, antique clocks and tractors, early phonographs and cameras, and even mock-ups of Victorian kitchens and bathrooms. Cafeteria. (If you've sufficient curiosity, visit also the neighboring *Geology Museum* [Exhibition Road], where you might enjoy sparkling displays of emeralds, rubies, sapphires, and diamonds.)

Commonwealth Institute (Kensington High Street at Holland Park): A post-World War II structure that looks as though it might have been displaced from a world's fair, the institute is only partially a museum. It's a commendable enterprise designed to put the various Commonwealth countries' best feet forward to the people of the United Kingdom. Its museum aspect embraces two vast floors of exhibits—of each and every one of the Commonwealth countries. (Nigeria, in my view, is the don't-miss of the lot.) Noteworthy, too, is an art gallery with frequently changing shows of Commonwealth artists, often two or three at a time. Cafeteria.

Madame Tussaud's (Marylebone Road): I dignify this establishment by including it in this section of selected museums only because you will have heard of it, and may want to go. Well, unless you see them, you can't believe how awful many of the wax statues are, particularly those of the contemporary personalities whose faces we are familiar with from newspapers, films, and television.

Memorial Houses

Thomas Carlyle's House (24 Cheyne Row, Chelsea) is small and on a street of small houses. It's as good an excuse as any to visit this good-looking Chelsea quarter—bordering the Thames and with more substantial Cheyne (pronounced *cheyney)* Walk its most noted thoroughfare. The house was more than a century old when Carlyle and his wife moved in, in 1834, remaining until the author died in 1881. Furnishings are the Carlyles' own. To be seen are the top-floor studio, living room, and bedroom and the basement kitchen.

Charles Dickens' House (48 Doughty Street) was Dickens' home for only two years (1837–39), but the prolific author, in that brief period, wrote *Oliver Twist* and *Nicholas Nickleby* there and worked on other books, too. There's a remarkably complete library of and about Dickens, as well as a Pickwick-type kitchen below-stairs.

William Hogarth's House (Hogarth Lane, Chiswick): Considering that it was badly damaged during World War II and had to be restored, this house conveys a graphic picture of what it must have been when Hogarth and his wife used it as a country retreat in the mid-eighteenth century. There is precious little furniture, but there is a quantity of the master's prints.

Dr. Samuel Johnson's House (17 Gough Square) is a four-story Queen Anne house on a square tucked behind Fleet Street and is reached by the same alley on which the venerable Cheshire Cheese pub has its entrance. Johnson chose it in order to be near the printer of his monumental dictionary. He lived in the house between 1748 and 1759, during which time the dictionary was a major project, with half a dozen copyists working on it exclusively.

John Keats' House (Keats Grove, Hampstead) is early nineteenth century, handsome, and full of mementos of the gifted young poet, who was only twenty-five when he died in Rome. Next door is a library full of editions of Keats' works and portraits of him.

SQUARES: A SUM-UP

Trafalgar Square is No. 1, with a landmark (170-foot-high Nelson pillar), playing water (the fountains are among London's loveliest), structures of note (National Gallery, St. Martin-in-the-Fields Church, nearby Charing Cross Railway Station), and the scenic view along Whitehall—to Big Ben and Parliament. *Piccadilly Circus,* its central statue of Eros notwithstanding, has all of the charm of New York's Times Square, which is to say, not much. Heaven knows, though, how many passengers throng its excellently run Underground station per day. And the Circus is central: theaterland east on Shaftesbury Avenue, Regent Street stores to the north, and Mayfair to the west via Piccadilly. *Soho Square* remains partly eighteenth-century and has given its name to the multicultural foreign quarter adjacent to the theaters, with two churches, one French Protestant, the other (St. Patrick's) Catholic and—on Greek and Frith and adjacent streets— restaurants serving cuisines of Italy, France, Greece, China, Hungary, and India. *Grosvenor Square* is important to North Americans. The former neo-Georgian American Embassy is now an annex of the Canadian High Commission, the Americans having moved to a striking Eero Saarinen-designed embassy, powerful, good-looking and appropriate to the site, with an oversized eagle over the entrance that had London agog when it went up in 1960. Note, too, Sir William Reid Dick's statue of President Franklin D. Roosevelt, a British tribute to the close Anglo-American cooperation of the World War II era. *Belgrave Square* is the epitome of elegant London, a Regency-era jewel, surrounded by fine houses, today sheltering embassies (Austrian, German, Japanese, Spanish) and scholarly societies. *Eaton, Cadogan,* and heavily American-populated *Chester* squares are nearby and similarly posh, and the area's streets—Wilton Crescent, Belgrave Place, Chesham Place, Pont Street—are, too. *Sloane Square* is synonymous with Chelsea. King's Road leads both east and west from it. Sloane Street leads north to Knightsbridge, and Lower Sloane Street heads south toward Chelsea Embankment and the Thames. *Bloomsbury Square* and its neighbors are dominated by the British Museum and the University of London. Exiting the museum, have a look at *Bedford, Russell,* and *Tavistock* squares and the quarter's streets.

PRETTIEST PARKS

St. James's, Green, and *Buckingham Palace Gardens* are the most central of the parks and are contiguous. St. James's is bisected by a lake where birds breed. Green Park borders on Hyde (below), with Wellington Arch and Hyde Park Corner the points of contact between the two. *Hyde Park's* spark is Speaker's Corner—what free speech in Britain is all about. But there are, as well, boating on the Serpentine, riding on Rotten Row, and band concerts at the Achilles Statue. *Kensington Gardens* is adjacent to Hyde Park, to its west. Originally Kensington Palace's front yard, it now draws small fry who will sail bathtub-size boats in the Round Pond. *Regent's Park's* big draw is *London Zoo*, with an aviary designed by Lord Snowdon and open-space confinement areas for big animals, as well as a reputed aquarium and, at the south end, the late Queen Mary's rose garden. *Battersea Park*, south of the Thames, is essentially a Fun Fair—roller coasters and the like, with a cross-section of London in attendance. *Kew Gardens* is officially the Royal Botanic Gardens, lovely to walk about (there are 25,000 botanic specimens), with a onetime royal residence—*Kew Palace*—an eminently inspectable retreat of no less a monarch than George III, whose consort, Queen Charlotte, died within, in 1818. *Hampstead Heath* has two things going for it: *Kenwood House* (both a stately home and an art gallery) and elevation—400 feet at its highest—that assures a smashing view of central London to the south. Relax at venerable Spaniards Inn pub; have a look at Georgian, village-like Hampstead adjacent.

PERIPHERAL LONDON: SELECTED COUNTRY HOUSES

Ham House (Richmond, Surrey) went up in the early seventeenth century. One enters a galleried Great Hall hung with paintings by Reynolds, Kneller, and Van Dyck, but that is only the beginning. Elsewhere you'll see textiles, plasterwork, wood carving, mantels, mirrors, wall coverings, parquet floors, painted ceilings, and furniture. There is not an inferior piece of work in the house.

Not to be missed: the Great Staircase; the Duchess's bedroom, with its immense red-canopied bed; the upstairs Long Gallery, with its Sir Peter Lely paintings of voluptuous ladies; and the North Drawing Room, with its English tapestries, gilded chairs, and a marble fireplace banked by twisted half-columns. Café.

Chiswick House (Burlington Lane, Chiswick) is probably the greatest pure Palladian villa outside of the prototypes in the Veneto region of northern Italy. Chiswick was built in 1725 by Lord Burlington after his return from a Grand Tour on which he saw the originals. Chiswick was designed by William Kent—the multitalented landscapist-cabinetmaker-architect—in collaboration with Lord Burlington. It is smallish, and today it is largely unfurnished. But Kent's elaborate ceilings and wall decorations compensate for the lack of chairs, tables, sofas, rugs, and paintings. There are three exceptionally striking chambers: Red Velvet Room, Blue Velvet Room, and, loveliest of the lot, central gallery in white and gold.

Osterley Park (Great West Road, Middlesex) is the earliest of several Robert Adam-designed country houses in the London area. Adam's goal was "delicacy, gaiety, grace and beauty"—hardly immodest, but he attained it. Osterley's principal rooms are just as Adam created them, and that includes furniture he had especially made for each. The entrance hall stuns with its magnificence—a ballroom-size, high-ceilinged chamber, with the decoration consisting solely of the gray-and-white marble floor and the plasterwork on the walls and ceiling, in Wedgewood blue and white. There is a severely beautiful library, a dining room where a series of console tables placed against the walls (with the chairs) take the place of a conventional dining table; a Long Gallery with pale green walls to match the furniture in the same hue, and a room in which tapestries cover the walls, like elaborate wallpaper.

Syon House (Brentford, Middlesex) has never, in all of its four centuries-plus, altered its stern gray Tudor facade. Edward VI was the first of many celebrated visitors to enjoy Syon's hospitality. Lady Jane Grey, who reigned as Queen for nine days before her beheading, was offered the crown at Syon. By the mid-eighteenth century, Syon had become the seat of the Dukes of Northumberland. In 1762, the twelfth duke hired Robert Adam to transform the interior of Syon, while retaining the Tudor facade. The entrance hall, influenced by that at Osterley Park (above), is similar to it and painted in pale gray, the only other hue provided by the black tiles of a checkerboard marble floor. The Anteroom, with black marble pillars supporting gold neo-classic statues that in turn support a gilded ceiling, is an eye-opener. The Red Drawing Room is dazzling, and so is its art: painting after painting by Lely and Van Dyck. And the Long Gallery has books lining its pale green walls and an intricate Adam ceiling.

Kenwood (Hampstead Lane, Hampstead) is the latest of our trio of London-area Adam-designed houses. Lord Mansfield, its then owner, retained Adam in 1764 to transform on older house. Its State Room leads off an oblong entrance hall into two equally proportioned wings. Detailing is minute. The Library, with its arched ceiling supported by Corinthian columns, is the showplace room. Kenwood is also an art gallery of consequence (see Museums).

Hatfield House (Hertfordshire): The present house's predecessor—still standing—was the royal palace in which Henry VIII's daughter, Bloody Mary, kept her younger half-sister, the Princess Elizabeth, prisoner during part of Mary's reign. It was at Hatfield—in the old palace that now serves as a restaurant—that Elizabeth learned of her accession to the throne. The newer—and main—house is a Jacobean manor built by the first Earl of Salisbury (whose descendants are still resident). Its two-story-high Great Hall—with one wall covered with a trio of Brussels tapestries and another with a carved wooden screen— is one of the superlative English rooms and is the locale of Hilliard's so-called ermine painting of Elizabeth I and the Oudry portrait of her adversary, Mary Queen of Scots. Hatfield abounds in fine rooms— King James Drawing Room, with its red-and-white ceiling and red-and-gold furniture; 180-foot-long Long Gallery; capacious library; and chapel.

Luton Hoo (Luton, Bedfordshire): Queen Elizabeth II and Prince Philip made it a habit, at least before the 1973 death of Sir Harold Wernher, to weekend at Luton Hoo. The house itself, begun by Robert Adam in 1767 and set in a Capability Brown-conceived park, stands behind a turn-of-century rose garden. Loveliest of the rooms are the eighteenth-century French Blue Hall and dining room, the latter equipped with crystal and silver that had belonged to English monarchs and with Beauvais tapestries covering the walls. Art treasures embrace furniture, porcelain, sculpture, ivories, Renaissance jewelry, and extraordinary Old Master paintings, including works of Italians like Lippi and Flemings like Memling.

Woburn Abbey (Bedfordshire) is a pioneer in the Stately Home business. The 300-year-old house is treasure filled, with such splendid interiors as the drawing, dressing, and bedrooms in which Queen Victoria and Prince Albert stayed on their visits and the Long Gallery, with such paintings as the noted Armada portrait of Elizabeth I, a likeness of Elizabeth's half-sister Bloody Mary, after Sir Anthony More, and a Holbein of Jane Seymour. Owner-operator not only of the house, but of ancillary commercial enterprises is the Marquess of Tavistock. If you go by car, Woburn may be comfortably combined in a single day with Luton Hoo. A recommended lunch break would be at Paris House, a luxury-category French restaurant on the Woburn estate, or at a venerable inn-restaurant called The Bell, in nearby Aston Clinton (First Class).

St. Albans, twenty miles northeast, is not a house but rather a near-to-London town with a celebrated cathedral—an ideal excursion. When the Romans ruled 2,000 years back, it was Verulamium, and among the townspeople was a soldier named Alban who, legend has it, was executed by the anti-Christian authorities in the course of protecting a priest. The Saxon church where the sainted Alban was killed has long since been replaced by what is now *St. Alban's Cathedral*, a Romanesque-Gothic meld with a narrow nave that, at 300 feet, is among the world's longest. The saint's shrine is what one wants to see first, along with the exquisitely carved choir, sculpted saints of the altar screen, and painted saints on walls and ceilings. Nearby *Verulamium Museum* shelters remnants of Roman St. Alban's, beautiful mosaics most especially. Lunch at the White Hart (Holywell Hill), a pub mellowed by age; it's twelfth century.

AFTER DARK

Theater and opera: Theater in London goes back to the sixteenth century, when the first public theater opened in Shoreditch. Its impresario was James Burbage, who came to be the employer of William Shakespeare, when the Bard left Stratford to become an actor in the capital. Within a couple of decades, the same Burbage opened a new theater on the Thames's south bank—the circular Globe that achieved immortality; the London theater tradition had become entrenched.

Today, the capital has more than half a hundred theaters, one of which—*Theatre Royal, Drury Lane*—is on the site of a predecessor that opened under Charles II's patronage three centuries ago. The Drury Lane is set behind an imposing neoclassic entrance portico. *Theatre Royal, Haymarket*, is another similarly aged, similarly atmospheric, and somewhat similarly porticoed beauty, its origin dating to the reign of George I, with its current home substantially the refurbishing of the Regent's John Nash. I am fond, too, of the *Royal Opera House, Covent Garden.* It is mid-nineteenth-century, at once a place of splendor but still with an intimacy rarely found in opera houses on the Continent. And mind, I say this despite the decidedly regal aspects of the theater, including a royal box that has its own private supper room. A personal favorite, too, is the Edwardian *Coliseum*, home to the English National Opera, which has pioneered in the presentation of grand opera sung in the English language.

Most London theaters show productions especially produced and cast for a single run. But London has several repertory companies. The *National Theatre*, for long also called the Old Vic because its home was in the theater by that name, is the most noted (earlier members of its company included Dame Edith Evans, Sir Laurence Olivier, Vivien Leigh, Sir John Gielgud, Charles Laughton, and Sir Alec Guinness—to name a few). Its home is a boldly handsome three-auditorium theater on the South Bank of the Thames, a stellar specimen of British contemporary architecture. There is, as well, the *Royal Shakespeare Company.* Its home base is the Royal Shakespeare Theatre in Stratford (Chapter 17), but it has for some time played London seasons, as well, moving in 1982—when it opened—to the revolutionary-design, 1,200-seat theater of the Barbican Centre for Arts and Conferences in the Barbican quarter of the City. The *Royal Court Theatre*, on Sloane Square in Chelsea, is highly respected for an innovative policy that has brought such playwrights as John Osborne (originally with *Look Back in Anger*) to public attention. Much earlier, a number of Shaw plays were first seen at the Royal Court.

Glyndebourne Festival is English eccentricity carried to its zenith and with great success over a period of two decades in the form of top-rank opera (generally five works per season), to the accompaniment of the London Philharmonic, at a country house 54 miles south of London, with the prescribed dress black tie (men can get away with dark suits) and the clincher a seventy-five-minute intermission to allow the formally dressed audience to picnic on the lawns or to dine in a more prosaic on-premises restaurant. Season is late-May through mid-August, with many customers transported by a special opera train that traditionally departs London's Victoria Station at 2:55 P.M. Harrods department store sells specially prepared picnic packs, or order a hamper from caterers near Glyndebourne. Information and advance booking: Glyndebourne Festival, Lewes, England.

The Royal Ballet: If London holds its own with opera, it distinguishes itself with ballet. The Royal Ballet was born as the dance wing for the opera company originally associated with the Old Vic Theatre. When, with the advent of the thirties, the Sadler's Wells Theatre opened, the ballet took the name of the theater and under the direction of Ninette de Valois—later awarded the title "Dame" in recognition of her achievement—began to achieve international celebrity, to the point where it was honored by being given a permanent home just after World War II in the Royal Opera House. Another name change—to Royal Ballet—came not long thereafter. Frederick Ashton—later knighted for his work with the company—joined Dame Ninette as the company's principal choreographer in 1935, to be succeeded by Sir Kenneth MacMillan.

All three of these balletic giants shaped the company. The de Valois beginnings were essentially classical. Ashton carried on with that tradition (a Royal Ballet *Giselle* or *Swan Lake* is to this day a major London treat) and added his own imprint with such works as the dramatic *Daphnis and Chloe*, *Lady of the Camellias* (his interpretation of *Camille*), the lilting *Les Patineurs*, and the exuberant *Jazz Calendar*. MacMillan's major works have included a full-length *Romeo and Juliet* to music by Prokofiev, a balletic retelling of the Anastasia story, and his own interpretation of Stravinsky's *The Rite of Spring*. Recent years have seen the company take the works of contemporary foreign choreographers into the repertory, including New York City Ballet's George Balanchine (*Agon*) and Jerome Robbins (*Dances at a Gathering*). The company has an auxiliary wing, *The Royal Ballet New Group*. And there is other ballet—*Ballet Rambert, London Festival Ballet*—

under the artistic direction of ex-Royal Danish Ballet soloist Peter Schanfuss; *London Contemporary Dance Theatre;* and *Royal Sadler's Wells Ballet,* headquartered in the original Sadler's Wells Theatre.

Concerts and recitals: London has no less than five symphony orchestras. The *Royal Philharmonic,* founded in 1813, has its home base in Royal Festival Hall and never gives a concert without a bust of Beethoven on the stage. Beethoven wrote his Ninth Symphony for the orchestra and had close associations with it, as did such composers as Mendelssohn, who wrote his Fourth for the Royal Philharmonic, and Dvorak, who did likewise with his Second. The *London Symphony* is even older than the Royal Philharmonic. The *London Philharmonic,* founded by the late Sir Thomas Beecham, has in recent seasons been under the direction of the Dutchman, Bernard Haitink; its home also is Royal Festival Hall. And there are, as well, the *BBC Symphony* and the *Philharmonia,* not to mention numerous chamber music groups, from the *London Mozart Players* to the *London Sinfonietta.* And symphonies from elsewhere in Britain. *Royal Liverpool Philharmonic, City of Birmingham Symphony, Bournemouth Symphony,* to name but three, make London appearances along with orchestras from abroad.

Royal Festival Hall was built for the 1951 Festival of Britain on the South Bank of the Thames, near Waterloo Bridge. It is an absolutely super building, early-fifties contemporary at its very sensible, functional best, of reinforced concrete, with superb acoustics. The river setting is taken advantage of with a vast terrace affording fine vistas and above it a glass-walled restaurant. The auditorium seats 3,000. Adjacent, as part of the *South Bank Arts Centre,* are the smaller, also-attractive *Queen Elizabeth Hall* (1,100 seats) and the 370-seat *Purcell Room,* for chamber music. There is, as well, the *Hayward Gallery* at which short-term art exhibits are held.

In contrast is *Royal Albert Hall,* in Kensington, built a century ago, named for the consort of Queen Victoria and just across the road from the alfresco memorial to him. The Royal Albert, unlike the Royal Festival, has never been loved for its acoustics. It has other things going for it, namely a capacity to seat 8,000 souls and a thousand-voice choir, all at once. Its organ is one of the biggest extant. The shape is circular—Royal Albert can be likened to a kind of fat silo.

London's newest concert hall—seating 2,000, and home base for the venerable London Symphony—is a part of the Barbican Centre for Arts and Conferences, a boldly designed $265-million complex in the City's Barbican quarter, which opened in 1982.

Chamber music concerts and recitals are given regularly in *Wigmore Hall* (Wigmore Street). London's beautiful *churches* are frequent settings for musical events—*St. John's,* Smith Square, and *St. Martin-in-*

the-Fields, on Trafalgar Square, are but two. Many, particularly in the City, give free lunchtime concerts. And in summer, at least when the weather cooperates, there are *outdoor musical events* at such locales as Holland Park, Victoria Embankment Gardens, and the Orangery of Kenwood House, Hampstead.

Booking theater, opera, and ballet tickets: There are few problems here, with the exception of concerts, particularly those of symphony orchestras in Royal Festival Hall and certain performances of the Royal Ballet and Royal Opera. The foregoing can be difficult to get seats for. Legitimate theater is usually easier. In all cases, the most direct and cheapest way of booking is in person at the theater box-office; many accept major credit cards. If this is inconvenient, there are the booking agencies, which add a service charge to the cost of each ticket; giant of the ticket-agency industry is Keith Prowse, whose head office is at Plantation House, Fenchurch Street, and from whose U.S. branch (234 West 44th Street, New York, NY 10036; Phone 1-800-223-4446) you may purchase tickets before you leave home. And every hotel of any size has a theater-booking cubbyhole. All of these establishments have supplies of weekly schedules of what's on in the theater, gratis. The daily press has the same information. *Leicester Square Ticket Booth* (Leicester Square) sells tickets for certain plays at half-price, plus a moderate service charge, on the day of performance; its usual hours are noon to 2:00 P.M. for matinee tickets, 2:30–6:30 P.M. for evening seats.

TRADITIONAL PAGEANTRY

Trooping the Colour marks the sovereign's birthday and takes place on an early June Saturday at Horse Guards Parade. The Queen is star of the show, mounted atop a royal horse. Prince Philip also participates, as do various units of the Royal Guard.

Royal Tournament is an annual event at Earl's Court, an immense arena-exhibition hall; entrants are members of the armed forces, and the show is at once music, derring-do, and pageantry.

State Opening of Parliament takes place early in November and embraces a procession beginning at Buckingham Palace, proceeding via the Mall, Horse Guards Parade, and Whitehall to the House of Lords, where the Queen reads her speech from the throne.

Order of the Garter Ceremony is an annual June event at Windsor

Castle, with the Queen leading a resplendent procession from the castle proper to St. George's Chapel.

City of London Lord Mayor's Procession takes place the second Saturday in November. He rides in his ancient coach from Guildhall to the Law Courts, where the Lord Chief Justice welcomes him.

SPECTATOR SPORTS

Cricket: Lords, in St. John's Wood, usually beginning in April and running into September.

Tennis: Wimbledon Championships are annual early-summer events at Wimbledon's Lawn Tennis and Croquet Club.

Racing: To be seen at Ascot, with dressy Royal Meetings à la *My Fair Lady* a June highlight; and Epsom, July and August.

Rowing: The Henley Royal Regatta is an annual early-July event, at the Thames-side town of Henley, not far from London.

Horseback riding: The Royal International Horse Show at Wembley is an annual late-July event—show jumping is the highlight, and the Queen, herself a skilled equestrienne, often attends.

Croquet: The Croquet Association Open Championships, with teams from abroad competing in this very English and very ancient sport, at the Hurlingham Club.

Polo is played at a number of clubs, including the Guards Polo Club, Windsor, and the Ham Polo Club, Surrey.

CASINOS

There are a number of London casinos. The catch is that they are operated as private clubs, and only members may play. For a foreigner to be able to gamble, he or she must have been a member at least 48 hours—according to British law. So if you are interested, apply at one of the clubs *two days* before you plan to play; *take your passport with you* and be prepared to pay a membership fee. Casinos include the *21 Club* and that occupying the opulent, onetime ballroom (now with its own restaurant and bar) at the *Ritz Hotel* (Piccadilly).

SETTLING IN

SELECTED LUXURY HOTELS

Athenaeum Hotel (Piccadilly) is a pre-World War II house, splendid-ly situated and small enough (112 nicely decorated rooms and suites) so as to be able to offer relatively personal service. The bar is inviting, the restaurant—in pastel greens and pinks—likewise. A Rank hotel.

Berkeley Hotel (Wilton Place, off Knightsbridge) is the relatively modern successor to an earlier hotel of the same name, at another location. The facade is restrained and unadorned. Interiors are a mix of the contemporary with the traditional, employing marble, crystal, and antique paneling. The Berkeley (pronounced Barkeley) is not large—159 rooms and suites with exceptional baths. There are a pair of top-rank restaurants (the Buttery's buffet lunches are detailed on another page, while the main dining room's fare is more formal French), congenial drinking spaces, and an unexpected indoor swimming pool-cum-sauna on the roof. Lovely service. Member, Leading Hotels of the World.

Brittania Inter-Continental Hotel (Grosvenor Square): I had been an enthusiast of the Brittania even before Inter-Continental took it over, thoroughly and tastefully refurbishing it. With its handsomely colonnaded, Georgian-style facade on one of London's legendary squares, this 356-room house has both location and looks in its favor. And its facilities attract, the range 24-hour room service and updated baths-cum-hairdryers, to a trio of reliable restaurants and as many bar-lounges—one a proper London pub. *Luxury.*

Brown's Hotel (Dover Street and Albemarle Street) has been a London fixture since the year Victoria acceded to the throne. That, if you have momentarily forgotten, was 1837. Brown's carpeted floors are evocatively creaky. There's a paneled lounge for tea or drinks, traditional-decor restaurant, and 135 bedrooms and suites. Brown's hall porters are celebrated, and with good reason. Where does one find better, more efficient, or more kind? Trusthouse Forte.

Capital Hotel (Basil Street) has for some years been appreciated for its intimate charm. (There are just 60 rooms and suites, and it's located on a convenient Knightsbridge street.) But its plain contemporary decor did not, alas, win it any beauty contests. That is all changing, with skilled interior designer Nina Campbell (whose first hotel was Hambleton Hall in the Midlands [Chapter 12]) transforming the interior, with typically exuberant treatment blending traditional textiles and furniture with witty Campbell innovations. You'll see what I mean in the guestrooms she's had a hand in, at the bar-lounge and the long-esteemed French restaurant, about which I comment in a subsequent paragraph.

Claridge's Hotel (Brook Street), in the heart of the smartest part of Mayfair, has made a specialty of royalty over the years (since 1838, to be precise). The original Claridges were a butler and his wife, a housekeeper who had worked for the gentry. But a solitary royal signed the register in 1860, to be visited by no less grand a lady than Queen Victoria. And the crowned heads have not stopped since. Part of the staff still is liveried—a nice Claridge's touch this—and one drinks (tea or stronger stuff) in the lobby rather than in a detached bar, the better to watch the clientele pass in review. Accommodations are elaborate and the proportion of suites is high. Two restaurants. Member, Leading Hotels of the World.

Connaught Hotel (Carlos Place) is quite as though some English friends were putting you up at their town house. Accommodations— of which there are not all that many (the total of rooms and suites is 106)—are quietly deluxe. You would not be terribly surprised to meet His Majesty, Edward VII, in the paneled bar, which is, in and of itself, a worthy destination for the thirsty. And the restaurant warrants additional comment on a later page. The Connaught accepts only MasterCard—no other plastic. Member, Leading Hotels of the World, Relais et Châteaux.

Dorchester Hotel (Park Lane) is, or at least always has been for me, an extraordinary hotel experience. The luxury is the kind that English interior designers—Oliver Messel, for one—create so well, combining traditional furnishings with contemporary fabrics and colors, with the results warm and welcoming. This is an exceptional place to eat, too: tea in the recently enlarged Promenade Lounge, casual lunches in the strikingly good-looking Cocktail Bar, exceptional meals in the svelte, French-accented Terrace Restaurant, and the English-fare Grill (see below). Ordinary bedrooms are particularly spacious. But suites—the many regular ones and the super-luxurious Roof Garden series—can be sumptuous. Ask for front accommodations, and your view is of Hyde Park.

Dukes Hotel (St. James's Place) is one you either look for or are taken to, but I'll wager it's not one you'll casually pass by. And therein lies its charm. St. James's Place is a cul-de-sac off St. James's Street, closer to Pall Mall than to Piccadilly. Of the 50-plus rooms, those on lower floors tend to be compact, those higher up (recently created) are good-size. There are, in addition, 14 super suites with big baths and, as a bonus, kitchens; a paneled bar and a restaurant about which I write more on a later page. Friendly. Member, Prestige Hotels.

Grosvenor House Hotel (Park Lane) went up in the late twenties. Its architect, Sir Edwin Luytens, was the very same whom the Crown had earlier commissioned to design a new capital for India when it was determined that it was time to move on from Calcutta to New Delhi. Lobby is big and humming. Residential wings—they are connected by the lobby and the public rooms—boast zingy accommodations. There are fine restaurants (that termed Ninety Park Lane is exceptional) and drinking parlors, and tea in the lounge remains a happy London pastime. A Trusthouse Forte Exclusive Division hotel.

Hyatt Carlton Tower Hotel (Cadogan Place): Credit Hyatt International for zeroing in on a class act of a London hotel—architecturally contemporary, albeit graceful, and situated in posh Belgravia, with shops and restaurants of both Knightsbridge and the King's Road equally close by—for its European flagship. When Hyatt took over, half a decade back, it embarked on an ongoing multimillion-pound refurbishment with style and flair. Much of the capacious lobby has become the Chinoiserie, traditionally furnished, but with Oriental accents, that's a café-lounge open early breakfast through casual lunch, afternoon tea, cocktails, and on into the late hours. One of the two restaurants, the Chelsea Room, was upgraded, while the other—specializing in beef—was wisely left alone. And guest rooms—228 all told—are being deftly restyled, with Spa Suites, each with whirlpool baths, especially handsome. Hyatt with a British accent? You bet. And it works.

Hyde Park Hotel (Knightsbridge) is surely—along with nearby Harrods department store—the most easily identifiable building in the Knightsbridge quarter, a perfectly splendid red-brick Victorian pile, towered and turreted and, alone among London hotels, with back rooms facing onto Hyde Park. You want to aim for one of those, to be awakened each morning by the clomp-clomp of the Horse Guards en route from barracks to the Admiralty. There are 180 soft-toned rooms and a score of spacious suites, high-ceilinged public areas that include a pair of restaurants (one of which is detailed in a later paragraph), and a congenial lounge, as agreeable for afternoon tea as for cocktails. A Trusthouse Forte Exclusive Division hotel that is also a member of Leading Hotels of the World.

Inter-Continental London Hotel (Hamilton Place) has a lot going for it. Location first—at Hyde Park Corner, looking over the park and just opposite Apsley House, built as a town house for the first Duke of Wellington and now an art-filled museum. Skilled management is second. And facilities—500 traditional-style rooms and suites with superbly equipped baths—is third. There are a pair of restaurants (one, Le Soufflé, is later counseled; the other is a late-hours coffee shop), a pair of bars—one on the roof turns disco after dark—and a chauffeur-equipped Rolls-Royce that will take you to or from the airport or, for that matter, on town and country tours. Along with the Inter-Continental Maui, in Hawaii, and the Inter-Continental New York, this is my favorite in the chain.

Inn on the Park (Park Lane) successfully melds a contemporary facade and dominantly contemporary look with just enough of the traditional to be distinctive. Rooms and suites, lobby, pair of restaurants—both the Four Seasons and Lanes—bar-lounge: all have style. And service, in my experience, is cordial and professional. A Four Seasons hotel that is a member of the Prestige Hotels group.

London Hilton on Park Lane (Park Lane) raised eyebrows among locals when it opened in the sixties. Muttering, muttering about those upstart colonials coming over to run a hotel—and a skyscraper of a hotel at that. Well, Hilton International pioneered in London, as in other parts of the world. After two fabulously successful decades, the hotel emerged into the late eighties with a new name—it had been called Hilton International London—and a new decor, as a consequence of a $7-million renovation. The clean-lined lobby took on a soft Georgian look with Chippendale and Hepplewhite furnishings; it opens onto a spacious open lounge that welcomes guests for breakfast, casual lunches, afternoon tea, and cocktails. A marble staircase leads to the high-ceilinged and handsome British Harvest Restaurant. And the 24th through 27th floors—with nearly 20 new suites and close to 40 upgraded rooms—embrace the Vista Executive section of the hotel, with separate check-in and complimentary breakfast, snacks, and beverages for its premium-category guests.

London Marriott Hotel (Duke Street at Grosvenor Square) is the onetime Europa Hotel, attractively mock-Georgian with respect to facade, splendidly situated, and with but one drawback: smallish rooms. Marriott management, to alleviate this problem, undertook elaborate renovations, eliminating many rooms in the process, to create larger guest quarters. The wood-paneled Diplomat Restaurant is French-inspired, and there's a good-looking cocktail lounge.

May Fair Hotel (Stratton Street, off Piccadilly): I first came to know the May Fair in the course of attending a play in the legitimate theater taking its name and sharing its building. Then, a few seasons back, Inter-Continental Hotels took over, completely refurbishing the 327 rooms and suites in elegant, traditional style, and updating their baths. There is a pair of restaurants—Le Châteaubriand is authentically French and quite grand; the Coffee House is casual. And there is a pair of bars. Very nice, indeed.

New Piccadilly Hotel (Piccadilly) goes back—in its original form—to London's Roaring Twenties. Its facade—arcaded at street level and topped by a dazzling colonnade of eight Corinthian pillars—is like no other in town. Over the years, though, the Piccadilly slid downhill. The principal restaurant, oak-paneled in the manner of the great hall of a country house, had become, on my last visit, a help-yourself-to-the-roast-beef carvery. Enter Gleneagles Hotels, as new owner. It spent £150 million to create the New Piccadilly. There are just under 300 traditional-style rooms and suites with opulent baths; Terrace Garden Restaurant set behind columns of the facade; Gleneagles Club with swimming pool, sauna, squash court, and café; boîte-disco, logically called the Music Room; and, for nostalgia buffs of the old Piccadilly like me, the Oak Room—with original paneling of the old main dining room retained—and an Anglo-Scottish menu.

Park Lane Hotel (Piccadilly) has been a luxury-category leader for more than a half-century. Recently refurbished rooms and suites now have a light and lively look; this is among the better values of the top houses, with capacious public spaces, including a restaurant and bar-lounge and views of Green Park from many rooms.

Ritz Hotel (Piccadilly), created by the legendary Caesar Ritz and for long both a London landmark *and* a London institution, has been refurbished at considerable cost. The glass-roofed Palm Court—all paneled walls and crystal chandeliers and plasterwork picked out in gold—has become so popular for tea that you must book in advance. All the public spaces—especially the Louis XV-inspired restaurant, are beautiful, as is the old ballroom, now seeing service as the separately entered Ritz Casino. By all means, pop in for a drink, tea, or a meal. Settling in is another matter, or at least has been, in my experience. I have found hall porters surly and/or inept and reception staff patronizing. Single rooms can be tiny. Corridor walls are hung with garish, posterlike paintings. And in an expensively refurbished, really costly, super-deluxe London hotel with but 144 suites and rooms, is there any excuse for bathrooms without showers (I drew one, on one visit) or for bathrooms with their showers' hot-water taps inoperable (my luck, on another visit)?

Savoy Hotel (Strand) is the epitome of Victorian London, dating to 1889, and in the hurly-burly quarter adjacent to the City that is chock-full of fine specimens of Victorian architecture. You're away from smarter Mayfair and the West End here, but the Savoy is convenient for theater and opera buffs and those with business in the City. There are 200 no-two-alike, quietly traditional rooms and half a hundred suites (those facing the Thames are the loveliest); two dining rooms (the Savoy Grill warrants comment on a later page; the River Restaurant features dancing at dinner); convivial bar; relatively recent Thames Foyer for tea and pre-theater snacks; and extraordinary private-party rooms, including eight named for Gilbert & Sullivan operas—appropriate, given the Savoy's founder: Savoyard impresario Richard d'Oyly Carte. Member, Leading Hotels of the World.

St. James's Club (Park Place, off St. James's Street) occupies a capacious Victorian town house that has been smartly fashioned into a private club that operates as a hotel—with nearly 30 smashing Art Deco suites, 16 similarly smart doubles, the lot with superb baths. There are lounges on the street floor and a cocktail bar and excellent French-accented restaurant in the basement, to which members may bring guests. "Club" in the title means just that. You must be a member—there are annual dues and elected officers and board—to stay at St. James's. *However*, first-time overseas visitors need not be members for an initial stay, so long as they've booked in advance.

Sheraton Park Tower Hotel (Knightsbridge), occupying a circular eighteen-story structure, has become a Knightsbridge landmark, with Hyde Park views from many of its period-decor, marble-bathed suites and rooms, a later-recommended restaurant, a bar-lounge, and a convenient location; with major stores like Harvey Nichols and Harrods near-neighbors. Very smart, indeed.

Westbury Hotel (New Bond Street) has two major pluses: an inspired location, as convenient for shops as for theater, and professional service. There is a good restaurant, much frequented by Londoners, and the popular Polo Bar. Rooms, however, run small, although efforts have been made to redesign them so as to afford a bit more space. Trusthouse Forte.

SELECTED FIRST-CLASS HOTELS

Basil Street Hotel (Basil Street) is so attractively decorated with antiques and so agreeably located in Knightsbridge that it is never wanting for clients. Book way in advance for this one. The lounges could be those of a great house in town or even in the country. There is a reasonably priced coffee shop. But, alas, the main restaurant is not what it once was; a recently sampled breakfast was sadly disagreeable. And note: Only about half of the 123 rooms have baths.

Belgravia Sheraton Hotel (Chesham Place): Sensing the need for an intimate hotel in the fashionable Belgrave Square quarter, Sheraton Hotels bought the London Belgravia and closed it down, the while spending £4 million on a stem-to-stern refurbishing, with the resulting Belgravia Sheraton, a 90-room house that caught on immediately, with business, as well as pleasure, visitors. Take your choice of one-bedroom or studio suites or king or queen-size doubles; all have spanking new phone-equipped baths, with the decor theme a kind of modified traditional, which carries into public spaces. These include a well-operated restaurant (whose prix-fixe lunches and dinners are sound buys and include wine and coffee) and lobby-bar-lounge in which is served morning coffee, a bargain-tabbed buffet lunch, and afternoon tea.

Cadogan Thistle Hotel (Sloane Street) is an older house of moderate size, Edwardian handsome, with super bedrooms and suites (Oscar Wilde was arrested in one of the later, the management advises), a bar named for Lily Langtry, a reliable restaurant, and a lounge made to order for well-priced afternoon tea or a drink.

Cavendish Hotel (Jermyn Street), just opposite Fortnum & Mason, is a modern version of a well-known oldie that had occupied the same space. Location is convenient. Rooms are functional. Public areas—including a restaurant and a cozy bar—are inviting. Trusthouse Forte.

Chesterfield Hotel (Charles Street) does not take its name lightly. An eighteenth-century Earl of Chesterfield was its builder and original occupant. There are today just over 80 charming rooms, all consistently well equipped, and delightful public spaces, the range a library-like lounge through a bar giving on to the garden. With an elegant—and excellent—restaurant.

Cumberland Hotel (Marble Arch) is British hotelkeeping at its moderate-level best. The idea is comfort rather than luxury. There are more than 900 rooms and all are cheery and well equipped; several restaurants and bars, as well. Trusthouse Forte.

11 Cadogan Gardens Hotel (Cadogan Gardens) occupies a quartet of contiguous Edwardian-era houses on a fashionable Chelsea street just off Sloane Square. All 50 of the rooms—no two of which are alike either in size or decor—have baths, and of these not quite half are shower-equipped. Main-floor lounge is antique-furnished, and a treat is inclusion of a whopping big English breakfast—served in rooms—in the daily rate.

Goring Hotel (Beeston Place, off Grosvenor Gardens, near Buckingham Palace) is a honey of a family-run (third generation) house in gracious traditional style, with capacious public areas, convenient restaurant with English favorites always on its menu, a hundred no-two-quite-alike rooms (ask for one overlooking the hotel's big garden), and a delightful staff, many of whose members are long on scene.

Grosvenor Hotel (Buckingham Palace Road) is the very model of a mid-category Victorian palace: high-ceilinged public areas, with a grand staircase dead center, open-late restaurant, spacious bar-lounge, and showers in some of the 356 well-equipped rooms' baths. Location—near Buckingham Palace—is such that when the Guard changes it marches past the Grosvenor. The value is good here.

Holiday Inn Chelsea (Sloane Street) looks nothing like your standard Holiday Inn because it was not built as one: tasteful, traditionally influenced decor, a couple of hundred well-equipped rooms, pleasant cocktail lounge, restaurant encircling the indoor swimming pool.

Holiday Inn Marble Arch (George Street) is a few short blocks north of the landmark that designates it. It has 245 comfortable rooms, round-the-clock room service, restaurant, coffee shop, and bar, as well as the every-floor ice machines that no self-respecting American motel would be without.

Holiday Inn Mayfair (Berkeley Street, off Piccadilly): My goodness, time flies. When I first knew this location, it housed the old Berkeley Hotel, before it built new quarters in Knightsbridge (below). Next, I found myself inspecting a rebuilt hostelry on the site, called the Bristol. On a recent stroll along Berkeley Street, I discovered that the Bristol had become the Holiday Inn Mayfair—a meld of modern and Louis XV, embracing not quite 190 rooms and suites with well-equipped baths, reliable restaurant, bar-lounge, and friendly staff.

Kensington Close Hotel (Wright's Lane): All 350 rooms' baths have showers and there are fine views from the upper floors, not to mention such amenities as a swimming pool, sauna, and terrace.

L'Hôtel (Basil Street) is not only a neighbor of the Capital Hotel (above) but shares the same owners, if not the same smart ambience. This relatively new establishment has but eleven rooms and a one-bedroom suite. Decor motif is college-dorm maple—nothing fancy, mind you—and each room has its own bath, with hand-showers attached to tubs. There's a wine bar-restaurant in the basement, French style and popular with neighborhood regulars.

Lowndes Thistle Hotel (Lowndes Street) has a stark, contemporary facade that does not prepare one for the interiors, which are late twentieth-century emulations of the Georgian genius of Robert Adam. Lobby, Adam Room Restaurant, and even bedrooms are Adam style, while the bar is rather giddy Chinese Chippendale.

New Mandeville Hotel (Mandeville Place) is an exceptionally tasteful, middle-category house but a stroll from Oxford and Regent streets. Rooms could be larger, but there is no denying their good looks and good baths—all shower-equipped. Four places to eat: formal restaurant, cheery coffee shop, traditional-style pub, and tearoom.

Pastoria Hotel (St. Martin's Street) has the advantages of an eminently convenient Leicester Square situation, and an overwhelming majority of its 50-odd rooms have a bath. Restaurant-bar.

Portman Inter-Continental Hotel (Portman Square) has a no-nonsense, contemporary look, from the lobby through 275 functional rooms with shower-equipped baths. Coffee shop and bar work well, but the star of the Portman show is its remarkable French restaurant.

Royal Garden Hotel (Kensington High Street) is a big mid-sixties palace, with an immense high-ceilinged lobby, quartet of restaurants, equally generous choice of bars, 500 rooms and suites, and situation at the edge of Kensington Gardens, with views of the park below and the city beyond. A Rank hotel.

Royal Horseguards Thistle Hotel (Whitehall Court) has going for it a location overlooking the Thames near Parliament and Whitehall. To the outer world, the Royal Horseguards is a Victorian block, colonnaded, arched, and turreted. Within is a contemporary hotel: sleek-lined lobby; compact red, black, and white guest rooms; and an ice machine on every floor. Bar and coffee shop.

Royal Lancaster Hotel (Lancaster Terrace, north of Hyde Park) is among the choicest of the skyscrapers, with a traditional decor, 467 nice-looking bedrooms and suites, pair each of restaurants and bars. A Rank hotel.

Royal Westminster Thistle Hotel (Buckingham Palace Road) might well be called the Royal Buckingham. It is a near neighbor of the palace, to the point where the Royal Guard passes by en route to Changing ceremonies at the palace's front gate. Behind the clean-lined facade are attractive public spaces, including an inviting bar and a steak restaurant, functional guest rooms, and ice machines on every floor.

Russell Hotel (Russell Square) is the Grande Dame of Bloomsbury— a magnificent Edwardian pile, with one of the great facades of London, a marble-arched and pillared lobby, and similarly impressive public rooms, including a restaurant, grill room, pair of bars, and a lounge where afternoon tea—particularly welcome after a visit to the nearby British Museum—is served. Bedrooms have been modernized: some baths have showers. Trusthouse Forte.

Selfridge Thistle Hotel (Orchard Street) is most definitely to be associated with Selfridges department store on Oxford Street. It is right next door, with 304 rooms, handsome restaurant, coffee shop, bar, and—hear this, shoppers—separate entrance of its very own to the vast, tempting department store adjoining.

Sherlock Holmes Hotel (Baker Street) is included here for two reasons. First is because it is a comfortable, medium-size (149 rooms) modern hotel in a reasonably convenient part of town, north of Oxford Street. Second is because it alone on Baker Street pays tribute to the fictional detective with whose name the street is synonymous. Volumes of Holmes are on sale, and there are public rooms named for the good Watson and the evil Moriarty.

Stafford Hotel (St. James's Place, just off St. James's Street) is but a hop and a skip from Dukes (see above) and is quite as old-school and as charming, with a loyal army of repeat customers, again like Dukes. There are 70 rooms, some more attractive and more recently redecorated than others. The inviting little bar has a Louis XV look. It and the adjoining restaurant have their own (optional) entrances on Blue Ball Yard. Member, Prestige Hotels.

Strand Palace Hotel (Strand) is value-packed. Its exterior is elderly, but its 800-room interior is up-to-date; there are varied eat-drink locales, including an all-you-can-eat roast beef restaurant. Trusthouse Forte.

Tower Thistle Hotel (St. Katharine's Way) is perhaps the most romantically located hotel in London—just across the street from Her Majesty's Tower of London. The hotel is up-to-the-minute modern, with more than 800 rooms and a slew of bars and restaurants. But mind, you are *way* east.

Waldorf Hotel (Aldwych) is a landmark on the arc-shaped thoroughfare that leads off the Strand and backs on to what has become Fleet Street. Its glory is a high-ceilinged lounge (a major destination for tea). The restaurant, all crystal chandeliers and Ionic columns, is smart. There are 310 bedrooms and suites, which Trusthouse Forte management has modernized.

SELECTED MODERATE-RATE HOTELS

Alexander Hotel (Sumner Place): Though with interiors by no means as stylish as those of its across-the-street neighbor, Number Sixteen Sumner Place (see below), the Alexander is agreeable; a clutch of refurbished elderly houses, in which all doubles have baths and some singles have showers. Restaurant, lounge.

Bedford Hotel (Southampton Row) is a favorite with visitors for whom the British Museum or University of London are prime destinations. There is a garden, with restaurant and bar overlooking it, and some of the 180-plus rooms' baths have showers.

Berners Hotel (Berners Street) is an oldie, but with a fair number—nearly 90—of private baths among its nearly 240 rooms. Ambience is Edwardian, location is convenient to Oxford Street.

Bloomsbury Centre Hotel (Coram Street) is just north and east of Russell Square, in the British Museum-University of London area. It may lack atmosphere, but it is big (all 247 rooms' baths have showers); restaurant, coffee shop, bar.

Charing Cross Hotel (Strand), attached to the Charing Cross Railway Station, is a turn-of-century souvenir of an era when hotels were built with high ceilings, elaborate plasterwork, palatial reception areas, and huge bedrooms. Today's visitors enjoy the style of the old with contemporary facilities like private baths (most rooms have them) and convenient wine-dine facilities, especially the Betjeman Carving Restaurant—an all-you-like beef-lamb-pork eatery.

Clifton Ford Hotel (Welbeck Street) is conveniently located on Welbeck Street, a bit north of Oxford Street; restaurant, bar.

DeVere Hotel (Hyde Park Gate) is a late nineteenth-century house that has been partially modernized to the point where something like 80 of its 95 rooms have baths. Withal, the place remains turn of the century, with views of Kensington Gardens from the better rooms. Restaurant, bar.

Ebury Court Hotel (Ebury Street) embraces a quartet of elderly joined houses. Corridors are irregular because of the way the houses are joined; not all have baths. The restaurant is exceptional. Victoria Station is close by, and both the Piccadilly and Knightsbridge areas are short bus rides away. Charming.

Eden Hotel (Harrington Gardens) is inelegant but spotless, with a restaurant, bar, obliging staff, and central Kensington location.

Embassy House Hotel (Queen's Gate) is nicely situated near Kensington High Street. Elderly from without, it surprises within: all 70 rooms have showers in their baths. Coffee shop, bar.

Flemings Hotel (Half Moon Street, just off Piccadilly) is so centrally placed that it is frequently full up. It's elderly and attractive, with restaurant, coffee lounge, and bar.

Green Park Hotel (Half Moon Street) is an across-the-street neighbor of Flemings, but bigger; with restaurant and bar.

Grosvenor Court Hotel (Davies Street) is well situated near Oxford Street. Most rooms have private baths, and there's a restaurant and bar, if not an excess of charm.

Hyde Park Towers Hotel (Inverness Terrace) is just off Bayswater Road, north of Hyde Park. It's an updated building, with cheery rooms (all of whose baths have showers), coffee shop, bar.

Ivanhoe Hotel (Bloomsbury Street) is no-frills, behind a rather forbidding facade in the British Museum area. Rooms—many of which have bath—are pleasant enough, housekeeping is good, and there are a moderate-priced restaurant, café, and bar.

Kenilworth Hotel (Great Russell Street) is, not unsurprisingly—given its name—an across-the-street neighbor of the above-described Ivanhoe in Bloomsbury. It, too, has a restaurant and bar and has had a thorough—and relatively recent—facelift.

Kensington Court Hotel (Nevern Place at Templeton Place) is near the Earl's Court exhibition center and the tube station of that name. Out of the way, but with the baths of all its modern rooms shower-equipped; restaurant and bar.

Kingsley Hotel (Bloomsbury Way) is a quiet British Museum neighbor. It's a good value, with well over half of its 175 rooms equipped with baths, if not showers. The restaurant is of the help-yourself-to-roast-beef variety, and there's a bar.

London Elizabeth Hotel (Lancaster Terrace at Bayswater Road) is just opposite the luxury-category Royal Lancaster Hotel. Rooms are satisfactory, but the big plus is the French-operated restaurant.

Londoner Hotel (Welbeck Street) is a same-street neighbor of the Clifton Ford. There are 120 rooms, a restaurant, and a bar, and the location, a bit north of Oxford Street, is convenient.

Mandeville Hotel (Mandeville Place) is still another conveniently situated, moderate-category hotel. Majority of its nearly 170 rooms have bath, but not showers. There are wine-dine facilities, and Oxford and Bond streets are nearby.

Milestone Hotel (Kensington Court) is late nineties, with vistas of Kensington Gardens, and 50 of its 80-odd rooms have baths; restaurant, bar.

Mostyn Hotel (Portman Street) is a Portman Square-area hostelry, more modest than its newer neighbors, with Oxford Street nearby. It's elderly, but with updated bedrooms, about half of which (out of a total of about 100) have baths.

Mountbatten Hotel (Monmouth Street)—for long the Shaftesbury Hotel, in the Covent Garden area—emerged after extensive 1985 refurbishing with a new name, new management, 127 comfortable rooms and public spaces—Burma Room restaurant, Broadlands lounge, for example—called after significant places and events in the life of the late Lord Mountbatten of Burma. *First Class.*

Mount Royal Hotel (Marble Arch) is a neighbor of the earlier described Cumberland, and though smaller—it has but 700 rooms to the Cumberland's 900—it is competitive in that it, too, emphasizes no-frills comfort at a good price and with a convenient address. Well-priced restaurant and bar.

Normandie Hotel (Knightsbridge) has been updated, offering period-decor public rooms and more contemporary bedrooms, the majority with baths. Breakfast meals are served.

Number Sixteen Sumner Place Hotel (Sumner Place) occupies a joined trio of elderly, attractively decorated, well-maintained Kensington houses. Breakfast only.

Rembrandt Hotel (Thurloe Place) is convenient to Harrods. It's Edwardian in origin, with more than half a hundred rooms (out of a total of about 175) with private baths.

Royal Court Hotel (Sloane Square) is at once conveniently situated and well equipped (restaurant, two bars), with those of its recently refurbished rooms the ones to specify.

Rubens Hotel (Buckingham Palace Road), with its opposite-the-palace location, has 150 rooms, mostly with baths. Restaurant and bar, appropriately enough considering the location, are embellished with likenesses of former residents of the big house across the street.

Rutland Court Hotel (Draycott Place) is just off Sloane Square. Only some of the 30 rooms have baths. There is no restaurant but a full breakfast, served in one's room, is included in the room rate.

St. Ermin's Hotel (Caxton Street) has 252 well-fitted rooms; high-ceilinged, still-Victorian main lounge; grill room; and bar.

Stratford Court Hotel (Oxford Street) is near department stores and Bond Street boutiques; has had a thorough and relatively recent refurbishing; and offers pleasant rooms, carvery-type restaurant, and bar.

Wilbraham Hotel (Wilbraham Place) is a perfect charmer of a Victorian house, all dark paneling and antiques, with a spic-and-span look to both public rooms (these include a good restaurant) and guest rooms, of which there are no two alike. More than half the nearly 60 rooms have baths. Location, near Sloane Square, is super.

Willett Hotel (Sloane Gardens) is small (17 rooms) and simple but clean, with a full English breakfast part of the tab.

STAYING AT THE AIRPORTS

Gatwick Hilton International Hotel is a part of the Gatwick Airport complex, with access to its terminal through a covered passageway from its striking atrium-lobby. The 380 rooms and suites are soundproofed and tasteful, with welcome American-style plumbing in the baths, restaurant, traditional-style pub, lobby bar, indoor pool and health club, and a slew of conference rooms for business meetings and meals. *Luxury.*

Sheraton Heathrow Hotel is a five-minute drive (via hotel shuttle bus) from the airport. This is a biggie: 440 really comfortable rooms, late-hours coffee shop, bar-lounge, indoor pool, sauna. *First Class.*

DAILY BREAD

SELECTED ENGLISH-CONTINENTAL RESTAURANTS

Beurre Fondu (Wilbraham Hotel, Wilbraham Place): Continental and English dishes served in a Victorian atmosphere of white napery, dark-wood paneling, fresh flowers. Roasts, grills, and desserts are very good, indeed. *Moderate.*

Café Royal (Regent Street): Edwardian opulence. Menu blends the classic style of France—a duck *pâté*, for example, or *truite meunière aux pistaches*—with English specialties like bread pudding or roast lamb. The wine list is long and expert. There is a choice of rooms, with the Grill the smartest. *Luxury.*

Camellia (Syon Park, Brentford, Middlesex) is the perfect luncheon choice on that day you're devoting to stately houses on the periphery of London—Syon House, for example, and neighbors like Osterley Park and Chiswick. The Camellia is capacious and bright, with, say, fresh asparagus if it is in season, for a starter, and steak, pasta, or broiled red mullet to follow. *First Class.*

Causerie (Claridge's Hotel, Brook Street) serves a celebrated luncheon buffet—smart, attractive, and tasty. *First Class.*

Connaught Hotel Restaurant (Carlos Place): If it is less exuberant than the Café Royal (above), this very proper dining room of a very proper hotel is no less Edwardian, with its look running to dark woods, starched white napery-cum-fresh flowers, gleaming silver, and impeccably tuxedoed waiters, every one of them, as far as I can perceive, skilled and smiling. Fare is overwhelmingly—and authentically—French, albeit with British overtones. By that, I mean you will be as happy with the extraordinary mix of *hors d'oeuvres au choix*, selected from a groaning two-tier trolley—*pâtés* and terrines, salamis and salads—as with the chicken pie that is an every-Sunday tradition. Roast beef and lamb chops are standbys, too; no less so are Gallic *quenelles de haddock* and *entrecôte grillée.* Waiters will happily let you choose mini-portions of two or three sweets from the wagon. French pastries are exemplary, but you ignore the Connaught's apple and black currant pie and its bread and butter pudding at your peril. The three-course prix-fixe lunch is one of the best buys in London. Precede it—or dinner—with a drink in the hotel's paneled bar. (And bear in mind that the Connaught, for some inexplicable reason, accepts but one credit card—MasterCard.) In my view, one of Britain's best restaurants. *Luxury.*

Dukes Hotel Restaurant (St. James's Place, off St. James's Street): Quarters tend to be cramped in this tastefully decorated restaurant— you overhear everyone else's conversations and some are worth eavesdropping on. More to the point, however, the food is good Anglo-French, with creative touches. How about opening, for example, with a pair of eggshells filled with scrambled eggs, one flavored with lobster, the other with smoked salmon and truffles? Consider an entrée of filet of beef in a Madeira sauce topped with oysters or breast of duck served in tandem with a crispy duck salad. Have chocolate cake to conclude. *First Class.*

Ebury Court Hotel Restaurant (Ebury Street) is a London sleeper, traditional in look if not always in menu. Dishes are as diverse as *poule basquaise* (chicken flamed in brandy, with red and green peppers, onions, and tomatoes), escallop of veal Cordon Bleu, minute steak, and a variety of omelettes. Home-baked bread. *First Class.*

Grange (King Street) occupies a building of indeterminate vintage, on a difficult-to-locate City street. But the search is worthwhile. The Grange is a looker—subtle tones of brown, black, and white are used in the decor from walls and ceiling to table linens and china. Starters include *boeuf bourguignonne*, a Middle-Eastern lamb kebab, or poached salmon. Roast duckling, with honey and orange, is delicious. After-theater. *Luxury.*

General Trading Co. Café (Sloane Street, at Sloane Square) is a worth-knowing-about source of sustenance, breakfast through tea, not excluding morning—and, for that matter, all-day—coffee and made-on-premises cookies. Shepherd's pie is a good bet at midday, but there are French-inspired dishes, too. *Moderate.*

Hyde Park Hotel Grill Room (Knightsbridge), one of the two spiffy restaurants of a spiffy hotel, is a happy choice at midday, when it offers a generous buffet lunch—both hot and cold choices, with desserts included—and still another three-course table d'hôte, which might run to *pâté maison* or the day's soup, roast beef with Yorkshire pudding or grilled lamb chops, and dessert following. Pricier à la carte at dinner, but at lunch: *First Class.*

Leith's (Kensington Park Road) occupies an elderly house with the decor no less original than the menu: game casseroles, for example, seafood bisques, a variety of made-on-the-premises *pâtés*, both meat and fish. *Luxury.*

Lyons Corner House (Strand, just off Trafalgar Square): First of the multilevel restaurant chain—long-beloved of foreign visitors (myself included) and Britons alike—to return after their 1970s demise, this Lyons has a main-floor coffee shop for breakfast, short orders, and tea; and a basement restaurant for more substantial lunches and dinners, built around favorites like steak and kidney pie, and fish and chips. *Moderate.*

Buttery (Berkeley Hotel, Knightsbridge) is recommended for its remarkably well-priced buffet lunch—cold meats, hot dishes, salads, sweets, the lot delicious. *Moderate.*

Ritz Hotel Restaurant (Piccadilly) is one of the most beautiful rooms in Europe, a generously proportioned Louis XVI chamber giving onto the hotel's walled garden, the severe black of the waiters' tails in pleasing contrast to the pale walls, ceiling, and plasterwork. Fare is essentially French and, in my experience, delicious. Good-value set lunches. *Luxury.*

Sheraton Park Tower Hotel Restaurant (Knightsbridge): This circular tower of a hotel, a Knightsbridge landmark, has replaced its two conventional restaurants—one a coffee shop, the other posher—with a single eatery, dubbed The (with a capital "T") Restaurant, that's open from early breakfast through late evening. A glass-walled-and-domed conservatory—Art Deco in style—it is worth knowing about after theater, when a supper of, say, onion soup and a brace of perfectly boiled lamb chops with a crisp salad fill the bill, accompanied by one of the wines from an excellent French list. Splendid service. Depending on when you go, *Moderate-First Class.*

Stafford Hotel Restaurant (St. James's Place) is quiet of ambience, traditional in decor, and almost completely French-staffed, with interesting French-accented dishes (lobster bisque, *salade niçoise,* calf's liver *à l'orange,* sweetbreads Gloria), as well as English standbys like potted shrimp and mixed grill. There are well-priced prix-fixe menus at both lunch and dinner. *First Class.*

SELECTED ENGLISH TRADITIONAL, INCLUDING PUB-RESTAURANTS

Anchor (Bankside), on the Southwark side of the Thames, dates to Elizabethan times. An engaging mix of clientele, both foreign and domestic, admire vistas of the City—there's an observation platform—across the water. Fare is pub-hearty, the ambience history-laden. *Moderate.*

Antelope (Eaton Terrace) offers the economy of a pub in a smart Belgravia setting. Lunch upstairs on roast beef. Dover sole, or beef and kidney pie; downstairs buffet, too. *Moderate.*

Audley (Mount Street) is a Mayfair pub and offers a choice: Gilded Cage in the cellar, main-floor pub proper, Annie's Attick upstairs. All three are amusing and provide solid fare. *Moderate.*

Barley Mow (Duke Street) is handy to Oxford Street, not to mention Mayfair. A traditional pub, it's ideal for a lunch of, say, grilled sausages or pork pie and a salad. *Moderate.*

Bendicks (Sloane Street, near Knightsbridge) is at once a source of the fine chocolates bearing its name and a tearoom-coffee house, small but inviting. *Moderate.*

Blue Posts (Bennet St. at Arlington Street) is an Edwardian pub, just off St. James's Street, and popular with workers in the neighborhood, in part because it's an agreeable source of casual meals, dinner as well as lunch. *Moderate.*

Bunch of Grapes (Brompton Road) is an unabashedly Victorian pub, with an attractive clientele and appealing, if conventional, pub-lunch fare. *Moderate.*

Bunpenny (Brompton Road) is no more conventional than its oddball name. Look is Exuberant Edwardian, with a garrulous, albeit prosperous, clientele, enjoying English-accented fare. *Moderate.*

Carveries (Cumberland Hotel, Marble Arch; Strand Palace Hotel, Strand; Regent Palace Hotel, Piccadilly Circus) are help-yourself-to-roast-beef restaurants, at which a waitress serves you everything but the main course, which you collect at a counter, with a chef to assist, and with the happy understanding that you may go back for more. Roasts of lamb (with mint sauce) and pork (with applesauce) supplement the beef. Excellent value. *First Class.*

Chelsea Potter (King's Road) lives up to its location—smart, with a clientele of modish neighborhood regulars, an engaging ambience, and good comestibles. *Moderate.*

Cheshire Cheese (Fleet Street): The glory of the Cheshire Cheese is that it's tourist-proof. There is not a locale in all of London more evocatively Olde English. It has operated, as it proclaims, "under 15 sovereigns," beginning with Charles II, during whose reign it was rebuilt. It occupies a building of its own at the corner of the narrow street that leads down to Gough Square and Dr. Johnson's House. Johnson was a Cheshire Cheese habitué. His portrait hangs in a place of honor in the Coffee Room. Roast beef is the star of a traditional menu, with all of the old favorites recommendable, most definitely including mutton chops. *Moderate-First Class.*

Dorchester Hotel Grill Room (Park Lane): Extensive refurbishing elsewhere in this hotel notwithstanding, the Grill Room retains its somewhat unlikely, but agreeable, mock-Renaissance decor—coffered ceiling, tapestried walls, red-leather chairs out of a King Arthur movie—all very comforting. So, indeed, is the cuisine, an inspired meld of traditional English dishes, with other specialties of the Cuisine Naturelle school, which uses no cream, butter, oil or alcohol. Beetroot and watercress soup with curd cheese and steamed stuffed leg of chicken with tomato confit are typical *cuisine naturelle* offerings. I am partial, however, to such British standbys as rabbit pie, scallop *soufflé*, or Kentish potroast, typical of entrées on the good-value three-course lunch. At both lunch and dinner, the opener is an oversized wagon piled high with baked-on-premises breads in amazing variety. Desserts—including sherry trifle and lemon syllabub—are special, too. So is the old-school service. In my experience, one of Britain's best restaurants. *Luxury.*

Down's Wine Bar (Down Street, off Piccadilly) is obliging when it comes to solid fare—coarse *pate*, sautéed mushrooms, hamburgers—at tempting prices. Wine by the glass or bottle. *Moderate.*

English House (Milner Street) is just that: an elegant Kensington town house, antiques-furnished, whose personable owner, Malcolm Livingston, serves traditional English dishes, mostly based on recipes from Michael Smith's excellent book, *Fine English Cooking.* The range is soused herring and chilled Stilton soup through fish pie, grilled home-made sausages, and mustard-baked chicken to maids-of-honor chocolate *pye* and hot apple crumble. Good-value table d'hôte lunches; dinner is pricier. In my experience, one of Britain's best restaurants. *First Class-Luxury.*

George Inn (Borough High Street, Southwark) is sufficiently venerable to be a property of the National Trust; it's the only galleried inn left in London. In the beamed tavern, a cold buffet is served at lunchtime. The dining room offers a set meal that invariably includes roast beef, as well as grilled fish and such traditional dishes as roast chicken with bread sauce. *Moderate.*

Grenadier (Wilton Row) is a pub that goes back to the early nineteenth century, when George IV was a customer. Clientele today is fashionable Belgravia. Lunches (and dinners, for that matter) are excellent, with decor on military lines—old uniforms, swords, and the like. *Moderate.*

Grove (Beauchamp Place) is a two-story pub with the bar downstairs—in warm weather, customers are out in front taking in the sun and the pedestrians. The restaurant above specializes in hot pies, grilled fish, and nice desserts. *Moderate.*

Hungry Horse (196 Fulham Road, at the end of an alley) occupies a pair of contiguous basement rooms in a Kensington town house. Hardly fancy, but with delicious traditional favorites: smoked trout, leek soup, roast beef, steak, kidney-and-mushroom pie, double lamb chops. Delicious puddings and other desserts. *First Class.*

King's Head and 8 Bells (Cheyne Walk) is a venerable pub on a venerable Chelsea street, with the food as good (I know of no pub in Britain with more delicious grilled sausage!) as the look is handsome. Combine lunch with a visit to Thomas Carlyle's House nearby on Cheyne Row. *Moderate.*

Lockets (Marsham Court at Marsham Street): Origins are seventeenth century. The menu makes the best reading of any in town (they'll let you have it if you will but ask) and points out that Vanbrugh referred to it in his play *The Relapse*, which was the rage of the 1696 season, and in which the character of Lord Foppington announces that he will "go to dinner at Locket's, and there you are so nicely and delicately served. . . ." You still are. Bill of fare is divided into Fore-Dishes, Soups (there is included at that point a venerable recipe for a potage known as Veal Glue). Fishes, Removes and Made Dishes, Grill and Side Dishes, and—on a separate card—Kickshaws (desserts, these), Savouries, and Cheeses. Start with potted shrimp, continue on to Cornish crab soup with brandy, following with baked English trout with bacon or jugged hare or venison, and conclude with brandy and sherry syllabub or Cambridge burnt cream, with a savory like mushrooms on toast for the last course. Clientele runs to MPs (Parliament is a neighbor). *Luxury.*

Maggie Jones's (Old Court Place at Kensington Church Street) is one of the most uncommonly good of the smaller London restaurants. Cauliflower soup to start; entrées like shepherd's or chicken-and-carrot pie; desserts like chocolate mousse or apple crumble; carafes of wine; homemade bread. *Moderate-First Class.*

Markham's (King's Road at Smith Street): The marvelously ornate Victorian facade of this busy pub is a neighborhood landmark, worth knowing about at midday, when its hamburgers and quiche appeal. *Moderate.*

Rose and Crown (Old Park Lane): is a convenient pub for a quick but relaxing lunch from the buffet at the bar—cold meats, cheeses, French bread, and the like, washed down with a pint of lager. *Moderate.*

Rules (Maiden Lane) has been a City landmark since the eighteenth century. Its heyday was during the reign of Edward VII when His Majesty was a customer. Look of the place—old prints, carved beams, massive silver serving trolleys, white-aproned waiters—could never be duplicated. If one sticks to standbys—roast Aylesbury duck, steak and kidney pie, mixed grill, grilled kidneys and bacon, filet steak—one does well. Go after the theater. *First Class.*

Samuel Pepys (Brooks Wharf, Upper Thames Street) is a modern pub-restaurant with more emphasis given to the restaurant than the pub. One drinks (and eats simply, if desired) in a bar on the ground floor; the high-ceilinged dining room—Thames view—is upstairs. Decor is neo-seventeenth century, the idea being to re-create the City's Restoration-era, which Pepys chronicled in his diary. Fare runs to oxtail soup and roast beef. *Moderate.*

Shelley's (Stafford Street at Dover Street) is a strategically situated pub but steps from Piccadilly, whose restaurant is indicated for a stick-to-the-ribs lunch or dinner. *Moderate.*

Upper Crust in Belgravia (William Street) sports a crisp look in main floor and basement dining rooms, with table d'hôte lunches its best buys, featuring entrées like fried chicken, roast pork, and beef sautéed in Guinness. Friendly. *Moderate.*

SELECTED SEAFOOD RESTAURANTS

Manzi's (Leicester Street) is an old-school seafood restaurant, with dining rooms on the main floor and in the basement, where the style is more casual, and there is counter service—worth knowing about, if you are alone. *Moules marinières* are very good, and so, for that matter, is the fish, Dover sole included. *First Class.*

Mr. Bill Bentley's Wine and Seafood Bar (Beauchamp Place) is amusingly conceived and with an attractive clientele. The bar is on the street floor, and the dining room, serving fish/seafood menu—is one flight up. *Moderate-First Class.*

Overton's (St. James's Street) is the kind of restaurant one sees in movies about fashionable London. Traditional specialty is seafood—lobster bisque, trout *meunière*, sole Overton's, *scampi en brochette*, fresh Scotch salmon, dressed crab. *Moderate-Luxury.* (Note: Should you find yourself at Victoria Station, hungry and with time to kill, search out the Overton's near the entrance.)

Poissonerie de l'Avenue (Sloane Avenue, behind Peter Jones department store) is a worth-remembering Chelsea entry. Fish is fresh and prepared to order as you like it; ambience is light. *First Class.*

Scott's (Mount Street), with oversize, brown leather chairs at its central tables, and broad banquettes lining walls hung with sporting prints, is the epitome of the Mayfair eatery. Or, I should say, seafood eatery. The well-organized menu makes half a dozen concessions for meat eaters—including roast pheasant and partridge. But you go to Scott's for oysters and caviar, smoked salmon or trout, or an exceptional lobster bisque—among starters. And for such entrées as grilled Dover sole (which I recommend heartily) and such other fish choices as haddock, turbot, skate plaice, halibut, and lobster in a variety of styles. The waiting staff, mostly Italian, is swift and cordial. *Luxury.*

Wheeler's (Duke of York Street) is one of a small chain of this name. Londoners who know the lot play their favorites. The Duke of York Street Wheeler's occupies a building so narrow it comes close to not making sense. There is a dining room on each of the several tiny floors, and the Italian waiters negotiate the stairs and the compact areas with consummate skill. House specialty is oysters on the half-shell. There are a dozen lobster dishes, scallops four ways, 25 sole dishes, and sublime fried potatoes. *First Class-Luxury.*

SELECTED FOREIGN RESTAURANTS

American

Garfunkel's (Duke Street, Leicester Square, and a number of other locations) pleases with the likes of a menu running to hamburgers; pizza; and ice cream billed as American-style, plain, or the basis of sundaes. *Moderate.*

Hard Rock Café (Piccadilly, near Hyde Park Corner) is a stylishly decorated room absolutely loaded with Londoners—young, most of them—devouring the cuisine of their American cousins as though there were no tomorrow. Menu is limited: hamburgers and frankfurters pretty much describe it. But they're good, not always the case with our national staples in the U.K. *Moderate.*

Parson's (Fulham Road) is indicated when you crave a hamburger. You may or may not like those to which Mexican embellishments like guacamole have been added, but *au naturel* and cum-cheese, they're tasty. *Moderate.*

McDonald's (Haymarket): We do not cross the Atlantic for Big Macs, and I accord space to this McDonald's only because it's near theaters (indeed, framed playbills decorate the upstairs walls) and convenient for a precurtain burger that will tide you through to a proper post-performance supper. *Moderate.*

Chinese

Dumpling Inn (Gerrard Street) is, to paraphrase one of Bette Davis's immortal lines, "a dump"—to look at, that is. It occupies a down-at-the-heels corner store in the Chinatown sector of Soho. If you are only two, you may have to share a cramped table, and, if the place is especially jammed, you may be directed to the airless basement. Regional specialty is Peking, and no matter what it is—pork or beef dumplings; scampi Peking-style, grilled with garlic; shredded beef and green peppers; a dish of Chinese vegetables—it is delicious. The bill comes itemized in Chinese, so you end up trusting your hosts' abacus. *Moderate.*

Ken Lo's Memories of China (Ebury Street) stands out on two counts. First is ambience: The look is very sophisticated, indeed. Second is ownership: Lo is an eminent Chinese-born writer on the cookery of his native land, long resident in Britain. The name of the restaurant is a personal one: Dishes served, from various regions, are those he recalls from his youth and wrote about evocatively in his book, *Chinese Foods*. Order à la carte or table d'hôte. Lunch is cheaper than dinner, but the category is *Luxury*.

Dumpling House (Beauchamp Place), though no relation to Dumpling Inn (above), might appeal, in the course of a Knightsbridge-area shopping bout, when the urge for Peking Duck overtakes you. Many Szechuan dishes, too. *Moderate.*

French

Au Jardin des Gourmets (Greek Street) is just the Soho ticket for after-theater—and has been for something like half a century. The Jardin's métier is bistro food—onion soup and escargots, *entrecôte grillée* and lamb chops, sound salads, desserts that include a fabulous *crème brulée*, and well-priced wines. *First Class.*

Brasserie des Amis (Basil Street, opposite Harrods) is indeed a brasserie, and in the best sense: with stick-to-the-ribs French favorites— onion soup, escargots, steak French style, super salads. In addition, though, there are authentic Italian pastas. And service is at once agreeable and proficient. *Moderate.* (*Mes Amis*, a more formal restaurant, is directly next door, and another relative, *Relais des Amis*, is heart of Mayfair, on Curzon Street.)

Brasserie St. Quentin (Brompton Road) evokes its south-of-the-Channel counterparts at their classiest. This is a looker of a Gallic-staffed house, with downright delicious victuals—starters like quail eggs and whatever the potage du jour, through entrées based on duck or trout or beef. Have the mixed sherbets for dessert. Lively, lovely, and *Luxury*.

Capital Hotel Restaurant (Basil Street): By and large, everything is masterfully prepared and served, delicious to taste, and—given the ambience of the restaurant, relatively recently refurbished in exuberant traditional style by the skilled decorator Nina Campbell—enjoyable to eat. Crab bisque and chef's *pâté* are fine starters. Among entrées, *steak au poivre* and roast lamb are authentically Gallic. Salads, cheese, desserts, and wines are of equally high caliber. And the prix-fixe-cum-coffee, both at lunch and dinner, is sound value. *Luxury*.

Chelsea Room (Hyatt Carlton Tower Hotel, Cadogan Place): You go to the Chelsea Room for the smart crowd (lots of neighborhood locals) and the smart ambience. It occupies beige-hued quarters up a flight from the lobby of a handsome hotel. Massive flower arrangements—calla lilies might be teamed with pussy willows and mums—are strategically positioned. You sit on Louis XV chairs upholstered in understated checks. Staff is essentially Continental, menu fairly standard Gallic with the occasional surprise—snails in a novel parsley sauce and fennel flavoring crab bisque, among starters; turbot in conjunction with lobster and cucumbers, and veal filet in a cognac-mustard sauce, grape-garnished, among entrées. *Luxury*.

Hilaire (Old Brompton Road, a couple of blocks from South Kensington tube station and an easy walk from the Victoria and Albert Museum) is small and neat—it comprises main floor and basement rooms in tones of gray and white, with bentwood chairs at the tables. The welcome may be tentative (most customers appear to be neighborhood regulars and the Anglo-French staff shy). But the service is kindly and the fare creative. The well-priced three-course lunch might open with terrine of preserved duck and *foie gras*, continue with roast lamb served with a delicious onion compote and superb *pommes dauphinois*, and conclude with Hilaire's own rhubarb ice cream. *First Class*.

Interlude de Tabaillau (Bow Street): It's been a long opera or a full-length ballet at neighboring Covent Garden—and you've worked up an appetite. Relax over a sumptuous Interlude de Tabaillau dinner, opening perhaps with one of this house's celebrated mousses, later concentrating on a seafood or poultry specialty. Special sweets, an intelligently selected, dominantly French wine list, and expensive but fairly priced table d'hôte lunches and dinners. *Luxury*.

Langan's Brasserie (Stratton Street, off Piccadilly) is a two-story establishment, with the near-ballroom-size main-floor room the one to book for. Ambience is humming Art Deco, and waiters dart about in ankle-length white aprons, as they might in a trendy Paris bistro. Indeed, the menu is bistro-inspired, essentially French, with delicious, no-nonsense openers like garlic-scented snails, *céleri remoulade*, and hearty soups, followed by equally satisfying entrées, with choices of veal (*paillard de veau*), lamb (*gigot d'agneau*), or beef (*entrecôte grillée sauce béarnaise*). French fries are masterful, likewise the potatoes styled *gratin dauphinois*, not to mention other vegetables like puréed spinach and glazed carrots. Have *poire belle-Hélène* or *baba au rhum* to conclude. And take advantage of the reasonably priced choice of French wines. In my experience, one of Britain's best restaurants. *First Class.*

Le Crocodile (Kensington Church Street): You've been doing the boutiques of Kensington Church Street, and you're famished. Pop into Le Crocodile for a French lunch that might embrace a hearty soup, roast pheasant, and the house's celebrated Grand Marnier mousse for dessert. Well-priced wines. *First Class.*

Le Gavroche (Upper Brook Street): A snazzy basement restaurant in Mayfair? Well, yes. And that is an understatement. Down you go to a subterranean chamber walled in green baize, its tables and banquettes oversize, with their floral centerpieces little works of art, their china delicate Wedgwood. An attentive Anglo-French staff, which seems to consist more of green-blazered captains than white-jacketed waiters, greets you with grins and brings crocks of sweet butter and baskets of *petit-pains*, hard French rolls unsurpassed in London. With your aperitif comes a planter of *amuse-gueules*, exquisitely wrought canapés to gently ease hunger pangs. If you are prudent, you will have gone for the three-course-and-coffee-cum-petits-fours lunch. Each dish is brought by a pair of waiters, with a captain in attendance; one chappie lays the platter on the table; another, poof!, removes its silver bell-cover. Cuisine is classically inspired but with Gavroche variations—a cream of crayfish soup flecked with caviar, or scrambled eggs with mussels in a kicker of a sauce, as starters; two species of fish from the morning's market bathed in butter-enriched champagne, or a rich navarin, or lamb stew, unlike any you have had in France. Desserts are masterworks—*mille feuilles* in a warm vanilla sauce, the house's own sherbets, *soufflés*, and tarts. And the wine list just has to be the most extensive in the kingdom, with some bottles under £10, a few as pricey as £600. In my experience, one of Britain's best restaurants. *Luxury.*

Le Soufflé (Hotel Inter-Continental London, Hamilton Place) deceives with its Art Deco environment. You like the look—bright and perky red and white. But you don't quite expect an *haute cuisine* French restaurant. Then you watch the staff of pros at work, and then you taste the food. *Soufflés* are the specialty, cheese through chocolate. But everything is exceptional here—appetizers, like a delicate salad of breast of chicken and watercress dressed with walnut oil, through entrées like grilled veal escalope with lobster sauce, and on to carefully selected cheese in peak condition and a trolley full of baked-on-premises pastries. With an expertly collected cache of wines. Exceptional. In my experience, one of Britain's best restaurants. *Luxury.*

Ménage à Trois (Beauchamp Place) has achieved something of a reputation by limiting its repertory to first courses and desserts. Among the former, there are salads and terrines in abundance, with soups, as well. And the sweets are nothing if not original. Fun for lunch. *First Class.*

Rotisserie Normande (Portman Inter-Continental Hotel, Portman Square) takes its French name seriously. You may order a grilled steak or roast beef. But the Gallic specialties, *poulet en cocotte*, for one, are delicious. So are the sweets. *First Class-Luxury.*

Greek

Trojan Horse (Milner Street) is Greek from one's aperitif of water-clouded *ouzo* on into an hors d'oeuvres platter embracing the white goat cheese called *feta* and the stuffed vine leaves known as *dolma*, entrées including the eggplant casserole classic called *moussaka*. Bread is good and wines are mostly Greek. *Moderate.*

Hungarian

Gay Hussar (Greek Street) is a Soho destination of distinction, a first-rate Hungarian restaurant. To order here are all of one's favorites—chicken paprika, *gulyás*, stuffed cabbage, strudel. There are good Hungarian wines and engaging Magyar service. *First Class.*

Indian

Last Days of the Raj (Drury Lane), a title that will surely appeal to aficionados of the TV series, *The Jewel in the Crown*, does well by tandoori specialties—shrimp, as well as more usual chicken; this last-named turns up prepared in other ways, too. The menu is imaginative, by which I mean you want to conclude with one of the made-in-house ice creams. *Moderate.*

Khyber Pass (Bute Street at Sumner Place) is not going to win a beauty contest, but the fare is down-home Indian, curries on to other staples, and satisfying. *Moderate.*

Tandoori (Fulham Road) takes its name from the specially baked chicken that is perhaps the greatest culinary contribution the Moguls made to the Indian cuisine. The restaurant features an authentic version of the chicken, with jumbo shrimp similarly prepared. *Moderate.* (Note: Tandoori of Mayfair, under the same management, is on Curzon Street and a bit more costly.)

Italian

Bianchi's (Frith Street) is perhaps a prototype of the middling Soho restaurant—convenient if one is in the neighborhood, with a conventional menu of antipasti, pasta in considerable variety, and a number of veal dishes. *First Class.*

Café Torino (Piccadilly, near Hatchards bookstore): It's been a busy morning in the shops, and you want a quick lunch. Café Torino is self-service, and if you don't think twice about the Italian city it's named for, you're apt to be surprised at how delicious the *lasagne* is. Non-Italian fare, as well. Bravo! *Moderate.*

Il Passetto (Shaftesbury Avenue) is indicated for a satisfying after-theater supper. Concentrate on typical dishes of the peninsula—minestrone, pasta, veal *scaloppine*. Italian wines. *Moderate.*

La Capannina (Romilly Street), on a typical after-theater evening, is quite possibly the noisiest restaurant in Soho. Which is going some. Food is tasty—*linguini al pesto*, for example, or the *saltimbocco alla Romana*, with chicken, seafood, and lamb dishes, as well. And excellent salads. *First Class.*

La Cucina (Rupert Street, Soho) is convenient after the theater when you're hungry for a hearty pizza or a well-priced plate of pasta and a robust wine. *Moderate.*

Sambuca (Symons Street) is a step from King's Road—modish and pleasant. Start with the hearty minestrone, and go on to pasta or a veal dish and possibly a dessert; they're good. *First Class.*

San Frediano (Fulham Road): Italian restaurants are a glory of gastronomic London; San Frediano is among the relatively new ones. The pastas are invariably reliable; so are meat entrées, most especially veal *scaloppine* in a variety of guises. *First Class.*

Terrazza (Romilly Street) has an ebullient Soho buzz to it on both of its handsome stucco-walled floors. Order one of the chicken or shrimp specialties; a meal here is the ultimate Italian experience—delicious, hearty, animated. *First Class.*

Trattoria Imperia (Charing Cross Road) is unassuming but authentic, with a cheery staff, appetizing antipasti, fresh salad greens, and pasta cooked *al dente.* Good for after-theater. *Moderate.*

Spanish

Martinez (Swallow Street) is apparently ageless—and has been since it opened in the twenties. I don't know it for anywhere near that long, but for as long as I have it has remained consistently good, occupying capacious quarters on a narrow little street just off Regent. Authentic Spanish dishes—*paella* of course, *calamares en su tinta, zarzuela de pescado y marisco, cazuela de merluza vasca, langosta en su aroma, arroz con pollo*—are reliable. Waiters must surely be the same engaging, courteous Spaniards who have been present since the opening. *Moderate-Luxury.*

Swiss

Swiss Centre (Leicester Square): There are four restaurants on the premises and a wide range, from *Chesa*—most costly of the group, with traditional specialties, fondue, *Berne platte, bundnerfleisch,* and the great potato dish called *rosti*—in a deluxe setting, to the quick-service *Rendezvous.* Decor is Swiss modern; service, Swiss-efficient. *Moderate-First Class.*

DEPARTMENT-STORE EATING

Barkers (Kensington High Street): *Terrace Restaurant* is on the second floor; its *Rendezvous* cafeteria is in the basement.

Debenhams (Oxford Street): Descend to *Springle's Restaurant* in the basement, for lunch or tea.

Fenwick (New Bond Street at Brook Street) has both a third-floor waitress-service restaurant and a basement cafeteria, for lunch, coffee, or tea on the run.

Fortnum & Mason (Piccadilly and Jermyn Street): The lower-level *Fountain,* on the Jermyn Street side, is eternally crowded. Besides sandwiches and cold plates, there are the famed Fortnum ice creams. Happiness of a summer sightseeing afternoon, I am here to tell you, is a chocolate soda with rum-raisin ice cream—and a blob of whipped cream for good measure—at Fortnum's. Alternatively, there is a café at the rear of the main floor; and there is, as well, the fourth-floor *Restaurant*—most serene and priciest of the trio—for morning coffee, lunch, or tea. *Moderate-First Class.*

Harrods (Knightsbridge) offers a wide choice. Begin with the *Health Food Bar* in the food stalls on the main floor; continue to the *Dress Circle Restaurant*, a self-service spot for coffee, afternoon tea, sandwiches, and pastries, that's up a flight. Move to the fourth floor, where there are two restaurants—the informal café in the *Way In* department and the traditional-decor *Georgian Room*, with its own cocktail lounge and where one lunches very pleasantly, indeed. The Georgian Room's buffet afternoon teas are one of London's top values. And note also a winning pub—*The Green Man*—in the basement, ideal for lunch. *Moderate-First Class.*

Harvey Nichols (Knightsbridge) offers a green-and-white coffee shop-wine bar in the basement and smart *Harvey's at the Top*—on five.

John Lewis (Oxford Street) has an attractive restaurant, reasonably priced, and fully licensed, on its second floor; try it for breakfast, as well as later in the day.

Peter Jones (Sloane Square) has a pair of eateries. The restaurant proper is à la carte, and the cafeteria on five affords fabulous views. *Moderate.*

Selfridges (Oxford Street) offers an extraordinary range: up-a-flight *Coffee Shop* (not only for lunch but for Devon-style cream teas in the afternoon); *Brass Rail* (for sandwiches and other hearty fare) in the main-floor food department; fourth-floor *Top of the Shop*—a vast cafeteria—and that same floor's waitress service, fully licensed, and most attractive *Grosvenor Room;* and, in the bailiwick that is Miss Selfridge's, the balcony coffee shop known as *The Bistro.* You may go broke in Selfridges, but you aren't going to go hungry. *Moderate-First Class.*

SUSTENANCE IN THE MUSEUMS

Most ambitious of the museum restaurants is that at the *Tate Gallery* (Millbank)—with an interesting Gallic-accented menu and extraordinary wine list, but rather too elaborate for the average museumgoer, who may instead grab a bite at the pedestrian and adjacent Café.

There's a nondescript self-service coffee shop at the *British Museum* (Great Russell Street), a long-awaited, new (in 1985) restaurant (to replace the dullish old one) in the *Victoria & Albert Museum* (Cromwell Road). An unexceptional source of sustenance is the cafeteria in the *National Gallery* (Trafalgar Square). Topping my list in this category is the self-service restaurant in the *Royal Academy of Art* (Piccadilly); have *pâté*, quiche, a sandwich, ploughman's lunch, or simply pastry with morning coffee or afternoon tea; everything tastes good and the prices are right.

TEA AND DRINKS

Afternoon tea is no longer the occasion it used to be, not at least in busy, urban London. Country places are the best locales for the so-called cream teas—home-baked scones served with butter and jam and tiny pitchers of cream so rich it has to be scooped out with a spoon, not for one's tea but as a topping on the scones. Still, that is not to say that London is without a number of especially inviting spots for an afternoon tea break. Decade in, decade out, the *Ceylon Tea Centre* on Regent Street serves the best-value afternoon tea in London.

Department stores' restaurant facilities are described above. Tea is particularly pleasant—if one can get a seat—at *Harrods' Georgian Room* (the lure is an extraordinary help-yourself buffet, with assorted breads-cum-butter-and-jam, cakes, and pastries galore), *Selfridges' Grosvenor Room, Peter Jones's Restaurant, Barkers' Terrace, John Lewis's Restaurant,* and last but hardly least, *Fortnum & Mason's* ground-floor *Fountain* and fourth-floor *Restaurant.*

Hotels remain the most elegant tea spots. Tea is a special treat when taken in the pricey *Winter Garden* of the *Ritz* (Piccadilly)—sandwiches and cakes, with white-glove service to match. But there's a catch, you must book in advance. The *Dorchester* (Park Lane) is still another deluxe locale, and you get a little more to eat. At *Claridge's Hotel* (Brook Street), a liveried waiter will serve you in the lobby so that you can watch the passing parade. The *Waldorf Hotel's* (Aldwych) elaborately high-ceilinged lounge is a good tea locale when you are in the City in mid-afternoon. *Grosvenor House* (Park Lane) serves a tasty tea in its humming lobby—a diverting way to watch a segment of London pass in review. *Brown's Hotel* (Dover Street) serves a really hearty afternoon tea of sandwiches and cakes—in its wood-paneled lounge; the atmosphere is very English. Still other hotels for tea are the *Hyatt Carlton Tower* (Cadogan Place), *Belgravia Sheraton* (Chesham Place), *Savoy* (Strand), *Connaught* (Carlos Place), *Hyde Park* (Knightsbridge), and *Cadogan Thistle* (Sloane Street).

Cocktails can be congenial in the hotel lounges. I particularly like the dark-beamed bar of the *Connaught* (Carlos Place), the *Dorchester* (Park Lane), the *London Hilton on Park Lane*, the *Inter-Continental London* (Hamilton Place), the *Savoy* (Strand), the *Hyatt Carlton Tower* (Cadogan Place), *Claridge's* (Brook Street), and the *New Piccadilly* (Piccadilly).

Pubs for drinking (as distinct from those earlier recommended for meals) are numberless. Those I have already singled out are eminently recommendable for drinking, as well as eating, purposes. Still, there are some others that I should like to call to your attention:

Black Friar (Queen Victoria Street, in the City)—with an opulent decor of mosaics and bas-reliefs.

Dirty Dick's (Bishop's Gate) boasts that it hasn't been cleaned up in a couple of hundred years: spider webs are its trademarks.

Duke of Albemarle (Dover Street) is a well-located pub for the West End visitor in Piccadilly. Look is modish, drinkers likewise.

Bunch of Grapes (Brompton Road) is a Knightsbridge watering hole, convenient to Harrods.

Lamb and Flag (Rose Street) is a theater-district landmark, a happy choice for after the play. This, the West End's oldest timber-framed drinking house, dates to the Tudor era.

Mayflower (Rotherhithe Street) is a half-timbered oldie named for the Pilgrims' ship, with a Thames view.

Piccadilly Nuisance (Dover Street) caters to well-got-up locals and drop-in visitors; pleasant.

Salisbury (St. Martin's Lane) is a between-acts drinks spot and an after-theater magnet, as well, with thespian types prevalent among the regulars. Look is opulent turn-of-century. Good eats.

Sherlock Holmes (Northumberland Street) is a monument to the fictional detective, with all manner of Holmesiana, even including an imagined mock-up of his Baker Street digs.

THE SHOPPING SCENE
Where to shop? I break Shopper's London down this way:

Piccadilly—between Piccadilly Circus and Green Park. *First Class-Luxury.*

Regent Street—from Pall Mall to Oxford Street. *First Class-Luxury.*

Oxford Street—from Marble Arch to Charing Cross Road. *Moderate-First Class.*

Knightsbridge—including Brompton Road, Sloane Street, and Pelham Road. *First Class-Luxury.*

King's Road—Chelsea—from Sloane Square to Beaufort Street. *Moderate-Luxury.*

Mayfair—roughly, the area bounded by Park Lane, Regent Street,

Piccadilly, and Oxford Street, and including Old and New Bond streets, Curzon Street, Savile Row, Mount Street, and Audley Street. *Luxury.*
Kensington—including Kensington Church and Kensington High streets. *First Class-Luxury.*
Strand and *Covent Garden*—from Trafalgar Square east, along with neighboring Covent Garden—splendidly refurbished as a shopping mall, facing St. Paul's Church. *Moderate-Luxury.*

Profiling the department stores: London's rank with those of the major American cities and a very few others—Tokyo, Copenhagen, Stockholm, Paris. They are an effortless lesson in the capital's and, indeed, in the country's standard of living, the while reflecting British genius at marketing, merchandising, display, and salesmanship, not to mention taste. *Harrods* (Knightsbridge) leads the pack, from the brilliant facade of its late nineteenth-century quarters through the merchandise and services of its four vast floors, with the extraordinarily stocked, tile-walled food halls, antiques, housewares (including garden equipment), and clothing departments outstanding, along with a variety of restaurants (including a handsome basement pub), barber shops, hairdressers, bank, theater-ticket bureau, and even a vet if you've a sick pet. *Selfridges* is queen-bee of the Oxford Street emporia, neoclassic, with a magazine-and-newspaper stand of exceptional diversity, exemplary food, London souvenirs, china-glass-housewares departments, not to mention more places to eat than any other store. *John Lewis, Debenhams,* and *Marks & Spencer,* the nationwide cut-rate chain, are among Selfridges' Oxford Street neighbors, with *John Lewis* the biggest and most impressive of this group (don't miss china and housewares in the basement). "Marks & Sparks," as Brits call it, is chock-filled with clothing buys. *Liberty,* with its distinctive half-timbered facade, leads the Regent Street lineup; indeed, only Harrods is smarter. Liberty's celebrated prints, mostly paisley designs in silk and cotton, are made up into articles of clothing (beginning with neckties) and sold by the bolt; super housewares. *Dickins & Jones* is Liberty's Regent Street neighbor—with no standout features, as far as I can perceive. *Fortnum & Mason* (Piccadilly) is eternally jam-packed with Americans, grabbing up its costly comestibles from tailcoated salesmen as though there were no tomorrow. It also offers a trio of restaurants and departments vending antiques (excellent), clothing, and assorted doodads. *Harvey Nichols* (Knightsbridge) is a near-neighbor to Harrods, with pricey women's clothing, some men's, too; china and glass. *Barkers* (Kensington High Street), recently refurbished and brightened up, is worth knowing about for its pharmacy, food, and china. *Peter Jones* (Sloane Square) occupies an architecturally striking pre-World War II building, but it disappoints within; Chelsea deserves smarter.

Strolling the street markets: Petticoat Lane (Middlesex Street) is the most amusing, Sunday mornings, between nine and noon. Countless stalls line Middlesex and adjacent streets, defying easy classification: china and clocks, linens and luggage, jeans and jewelry, with the traditional whelks and cockles and mussels—old-time London's seafood favorites—always on hand, not to mention sandwich boards attached to grim-visaged elderly men, with the hardly optimistic intelligence to the effect that "The End Is at Hand." *Portobello Road* is a two-part affair: flowers, fruit, and vegetables early weekday mornings; antiques—among a lot else—Saturday, the day long. *Camden Passage:* hundreds of shops bulging with elderly—and really aged—objects, 10:30 A.M.–5:30 P.M. weekdays, with additional outdoor stalls open only Monday, Wednesday, and Saturday. *New Caledonia Market* (Bermondsey Square): alfresco, Fridays only, from 7:00 A.M. until about 3:00 P.M., with some 250 vendors of antiques and assorted bibelots.

SELECTED SHOPS BY CATEGORY

ANTIQUES: London is one of the great world antiques centers for seventeenth-, eighteenth-, and nineteenth-century furniture, ceramics, porcelain, maps, paintings, clocks, tapestries, and other objects, not to mention non-British antiques from France, Italy, the Middle East, and Asia. Besides the big dealers and auction houses, consider shops—often with good prices—on Knightsbridge's Brompton Road, Chelsea's King's Road, Kensington's Fulham Road and Church Street, and Portobello Road. To be noted, too, is the big, annual, high-caliber Antiques Fair, held for a fortnight in mid-June at Grosvenor House Hotel. *Mallett & Son* (New Bond Street), *Stair and Company* (Mount Street, along with a number of other Mount Street shops), and *Frank Partridge* (New Bond Street) are representative of the top stores, often with museum-caliber merchandise. There is a group of antiques markets—indoor affairs, with scores of dealers' shops—that are fun to browse and can yield important purchases, very often at good prices. These include *Antiquarius,* perhaps the best known, on King's Road; *Chelsea* (also on King's Road), and *Hypermarket* (Kensington High Street). Shops with specialties are virtually limitless; some, to give you an idea, are *Aubrey Brocklehurst* (Cromwell Road), clocks and watches; *S. J. Phillips* (New Bond Street) and *Eckstein's* (Jermyn Street), jewelry; *Spink & Son* (paintings, drawings, Asian art); *Hotspur* (Lowndes Street), English eighteenth-century furniture; *Valerie Wade* (Ebury Street), English nineteenth-century furniture; *John Sparks* (Mount Street),

Oriental porcelain; *Victor Franses* (Jermyn Street), tapestries; *Wildenstein* (New Bond Street) and *Arthur Tooth & Sons* (Bruton Street), fine paintings; *Weinreb & Douwind* (Great Russell Street), prints and maps; *John Jesse & Irina Laski* (Kensington Church Street), Art Nouveau and Art Deco objects; and *London Silver Vaults* (Chancery Lane), silver. Two stores with top-rank antiques departments are *Asprey* (New Bond Street) and *Fortnum & Mason* (Piccadilly). *Antiques Auction Houses* advertise their sales in advance, in the press; the range is wide— furniture, paintings, porcelain, old books and maps, silver, carpets. Generally, sources of the merchandise are stated; these are usually estates of collectors. Contents of each sale are on view in the auctions rooms, usually two days before the auctioneer bangs his gavel. Often, there are illustrated catalogues of sales, obtainable in advance by mail at advertised prices. Major houses are *Sotheby's* (New Bond Street)— the largest and with overseas (including U.S.) branches; *Christie's* (King Street)—also in America; *Phillips* (Blenstock House, Blenheim Street, off Bond, and also in New York); and *Bonhams* (Montpelier Street, near Harrods).

BARBERS (MEN'S) AND HAIRDRESSERS (WOMEN'S): Choice barber shops include *Ivan's* (Jermyn Street), with a veritable platoon of barbers on two levels; *Michaeljohn's* (Albemarle Street); and, the most atmospheric and Olde English of the lot (vending its own lime cologne, which is exported to the U.S.), *Trumper* (Curzon Street). Women's hairdressers include *Nevile Daniel* (Sloane Street)—should you want to have your hair done by the very same salon that sets the Queen's; and *Vidal Sassoon* (Sloane Street). Note, too, that there are big shops for both men and women in *Harrods* (Brompton Road).

BOOKS: *Hatchards* (Piccadilly) has been my favorite source these many years, trip in, trip out; three floors and a very knowledgeable staff. *Foyles* (Charing Cross Road) is long-on-scene, as well, with vast stocks in limitless categories. *Heywood Hill* (Curzon Street) specializes in rare editions and will search out an elusive title. *Her Majesty's Stationery Office* maintains a diverse list not unlike the U.S. Government Printing Office; main shop on High Holborn; others, kingdomwide.

CASHMERE AND OTHER SWEATERS AND WOOLENS: *Westaway & Westaway* (Great Russell Street, opposite the British Museum) has extraordinarily diverse stocks and fabulously low prices. *S. Fisher* (Burlington Arcade): If my purchases are typical, Fisher's Shetlands wear and wear and wear.

CHINA AND GLASS: *Reject China Shops* (three detached shops on Beauchamp Place, another on Regent Street, branches in such unlikely cities as Bath and Oxford) is the ultimate bargain-china source; at any given time you'll find diverse stocks of well-known English makers, along with assorted doodads—also cheap—including cork-based drinks coasters and place mats. *Jared* (Piccadilly) is long reputed for quality and diversity; very big on Spode and reliable at shipping. *Chinacraft* (with outlets on Oxford Street, Brompton Road, Burlington Arcade, Regent Street, and at other locations) prides itself on having just about any pattern of any manufacturer. Don't forget department stores—not only *Harrods* and *Selfridges* but *Barkers, Peter Jones, Liberty,* and *John Lewis,* to name a few. And treat yourself to a perusal of extensive selections in such smart shops as *Thomas Goode* (South Audley Street) and *General Trading Co.* (Sloane Street).

CHOCOLATES: Most delicious sources include *Bendicks* (Sloane Street—also a tearoom), *Charbonnel et Walker* (Old Bond Street), and *Rococo* (King's Road). Food halls of department stores like *Harrods* and *Selfridges* have diverse stocks, as does *Fortnum & Mason.*

ENGLISH PERFUMES, TOILET WATERS, AND SOAPS: *Floris* (Jermyn Street) and *Penhaglion* (Wellington Street) make their own, package them beautifully, and export them to America.

ENGRAVED STATIONERY: *Frank Smythson* (New Bond Street) is known for its pale blue writing papers, but you may have white or ivory stock, as well.

FABRICS: *Liberty* (Regent Street): Fabrics by the yard—in traditional cotton and silk patterns—were the original stock in trade of this department store.

FLOWERS: *Joan Palmer* (Jermyn Street) has attractive arrangements, should you require a hostess gift; they deliver.

JEWELRY, SILVER, AND FINE GIFTS: *Asprey* (New Bond Street) and *Mappin & Webb* (Regent Street) are full of beautiful things; no stores in town are more eminently browseable.

KITCHEN EQUIPMENT: *Reject Shops* (Brompton Road) is to kitchenware what *Reject China Shops* is to porcelain. Big stocks, small tabs. *David Mellor* (Sloane Square) has two floors full of the very latest and smartest objects. *Elizabeth David* (Bourne Street) writes beautiful cookbooks, sells beautiful kitchenware. *General Trading Co.* (Sloane Square) has extensive—and interesting—stocks. Again, don't overlook department stores, *Liberty* especially.

CLOTHING: The internationally reputed *"There'll Always Be an England" stores*—all of them unisex and costly—include *Aquascutum* (Regent Street), in my view, the smartest of the lot, and with a New York branch; *Burberrys* (Haymarket, Regent Street, and with their merchandise in their own and other shops throughout the planet); *Jaeger* (with half a dozen-plus stores in London, on Regent, Sloane, and Baker streets, to name three)—most boutique-like of our group; and, finally, *Simpsons* (Piccadilly) and *Austin Reed* (with its main store on Regent Street).

For clothes by well-known British designers like Jean Muir, Margaret Howell, and Zandra Rhodes, look in top department stores like *Harrods* and *Harvey Nichols*, but also in *Margaret Howell's* own shop (St. Christopher Place), *Zandra Rhodes'* own shop (Conduit Street); *Brown's* (a cluster of South Molton Street boutiques); and *Fenwicks*, a multifloor clothing store on Bond Street that goes oddly underappreciated by transatlantic visitors (it has two good restaurants). The ubiquitous, Welsh-origin *Laura Ashley* has a number of shops; the one on Fulham Road is the main clothing outlet. Finally, women's hats. You might enjoy an original from *Simone Mirman* (West Halkin Street)—milliner to both the Queen and the Queen Mum.

Men's clothes are very big in the first, unisex group of stores heading this category. So-called bespoke (custom) tailors are celebrated and include *Gieves and Hawkes* (Savile Row)—long established and with a traditional point of view; and more contemporary *Blades* (Burlington Gardens). *Moss Bros.* (Piccadilly), formerly a tuxedo-rental chain, has become an exemplary all-around clothier. *Kilgour French & Stanbury* (Dover Street) tends to be high style and pricey. *Bates* (Jermyn Street) specializes in tweed hats and grouse-shooting caps, while *Lock* (St. James's Street) is the world's premier source of derbies, called bowlers in Britain. Haberdashers are at every turn. I am partial to two on Jermyn Street—*T. M. Lewin*, with super neckties, especially those of challis wool; and *Hilditch & Key*, celebrated for its shirts. Of the department stores, *Liberty* and *Harrods* are menswear leaders; *Fortnum & Mason's* men's department is smart, especially for ties and cashmere sweaters; and *Marks & Spencer* is always worth exploring.

MINIATURE ENAMEL BOXES: Halcyon Days (Brook Street).

RAINCOATS: Aquascutum (Regent Street) and *Burberrys* (Haymarket and Regent Street).

SCOTTISH TARTANS: Scotch House (Brompton Road and Regent Street)—with other Scots woolens and knitwear, including cashmere and Shetland sweaters; branches in Edinburgh and Glasgow.

SPORTING EQUIPMENT: Lillywhite's (Piccadilly Circus)—with men's and women's sports duds, as well.

TOYS: Pollocks (Scala Street)—which just has to be the world's loveliest old-fashioned toy store; adults love it.

UMBRELLAS: Swain Aderley Briggs & Sons (Piccadilly).

INCIDENTAL INTELLIGENCE

Airports: Heathrow Airport is fourteen miles from town, making taxis a fairly expensive proposition; buses into town run frequently, and they're cheap and efficient. *Gatwick Airport* is more distant from the city, but, to compensate, is linked with it by rapid trains to and from Victoria Station.

Railway stations: London has more than a dozen railway stations—surely it sets a world record among cities in this respect—so it is essential to understand clearly where you'll be departing from. Of this large group of terminals, the most important are *King's Cross* (trains to the north, through to Edinburgh), *Euston* (trains to the north, through to Glasgow, and boat trains to Ireland via Liverpool), *Charing Cross* (with trains mainly for the southeast), *Liverpool Street* (trains heading east and northeast), *Paddington* (for west and southwest points), *Waterloo* (south), and *Victoria* (southern points and the Continent).

Public transportation is excellent. The subway—officially the *Underground* but also known as the Tube—is one of the best such systems in the world; free route maps of the system are available from ticket-sellers at every station. The Underground embraces eight major lines, each of whose routes has a color of its own on the system maps. Ascertain the Underground station nearest to your destination, determine which line it is on, and plot your route by means of the system map, noting whatever transfers en route may be necessary. The stations indicated by big circles on the map as "Interchanges" are where you may transfer to connecting lines. There is only one class of travel, with fares determined by the length of the trip. You announce your destination to the ticket agent when purchasing your ticket, and he or she will tell you the amount of your fare. Remember to hold on to your ticket for surrender at journey's end. And remember, too, that

Underground ticket agents and conductors are invariably helpful. If at all in doubt about your trip—particularly if you will have transfers to make en route—don't hesitate to ask for help.

Buses can be a more complicated matter. But the stops on each route are clearly listed at each and every bus-halt. Among routes traversing central London (with some major stops indicated): *Route 9* (Kensington High Street, Knightsbridge, Hyde Park Corner, Piccadilly, Trafalgar Square, Aldwich, St. Paul's); *Route 11* (King's Road, Sloane Square, Buckingham Palace Road, Whitehall, Trafalgar Square, Aldwych, St. Paul's); *Route 14* (Fulham Road, South Kensington, Brompton Road, Knightsbridge, Hyde Park Corner, Piccadilly Circus; Shaftesbury Avenue, Tottenham Court Road); *Route 74* (Earls Court, South Kensington, Knightsbridge, Hyde Park Corner, Marble Arch, Baker Street, Regents Park Zoo); *Route 88* (Bayswater Road, Marble Arch, Oxford Circus, Piccadilly Circus, Trafalgar Square, Whitehall, Tate Gallery). Bus fares are calculated by distance. You board from the rear, seat yourself either on the main level or upstairs (where you may smoke). Simply state your destination to the conductor when he or she approaches and pay the requested amount, retaining the ticket you are given, in case you are later asked to produce it. Bus conductors— traditionally Cockney and either male or female—are now West Indian and East Indian, as well. Like their Underground colleagues, they are the traveler's best friends in London; feel free to ask their counsel. If your stay in London will be lengthy, consider purchasing Underground and/or Bus passes, which are available for varied periods of time.

Taxis are especially designed as taxis, with plenty of leg room and headroom so that it's easy to stretch out and easy to step in and out; they are the most civilized such conveyances of any country on the planet. They are metered, but nominal extra charges are made for luggage, and drivers are tipped 15 percent. They may be hailed as they pass or picked up at taxi-ranks, of which there are many. Taxi-ranks have phones; two worth knowing are St. George's Square (834-1014) and Sloane Square (730-2664). The phone for All-London Radio Taxis is (01)286-4848. Hotel doormen are expert at securing taxis, and you need not be a guest at the hotel to ask the doorman's help in this regard; naturally, he will expect a tip for his service.

Self-drive cars are obtainable from a great number of firms. The two American leaders, *Avis* and *Hertz*, are both on the scene, but so are many English firms, of which *Godfrey Davis* and *J. Davy* are among the best known.

Private escorted sightseeing: Several firms specialize in tailor-made touring. One such, *Grosvenor Guide Service* (30 Harwood Road, London SW6; phone (01)736-9779), is operated by the knowledgeable

Judy Hoade and a staff of sophisticated, attractive women, all of them trained and licensed guides. Mrs. Hoade or one of her colleagues will take you where you want to go; they use their own cars and act as guide-drivers. If you like, they'll come up with imaginative suggestions for excursions—shopping in town, inspecting an Inn of Court with one of its members, and lunching with him in that Inn's Great Hall; touring Parliament with an insider, privately; taking in Royal Ascot or a polo match at Windsor Great Park.

Tour operators run a variety of sightseeing tours by bus, both of London proper and of attractions nearby and longer excursions, as well. These include *American Express* (Haymarket), *Frames* (Herbrand Street), and *London Transport* (Broadway).

London is eminently walkable by oneself, map in hand. But there are organized *walking tours* of the various sections of town. Contact *London Walks* (Conway Road) or *Discovering London* (Pennyfield's, Brentwood, Essex).

London and environs from the Thames is eye-filling and easily undertaken by means of scheduled river boats, during the warm-weather months. Launches depart from Westminster and Charing Cross piers, to such points as Hampton Court, Kew, and Greenwich. Ask *Thames Passenger Services* (Charing Cross Pier, Victoria Embankment) for details.

London business hours: 9:00 A.M.–5:30 P.M., Monday–Saturday; however, some shops close Saturday at 1:00 P.M. Department stores, bless 'em, remain open Saturday until 5:30 P.M.; they have one open evening; I say "evening" rather than "night" because it's not very late—7:00 P.M. With Harrods (Knightsbridge), this traditionally has been Wednesday. Oxford Street department stores stay open later on Thursday. Banks: Monday–Friday, 9:30 A.M.–3:30 P.M.

London addenda: Besides the banks, there are change bureaus at Victoria Station (Thomas Cook) and such department stores as Harrods, Selfridges, and Barkers, among others. If you hold an American Express credit card and need money, present it at *American Express* (Haymarket). The *Trafalgar Square Post Office* never closes. The *London Taxi Lost & Found* is at 15 Penton Street. The *All-Purpose Emergency Telephone Number*—for police, fire, and ambulance—is 999. You may dial it from any telephone—and for free; no coin is necessary. Dial 246-8041 for the *London Tourist Board's* daily recorded roundup of visitor attractions; dial 730-0791 for answers to specific tourist's questions by the Board. *London Transport's* phone number—for information on the Underground and buses—is 222-1234, round-the-clock. *American Embassy* (including Consulate General and Commercial Attaché) is on Grosvenor Square (telephone: 499-9000). *Canadian High Commission* is at Canada House, Trafalgar Square (telephone: 930-9741). And lastly, the weather. Dial 246-8091 for the latest prediction.

Further information: London Tourist Board Information Centres are at Victoria Station and Heathrow Airport and in Harrods (Knightsbridge) and Selfridges (Oxford Street) department stores. City of London Information Centre is in St. Paul's Churchyard.

3

Bath and Wells
Georgian and Medieval

BACKGROUND BRIEFING

Let us sidestep, for the moment at least, the proposition as it pertains to all of England. But surely there *will* always be a Bath. The Romans made of it a spa, naming it for still-therapeutic waters. Medieval Britons adorned it with what is perhaps the most sublimely proportioned of Britain's abbey churches. And then, in the early eighteenth century, a long-somnolent Bath reemerged into a Golden Age dazzler of a watering hole: architecturally stunning (credit the John Woods, Senior and Junior), socially the capital of the kingdom (credit unofficial ruler Beau Nash), intellectually absorbing (credit such house-renters as Richard Brinsley Sheridan, William Wordsworth, Jane Austen, and Thomas Gainsborough), and politically potent (with settlers-in including George III's consort, Queen Charlotte; George IV's morganatic wife, Mrs. Fitzherbert; William Pitt; and Lord Nelson).

Queen Elizabeth I visited late sixteenth-century Bath—by which time it had begun to decline—and ordered a refurbishing. The following century, James I and VI's queen, Anne of Denmark, became the first royal to employ Bath's waters for health purposes. It was Queen Anne—ailing more than well, pregnant more often than not, during the dozen years of her early eighteenth-century reign—who made Bath a resort of consequence when she began making visits with courtiers, the while inspiring among an enterprising trio of newcomers a scheme for rehabilitation of the ancient city.

Sensibly quarrying the local stone, entrepreneur Ralph Allen and architect John Wood (and later his son) joined forces with London expatriate (and gambler) Beau Nash to create a Bath based upon the neoclassic northern Italian designs of Andrea Palladio. The Woods' Bath, mercifully preserved, is a complex of exquisitely wrought residential terraces, squares, and circles, punctuated by elegant public buildings, the lot utilizing the ancient Roman Baths and medieval Bath Abbey as an inspired nucleus.

Under Beau Nash's aegis as social arbiter, Bath was rivaled only by London as a focal point of eighteenth-century Britain. Everyone put in Bath appearances, from ambitious young men anxious to seek their fortunes whatever their fields of endeavor, through to monarchs and their courts, politicos, artists, and writers.

With the Industrial Revolution and the burgeoning railroad, British society became more mobile and wandered farther afield. Only after World War II, when conservation-minded groups like the Bath Preservation Trust set to work, did the opulence of the eighteenth century begin to reemerge. Recent decades have seen Bath shed the grime of centuries, restore its architectural and artistic treasures, develop a proper accommodations industry (its hotel rooms had lacked, of all things, baths), and encourage visits from the traveler curious to investigate a re-created jewel of a town, rivaled by few anywhere in Europe. And it offers the bonuses of a southwest England situation near a charmer of a cathedral (Wells), a culture-rich city (Bristol), outlying villages little changed over the centuries, and not a few country houses of exceptional caliber.

ON SCENE

Lay of the Land: Bath's ravishing squares and crescents serve as landmarks, as one proceeds from the core of town: Bath Abbey and the neighboring Roman Baths. Bath Spa Station, the train terminal, is due south. High Street is just north of the Abbey. Allow time for walks. A classic one would take you across the Robert Adam-designed, shop-lined Pulteney Bridge, over the River Avon, past Lauriston Place, and on to mansion-lined Great Pulteney Street, at whose end is the colonnaded facade of the Holburne of Menstrie Museum, with Sydney Gardens out back. More eye-filling is a walk from the Abbey north along Union and Milsom streets (they have smart shops), with a turn west to George Street; thence north on Gay Street to The Circus, lined by classic-style houses with the Assembly Rooms at its northern extremity; and due west via Brock Street—the Royal Crescent. Pause, en route, at the colonnaded houses of The Circus. Each is an entity, yet the cluster is united, with a different classic order of architecture on each floor: Doric at street level, Ionic up a flight, Corinthian at the top. Royal Crescent—unsurpassed among counterparts, Europe-wide—is the masterwork of the architects Woods, father and son: no less than 30 joined mansions united by a series of Ionic columns, 114 all told. Landsdown Crescent, farther north and elevated so as to afford a panorama of the city, is lovely, too. Other pedestrian destinations: the park called Parade Gardens, obeliskcentered Queen Square, Victoria Park's Botanical Garden, antiques shops lining Bartlett Street, and nearby St. Swithin's Church, where Jane Austen's father was rector.

Roman Baths and Museum and Pump Room (Stall Street): The baths' most spectacular remain is a great pool—it would be called Olympic-size today—that, though now uncovered, was arch-roofed some twenty centuries back. The museum, adjacent, is not to be rushed through. As a result of continuing excavations by the Bath Archaeological Trust, it brims with bits and pieces of Roman Bath, some from the temple that stood alongside the baths. A gilded bronze head of Minerva is star of the show, but there are miniature gemstones, earrings of gold, tin masks, pewter pitchers, stamped lead pipes, sculpted heads, and tombstones. The Pump Room, some seventeen centuries newer, is named for the pumps that coaxed the spring water up a level, into Beau Nash's salon, where white-wigged patrons sipped it, the better to cure bouts of gout.

Bath Abbey (Abbey Churchyard) is a fifteenth-century successor to an earlier church that had full cathedral status and was twice the size. The Abbey is the last of the major churches to go up in Perpendicular, the third—and most elaborate—of the three categories of English Gothic. Pause, before going in, to study the facade, noting the sculpted angels ascending and descending ladders—stairways to heaven—on either side of the great window, itself surmounted by an angelic choir. Within, the long nave is unbroken in its path to the high altar and the massive east window, depicting half a hundred scenes in Christ's life. Three other Abbey standouts: fan vaulting over the nave; a modern stained glass window depicting the tenth-century coronation (in Bath) of King Edgar, the ceremony for which serves as the pattern for coronations of British sovereigns; and last, and perhaps most atypically, a memorial tablet to Bath's eighteenth-century social leader, Beau Nash.

Holburne of Menstrie Museum (Great Pulteney Street) occupies a palace-like structure that had been a hotel when it went up in the eighteenth century. Within, the University of Bath operates one of the most beautiful small museums in Britain. Concentrate on the second-floor paintings: Queen Charlotte, a frequent Bath visitor, by Zoffany, court painter to her husband, George III; works by Gainsborough, Romney, Ramsay, Stubbs, and even Gilbert Stuart. Furniture throughout—including Sheraton and Chippendale—is of the period. So are the china—Bristol, Chelsea, Worcester—and silver.

No. 1 Royal Crescent Museum (Royal Crescent) stands at the east end of the house-rows of eighteenth-century Bath. The Bath Preservation Trust has turned the house into a museum, furnishing it as it might have been when first inhabited—dining room on the ground floor, drawing room one flight up, bedrooms on two, with servants' quarters in the attic. Special.

Museum of Costume and Assembly Rooms (The Circus): Look first at the main-floor rooms of this eighteenth-century venue for balls and parties: a reception room in pale gray and green, beneath a spanking chandelier; a beige tearoom, quiet but smart; and the Octagon Room, stunner of the group, with superb paintings. Down to the basement, then, to see the costumes, with the gamut Elizabethan through Bath's heyday, into the Victorian decades, the 1920s and 1930s, the post-World War II New Look, and this very season's *haute couture*.

Bath Carriage Museum (Circus Mews): More than 30 carriages; a ducal coach, early police vans, and a hansom cab among them.

Guildhall (High Street): Up you go a flight, for a look at the banqueting room, a Georgian masterwork that is called, with reason, the best-looking public space in town. The Adam-style plasterwork of the ceiling is a major reason.

American Museum (Cleverton Manor) occupies a classic-style country house a few miles out of town, and, rather infuriatingly, closes down in winter and opens only three hours each afternoon—with the exception of a few holidays and Sundays—the rest of the year. To be seen are no less than 18 rooms furnished with American furniture, draperies, glass, and silver, representing various design eras of the United States, between the seventeenth and nineteenth centuries. Café.

Lacock and Castle Combe villages make for a pleasant day's outing. The former, Lacock, has changed nary a whit since the eighteenth century and has buildings going back to the thirteenth. Indeed, it is such an all-of-a-piece antique that it's operated, in toto, by the National Trust, with its various dwellings mostly let out to individuals. Ask at the Trust's Information Centre on the High Street as to what interiors happen to be open; ancient *Lacock Abbey* is the most important. Pause for tea at *King John's Hunting Lodge* (Church Street). Proceed then to Castle Combe, a real live village, not under National

Trust aegis, where there's a charming little Gothic church—invariably open—just opposite the fifteenth-century Market Cross, itself a neighbor of the little Castle Hotel, where you could do worse than have a cream tea.

Wells and its Cathedral: But 20 miles southwest of Bath, little (pop. 10,000) Wells bases itself upon its centrally situated Cathedral. Consecrated in 1239, *Wells Cathedral* is Early English, oldest and least detailed of the three types of English Gothic. It is at its most spectacular from without, when one pauses on the broad lawn and takes in the West Front, a sprawling alfresco stone screen, or reredos, in whose half-dozen levels of niches are nearly 400 statues depicting the Last Judgment, framed by a pair of strong square towers. What first strikes one, within, is the architecturally unique pair of inverted arches separating the nave from the chancel, each pure Gothic in shape, the upper one—upside down—directly above the lower, erected to strengthen the central tower. Have a look at the cloister, the misericords—carved wooden slats—in the splendidly scaled choir, and the stone steps—worn smooth from countless feet treading them over the centuries—that lead to the octagonal chapter house. The *Wells Museum*, to the left of the Cathedral's west front, is chock-full of local lore but open only in summer. Out back of the Cathedral, across a water-filled, duck-populated moat, you may look over a wall to the four-teenth-century *Bishops' Palace*. Stroll down *Vicar's Close*, framed by stone row houses on both sides, the lot dating to 1348 and all inhabited.

Badminton House (Badminton, 20 miles north of Bath) has severely limited open hours—traditionally Wednesday afternoons—but it is such an outstanding example of Palladian architecture—it went up in the seventeenth century—that you almost forgive the Duke of Beaufort his desire for privacy. Noted English architect-designer William Kent made eighteenth-century changes and was the original planner of the grounds—later enlarged by Capability Brown. Within, there are museum-caliber paintings, continental European as well as English, and superb furniture.

Corsham Court (Corsham, nine miles east of Bath) is, like Badminton, set in a park designed by Capability Brown. But the house dates to Elizabethan times, albeit with Georgian additions. There is eighteenth-century furniture, much of it Chippendale, but the top treat is a picture gallery packed with Old Masters—English, Spanish, Italian, and Flemish—a bearded Van Dyck gent in a white ruff quite possibly the star of the show.

Montacute House (near Yeovil, 40 miles south of Bath): The stone-work of Montacute's Elizabethan exterior is impressive enough. Within, plasterwork, paneling, and tapestries are exceptional. So are paint-ings—by masters like Ruisdael, Lawrence, Hoppner, and Reynolds. The Long Gallery—189 feet running the length of the house—is the longest such extant of any Elizabethan or Jacobean house. Café. National Trust.

SETTLING IN
Royal Crescent Hotel (Royal Crescent, Bath): Start with a central pair of the thirty joined houses of architect John Wood the Younger's mid-eighteenth-century masterwork, the 530-foot-long Royal Crescent. Come up with a multimillion-pound budget for restoration by experts (including art whiz Lord Crathorne to select paintings). Invest in museum-caliber antique furniture and accessories. Purchase the finest textiles, porcelain, and crystal. You end up with what is one of Britain's most beautiful hotels. Suites are unsurpassed, so far as I know from my researches, in any British hotel, given the stuccowork of their ceilings, canopies of their four-poster beds, and eighteenth-century furniture. Bedrooms—no two of which are alike—are similar-ly significant and those in the main building have been supplemented by half a dozen (plus two smashing suites) in the Pavillion—a re-stored Palladian villa in the garden. Public rooms—entrance hall, lounges, basement restaurant—manifest the meld of opulence and comfort that was a hallmark of the period. Member, Leading Hotels of the World, Prestige Hotels. *Luxury.*

Francis Hotel (Queen Square, Bath) occupies a cluster of connected Queen Square mansions, venerable to be sure, but attractively up-dated—albeit in period style. Many of the 90 bedrooms' baths have showers. The restaurant is reliable, bar congenial, and location could not be more central. Trusthouse Forte. *First Class.*

Lansdown Grove Hotel (Lansdown Road, Bath) is away from the center but compensates with a garden setting that affords views of the city. This is an old-school house charmingly modernized. Not all rooms have baths. Good-value restaurant. *First Class.*

Priory Hotel (Weston Road, Bath) went up in the 1830s in Gothic Revival style. Away from the center, in its own lovely garden, it has been a hotel for only a couple of decades. Each of the 15 bedrooms is antiques-accented. So are the lounges, the bar, and the outstanding restaurant, described later. You have the feeling of being a guest in a country house, complete with outdoor swimming pool and drinks terrace. Member, Relais et Châteaux. *Luxury.*

Beaufort Hotel (Walcot Street, Bath): You don't anticipate—given its antiseptic contemporary facade in Bath, of all cities—that you're going to like the Beaufort. Within, the modern motif continues, but it's modified with traditional (the bar, for example, is Chinese Chippendale), and it works very well, with 123 bedrooms—all of whose baths are shower-equipped—a river view, central situation, restaurant, and smiling staff. *First Class.*

Royal York Hotel (George Street, Bath) comprises a quartet of side-by-side eighteenth-century Bath houses. There's a convenient restaurant and bar-lounge. Not all bedrooms have bath. *Moderate.*

Christopher Hotel (High Street, Bath) is heart-of-the-Bath-action, to the rear of the Abbey. This is a smallish house, with but a score of bedrooms, about half of which have baths. The bar is popular with locals, and there's a restaurant. *Moderate.*

St. Monica's Hotel (Great Pulteney Street, Bath): The address for this eighteenth-century house-turned-hotel is a landmark street. Nothing fancy within, to be sure. But most of the 22 rooms have baths, and there are both lounge and restaurant. *Moderate.*

Pratt's Hotel (South Parade, Bath) is an old-reliable. Setting is a cluster of historic houses on a historic street. Almost all of the 42 rooms have baths. Restaurant, bar. *Moderate.*

Fernley Hotel (North Parade, Bath): What Pratt's, above, is to South Parade, the Fernley is to its northern counterpart. This is an attractive hotel in a nicely updated setting. Many rooms have baths, and there's a pub that serves casual meals. *Moderate.*

Edgar Hotel (Henrietta Street, Bath) is a case of big things in small packages. Most of the 35 rooms have baths; the restaurant, bar, and lounges are smart Regency style; and the setting is a Georgian-era terrace in central Bath. *First Class.*

Homewood Park Hotel (Freshford, near Bath): What I like most about this architecturally undistinguished, essentially Victorian hotel is chef/co-owner Antony Pitt's authentically French cooking. A Pitt-prepared lunch—Marseilles-style fish soup, breast of duck with a Cassis-based sauce, the Gallic potato masterwork called *gratin dauphinois*, and a hot chocolate *soufflé*—is long-savored, indeed. I consider Homewood Park's restaurant one of Britain's best. There are eight adequate bedrooms. *First Class.*

Ston Easton Park Hotel (Ston Easton, near Bath) is an exercise in Palladian splendor, an extraordinarily good-looking eighteenth-century house meticulously transformed into a seventeen-room hotel. Withal, the tone of the place—formal and, if not frigid, certainly not spontaneous, at least in my experience—is such that I would prefer a quick inspection, in the manner of a visit to an uninhabited National Trust-operated house open to the public, rather than an overnight stay. The restaurant, with Anglo-French fare, is the least elaborate of the public spaces; drinks are served in the drawing room. *Luxury.*

Castle Hotel (Castle Green, Taunton): An agreeable small town 30 miles southwest of Bath. Taunton is convenient, as well, to Bristol and Wells, not to mention southwestern points like Exeter and coastal Devon. The Castle Hotel is built around a onetime castle that goes back a dozen centuries. There are 45 no-two-alike suites and rooms, smartly traditional but with superb baths. Relax, when the weather is fine, in the garden. The bar-lounge is a joy, and the restaurant is—to understate—exceptional; one of the best in the west. In a word, one of Britain's best small hotels. Member, Prestige Hotels. *Luxury.*

County Hotel (East Street, Taunton) is not as distinctive as the Castle (above). Nevertheless, it occupies quarters in a Georgian house, most of its rooms have bath, and the chandeliered, up-a-flight restaurant is a pleasure. Trusthouse Forte. *First Class.*

Castle Hotel (Castle Combe): Take away the Castle Hotel and the only other principal monuments remaining in this hamlet are the Market Cross and parish church, just opposite. This is a thirteenth-century stone house with a dozen charming rooms—most have baths—and one is a honey of a honeymoon suite. Have drinks or tea in the lounge, dinner in the stone-walled restaurant. *First Class.*

DAILY BREAD

Popjoy's (Sawclose, Bath) occupies the onetime residence of none other than Beau Nash, Bath's eighteenth-century social leader. And it bears the name of his eccentric mistress, Juliana Popjoy. Menu is eclectic, at once English and French-influenced. Open with the most unusual eggs Benedict you'll have had; smoked mackerel is an ingredient. Beef is excellent; desserts, elaborate. *Luxury.*

Royal Crescent Hotel Restaurant (Royal Crescent, Bath): Precede your meal with an aperitif in the cocktail lounge of this extraordinarily beautiful hotel (above). Move, then, to the stylish, eighteenth-century dining room. Open with soup or a *pâté*, proceeding with veal, lamb, or seafood—all inventively prepared. Skip a sweet at your peril. The wine list is one of the best in the region. *Luxury.*

Hole in the Wall (George Street, Bath): Setting is the basement of an eighteenth-century house, with the cuisine of France its inspiration. Open with seafood terrine, selecting *poulet canaille*—an inspired way of preparing chicken—as the main course, concluding with syllabub as a sweet. Fine wines. And—a relatively recent development—there are twin- and double-bedded rooms-cum-bath on the upper floors of this "Restaurant with Rooms." *Luxury.*

Priory Hotel Restaurant (Weston Road, Bath) embraces two dining rooms—one traditional, the other contemporary and garden-view. Fare is Gallic—lamb roasted with rosemary, veal kidney in a mustard sauce, with smoked salmon terrine to start, house-baked pastry to conclude. Order à la carte, and tab is *Luxury.* Choose the table d'hôte, and it's *First Class.*

Francis Hotel Restaurant (Queen Square, Bath) is attractive, with eighteenth-century overtones, and good value, if you select the three-course luncheons or dinners, with such main dish possibilities as steak and kidney pie, and roast turkey. *First Class.*

Beaujolais (5 Chapel Row, Bath): Stick-to-the-ribs French standbys—onion soup, *entrecôte* with *frites*, hearty desserts, sound wines—are what make Beaujolais recommendable. *First Class.*

Trattoria Pietro (39 Gay Street, Bath): You could do with a reviving bowl of minestrone, spaghetti to follow, with, say, a bottle of Chianti Classico to accompany. Head for Pietro's. *Moderate.*

La Venange (Margarets Buildings, Brook Street, Bath) is just the ticket when it's an unpretentious meal of, say, soup, quiche, and salad or cheese with French bread and a glass of wine. *Moderate.*

Pump Room and Terrace Restaurant (Roman Baths, Bath): The capacious Pump Room, chandelier-hung and supported by Corinthian columns, has been busy since the eighteenth century, when its customers were drinkers of the salubrious Bath waters. Today's beverages are morning coffee (with a traditional Bath bun) or afternoon tea. Adjacent is the Terrace Restaurant, overlooking the principal Roman bath; for this last, arrive early to avoid crowds. *Moderate.*

Old Red House (High Street, Bath) has been drawing the thirsty (for tea or coffee) and the hungry (for pastries and lunch) since 1798. Near Bath Abbey. *Moderate*.

Sally Lunn House (Old Lilliput Alley, Bath) bills itself as the oldest house in town (A.D. 1482). You go not only for the environment, but to have a sugary Sally Lunn bun with morning coffee or afternoon tea, a casual lunch or, for that matter, dinner, at which you might want to try an English wine. *Moderate*.

Castle Hotel Restaurant (Castle Green, Taunton): An outstanding hotel (above) is the setting for an even more outstanding restaurant. The menu deftly melds French with English cooking and baking. The à la carte offers treats like a duck *pâté*, and *ragout des fruits de mer à la crême*—seafood in a vermouth and cream sauce—through to entrées including a trio of lamb chops sautéed in butter with Charon sauce, a variation of hollandaise. But the three-course lunches and dinners are quite as exceptional and top value. In my experience, one of Britain's best restaurants. *First Class-Luxury*.

Swan Hotel (Sailor Street, Wells) faces the western facade of Wells Cathedral and dates to the fifteenth century. An ideal locale for lunch, a drink, tea, or overnight; several of the rooms have antique four-poster beds. *Moderate-First Class*.

Red Lion Hotel (Market Place, Wells), in a fine old Georgian house, fronts the town's main square, alongside the cathedral. Pop in for a snack, lunch, or tea. *Moderate-First Class*.

Vicar's Hall (Vicar's Close, Wells), a setting that evokes the Wells of yore, as well it might, given fourteenth-century origins—that's just the ticket for morning coffee, lunch, or afternoon tea. *Moderate*.

AFTER DARK
Theatre Royal (Sawclose Barton Street, Bath) is no less felicitous in look than the city's other main monuments; plays, entertainments.

Bath Festival (violinist Yehudi Menuhin was its founder) is an annual spring (usually late May–early June) event; talent is often world-class, with historic buildings in and around town settings for concerts and recitals.

INCIDENTAL INTELLIGENCE ═══════════

Further information: Bath Tourist Information Centre, Abbey Church-yard; Wells Tourist Information Centre, Town Hall, Market Square.

4

Birmingham
And Westward to Shropshire

BACKGROUND BRIEFING

Time was, and not so very long ago, when Scotland's first city was Britain's second. But it has been some years now since Birmingham overtook Glasgow for the United Kingdom's No. 2 spot. It has, for long, taken full advantage of its location—equidistant from four key cities: London, Liverpool, Manchester, and Bristol—and a focal point for transport via canal, rail, and road.

Birmingham has always built upon its accomplishments. Its strategic West Midlands location facilitated development, even before the Norman Conquest, as a trading point. By the time William II granted the first royal charter to Peter de Bermyngham—scion of the family from which the city took its name—it was a busy distribution center, with prosperous farms surrounding it and an increasingly savvy populace of artisans and merchants. Richard the Lionhearted bestowed a second charter the first year of his reign—in 1189—and Henry III followed suit in the ensuing century.

As the Middle Ages became the Renaissance, Birmingham prospered, manufacturing leather products and trading in wool. In the mid-eighteenth century, James Watt and Matthew Boulton's factory was producing steam engines. By the mid-nineteenth century, Birmingham had become a proper city, with a government progressive enough to pioneer in areas like slum clearance, water supply, and other municipal services that at the time were novelties.

While it grew—today's Birmingham is a manufacturing and distribution center of world class—it did not shy away from an aggressive role in culture and the arts, fine, as well as performing. The landmark City Hall, which it erected as long ago as 1834, contains an auditorium in which the city's internationally esteemed symphony continues to perform. By 1867, it had opened an Art Gallery that has become an

all-Britain leader. The University of Birmingham, founded at the turn
of the century, is complemented by the more recent University of
Astin. World War II devastation did not crush Birmingham—at least
for long. Its rebuilt center is at once boldly contemporary and reten-
tive of the traditional.

ON SCENE

Lay of the Land: Central Birmingham, ringed by a circle of ultramodern freeways, is bisected by wide and busy New Street, running east-west with New Street Railway Station at its center. Flanking
the station is Birmingham Shopping Centre, vast and ultramodern,
albeit not as vast or ultramodern as its almost-next-door neighbor,
even newer, 150-store Bull Ring Shopping Centre, identified by the
circular skyscraper at its main entrance and named for adjacent Bull
Ring, the venerable square that is where Birmingham began. Bull
Ring still is the setting for daily open market, its range of wares
clothes to candy.

Streets leading north from these shopping complexes—Bull Street,
High Street, Corporation Street—are, by and large, pedestrians-only
and lined with shops and department stores: Debenhams, Lewis's,
Marks & Spencer, and Rackhams, poshest of the lot and related to
London's Harrods.

Walking is a pleasure in central Birmingham from, say, the sprawling, neoclassic Town Hall-Art Gallery & Museum complex at New
Street's western extremity, eastward to and through streets like Colmore Row and Waterloo Street, to the placid park-like square that
surrounds St. Philip's Cathedral.

Birmingham Museum & Art Gallery (Congreve Street) is an extraordinary mix. Begin in its archeology galleries—remnants of Roman
and Saxon Britain, gold jewels and sculpted heads from ancient Greece,
a T'ang horse out of early China, Assyrian ivory, an enormous Bud-
dha out of India, ancient Peruvian textiles, and even North American
Indian artifacts. Look, then, at relatively recent rooms devoted to the
history of the city—watercolors and maps, prints and pottery. Then
go on to the special treats: Birmingham's paintings. Hans Memling's
Nativity is probably the single greatest of the lot. But there are works
by Bellini and Botticelli, Guardi and Canaletto, among the Italians;
Rubens and de Hooch, among Low Countries masters; Poussin, Boucher, Courbet, and Corot, from pre-Impressionist France; Impressionists like Sisley, Pissaro, Renoir, and Mary Cassatt. English work?
Consider a Peter Lely of Cromwell, half a dozen Gainsboroughs,
Ramsay and Reynolds, Hogarth and Zoffany, and one of the largest
collections extant of English nineteenth-century pre-Raphaelites—

Millais, Ford Madox Brown, Edward Burne-Jones. With silver from all over Europe, and furniture—eighteenth-century Italian and French, especially. End-of-visit surprise: pots of real tea—not tea-bags—served with individual strainers (a rarity in today's Britain!) in the cafeteria.

Barber Institute of Fine Arts (University of Birmingham): The late Queen Mary, among the more art-savvy of the Royal Family in modern times, opened the Barber in 1939; it was a gift of the widow of a governor of the university, which included funds for acquisition of just about anything in the fine and decorative arts categories except pottery or china—which is hardly missed, given the caliber of the paintings. The Barber is an all-Britain sleeper, with the quality as exciting as the broad scope of the collection—a Degas jockey, a typically Teniers village out of the seventeenth century, Botticelli's *Madonna and Child with the Infant St. John*, a Bellini painting of a young lad—instead of his more usual Madonna, a Della Robbia sculpture, a *St. John* by Simone Martini, and Boudin's beloved Normandy coast. And more brilliance as you walk about: Veronese and Guardi, Delacroix and Rodin, Hals and Steen, Turner and Reynolds. Dame Martha Constance Hattie Barber, we are in your debt!

St. Philip's Cathedral (a.k.a. Birmingham Cathedral, Colmore Row) is one of a number of city cathedrals—Portsmouth, Newcastle, and Manchester are among the others—that started out as ordinary churches but were promoted to cathedral status when the cities in which they are situated were made seats of bishops heading newly created dioceses of the Church of England. Such was the case with St. Philip's. This single-towered, neoclassic structure is elegant in the sense of the smaller Wren churches in London and others by Gibbs and Hawksmoor. Along with Wren's vastly bigger St. Paul's in London, it is the only Baroque-era British cathedral. Four of its windows—*Ascension, Crucifixion, Nativity,* another called *Doom*—are by the last century's pre-Raphaelite master, Burne-Jones, a native of Birmingham, who was baptized in St. Philip's. And there is a plaque honoring a judge from Massachusetts, loyal to the Crown during the Revolution, who died in exile in Birmingham.

St. Chad's Cathedral (Bath Street) is, in its way, no less interesting than St. Philip's (above). St. Chad's was the first Catholic cathedral to be built in England after the Reformation in the sixteenth century. It opened in 1841, a most unusual species of Gothic Revival in that it has Germanic overtones—paintings, for example, attributed to Dürer, along with a superb German Renaissance pulpit, bishop's throne, and altar stalls. Note the Stations of the Cross, executed in rich detail. And look up at the lovely twin steeples.

St. Martin's Church (Bull Ring): Birmingham has a soft spot for St. Martin's as it's the original parish church of the town, going back a thousand years, but mostly the consequence of a late nineteenth-century restoration. Still, there are three memorials to early Bermyng-hams—the family that inspired the city's name. And a Burne-Jones window supplements those at St. Philip's.

Museum of Science and Industry (Newhall Street): A natural in a city where science and industry are the bases of development. If you're turned on by the likes of instruments, arms, engines, tools, cars, and motorcycles, the S and I is for you.

Birmingham Nature Centre and Birmingham Botanical Gardens are neighbors in the Edgbaston part of town and are nicely explored in tandem. The former is Birmingham's nomenclature for zoo, with—in natural habitat settings—lynxes, badgers, owls, and polecats, with ponds full of fish and waterbirds and a bonus of beehives. The latter embrace 10 pretty acres and include rose, rock, and rhododendron gardens. And a pavilion full of chattering tropical birds livens things up. Restaurant.

Aston Hall (Trinity Road), set in its own well-manicured park, could not contrast more with the tacky part of town that surrounds it. Along with the Barber Institute (above), this is a Birmingham sleeper of the first magnitude—a Jacobean country house, now engulfed by a city, to be sure, but beautifully operated by that city, to its great credit. And for quite some time, too. Queen Victoria opened it to the public as long ago as 1858, although she was not its first royal visitor. King Charles I was a guest in 1642. Throughout, the carved wall paneling, extraordinary stuccowork of the ceilings, furniture, and paintings are first rate, with the grand stairway, pair of drawing rooms, King Charles's tapestry-lined bedroom, and Long Gallery the standouts.

Coventry (20 miles east of Birmingham), heavily bombed during World War II, built a new cathedral so imaginatively that visitors flock to it. The town itself is ringed by a road called, logically enough, Ringway. High Street is smack in the center, with *Coventry Cathedral* lying due north, off Priory Street. Instead of razing what remained of the damaged Gothic structure, the architects of the new cathedral left the old walls, tower, and 300-foot spire quite as they were when the bombs hit in 1940. They form an entry to the new building, the award-winning work of architect Sir Basil Spence, that opened in 1962. It is among top-rankers of its kind, with respect to scale (Coventry is heroically proportioned); boldness of design that disregards symmetry; and exceptional contemporary art, including Sir Jacob Epstein's bronze sculpture of St. Michael, Graham Sutherland's massive tapestry of Christ in Glory (more than 70 feet in height), and John Piper's 200-panel baptistry window. Consider looking at a collection of studies made in preparation for the execution of the cathedral's Sutherland tapestry in the *Herbert Art Gallery* on the street called Jordan Well and at fourteenth-century *St. Mary's Guildhall* and its crypt on Bayley Lane.

Ludlow (48 miles west of Birmingham): Its proximity to the frontier with Wales—but a few miles to the west—assured this small (population 8,000), now-tranquil town a disproportionately substantial role in Anglo-Welsh affairs during the Middle Ages, when its now partially ruined castle was a border stronghold held either by rival barons or by the Crown. In the course of the centuries following—fifteenth through late seventeenth—the castle was seat of the Council of the Marches of Wales and Wales's virtual capital.

The council was the English governmental body that administered Wales and the border countries for most of the period (Commonwealth era excepted) from its establishment by Henry VII until the reign of William and Mary began in 1689. Although Edward IV spent most of his boyhood as Prince of Wales at Ludlow Castle, Catherine of Aragon was the castle's most celebrated royal resident; she stayed there as a princess with her first husband, Prince Arthur, elder son of Henry VII. After Arthur died at Ludlow Castle (you may see his tomb in nearby Worcester Cathedral [Chapter 22]), Catherine became queen—as first wife of his successor-brother, Henry VIII, living again at Ludlow (the second time with her daughter, later to become Queen Mary I) between 1526–1528.

Wealth was a medieval concomitant of political prowess in Ludlow, as a wool-manufacturing center. Indeed, it is wool rather than the castle bureaucrats of the Marches Council that was responsible for the architectural distinction the town achieved during the Tudor era—it abounds still in half-timbered structures—and retained well into the eighteenth century, by which time it had become a winter social center for Shropshire gentry, who quartered themselves in still-standing houses of that gracious period.

Agreeably compact, Ludlow revolves around its main square, *Bull Ring*, as good a place as any to begin an ambulatory town tour. Start at the *Ludlow Museum*, which is situated in an elegant eighteenth-century building, topped with a cupola and fronted by a classical portico—called Butter Cross. Exhibits run a broad range—medieval crafts to memorabilia of the politically powerful Tudor era, with later Georgian pieces and a pair of Victorian period rooms. Continue to *St. Laurence Parish Church*, just opposite, noting from without its fabulous 135-foot-high tower and, within, its size; St. Laurence is 200 feet long—the largest church in Shropshire and one of England's outstanding examples of Perpendicular Gothic. Sir George Gilbert Scott effected a mid-nineteenth-century restoration, wisely leaving the choir's misericords, or folding seats. And a good bit of original stained glass remains. Ludlow facades—along streets like Broad, College, and King—are of splendid half-timbered (and later) structures. Look around. Proceed west, then down the High Street, past the Victorian-era Town Hall to Castle Square and *Ludlow Castle*, owned, rather ironically, since the early nineteenth century by Wales-based Earls of Powis (see Powis Castle, Chapter 28), who have maintained it and kept it open to visitors. Although it might be said that the castle is at its best from without—now-paneless frames of once-elegant Gothic windows, towers, battlements, dry moats, and crenelated walls—it is not unpleasant to stroll the inner precincts. Note especially what remains of the royal apartments wherein lived Prince Arthur and his Spanish-born betrothed, Katharine of Aragon, and ponder in the process how different might have been the fate of Catholic England had Arthur lived to reign as king instead of his brother, who, as Henry VIII, broke with Rome and established the Church of England.

Shrewsbury (50 miles northwest of Birmingham and locally pronounced *Shrows*-b'ry) is bigger than Ludlow (above)—population hovers around 50,000—and gives the impression of being contemporarily more prosperous. But if it is hardly less ancient than its Shropshire neighbor to the south—founding was in the fifth century, and earlier names, each memorable, were Scrobesbyrig and Sloppesbury—Shrewsbury, although it battled often with just-next-door Welsh neighbors (the 1403 Battle of Shrewsbury, immortalized in Shakespeare's *Henry IV, Part 1*, took place just north of town), cannot boast, as can Ludlow, that Wales was governed from its castle.

Not that the Shropshire County seat gives the impression of plastic modernity. Walk around its core and you will find yourself saying, "This could be a movie set!" You learn, in short order, that indeed it was. TV crews settled into its top two hotels for several mid-1980s months to shoot the version of Dickens' *A Christmas Carol*, starring George C. Scott as Scrooge, which you may well have seen on your home screen.

The video producers were lured by architectural remnants of Shrewsbury's two Golden Age periods—the earlier Tudor era, which saw rich merchants build still-splendid, half-timbered mansions, and the later Georgian epoch, when gentry came for winter social "seasons" and erected elegant town houses, many still seeing service. This is a handsome town with a bonus of uncomplicated geography that makes self-guided exploration a joy. The central square—flanked by pedestrian shopping precincts—is called simply The Square. It lies at the confluence of High Street and a thoroughfare variously called Shoplatch, Pride Hill, and Castle Street. Nearby thoroughfares—Wyle Cop, Dog Pole, Town Walls—are no less interestingly labelled.

Shrewsbury Abbey is a onetime Benedictine monastery that is essentially Perpendicular Gothic, but with lovely Norman arches and columns in its somber nave. *St. Mary's Church* boasts the third tallest spire in England, and the stained glass in its vast Perpendicular Gothic windows is brilliant. *Shrewsbury Castle* goes back 900 years; there have been several restorations and what you see today is part history museum (do go in), part municipal offices. I would miss neither of the two principal museums. The elder, *Rowley's Museum*, occupies a honey of a half-timbered house, with remnants of regional Roman settlements its most spectacular exhibits, along with a costume collection. *Clive House Museum* celebrates Georgian Shrewsbury; Lord Clive (Clive of India) lived in it while mayor in 1762. Note the exceptional collections of Coalport china and derring-do military regalia.

Two additional churches beckon. One—*St. Chad's*—typifies Palladian Shrewsbury; it is England's largest circular church, and the eighteenth-century architect, George Steuart, is the very same who designed Attingham Park (below). The other—the *Roman Catholic Cathedral*—is an outstanding specimen of nineteenth-century Gothic Revival, the dramatically high and steep gables of its roof a clever substitute for a steeple.

Attingham Park (Telford Road, four miles southeast of Shrewsbury) is a country extension of the town's stylish Georgian period—a sumptuously detailed mansion fronted by a three-story-high portico supported by a quartet of Corinthian columns, by the same architect, George Steuart, who designed St. Chad's Church (above). Landscape architect Humphrey Repton created the verdant park. Early nineteenth-century Regency and Italian furniture, collected by one of the resident Barons Berwick, grace grandly proportioned state rooms, and there's a John Nash-designed circular staircase. Café. National Trust.

SETTLING IN
Grand Hotel (Colmore Row, Birmingham) is the epitome of the grand hotel. This is a handsome old-timer (it was built in 1875), deftly refurbished, albeit in traditional style, with a welcoming staff,

felicitous public spaces, a choice of good places to eat and drink, showers in the baths of all 180 rooms and suites, and—if you have a chance, take a peek—a ballroom called the Grosvenor Suite, which has to be one of the most opulent in the kingdom. *Luxury.*

Albany Hotel (Queensway, Birmingham) is, to be sure, nondescript modern from without. But go on in and give it a try. The 250 bedrooms—at least those I have inspected—are tastefully contemporary, and all their baths have showers. Facilities, among the most extensive of the British luxury houses, include a health club-cum-swimming pool and restaurant/bar, four squash courts, a pub that serves super bar-lunches, an all-you-can-eat roast beef Carvery, and an exemplary main restaurant. Trusthouse Forte. *Luxury.*

Midland Hotel (New Street, Birmingham) is a longtime Birmingham institution, heart-of-town, attractively old-school, with 114 rooms, all but 10 of which have baths, with showers in some of the twins. Public spaces here are ample, as they would have to be, given the number of restaurants (one French-accented, another for roasts and grills) and bar-lounges (four all told, with casual meals obtainable in three of these). *Luxury.*

Royal Angus Hotel (St. Chad's Queensway, Birmingham) has the disadvantage of being not quite central—it's an across-the-street neighbor of St. Chad's Cathedral (above). But it is spanking modern, with good-size rooms (all of whose baths have showers), attractive restaurant, two bar-lounges. *First Class.*

Birmingham Centre Hotel (New Street, Birmingham) is solid-value contemporary. All 200 of its compact rooms have shower-equipped baths; two restaurants and as many bars. *Moderate-First Class.*

New Imperial Hotel (Temple Street, Birmingham): This is a neat-as-a-pin house, with restaurant, bar, and everything but a quantity of bath-equipped rooms; only 10 of 110. *Moderate.*

Metropole and Warwick Hotel (National Exhibition Centre, Birmingham) is convenient for visitors with business at this away-from-downtown convention complex. This is Birmingham's biggest—with 500 well-equipped rooms, restaurants, and bar-lounges. *Luxury.*

Holiday Inn (Holliday Street, Birmingham): Rare is the Holiday Inn in Britain that will win a beauty contest. Still, most that I know are at least friendly and well operated. Birmingham's, in my experience, is neither. I can recommend only the generously proportioned bed-rooms, most with two double beds and showers in all the baths. *Luxury.*

Plough & Harrow Hotel (Hagley Road in Edgbaston, southwest of Birmingham's core) is popular with motoring travelers who like its country-house atmosphere. There are 40-plus rooms, attractive public spaces, including an agreeable bar and a smart restaurant wherein Anglo-French specialties—veal chops done the Gallic way and English mixed grill—are exceptional. *First Class.*

Feathers Hotel (Bull Ring, Ludlow) is so extraordinary from without that I suggest you study its facade for a few moments before you check in. This half-timbered building is one of Britain's all-time greats of its type. It took on its present richly detailed look in 1619 when an attorney in the employ of the Council of the Marches bought, en-larged, and refurbished it. The front door dates to 1830, and the front balcony was appended a few years later by a speech-giving politician. But your bags are heavy and you want to check in. Why not? Manager Peter Nash is ever-present, seeing to it that this 35-room house runs beautifully. A few rooms have four-poster beds, although most are contemporary, with showers in all the baths. Public spaces are atmo-spheric and ancient; you don't want to miss the intricately carved paneling in the residents' lounge. The bar is friendly, and the restau-rant—with a fabulous cathedral ceiling—is worthy of comment in a later paragraph. *First Class.*

Angel Hotel (Broad Street, Ludlow) is even older than the Feathers (above). It has a half-timbered facade, 17 neat rooms (there is one four-poster), a restaurant, and a wine bar whose lunches are a good value. *Moderate.*

Lion Hotel (Wyle Cop, Shrewsbury) bespeaks the good looks of Shrewsbury's eighteenth century. The king of the jungle, for which it is named, in gilded plaster, surmounts the little portico over the entrance, itself supported by Doric columns. Public spaces are hand-some—high-ceilinged lounge for tea, convivial bar, pleasant restau-rant, and (ask if you may have a look) original Robert Adam-style Assembly Room, now used for private parties. There's lots of history in this house. William IV came before ascending the throne, Paganini played, Dickens settled into the suite now bearing his name. And there are nearly 60 rooms, most of which have been recently—and tastefully—updated. In my experience, one of the best-operated small-city hotels in Britain. Trusthouse Forte. *First Class.*

Prince Rupert Hotel (Butcher Row, Shrewsbury) predates the Lion
(above); for the latter's Georgian facade, substitute originally fifteenth-
century half-timbering at the Prince Rupert. Public rooms' ancient
floors slope a bit, and their ceilings are oak-beamed. Sixty of the 70
rooms have baths; they're neatly contemporary in look. Casual lunches
are served in the bar-lounge, and there's a good restaurant about
which I comment in a later paragraph. *First Class.*

DAILY BREAD

Four Seasons (Albany Hotel, Queensway, Birmingham): First, credit
the Albany's interior designer; the Four Seasons is sleek and sophisticated. Second, be grateful for the serving staff, maître d'hôtel through
buspersons; they're pros and they smile. Third, compliments to the
chef. His two-course-and-coffee lunch—hors d'oeuvres from a groaning board to which you help yourself, entrées with the range lamb
chops and steak to panfried trout or *fritto misto* as you know it from
Italy. Tack on a sweet; they are top rank. At dinner, consider the à la
carte—duck terrine or a seafood casserole to start, sliced duck breast
or roast lamb to follow, *crêpes Suzette* made at table to conclude.
Exceptional wines. In my experience, one of Britain's best restaurants.
First Class-Luxury.

Castillane Restaurant (Midland Hotel, New Street, Birmingham):
This handsome room, with French-accented cuisine, is the only restaurant that I know of, anywhere in Britain, that offers a four-course-
and-coffee, table d'hôte dinner that includes a half-bottle of house
wine for each diner and a postmeal liqueur; at lunch, there's one less
course and a correspondingly lower tab. *First Class.*

La Capanna (Hurst Street, Birmingham) is a warm and welcoming
Italian spot, with tasty—and authentically sauced—pasta, good veal
and fish entrées, and sound Italian wines. *First Class.*

Great American Disaster (Cannon Street, Birmingham) is not the
only restaurant so named in Britain. Have a hamburger, steak, or fried
chicken, with chocolate cake for dessert, and a milk shake, if you like.
The look is amusing. *Moderate.*

Los Canarios (Albert Street, Birmingham): Britain has a considerable
Spanish population, much of it involved in the restaurant industry.
Los Canarios is at once *auténtico* and *simpático*. Ask for *sopa de maris-
cos*, a delicious seafood stew. *First Class.*

Gaylord (New Street, Birmingham): A logical source of the northern Indian specialty, chicken tandoori, so called for the special oven in which it is prepared. Curries, too. *First Class.*

Sylvania (St. Martin's House Parade, Bull Ring Shopping Centre, Birmingham) may not sound Chinese—but it is. Mostly Cantonese specialties; table d'hôte lunches and dinners. *Moderate.*

La Galleria (Paradise Place, Birmingham) is that delightful combination—a wine bar with Italian food. The pizza is good, but so is the pasta. House wine by glass or bottle. *Moderate.*

Corks (Whitefriars Street, Coventry) is an agreeably Gallic-flavored wine bar. Wine by the glass or bottle. *Moderate.*

Feathers Hotel Restaurant (Bull Ring, Ludlow): The giant menu, to start. Its cover sports a full-color photo of the Feathers's half-timbered facade that is eminently frameable. The space sheltering the restaurant is dramatically high and is topped by a beamed cathedral ceiling. Then comes fare. Prix-fixe lunches and dinners are sound values, and they're tasty, with starters like smoked trout with horseradish sauce and herbed cheesecake with fresh coriander sauce, entrées including steak and kidney pie and sliced duck breast with lime and green peppercorn sauce. Vegetables are expertly prepared; sweets and service are super. *First Class.*

Cavalier Restaurant (Prince Rupert Hotel, Butcher Row, Shrewsbury): Dark-beamed ceilings complement dark-wood, ladder-back chairs in this welcoming restaurant, where table d'hôte lunches and dinners—with such starters as onion soup, smoked mackerel and the house's own ravioli *au gratin*, and such entrées as roast pork or lamb and baked ham in madeira sauce—are good bets. Sprightly service. *First Class.*

Criterion Steak Bar (High Street, Shrewsbury) is more restaurant than bar. You've a choice of sirloin, filet, or T-bone steaks, with grilled scampi or sole as alternatives. Agreeable. *First Class.*

AFTER DARK
Birmingham Repertory Theatre (Broad Street) is a looker of a modern building, semicircular, with levels of arched windows its trademarks. The "Rep" produces thoughtful works by Birmingham playwrights and presents, as well, visiting troupes' offerings, plays through ballet. With a restaurant open to the public for lunch and

dinner. There are other theaters, including the *Alexandra Theatre* (Suffolk Street), No. 1 after the Rep.

City of Birmingham Symphony Orchestra—"CBSO" to its fans— performs regularly in *Birmingham Town Hall* (Paradise Street). To watch this respected ensemble perform on the Town Hall platform— backed by the pipes of its giant organ and framed by Corinthian columns supporting a splendid ceiling—is to watch quite a show.

Belgrade Theatre (Corporation Street, Coventry) carries on the year-round with a full schedule of plays—Neil Simon to Henrik Ibsen. Restaurant. (Note: Ask your hotel porter for a free copy of *What's On In & Around Birmingham*, published twice monthly.)

INCIDENTAL INTELLIGENCE

Birmingham Airport is the principal regional airport, with flights to domestic points, Ireland, the Netherlands, and Italy. *Further information:* Birmingham Tourist Information Centre, Colmore Row; Coventry Tourist Information Centre, Broadgate; Ludlow Tourist Information Centre, Castle Street; Shrewsbury Tourist Information Centre, The Square.

5

Brighton
And Surrounding Sussex

BACKGROUND BRIEFING

Brighton is hardly without competition among south coast resorts. Next-door Hove, Eastbourne, and Hastings due east, big Bournemouth, and the coastal ports of Devon and Cornwall are all in the running. Still, Brighton stands alone for two good reasons. Location is one—London is less than an hour's train ride north—and a strong royal association is the other.

King George IV, while he was Prince Regent in the closing decades of the eighteenth century, selected Brighton as the site of a pleasure palace that put it on the visitors' map—apparently for all time. Not that he selected Brighton out of the blue. An ancient, originally Anglo-Saxon fishing village, it was fortified against French marauders in the sixteenth century; knew its first royal visitor—Charles II crossed over to France from Brighton, after escaping the Battle of Worcester—in the seventeenth century; and came into the public eye in the mid-eighteenth, when a resident physician named Russell wrote a best-seller recommending seawater in the treatment of glandular diseases.

And so began Brighton's spa years. George III's eldest son, then Prince of Wales, went to visit an uncle in 1783. He was so taken with the place that he bought a small house, on the site of which he erected the first Royal Pavilion in the then-popular mock-classic style by the architect Henry Holland.

Not long thereafter, the Prince hired still another architect, John Nash, who designed an Indo-Chinese pavilion around the Holland house. The dual construction—one royal residence after the other in a heretofore uncelebrated provincial port—had its effect. Brighton became a fashionable resort. The Prince Regent's morganatic wife, Mrs. Fitzherbert, built a house that remains standing as the YMCA. And others of the Prince's retinue became residents.

The Prince Regent ascended the throne as George IV in 1820 and continued his regular visits until a couple of years before his death in 1830. His brother, who succeeded as William IV, liked the town, too, as did William's consort, Adelaide. But William's niece, the young Queen Victoria, did not like the Royal Pavilion, and sold it to the city in 1850. By that time, though, the railroad had long since arrived, and Brighton's reputation had long been made. In winter, it is today a leading conference and convention center. In summer, vacationers favor it. All told, this city, which with adjacent Hove has a population of about a quarter-million, sees some seven million visitors annually. Not surprisingly, it is reasonably well equipped with hotels, which is why I recommend it as a base for exploration of a richly rewarding patch of southern England.

ON SCENE

Lay of the Land: Brighton is delightfully walkable. Not surprisingly, the Royal Pavilion of the Prince Regent—"Prinnie," as he still is called locally—is the focal point, giving on to Castle Square, to the south. Several streets called Steine—just plain Steine, Steine Street, Steine Lane—are adjacent, along with North Street, Churchill Square shopping center, and, in agreeable contrast, the Lanes: a quarter of pre-Regency streets deftly refurbished as a venue for antiques and other shops, as well as interesting places to dine. The beach is south of the commercial core. Four waterfront landmarks you should know, going west to east: King Alfred Sports Centre (indoor swimming to badminton); Brighton Centre (concerts and congresses); Palace Pier, turn-of-century and still a crowd-pleaser, with amusement machines and the even older Volk's Seafront Railway, which links the pier with our fourth landmark; Brighton Marina—a yacht harbor and terminus for jetfoil ferries to France.

Royal Pavilion (Castle Square): Not unlike its builder, the pavilion is extravagant and impractical (Queen Victoria abandoned it because it afforded little privacy), but with a sense of style. The Prince of Wales gave architect John Nash full sway. He produced a Mogul Indian palace—plump towers, slim minarets, intricately detailed arches without, and outrageously exaggerated Euro-Chinese within. The overblown proportions and grand sweep of the pavilion are so overwhelming that the tendency is for visitors to ignore design details. Furniture, wallpaper, carpets, textiles, walls and ceilings, pillars and chandeliers—all are of a caliber to have impelled the exportation of a generous sampling across the Atlantic for a 1977 exhibition at the Cooper Hewitt Museum, the Smithsonian Institution's design branch, in New York. So take your time as you stroll through bamboo-accented corridors; grandiose banqueting room; kitchen with a ceiling supported by amusing fake palm trees; music and drawing rooms; and—by no means to be slighted—the more livable private apartments, particularly the suite created for the Prince when he finally—at the age of fifty-eight—ascended the throne; the bedroom of his short-lived only child, Princess Charlotte; a sitting room that might have been Mrs. Fitzherbert's; and quarters of two queens— Charlotte and Victoria.

Brighton Art Gallery and Museum (Church Street) is, in a sense, a part of the Royal Pavilion, in that its quarters went up at the turn of the nineteenth century—actually ahead of the John Nash-created pavilion—as the Prince Regent's stables. This is one of provincial England's most diverting museums—not so complex as to overwhelm after the overwhelming strength of the pavilion. Concentrate on portraits of "Prinnie"—among them a remarkable mosaic study of him while he was Prince Regent (the years 1811–1820, when he was a stand-in for deranged George III), the other a Sir Thomas Lawrence oil, in coronation robes, upon his becoming George IV. They are in the company of works of artists as diverse as Salvador Dalí and William Hogarth, with other attractions of note: a vast—and important—gallery of Art Nouveau furnishings (including a 1916 dining room by Scotland's Charles Rennie MacIntosh), with clothes of the same turn-of-the-twentieth-century period; similarly smashing displays of artifacts from the 1920s and 1930s; a fine cache of English ceramics; and an attractive café.

Preston Manor (Preston Manor Park) is an eighteenth-century house that is now a decorative arts museum, jam-packed with furniture, silver, and glass, seventeenth through early nineteenth centuries. Superb specimens are dotted about—a Regency room is outstanding—but the arrangement is infelicitous and disappointing.

Booth Museum of Natural History (Dyke Road) opened well over a century back and its original displays—more than 500 meticulously created settings for as many species of birds—are unique in the kingdom. Well combined with Preston Manor (above).

Rottingdean Village is a venerable hamlet four miles eastward, along the coastal cliffs. It surrounds a serene square, with its draw an open-to-visitors-house—*The Grange*, by name—that for a period served as home to author Rudyard Kipling before he moved to Bateman's, about which I write on a later page of this chapter.

Chichester: It's no wonder this town, twenty-five miles west of Brighton, is the site of an annual May–September arts festival that's among the most popular in Britain. Equate Chichester with charm. Start with its sixteenth-century *Market Cross*, straddling the intersection, appropriately cross-shaped, of the four principal streets—North, West, South, and East. The latter two constitute a pedestrian shopping zone; the former two frame the grounds of *Chichester Cathedral*, essentially Romanesque, with additions covering a span of centuries all the way to the late twentieth. The early—and original—nave is, to me, the loveliest part; three tiers of severe arches support an unadorned vault and lead to a treasury on one side of the high altar and to medieval stone carvings depicting the *Raising of Lazarus* and *The Arrival of Christ at Bethany*, on the altar's other flank. Biggest surprises represent the art of our own era: a stained glass window by Marc Chagall; a tapestry over the high altar by John Piper; and a striking Graham Sutherland painting of Christ with St. Mary Magdalene. Walk through the serene cloister to the refectory for lunch or a snack. Amble about this essentially Georgian town and then to such nearby points as the *District Museum* (on the street called Little London) exhibiting local lore, the better to provide a bit of Chichester background; and *St. Mary's Hospital* (Church Street) for a glance at the medieval-era misericords—carved-wood, fold-up choir seats depicting men, as well as monsters.

Goodwood House (three miles northeast of Chichester) is an essentially eighteenth-century-mansion in a 12,000-acre park containing a reputed racecourse and flying school, among much else. But it is the house that beckons, what with treasures amassed over nine generations by resident Dukes of Richmond. James Wyatt was a major force behind the architecture (the entrance portico is his work) and the state rooms, high-ceilinged, capacious, and in several instances, with ceilings supported by Corinthian columns. Show-off chambers are the cardroom (with its Sèvres porcelain); floral-motif, yellow drawing room; Long Hall—with paintings by Canaletto, Van Dyck, Reynolds, and Stubbs; and Tapestry Drawing Room, named for the Gobelins surfacing its walls.

Uppark (10 miles north of Chichester, near Singleton) is a symmetrical mansion, classic in style even to the pediment framing its main entrance, which went up in the late seventeenth century. Emma Hamilton lived there before she became Lord Nelson's mistress. King George IV, while he was Prince Regent, visited more than once. The ballroom-size saloon, with an Adam-style plasterwork ceiling, eighteenth-century furniture, and mostly Italian paintings (Giordano,

Batoni, Zuccarelli), is spectacular. But Red and Small drawing rooms
and the dining room are memorable, too. Look beyond the beautiful
gardens, and on a clear day you can see the sea, to the south, and the
Isle of Wight. National Trust.

Petworth House (20 miles northeast of Chichester) is positively palatial—an inspired rebuilding, completed in 1696, of a much older house.
The art is exceptional: paintings by Sir Godfrey Kneller of the ladies
of Queen Anne's court in the aptly named Beauty Room; and, among
mostly Flemish painters, van der Weyden, Bosch, Bourdon, Metsys,
Van Cleve, and de Lyon in the Little Dining Room. The Carved
Room's name honors Grinling Gibbons' woodcarving; the Turner
Room is so called after a baker's dozen paintings by Turner, who was
a frequent Petworth guest; and the North Gallery has works by Gainsborough, Romney, Zoffany, and Reynolds and a massive collection
of sculpture, much of it ancient Greek. Furniture is mostly eighteenth
century—and superb; so are the Capability Brown-designed grounds.
National Trust.

Clandon Park (20 miles north of Petworth) is a jewel out of the early
eighteenth century, one of the few examples in England of Italian
architect Giacomo Leoni and steeped in the tradition of that country's
Palladio. From the marble-surfaced entrance hall, one gains half a
dozen ground-floor salons, of which the Palladio Room, with an
intricate plasterwork ceiling, original wallpaper, and portraits by Kneller—is outstanding. But the saloon—its blue walls setting off extraordinary fireplace and ceiling—stands out, too. As do the canopied bed
and inlaid tables of the State Bedroom. A bonus: The Gubbay Collection—furniture, porcelains, jade, metalwork, textiles, carpets separately willed to the National Trust—has been used to furnish and
accessorize the interiors. If your visit is in the afternoon, stop for tea
at *Gomshall Mill*, in the adjacent hamlet of Gomshall, proceeding, if
you like, to the nearby town of *Guildford*, whose *Cathedral* (1961) has
the dubious distinction of being the only seat of an Anglican bishop
in Britain—with which I am familiar, at least—that is esthetically
unsuccessful. Built atop a mountain-like hill, geographically detached
from the community, it is based upon the Gothic style—red brick,
emptily immense, and plain. The contrast with also modern, also
Gothic-style, and utterly beautiful Liverpool Cathedral (Chapter 13)
could not be greater.

Arundel (midway between Brighton and Chichester, about 15 miles
west of the former) makes for a diverting outing. *Arundel Castle* is one
of Britain's medieval strongholds. Windsor, bigger and still a royal

residence, surpasses it in importance. Warwick is less restored and more treasure-filled. Still, Arundel, as the longtime seat of the long-time-Catholic Dukes of Norfolk, warrants attention. Never mind that much of it is a consequence of eighteenth- and nineteenth-century refurbishing. The point is that the work was done in the style of the Middle Ages—and done well. Arundel evokes the history played out within its crenelated walls. Surrounding a large quadrangle beneath an elevated keep, it embraces a suite of state rooms; not one, but a pair of chapels; oak-beamed Barons' Hall; dining room that looks like a chapel—its roof is high, stone, and Gothic-arched—because it *was* a chapel; wood-paneled library; bedroom in which a young Queen Victoria slept as an Arundel guest; and an extraordinary collection of paintings—Van Dycks in abundance, Gainsborough and Reynolds, Peter Lely and Sir Thomas Lawrence. Down the hill, in Arundel Town, is *Arundel Cathedral*, splendidly scaled mock-Gothic out of the last century and seat of the district's Catholic bishop, wherein repose remains of the 13th Earl of Arundel, executed in the Tower of London in 1595 as a militant Catholic and canonized as Philip Howard in 1970. Little Arundel has other lures in and about High Street, including the *Arundel Museum and Heritage Centre*, with a mixed-bag collection relating to the long centuries of collaboration between the people of the town and the noble families of the castle.

Bateman's (near Burwash, 20 miles northeast of Brighton) is the centuries-old name of the Jacobean house that, though unexceptional esthetically, served as the home of author Rudyard Kipling and his family from 1902 until Kipling's death in 1936. Kipling had been living in tiny Rottingdean (I recommend a visit to The Grange there, on an earlier page of this chapter) when he came across the empty Bateman's and moved in. If Kipling has been a part of your childhood—stories like *Kim* and *Captains Courageous*, poems like "If"—you want to make a pilgrimage to Bateman's, less for the principal rooms than for Kipling's book-lined study, full of mementos from his Indian years (he was born in Bombay, worked on a newspaper in Lahore, and lived for a time in his wife's home state of Vermont), first editions (some Indian-published) of his books, the chair from which he wrote elevated by blocks on each leg (Kipling stood less than five feet), his desk, and typewriter. Bateman's is likeable because, by the time you leave, you feel you know—and would have liked—the Kipling family. Café. National Trust.

Rye is Sussex's time-stood-still town: an enchanting period piece that has as few reminders of our modern era as in any urban area—small or large—with which I'm familiar in Britain. Its origins—given a near-

Channel location that it shares with smaller, neighboring Winchelsea—are ancient. Walk its compact core. The railway station is just north of Cinque Ports, High, and Mermaid streets, parallel with each other, and perpendicular with still other atmospheric thoroughfares—Rope Walk and Market Road, to name two. Of the lot, cobbled Mermaid Street is most requisite, with nary a modern appurtenance to mar its profile. Thirteenth-century Ypres Tower (Church Square) houses the *Rye Museum*—weathered documents, remnants of army and navy garrisons of yore, local ceramics and furniture, maritime mementos. *Lamb House* (West Street) is a National Trust-operated Georgian mansion; American author Henry James was a tenant from 1898 to 1916, during which time he wrote such works as *The Wings of the Dove* and *The Ambassadors.* You'll see not only his study, but additional, handsomely furnished rooms and the garden. *St. Mary's Church* (Church Square) went up in the eleventh century, and its Romanesque origins still are evident. But there have been Gothic embellishments, including a pair of mechanical angels that strike the tower clock each hour. The *Town Hall* (Market Street) is relatively modern Rye—by that I mean eighteenth century; duck in and ask if you may see the four maces, silver symbols of office of which Rye is proud.

SETTLING IN

Grand Hotel (Kingsmill Road, Brighton) is aptly titled and has been just that since it opened in 1864, when it impressed visitors with its five elevators. The hotel has reprinted an account of the opening from the *Brighton Herald*, which reads in part: "The visitor. . .has only to take his seat (with half a dozen others) in a comfortable little room, and his commands will be obeyed. . . . Unless he looks at the adjacent wall he will not know that he is in motion, and even then he will think, not that he is rising, but that the adjacent wall is going down. . . ." Even updated, the Grand evokes Victorian Brighton. Lobby is lovely (go for morning coffee or afternoon tea), dome-covered wrought iron staircase still superb, rooms comfortable, and baths modern—some even with continental-style hand showers, a rare occurrence in a British hotel. Corinthian columns support the chandeliered ceiling of the restaurant. *Luxury.*

Metropole Hotel (King's Road, Brighton) is another elderly house, not as history-laden as the Grand (above), to be sure, nor, for that matter, as traditional in its decor. Which is not to say that it can be found lacking. Public spaces are handsome: lobby-lounge (for tea and drinks), cocktail lounge, and two recommended restaurants—the Starlit Room, with views from on high and its own attached bar; and the less pricey, open-late Buttery. *Luxury.*

Royal Albion Hotel (Old Steine, Brighton) is an updated old-timer, seafront. Pleasant public spaces include restaurant and bar. Good value. *First Class.*

Wheeler's Sheridan Hotel (King's Road, Brighton) is cozy in look and not too big: 60 agreeable rooms, restaurant. *First Class.*

Queen's Hotel (King's Road, Brighton), with a super location and inexpensive tabs, is full-facility; some of the rooms' baths have showers. Restaurant, bar. *Moderate.*

Old Ship Hotel (King's Road, Brighton) could have done with some brightening up when I last inspected it. But it is friendly and has a history going back several centuries. (Management avers that an early owner was Nicholas Tettersell, the chap who sailed Charles II from Brighton across the English Channel to exile in France.) Two restaurants and as many bars. 156 rooms. *Moderate.*

Prince Regent Hotel (Regency Square, Brighton) had just better be a Regency-era hotel, given its name. And it is, refurbished with showers in the baths of all its 18 rooms. Breakfast only. *Moderate.*

Granville Hotel (King's Road, Brighton): I wish all the bedrooms had baths in this imaginatively decorated house turned hotel. Still, just over half do, the seaview lounge—up a flight—is congenial, and the basement restaurant is convenient. *Moderate.*

Dolphin & Anchor Hotel (West Street, Chichester) occupies a pair of ancient, contiguous inns, one of which—the Dolphin—has seventeenth-century origins. All 60 rooms are contemporary, and some of their baths have showers. Trusthouse Forte. *First Class.*

Ship Hotel (North Street, Chichester): The Ship went up in the late eighteenth century as a home for one of Lord Nelson's admirals. There are fine architectural details—especially the staircase—and 30 rooms, some with bath. Restaurant, bar. *Moderate.*

Richmond Arms Hotel (Goodwood, adjacent to Goodwood House, three miles from Chichester) is an originally eighteenth-century inn refurbished in traditional motifs. Cocktail lounge (wherein lunch is served), restaurant, and 22 lovely bedrooms. *First Class.*

Norfolk Arms Hotel (High Street, Arundel) is the handiwork of the tenth Duke of Norfolk, who—finding the need of a coaching inn while resident at nearby Arundel Castle—put it up in 1787. It exudes atmosphere. The main entrance is through the very same arch under which the horse-drawn vehicles passed. You'll like the restaurant, not to mention the two bars. And two-thirds of the three dozen rooms have baths. *Moderate.*

Mermaid Inn (Mermaid Street, Rye) is proud—as who can blame it?—of having been *re*built in 1420. Facade is half-timbered, street out front is cobbled, bar has an open fireplace, restaurant's ceiling is lined with ancient beams, and I don't know of any four-poster bedrooms in Britain—whose old hotels' four-poster rooms are a badge of honor— that surpass the Elizabethan bedchamber at the Mermaid. One can quibble about the bathrooms; I wish the fixtures would be replaced with newer ones in those rooms—the majority—that have baths. But that's carping. *First Class.*

George Hotel (High Street, Rye) has not quite the one-of-a-kind quality of the Mermaid Inn (above). Still, it goes back some four centuries, and there is no denying its good Georgian looks in both the beamed restaurant and the intimate bar. There are nearly two dozen well-equipped rooms. *First Class.*

Durrant House Hotel (Market Street, Rye) was Methodist John Wesley's home while he preached in the area. It goes back to the seventeenth century, but takes its name from an eighteenth-century owner, a friend of the first Duke of Wellington, who put it to use as a relay station for carrier pigeons bearing news of operations during the Napoleonic wars. How about *that* pedigree? Most rooms have baths (showers, actually). Restaurant, bar. *Moderate.*

Gravetye Manor Hotel (near East Grinstead, West Sussex) went up in the last years of the seventeenth century and became known, in the late nineteenth century, for gardens created by the owner of the period, William Robinson. Robinson's gardens, along with trout lakes, orchards, and woodlands, embrace the 30-acre setting of the house— which, in recent years, under the creative direction of owner Peter Herbert, has become one of the most distinguished in the British countryside. The stuccowork and paneled walls of the sitting room are stunners. The restaurant is as good looking as its fare is delicious, and there are 14 attractive bedrooms, each distinctive. Member, Relais et Châteaux. *Luxury.*

Little Thakeham Hotel (Merrywood Lane, Storrington, West Sussex) was designed in the early years of this century by the same architect

—Sir Edwin Lutyens—who created the Indian capital, New Delhi (and London's Grosvenor House Hotel, as well). It evokes Tudor palaces of half a millenium back, with spindly chimneys amid a profusion of towers and even a minstrel gallery overlooking the two-story-high drawing room, with some original Lutyens-designed furniture in the eight spacious bedrooms. There is an amusing paneled bar, exceptional fare (entrées include Scotch salmon, rack of lamb, and breast of duck, with super sweets) in the atmospheric restaurant, and delightful ambience, thanks to owner-managers Tim and Pauline Ratcliff's direction. *First Class.*

DAILY BREAD

Le Grandgousier (15 Westem Street, Brighton): You didn't come to Brighton to find a *restaurant bourgeois* transplanted from across the Channel. But Le Grandgousier is one such, serving up table d'hôte lunches and dinners. *Moderate.*

Wheeler's (The Lanes, Brighton): If you have nothing else to eat in Brighton, it should be the grilled Dover sole at Wheeler's. The list of white wines is formidable. *First Class.*

English's Oyster Bar (The Lanes, Brighton) is still another commendable seafood house. Best value is the two-course lunch. At any time: the hot lobster pâté. *Moderate-First Class.*

Pump House (The Lanes, Brighton) evokes the Brighton of old in its decor and comes through with solid victuals, at their most temptingly tabbed in the four-course table d'hôte, with entrées including *coq au vin*. *Moderate-First Class.*

Peter's (The Lanes, Brighton) has a Franco-Italian twist; French-style mussels—*moules marinières*—are delicious. And the Italian-entrée three-course table d'hôte is tasty. *Moderate.*

Market Wine House (The Lanes, Brighton): Order wine by the glass or bottle. Concentrate on the specialty—seafood. And have the three-course lunch, a buy. *Moderate.*

Royal Pavilion Tavern and Wine Bar (Castle Square, Brighton) is a neighbor of Prinnie's palace, but it's not all grand as regards tabs; salads, cold pies, sausages. *Moderate.*

Whig & Tory Restaurant (Dolphin & Anchor Hotel, West Street, Chichester) is a period-style setting for lunches and dinners. *Moder-*

ate-First Class. The same hotel's *Roussillon Buttery* is indicated for casual meals and most especially for afternoon tea. *Moderate.*

Hole in the Wall (St. Martin's Street, Chichester) has a specialty that appeals: fresh grilled fish. *Moderate-First Class.*

Royal Arms (East Street, Chichester) is just the ticket for a lunch of scampi and french fries or, for that matter, pizza. *Moderate.*

A & N Department Store Restaurant (East Street, Chichester) is just opposite Chichester Cathedral; lunch or tea. *Moderate.*

St. Martin's Tearoom (St. Martin's Street, Chichester) is for when you crave an Olde English afternoon tea or a light lunch. Atmospheric. *Moderate.*

Theatre Restaurant (Chichester Festival Theatre, Oaklands Park, Chichester) is open only during the annual festival, spring through summer. Smorgasbord, hot and cold, before and after performances in the evening or at lunch Thursday and Saturday. *First Class.*

Mermaid Inn Restaurant (Mermaid Street, Rye) is a retreat to the Middle Ages. Wood paneling on the walls is of the relatively rare type called linen-fold. There are beamed ceilings, wrought iron chandeliers, Windsor chairs, and carved-stone fireplaces. Table d'hôte lunches and dinners are reasonable and might include consommé with leeks and mushrooms, sautéed Kentish chicken, stuffed shoulder of pork, or panfried lamb noisette, and sweets from the trolley—an orange fool might be one such. *Moderate-First Class.*

Flushing Inn (High Street, Rye) has been packing them in, Middle Ages onward. Go for a proper lunch or dinner—steak and kidney pie, roast beef, seafood. Good wines. *First Class.*

John Fletcher Tea Shop (Lion Street, Rye): I can't imagine a Rye visit that does not include an interlude at Fletcher's for morning coffee, lunch, or sumptuous afternoon tea, with cakes and meringues delicious, sandwiches tasty, and old-fashioned service a delight. Setting? The building is contemporary with John Fletcher—and Fletcher was a contemporary of Shakespeare. *Moderate.*

Elizabethan (Cinque Ports Street, Rye): John Fletcher's (above) can be crowded. This half-timbered house, which dates to the period of Elizabeth I, is a worthy alternative; lunch through tea. *Moderate.*

AFTER DARK
Theatre Royal (Castle Square, Brighton) has a Victorian interior; it offers theater, ballet, and very often pre-London runs of new plays.

Brighton Festival is an annual May event, with international-caliber theater, ballet, and symphonic orchestras in a variety of settings— Theatre Royal, of course, as well as the Banqueting Room of the Royal Pavilion; the Dome (a part of the Royal Pavilion complex); the pavilion's lawns; and the Gardner Centre Theatre.

Chichester Festival Theatre (Oaklands Park, Chichester) is a starkly contemporary octagon away from the center, which is the principal venue for the town's spring-through-summer festival of the performing arts, but is open, as well, the rest of the year for symphonic and pop music, ballet, and opera.

INCIDENTAL INTELLIGENCE

No out-of-London city has better connections with the capital than does Brighton; trains take less than an hour (the station, as of course you know, if you're familiar with the Wilde comedy, *The Importance of Being Earnest*, is Victoria), and they run round the clock. Ships link Dieppe (Sealink Car Ferry) with Newhaven, nine miles from Brighton, while Seajet jetfoils cross between Brighton Marina and Dieppe in two hours. *Further information:* Brighton Tourist Information Centre, Old Steine; Chichester Tourist Information Centre, Council House, North Street; Arundel Tourist Information Centre, High Street; Rye Tourist Information Centre, Cinque Ports Street.

6

Bristol
Hub of Southeast England

BACKGROUND BRIEFING

The city from which John and Sebastian Cabot sailed to the New World in 1497 and the very same that today globally exports the celebrated sherry that takes its name, Bristol—principal port, hub of commerce, and cultural seat of southeast England—deserves better acquaintance, especially in the case of visitors to its infinitely smaller but currently more celebrated neighbor, Bath (Chapter 3), but a dozen miles distant.

Badly bombed during World War II—Nazis pounded it unremittingly in 1940 and 1941—and with an unfelicitously rebuilt core, Bristol is, withal, a substantial metropolis of half a million, brimming with vitality and, upon occasion, beauty.

Strategically situated—it edges the west shore of Bristol Channel, flowing into the Atlantic, with the Welsh capital of Cardiff its cross-channel neighbor—Bristol was chartered as a city eight centuries ago. By the time the Cabots departed its harbor for Newfoundland, it had thrived as the center of an international cloth trade. Forces of the crown captured it in a seventeenth-century Civil War battle. In the eighteenth, Bristol achieved new wealth through the so-called triangular trade, under which English wares were shipped from its port to west Africa; Africans, as slaves, were packed off to West Indian colonies, the while Caribbean tobacco, sugar, and rum went east to Bristol. At about the same time, it was in Bristol that John Wesley preached against slavery—not without effect—and it was in Bristol that Wesley ordained the first minister to serve the Methodist Church in America.

Its harbor was to yield premier place to that of Liverpool in the nineteenth century, but, still, it was from Bristol that another link to America was forged when the first transatlantic passenger steamer, the *Great Western*, sailed in 1838 to New York; wooden-hulled, it was the work of the engineer Isambard Kingdom Brunel, designer of the extraordinary suspension bridge over the Avon Gorge (below). A later Brunel ship, the then-revolutionary, iron-hulled, propeller-driven *Great Britain* (restored, and open to visitors in Bristol harbor) followed in 1843.

Twentieth-century Bristol founded a university that has become widely respected. A range of enterprises dedicated to the fine and performing arts (the Bristol Old Vic theatre company is world-famous), coupled with what remains of a rich architectural past, combine to make of it a city of no little visitor interest.

ON SCENE

Lay of the Land: Resign yourself to the fact that no matter where you headquarter, you will not be central, really central, that is. Points of interest are spread all over the lot, and more than in any other British city that I know (including vast London with its marvelous Underground), Bristol is a city where a car is of inestimable value. It is fringed on the south by a snakelike body of water, the so-called Floating Harbor, which more or less encloses the oldest part of town, whose most atmospheric streets are Corn and King (you want to walk them both). Move to the northeast, then, for the Broadmead area, a post-World War II addition where department stores—John Lewis, Debenhams, Marks & Spencer, and Littlewoods—are quartered. (But still another area, in and around hilly Park Street, whose landmark is the mock-Gothic University of Bristol tower, is shop-filled, too.) St. Mary Redcliffe, at least as important architecturally as Bristol Cathedral, is quite detached in the southeast corner of the city. The cathedral and several museums cover an extensive west-to-northwest region, a few miles beyond which is the suburb of Clifton, with its celebrated suspension bridge and other lures, including Greater Bristol's smartest shopping streets. Because you may not have time to explore this city, quarter by quarter, the order of visit-worthy destinations, below, is according to my priorities.

Bristol Cathedral (College Green): You will find purists—even including locals who are fond of their city—pooh-poohing Bristol Cathedral as too hybrid a mix of centuries (medieval through Victorian) to be taken seriously; I am not among them. This is one of the loveliest big-city cathedrals in Britain, successful at evoking Bristol's long history. The nave is mid-nineteenth century—and handsome. Older parts that you don't want to miss include a smasher of a twelfth-century chapter house; a pair of somewhat more recent Lady Chapels; and the misericords—fold-up wooden seats—of the choir, fascinatingly carved. Café.

City Museum and Art Gallery (Queen's Road) opens with an excla-
mation point, by which I mean that you enter it by means of an atrium
four stories high that is smaller and less spectacular than that at the
Glasgow Art Gallery and Museum (Chapter 25), but hardly forgettable. Start in the Applied Arts section—for lovely blue, green, and clear
Bristol glass, as well as silver. Then move along to the paintings.
France comes out ahead—with early painters like Corneille de Lyon
and Le Nain, later artists like Delacroix and Courbet, and Impressionists like Seurat, Boudin, and Renoir. There is a fine Cranach of Luther,
a *Nativity* by Jordaens, Italians like Carpaccio, Giordano, and Giovanni Bellini. Note the Bristol School's Francis Darby and fellow eighteenth-century Britons like Gainsborough, Reynolds, Ramsay, and
Richard Wilson.

St. Mary Redcliffe Church (Redcliffe Way) comes close to taking
honors as England's most all-around beautiful parish church: utterly
and exquisitely pure Perpendicular Gothic; bright and light thanks to
two levels of the vast windows typical of the genre; cut through by
a nave, whose vault is embellished by a thousand intricately painted
and gilded bosses (the decorative elements to which the vaults are
joined); and with a choir worthy of a cathedral and surprises at every
turn, not the least of which is the armor of Admiral Sir William Penn,
father of the Bristol-born Quaker who founded Philadelphia.

Georgian House (Great George Street) is a Bristol variation of Bath's
No. 1 Royal Crescent and Edinburgh's Georgian House—a sumptuous late eighteenth century mansion, in this case the original home
of a moneybags merchant—with rooms on three floors, including
study, so-called eating room, and breakfast parlor on the ground
floor; Adam-style drawing room, bedroom, and library upstairs; and,
in the basement, both a charming kitchen and—most unusual in
Georgian times—a cold-water plunge bath made of local stone, with
its original piping and drain, as well as a framed quote from a letter
of landlord John Pinney: "I now subscribe to a Cold Bath and goes
in every morning which I finds to be of great service to me."

Red Lodge (Park Row): Sixteenth-century houses operating as museums are rare in British cities; Red Lodge is a find. The ground floor's
Reception Room is, to be sure, of a later period—Queen Anne—but
very grand. Special treats are upstairs: three gorgeous rooms with
original, sublimely carved oak paneling; largest of the trio, the Great
Oak room, has a superb stone fireplace. Note the paintings; they
include a gent by Sir Peter Lely and a Godfrey Kneller of the first
Duchess of Marlborough.

St. Nicholas Church Museum (St. Nicholas Street): Operated by the Bristol City Museum & Art Gallery, like Red Lodge and the Georgian House (above), St. Nick's is a desanctified Georgian-era, Gothic-style church, bombed in 1940 and rebuilt, with its theme ecclesiastical art. Star exhibit is a massive and atypical religious triptych by the eighteenth-century English painter William Hogarth, originally placed in St. Mary Redcliffe Church (above).

Arnolfini (Narrow Quay) is modern looking and multifunctional, with its most important feature an art gallery for temporary exhibitions, some of them first rank. There are, as well, live concerts, a cinema, a bookshop, and a restaurant (below).

John Wesley's Chapel (Horsefair) goes back to 1739 and is the first chapel specifically constructed for Methodist worship. The interior is unembellished, but not unattractive, with an unusual elevated pulpit. This was where Wesley designated Francis Asbury to serve as the first Methodist minister in America.

Lord Mayor's (a.k.a. St. Mark's) Chapel (College Green) is all that remains of a hospital dissolved by Henry VIII and sold by him to the city of Bristol, which has retained it for use by the Lord Mayor. But it's open to the public, who enjoy viewing the Renaissance-era Flemish and French stained glass and even older architectural elements.

St. Stephen's Church (Corn Street) impresses, first, with a brilliantly conceived 130-foot tower. There are lovely Perpendicular Gothic windows and a high-arched nave whose vaulted ceiling is studded with gold bosses.

Suspension Bridge (Clifton): It seems inconceivable that this 702-foot-long bridge, 245 feet above the Avon Gorge, was designed as long ago as 1829. The same Brunel, who designed the pioneering transatlantic steamer (above), planned the bridge—a tower at each end—while in his twenties; it wasn't completed until 1864. Drive across!

Clifton Catholic Cathedral (Clifton Park)—opened in 1973—is superb, in large part, I suspect, because it ignores symmetry in favor of the unusual, with respect to the design of its steeple; the positioning of the altar in its irregularly delineated interior; and the play of materials used in its construction—granite and marble, glass and concrete—with brilliant stained glass windows, which, wall-like, enclose it.

SETTLING IN

Unicorn Hotel (Prince Street, Bristol) is interestingly situated on the waterfront, core of town, with a little lobby that belies a range of agreeable public spaces—well-operated Unicorn Restaurant, with good-value table d'hôte lunches and dinners; amusing Waterfront Tavern facing the quay; Lounge Bar; and close to 200 thoughtfully equipped, if not capacious, bedrooms, with the recently refurbished ones preferred. A Rank hotel. *First Class.*

Holiday Inn (Lower Castle Street, Bristol) would head my group of selected Bristol hotels if only it were more central. Location is near the Broadmead department stores (above). This is one of the better-looking links of this chain in Britain, with close to 300 generous-size rooms, pleasantly designed, most with two double beds, and the ever-reliable Holiday Inn baths, by which I mean with proper showers above the tubs and plenty of towels. Public rooms are more traditional than contemporary in look. I like Panache, the rataan-furnished restaurant, and the relaxing cocktail lounge. There's a looker of an indoor pool, leisure center-sauna, 24-hour room service, and a staff at once proficient and kind. *First Class.*

Ladbroke Dragonara Hotel (Redcliffe Way, Bristol), a neighbor of away-from-the-center St. Mary Redcliffe Church (above), might be faulted for an overexuberant contemporary decor and small bedrooms. But the staff is cheerful and professional, and the facilities are convenient, with both a restaurant (Kiln, by name, and occupying a circular brick-walled space wherein Bristol glass was for long fired) and a generously proportioned café-lounge. *First Class.*

Grand Hotel (Broad Street, Bristol) has not, in my unhappy experience, proved very grand. Enviably well situated and impressively venerable (it goes back a century), it seems tired. Refurbishings notwithstanding, corridors need paint; and the restaurant at breakfast wants a more appetizing buffet and supervised staff. I would hope, too, for an offer of a bellman at check-in, for heavy baggage; a room doorlock that worked without having to call for staff help to effect entry; a toilet that flushed properly; a hall porter who would smile and provide requested information on train departures; a switchboard that would come through with asked-for wake-up call; and a bedside lamp with a bulb strong enough to read by. *First Class.*

Avon Gorge Hotel (Sion Hill, Clifton) is an elderly house with attractive public spaces and nearly 80 bedrooms, not all of which had been refurbished when I last inspected; needless to say, it's an updated room you want to request, preferably one facing Clifton Suspension Bridge (above). Facilities include a restaurant (roast beef is the specialty) whose picture windows face the bridge, cocktail lounge, and broad, bridge-view terrace on which drinks are served in summer. *First Class.*

Thornbury Castle Hotel (Thornbury, near Bristol) has been on scene since the first decade of the sixteenth century, when the then-Duke of Buckingham received approval from King Henry VIII to fortify and crenelate his manor house. King Henry paid a visit, with Queen Anne Boleyn in 1535. Henry's daughter, ill-fated Queen Mary I, lived at Thornbury as a girl. Switch to the sixth decade of the present century. That was when Kenneth Bell became landlord. He opened a restaurant that became so renowned because of his Anglo-French cuisine that the early eighties saw him transform Thornbury into a proper hotel. The restaurant remains justifiably celebrated. A range of lounges complement it on the ground floor, and upstairs there are ten perfectly lovely rooms, each individually—and charmingly—decorated. The staff—welcoming, alert, and skilled—is as agreeable as the hotel. Member, Prestige Hotels. *Luxury.*

DAILY BREAD

Harveys (Denmark Street, Bristol) occupies space in the high-ceilinged, brick-walled cellars of the famous Bristol-based sherry firm, with the same company's open-to-the-public Wine Museum adjacent. The restaurant has the ambience—brisk, attractively populated, with a lively decibel count—of a restaurant in, say, London's City or West End. Service is cordial, swift, and skilled. And fare is exemplary. The extensive menu is in French, with each dish accurately translated into English. *Côte de Boeuf Rotie*—ribs of beef—are roasted to order; no wagon is wheeled up at Harveys. But you might prefer a more Gallic meal—*pâté du chef* or *coquilles St. Jacques ostendaise* (shrimps, as well as scallops, in a lobster sauce) to start and such entrées as *caneton à l'orange* (duck in orange sauce), *steak au poivre* (the sauce is brandy/cream), *cotelettes de chevreuil au genièvre* (venison with juniper sauce), or *côte de veau provençale* (veal chop with tomatoes, garlic, and oregano). Seafood entrées are super, too. Desserts *do* come to the table on a wagon: they do not disappoint. Splendid wine list. In my view, one of Britain's best restaurants. *Luxury.*

Barbizon (Corn Street, Bristol) occupies basement quarters in an aged, neoclassical building. Go for the good-value set lunch, three courses that might run to onion soup, sautéed lamb, and the upside-down apple-pie masterwork, *tarte tatin. First Class.*

Vintners (St. Stephen Street, Bristol) is a heart-of-town wine bar, stone arched and atmospheric, where the draw is a satisfying buffet, hot, as well as cold, to the accompaniment of a glass of the house wine. *Moderate.*

Carwardines Coffee House (Corn Street, Bristol) dates to the eighteenth century. Indicated for a snack or casual lunch. *Moderate.*

La Taverna Dell'Artista (King Street, Bristol) is charming and congenial, with Italian-accented fare that is not necessarily going to remind you of meals you've had in Florence or Rome. Okay if you stick to simpler things. *First Class.*

Guild Restaurant (Park Street, Bristol) is located in the Bristol Guild—the classiest store in town, a multifloor emporium with its range kitchenware, china, and glass through jewelry, clothes, and toys, which puts me in mind of the General Trading Co. on Sloane Street in London. The restaurant is indicated for a lunch of soup and salad, quiche, or a casserole, and you dare not skip a sweet—lemon cheesecake, chocolate brandy mousse, and apple crumble are celebrated, as are the nut brownies. And, yes, these pastries are available with afternoon tea. *Moderate.*

National Trust Shop Tearoom (Berkeley Square, Bristol): Setting is a Georgian house on a beautiful Georgian square, where the Trust sells its linen teatowels and the other doodads that transatlantic visitors so enjoy buying as gifts. Tasty sandwiches and pastries accompany tea or comprise a casual lunch. *Moderate.*

Llandoger Trow (King Street, Bristol) rates A for Atmosphere; it's a triple-gabled, half-timbered house dating to the mid-seventeenth century, where Stevenson is said to have written *Treasure Island*. Go for a beer or a ploughman's lunch. *Moderate.*

Rainbow Café (Waterloo Street, Clifton): The streets and squares near the suspension bridge are fun for strolls and shopping, and the Rainbow is worth knowing about when it's time for a pause for lunch (try the quiche or a salad) or the Rainbow's own cakes with a cup of tea or coffee. *Moderate.*

Arnolfini (Narrow Quay): The restaurant of this art gallery-cinema complex is conveniently central and ideal for a casual lunch or dinner—hot specials, salads, sandwiches—and for afternoon tea, as well. *Moderate.*

Thornbury Castle Hotel Restaurant (Thornbury, near Bristol) makes for a delightful excursion from town, with the three-course-and-coffee, prix-fixe lunch the raison d'être. Precede your meal with a drink in this beautiful hotel's lounge. Then consider opening with, say, cannelloni stuffed with spinach, continuing with an authentically Gallic navarin, or stew, of lamb, its sauce properly hearty. Choice of desserts can present problems, but the staff is so cordial they will let you sample two or, if you smile sweetly, even three. In no event, miss the hot butterscotch pudding. Dinners are more elaborate and more costly. *Luxury*.

AFTER DARK
Theatre Royal (King Street, Bristol) has operated continuously since 1776; take in a current bill—it could be a play by the reputed Bristol Old Vic company or a visiting ballet troupe—if only to experience the theater.

New Vic Theatre (King Street, Bristol) is another venue for the Bristol Old Vic; visiting attractions, too.

Hippodrome (St. Augustine's Road)—opera, concerts, plays, dance.

INCIDENTAL INTELLIGENCE ═══════════════

Further information: Bristol Tourist Information Centre, Colston House, Colston Street.

7

Cambridge
And Its Countryside

BACKGROUND BRIEFING

The whole point about Cambridge is Oxford.

By that, I mean that the former would not be the seat of a celebrated university were it not for the even longer-celebrated university of the latter.

What happened—all the way back at the start of the thirteenth century—was that a group of students at Oxford felt it expedient to get out of town after local authorities had hanged some classmates on charges of murder. A messy business to be sure. But the migrant Oxonians settled in Cambridge. In little more than a decade, they had founded their own university, and Oxford had competition. The obscure east-central market town on the River Cam—which had known occupations by Romans, Danes, Saxons, and Normans—came to grips with a new species of invaders: young men in search of knowledge.

Town-gown antagonisms over the centuries have been quite as pronounced as in the case of Oxford. Cambridge, like its sister-university city, has grown with a range of light industry to supplement the income generated by students. But it is the university that has made Cambridge the handsome, stimulating city it is, and that draws visitors. I've met none who leaves disappointed.

ON SCENE

Lay of the Land: Discard any notion you may have of a North American campus, detached from the city in which it is situated, on its own park-like grounds. Cambridge University—not unlike older and to my mind less beautiful, somewhat scruffy-appearing Oxford—spreads itself around the core of the city whose name it takes and whose single great natural asset, the River Cam, it takes full advantage of.

Think of central Cambridge's principal arteries as a giant letter Λ running north-south. The street going southeasterly is variously named Bridge, Sidney, St. Andrew's, and—here it becomes the site of the big department stores like Marks & Spencer—Regent. Its southwest counterpart—the other side of the big A—begins in the north as St. John's Street, changing as it veers southerly to Trinity Street, King's Parade (this area contains Cambridge's smarter shops), and Trumpington Street. There are two major east-west crossings, Market Street (with a centuries-old market in adjacent Market Square) and Pembroke/Downing streets. River Cam—still so placid it could be a stream in a bucolic meadow—runs north-south, on the western flank of town, while the Railway Station is detached—to the southeast.

Cambridge for the nonscholar, nonspecialist visitor is an easy-to-organize proposition. As background, you want to be aware that this ancient university has a federated structure embracing a central administration that's an umbrella for thirty-one colleges, each with its own cluster of buildings—usually garden-flanked and courtyard-centered and often of considerable architectural distinction—not to mention its own history, administration, and, to a far greater extent than in the case of American universities, autonomy. Like most fellow British university students, those at Cambridge study during the course of three terms each year—early October through early December, mid-January through mid-March, and mid-April through early June.

Range of the colleges' ages is extraordinary. Peterhouse, the oldest, opened seven centuries ago—in 1284; its founder was the bishop of nearby Ely (to this day Cambridge is a part of the Ely diocese). Newest is Churchill College; Sir Winston was on hand at its 1959 dedication. Only slightly older—and with a domed hall that is contemporary Cambridge at its most striking—is New Hall, a women's college, one of two such. There are eight men-only colleges; the others, in recent years, have become coed, although some 7,000 of the 9,000 undergraduates are male. And North Americans, note: Length of undergraduate course is three years, rather than four, as across the Atlantic.

Only the most avid of pleasure visitors wants to inspect all of the colleges. My suggestion is that you concentrate on the eleven I outline here, making certain that you earmark sufficient time for an art museum that is among Europe's greatest and that, like its counterpart at Oxford, too often is given short shrift by visitors intent on visiting the colleges. Cambridge, unlike Oxford, has no cathedral, but that at Ely is nearby, and the chapel of one of the Cambridge colleges—King's—is, with respect to its architecture, world-class.

Visiting the colleges: A city map in hand (from your hotel or the city tourist information center), start at *Corpus Christi College* (Trumpington Street), dating to the fourteenth century, with the elder of its quadrangles of that period. The library is special and full of college treasures; ask if you may see it. *Emmanuel College* (St. Andrew's Street) stuns, as one enters its main courtyard, with the facade straight ahead—that of Sir Christopher Wren's elegant Baroque Chapel, built a century after the college was founded in 1584. Do go inside, to see not only the chapel, but a plaque therein honoring alumnus John Harvard, who went on to found the New World university bearing his name. *Christ's College* (St. Andrew's Street) was John Milton's college, and the rooms believed to have been his are on the second floor on the left side of the building facing you upon entering the principal quadrangle. There is sixteenth-century stained glass in the chapel. *Sidney Sussex College* (Sidney Street) is among the more architecturally felicitous of the colleges. You want to look at its splendidly scaled dining hall, if only to see the contemporary portrait of Oliver Cromwell, painted while he was a student. Paneling of the small chapel is lovely, and so is the Gothic courtyard leading to it. *St. John's College* (St. John's Street) is the first of our colleges that back onto the River Cam. It's several centuries older than the Gothic-style, nineteenth-century Bridge of Sighs spanning the river and linking two of its buildings. But it's that bridge, named for the bridge in Venice that inspired it, that you want to note. Go inside, then, to see paintings by Romney and France's Rigaud in the dining hall, the richly paneled Combination Room, and—assuming you'll be allowed in—the seventeenth-century library. Note, too, the Tudor courtyard, as well as the garden; its designer was Capability Brown. *Magdalene College* (pronounced, like its Oxford counterpart, *Maudlen*) (Magdalene Street) is entered through a somber Tudor court. Its best-known treasure is the collection of books in its library that was a gift from Samuel Pepys, author of the still-delicious-to-read—and racy—diaries that were seventeenth-century best-sellers; Pepys's original diary manuscript is on view, too. Look in the dining hall; there's a Peter Lely portrait of Pepys. *Trinity College* (Trinity Street) is the university's largest, behind a broad expanse of garden, on the Cam. Don't deny yourself a walk along the river. And do go inside—noting en route the massive and magnificent Great Court, one of the largest such extant—to inspect the Gothic chapel (a standout in a university full of fine chapels) and the dining hall, with its seventeenth-century wood carving and riveting portrait by Holbein of Trinity's founder, King Henry VIII. End in the library, a sumptuous work by Sir Christopher Wren, with its bookcases carved with floral and fruit wreaths, the work of Grinling Gibbons. It's agreeable to walk along the Cam from Trinity to

Clare College (King's Parade), the better to gain access over Clare's seventeenth-century bridge to its gardens, quite the most spectacular at Cambridge, missing neither its chapel, treasure-filled library, nor the decorated ceiling and paneled walls of its dining hall. It's a brief walk along the river to Cambridge's most celebrated interior: *King's College Chapel* (King's Parade). No Cambridge college has more royal associations. King's was begun by Henry VI in the mid-fifteenth century, and work on its chapel continued during the reigns of four succeeding kings—Edward IV, Richard III, Henry VII, and Henry VIII. The chapel began as early Gothic and ended as a species of later Perpendicular of such beauty—especially the fan vaulting of its un-broken 289-foot-long ceiling—that it attracts visitors from all over the world. Pause over the carved-wood of the choir and at the high altar, where, framed as a triptych might be, is one of the sublime Rubens paintings, *Adoration of the Magi*. *Pembroke College* (King's Parade), anticlimactic after King's, offers, as if it had to compensate, *two* chapels: one, very ancient (1355); the other, still *another* Wren creation. *Peterhouse College* (Trumpington Street) is a case of ending at the beginning: at the university's first college, dating to 1284. The first dining hall went up some years later, and it remains, now in the company of buildings from eras throughout Peterhouse's history.

Fitzwilliam Museum (Trumpington Street): Like still another mul-tidepartment museum of the very first rank—the Metropolitan in New York—the Fitzwilliam chooses to close part of its galleries half of each day. Which means, rather infuriatingly, that, if you devote a morning to it, you'll see only its non-painting sections on the ground floor, and, conversely, if you have an afternoon earmarked, you'll see paintings—occupying the second floor—but not the other treasures.

The paintings run a wonderfully diverse gamut—a Brueghel village fete; a portrait of Queen Mary I, unhappy even as a princess, before she ascended the throne; a luminous Veneziano of the Annunciation; early Italian temperas of religious scenes, on through Titian (*Venus and Cupid With a Lute Player*); a Lorrain landscape; a mythical Vero-nese; Low Countries luminaries like Rembrandt and Van Dyck; later French greats—Pissarro and Renoir, for example; and prodigious Brit-ish representation—Hogarth and Turner, Gainsborough and Consta-ble. Other treasures? There are Phoenician stone reliefs, heads of Egyptian monarchs, Greek gods in bronze and goddesses in marble, coins from the ancient world, jade and porcelain from China, and decorative arts of the European Renaissance—Italian velvet, English crystal, vases from Meissen, tableware from Vincennes. And the Fitz-william building is a beauty. Restaurant, shop.

Other Cambridge museums include the *Cambridge Folk Museum* (Northampton Street), a nonuniversity presentation of objects—furniture (in period rooms), toys and dolls, farm implements, and weathered documents, that tell of the past, town, as well as countryside. University museums include *Archaeology* and *Anthropology, Geology,* and *Zoology* (all on Downing Street), *Classical Archaeology* (Little St. Mary's Lane), *History of Science* (Free School Lane), and *Polar Research Institute* (Lensfield Road)—for scholars and visitors with special interests.

Cambridge churches: Great St. Mary's (King's Parade) is the University Church, though it's not as architecturally exciting as King's College Chapel, with striking Perpendicular-style features, including a veritable skyscraper of a tower and oak-beamed roof. *Round Church* (a.k.a. Holy Sepulchre, Bridge and Round Church streets) is, to be sure, round—one of very few such in Britain—and its oldest parts go back eight centuries. *Little St. Mary's Church* (Trumpington Street at Little St. Mary's Lane) is medieval with mostly undistinguished additions. It's recommended principally because of a plaque within, erected in memory of Godfrey Washington, an eighteenth-century rector believed to have been a great uncle of the first American President. The plaque bears the same Washington coat of arms—containing stars and stripes—as is to be seen at the Washington family home, Sulgrave Manor, in Northamptonshire (Chapter 17); and which, it is conjectured, served as a basis for design for the United States flag.

American Military Cemetery (Madingley, three miles west of Cambridge) is the resting place of more than 3,800 U.S. military who lost their lives during World War II while based in Britain. On a memorial wall are carved the names of some 5,000 additional servicemen, missing in action. And on the portico of the severe, but handsome, stone chapel is inscribed the legend: "To the Glory of God and in Memory of Those Who Died for Their Country, 1941–1945."

Ely and its Cathedral (16 miles east of Cambridge) seem another world from the bustle of the university city. Ely is a small, ancient market town whose cathedral's silhouette punctuates the flat *fens,* or lowlands, of the Cambridgeshire countryside. It is, to be sure, agreeable to amble about the town's principal thoroughfares—High and Market streets—with their shops; old houses—some Georgian, some older—are on Minster Place and St. Mary's Street. There's a small museum of local lore that traditionally keeps limited hours except on weekends. But it's to experience the beauty of *Ely Cathedral* that one visits Ely. From without—and the perspective is superb from every direction—it is the cathedral's central tower that warrants perusal. A fourteenth-century replacement of an earlier one that fell apart, it is unique among British churches, being octagonal, and the base for an octagonal lantern—a kind of tower atop the tower—that is even more beautiful from within. The nave is a 208-foot-long space, unbroken as in many cathedrals, and surmounted by a painted frame roof, a nineteenth-century addition that blends well with the rest of what is essentially a Norman interior of generous proportions and exquisite detailing. Have a look at the decorated stone arches of the portals, the capitals of the columns, the misericords of the choir, and the chapels, most especially the 100-foot-long Lady Chapel. Surrounding the cathedral is a host of medieval and later structures, many now a part of King's School; the onetime Bishop's Palace—Jacobean—is now a school for handicapped children. Oliver Cromwell lived for a few years in the half-timbered house that's now the rectory of *St. Mary's Church* on St. Mary's Street; you can't go in the house, but the early Gothic church is visitable.

Audley End (at Saffron Walden, 15 miles south of Cambridge): Royal residences in Britain—or in this case, former royal residences—are always worth visiting. Audley End went up in 1603, as the seat of the then-Earl of Suffolk. It was even bigger than it is now, and its attributes caught the ear of King Charles II, who bought it after his restoration in 1669, possibly influenced by its proximity to the races then held at Newmarket (below), as they still are today. In the early eighteenth century, Sir John Vanbrugh, architect of Blenheim Palace and Castle Howard, demolished one of the courtyards and made interior changes. Later in the eighteenth century, Robert Adam was called in as architect-designer. The house—cared for by the Department of Environment—remains outstanding, thanks to the pleasing complexities of its turreted facade, a spectacular great hall with a stunning carved screen, and another dazzler—the intricate ceiling of the saloon. Exceptional paintings, too. Restaurant.

Newmarket (13 miles east of Cambridge), historic horse-racing capital of the kingdom, was at its raciest during the reign of Charles II, who lived for a while at nearby Audley End (above) and played the horses regularly, in the company of such mistresses as Lady Castlemaine and Nell Gwynn. Newmarket knew other royals—Charles I, William III, Queen Anne—of that period, and the association has continued to this day: Queen Elizabeth II races horses at Newmarket, and there is traditionally a royal box at the spring races and royal mares from nearby Sandringham House (Chapter 16). See—besides the track—High Street landmarks, including the historic Jockey Club,

Rutland Arms Inn, and—just outside the town, near the racecourse—
the National Stud, wherein the cream of the kingdom's crop of horses
are bred.

SETTLING IN

Garden House Hotel (Granta Place, off Mill Lane, Cambridge): Getting to the Garden House is the tough part, unless you're in a taxi;
local cabbies know the way. If you're in your own car, be advised that
not all other locals do. But the superb location—which makes it all
worthwhile—is alongside a perfectly beautiful garden that slopes
gently down to the River Cam. With a riverside room, you believe
you're in the country rather than in a university city. This is a modern
hotel, superbly equipped—all of the baths have showers, as well as
tubs—and professionally operated, although it could have done with
a more talented interior designer. Restaurant, bar-lounge; delightful
afternoon tea. *Luxury.*

University Arms Hotel (Regent Street, Cambridge) embraces elderly
and contemporary segments, is heart of town, and was for long the
No. 1 Cambridge hotel, pre-Garden House. It remains very nice,
indeed, with a broadly scaled lobby (go for morning coffee or afternoon tea) and a trio of bars (one serves casual lunches; another—
called Whisky Galore—stocks eighty brands). Only some of the singles among its 120 rooms are without baths, and most of the baths
are shower-equipped. Handsome paneled restaurant. *First Class.*

Gonville Hotel (Gonville Place, Cambridge) is low-slung, congenial,
and full-facility, with pleasant public spaces, restaurant, bar, 62 rooms,
and location so close to the center you may walk. *First Class.*

Arundel House Hotel (Chesterton Road, Cambridge) has a pretty
setting—front rooms overlook the River Cam; an attractive facade—a
cluster of century-old houses; comfortable rooms, 60 all told, a majority of which have baths; and a restaurant and bar that serves well-
priced lunches. An easy walk to the colleges. *Moderate.*

Royal Cambridge Hotel (Trumpington Street, Cambridge) occupies
several joined nineteenth-century houses. I wish more of the 85 rooms
had baths—about a third do—but otherwise the Royal Cambridge is
satisfactory. Restaurant, bar. *Moderate.*

Blue Boar Hotel (Trinity Street, Cambridge) is so delightfully mellow
(it dates to the late seventeenth century) that I regret Trusthouse
Forte, with all of the skill and wherewithal at its disposal, has not seen

fit to equip more than 11 of the nearly 50 rooms with baths. Restaurant, bars. *Moderate.*

Lamb Hotel (Lynn Road, Ely): Ask for a cathedral-view room in this authentically Georgian inn, and I suspect you'll be happy overnighting in Ely. The bar is a pleasure. Restaurant. *Moderate.*

DAILY BREAD

Eagle (Benet Street, Cambridge): On a sunny day, Cambridge's preferred lunch venue is the ancient cobbled courtyard of this ancient coaching inn. Order the house's pork pie with salad and half-pint of lager. Or the beef stew. Meals inside this Tudor-era pub, I should point out, are also a pleasure. *Moderate.*

Wilson's (Trinity Street, Cambridge): You choose, here, from a trio of rooms—restaurant-cum-bar, with a French-accented menu and extensive wine choices; carvery for roast beef with Yorkshire pudding; and more casual Granary. *Moderate-First Class.*

Arts Theatre Restaurant (St. Edward's Passage, Cambridge): You needn't be a ticket-holder to lunch or dine in the Pentagon Restaurant or the Wine Bar. The cold buffet makes for a good lunch, and there's more substantial fare at dinner. *Moderate-First Class.*

Shades (King's Parade, Cambridge): Down a flight you go to this basement wine-bar for a steak or the day's special. Congenial. *First Class.*

Guilder's (Wheeler Street, Cambridge) may not sound like a likely source of pizza. But it is. *Moderate.*

University Arms Hotel Restaurant (Regent Street, Cambridge) provides as handsome a mealtime setting as you'll find in Cambridge (excluding, of course, the dining halls of the university's colleges). And the price is right, if you order the wide-choice, three-course lunches or dinners; entrées range from lamb chops and roast beef to cold salmon and fried plaice. *First Class.*

Fitzwilliam Museum Café (Trumpington Street, Cambridge): That of the Royal Academy of Art in London excepted, I don't know of a museum cafeteria in Britain with such perfectly delicious food: homemade soups; open-face sandwiches, Danish-style; memorable cakes and pastries. *Moderate.*

Old Fire Engine House (St. Mary's Street, Ely): The fire engine is still to be seen in the yard. But the food's the thing, in this historic dwelling turned restaurant, with the kitchen center of the action. (You pass through, en route to your table.) It's hard to go wrong here—appetizing appetizers, roast lamb or beef, and fresh fish. And desserts! Think of me when you order the rhubarb pie. Try lunch, dinner, or simply afternoon tea in conjunction with a visit to the nearby Cathedral. For tea: *Moderate;* otherwise: *First Class.*

Eight Bells (Bridge Street, Saffron Walden) dates back some six centuries, the better to provide a little atmosphere in the course of, say, lunch, in advance of a visit to Audley End (above), or tea, afterwards. *Moderate-First Class.*

Rutland Arms (High Street, Newmarket): This history-laden inn is indicated for lunch or, at the very least, tea, in the course of an exploratory foray through Newmarket. *Moderate-First Class.*

AFTER DARK

Arts Theatre (Peas Hill, Cambridge) is the principal Cambridge venue for plays and musicals (some prior to London), ballet, modern dance, opera, and movies.

ADC Theatre (Park Street, Cambridge) is home base for the university's Amateur Dramatic Club, but other theatrical troupes use it.

Classical music: There are both a *Cambridge Philharmonic*, which usually performs at Guildhall, and a *Cambridge Symphony*, which plays in King's College Chapel. That and other college chapels, as well as the Round Church, are settings for concerts and recitals.

May Week and Cambridge Festival: These two annual events are packed with concerts and plays in beautiful settings. May Week—please note—occurs in June and is university-sponsored. The festival is a community effort, traditionally held in the first half of July.

INCIDENTAL INTELLIGENCE ═══════════════════

Further information: Cambridge Tourist Information Centre, Wheeler Street, Cambridge; Ely Tourist Information Centre, St. Mary's Street, Ely.

8

Canterbury
And the Pleasures of Kent

BACKGROUND BRIEFING

Tucked away in the southeast corner of England it may be. Still, Kent is not what you would call isolated.

Roman troops invaded it in the first century. In the sixth, Pope Gregory dispatched St. Augustine to convert the King of Kent to Christianity. In the year 1170, four knights, acting for Henry II, murdered the Archbishop of Canterbury in his own cathedral. In 1520, Henry VIII, leading a resplendent fleet, sailed from Dover to meet with France's King François I on the Field of Cloth of Gold.

The long Kentish centuries have not gone unchronicled. Chaucer, writing in the fourteenth century of the pilgrims who paid their respects at the tomb of the martyred Archbishop Becket, immortalized Canterbury. A Rochester mansion is credited as the inspiration for Miss Havisham's cobwebby house in *Great Expectations;* and Dickens would write more of Kent—in *David Copperfield,* for example, the young hero of which he sent to Dover, for a propitious meeting with Miss Betsy Trotwood.

Even Kent houses have gained literary celebrity. Palatial Knole's story was told by a family member, Victoria Sackville-West, and, more recently, Sissinghurst Castle was the setting for the eccentric marriage of his famous parents, as recounted by Nigel Nicolson.

Pleasure visitors like ourselves on nonhistoric missions, without literary bents? We make considerable pilgrimages, as well we might, beginning, logically enough, in the onetime capital of the onetime Kingdom of Kent.

ON SCENE

Lay of the Land: Canterbury is compact. Position yourself in a central hotel, and you may undertake most of your exploration on foot in a city delightfully weathered and immediately evocative of past centuries. The oval-shaped core of town follows the contour of ancient city walls, some of which still remain in the northwest corner. The major landmark—Canterbury Cathedral—is backed by the walls and fronted by High Street, which becomes St. Peter's Street as it goes northwest. St. George's Street as it proceeds southeast, Stour, and Castle streets are the principal thoroughfares running perpendicular to High Street. A charming network of lanes—Pound, Best, Mercery, Butchery, and Longmarket—extend from the other side of High Street. It is worth noting that, small as it is, Canterbury has two railway stations—West and East.

Canterbury Cathedral (Christchurch Gateway), even if it were plain as an old shoe—hardly the case—is the single most important church in England. It is the seat of the Archbishop of Canterbury, leader—with the title Primate of All England—not only of the Church of England, the established church of the kingdom, but also of the worldwide Anglican Communion, a kind of federation of churches subscribing to the 1930 Lambeth Conference and including not only the other Anglican groups in the British Isles—Scottish Episcopal Church, The Church in Wales, Church of Ireland—but affiliated churches abroad, including the Protestant Episcopal Church in the U.S. and the Anglican Church in Canada, with a total of some 46 million communicants planet-wide. (It is, perhaps, worth noting at this point what might be called the pecking order of bishops in England. The Archbishop of York, in northern England [Chapter 23], follows Canterbury, with the title Primate of England [note that the important adjective *all* is missing, being reserved for Canterbury], with the bishops of Winchester [Chapter 21] and Durham [Chapter 15]—each of whose seats are superb, history-rich cathedrals —traditionally following, along with the Bishop of London, based in Sir Christopher Wren's seventeenth-century St. Paul's Cathedral.) An anomaly of the church is that even though its clergy are appointed by the Crown (you will see announcements to this effect regularly on the Court page of *The Times* of London), their salaries are paid from the church's own coffers. Operation of the C. of E. (as it is frequently called) is through the Church Assembly, a three-house body, two of these clergy, one laity. It is worth noting, too, that the Archbishop of Canterbury has two official residences—the Archbishop's Palace in Canterbury and Lambeth Palace in London.

Given this background, Canterbury Cathedral's massive size and corresponding grandeur should not come as a surprise. The cathedral embraces a meld of styles and centuries, early Norman (its western crypt) through Victorian Gothic (its northwest tower). To many observers, its quite literally crowning achievement is its central—or "Bell Harry"—Tower, whose 235-foot height dominates Canterbury and is complemented by lower towers framing the front entrance. Inside, the nave overwhelms an indisputably outstanding specimen of Perpendicular, the third and final of the three English Gothic periods—long, narrow, severe, and superbly vaulted. Have a look, as you walk about, at the fan vaulting of the interior central tower; at the immense, almost church-within-a-church choir; at the steps worn by centuries, aptly called Pilgrim steps, leading to Trinity Chapel—for long the location of St. Thomas Becket's tomb; at the oddly cold and jarringly contemporary stone tablet, identified simply as The Martyr-dom, marking the spot where Archbishop Becket was murdered in the late twelfth century; and at the parts of the cathedral to which I return on each visit: a perfect square of a cloister dating to the time when the cathedral was a Benedictine monastery; at St. Gabriel and Our Lady chapels in the crypt—each a jewel of Romanesque, with strikingly carved columns and capitals and walls embellished with original frescoes.

St. Augustine's Abbey Ruins and St. Martin's Church (Longport) are ideally combined in the course of an eastward stroll from the cathedral. St. Augustine's ruins are what remain of a monastery of supreme historic significance. It was founded by St. Augustine in the course of his seventh-century mission to convert Kent to Christianity, which made of Canterbury a major northern European outpost of the church. The Fyndon Gate complex, dating to Tudor times, served as Canterbury quarters for Queen Elizabeth I and Charles I and now sees service as a detached annex of King's School, whose main quarters are adjacent to the Cathedral. But look, too, at the ancient abbey, or what remains of it: church, chapels, cloister, refectory. St. Augustine's gives you an idea, as the cathedral cannot, of Canterbury's advanced age. So, for that matter, does nearby St. Martin's Church, which Bede, the ancient and respected church historian, records as going back to the seventh century and which is therefore considered to be the oldest church in England still operated as such. It is small and plain, with segments dating to the period of the Roman Christians, before St. Augustine's arrival.

Blackfriars Church (St. Peter's Lane) is a chapel that was part of the monastery of the fourteenth-century Dominicans and so called for the black robes of that order. Surely there is irony in the fact that its current occupants are practitioners of a religion—Christian Science—founded in the New World by an American woman, as recently as the seventh decade of the last century.

Greyfriars (Stour Street) is what remains—probably the dormitory—of still another early Canterbury monastic settlement, that of the gray-robed Franciscans. Evocative. Thirteenth century.

Westgate Museum (St. Peter's Street) is an ancient city gate, later a prison, deftly—and very sensibly—transformed into a small museum of Canterbury history.

Royal Museum (High Street): This rather elaborate Victorian pile is at least as interesting for its architecture as for its exhibits. Still, the Royal displays some delightful turn-of-century watercolors and etchings of the cathedral and a group of paintings, some of which delineate the city's monuments. There's porcelain, too.

Rochester, the cathedral town too often bypassed in favor of more celebrated Canterbury, nearby, charms with the quiet, well-mannered patina it has acquired—with apparent ease—over a span of centuries. It is not at all difficult, geographically. Simply hie yourself to High Street, lined with fine old houses. That thoroughfare's main monument, *Rochester Cathedral,* goes back a thousand years, and if it is among the more somber of Britain's cathedrals—the periods are Romanesque and Early English—it is not without attributes, beginning with an intricately embellished west door, continuing with a breathtaking nave, flanked by three levels of arches of the same period; an Early English crypt, beautifully vaulted; and with columns embellished by ancient ecclesiastical graffiti. The formidable tower on a hill, over the cathedral, is the keep—all that remains of the Norman-built *Rochester Castle*—which, with its 120-foot height, is the tallest such in England. Go up for a look inside and for the smashing panorama of town and cathedral below. There are two museums. *Eastgate House* (High Street) is sixteenth century, but with a nineteenth-century Swiss-type chalet in the garden—in which Charles Dickens did a good bit of writing, and a house opposite that figured in Dickens's *Great Expectations. Guildhall* (High Street), the other museum, about as old as Eastgate House, abounds in Rochester lore.

Dover: The canny Romans were the first to appreciate Dover's situation as the English Channel port providing the shortest sea crossing to continental Europe. Indeed, a Roman-constructed lighthouse, dating back two millennia, remains as a remnant of five Channel towns united as the Cinque Ports in a joint coastal defense effort (and to this day confederated under an honorary Lord Warden). Dover's location—adjacent to its landmark White Cliffs, the closest bit of Britain to France—has always made it special.

Monarchs, from Henry VII onward, contributed to its development as a harbor and a bastion of defense. Those two aspects of the city are what most interest today's visitor. *Dover Castle* is one of Britain's underappreciated medieval monuments, easily on a par with better-known counterparts in, say, Wales, and northern England. Operated by the Department of the Environment and straddling a chalky cliff that backs the town and port, it is built around a twelfth-century keep and protected by magnificent walls that could be out of an Errol Flynn movie. You want to drive up and go inside. First, visit the keep, proud and square and with crenellated towers at each corner, with splendidly constructed circular stairs leading to the roof, and a second-floor chapel—a tiny Romanesque jewel—in between. Move along, then, to the Roman-built *pharos*, or lighthouse, dating to the first century, and end at St. Mary's Church, a thousand years newer than the lighthouse and infelicitously gussied up in the last century, to be sure, but withal Saxon in basic design, with walls of ancient Roman brick.

Down below, it's exciting to look at modern Dover's seafront *Marine Parade*—lined by venerable houses now serving as modest hotels—and its busy *Eastern Docks*, from which car ferries link England with French, Belgian, and Dutch ports. *Shakespeare Cliff*—most celebrated of the White Cliffs and with a silhouette not unlike that of Honolulu's Diamond Head—is due west, rising 350 feet skywards. And in town, on High Street, you want to pop into *Maison Dieu*, erected in the thirteenth century as a resting place for pilgrims en route from the Continent to the shrine of St. Thomas à Becket in Canterbury. It is now Dover's Town Hall. In a vast wood-beamed gallery, city fathers display arms and armor, brilliant pennants, and, most important—in the big hall and Council Chamber—paintings of monarchs associated with the town (including Queens Elizabeth I and Anne) and lord wardens of the Cinque Ports, including Sir Winston Churchill and the first Duke of Wellington.

Chiddingstone and Chilam are a pair of alliteratively titled Kentish villages—the former in west Kent, the latter in east Kent. Chiddingstone—primarily a single-street proposition under National Trust aegis—is a certifiable antique with only two buildings, village hall and church rectory, erected in this century. Almost everything else goes back to the 1400s and 1500s, with one half-timbered house after another from those eras, the lot complementing a honey of a fifteenth-century church, snug and square-towered.

Just beyond is *Chiddingstone Castle*, a late eighteenth-century Gothic Revival mansion built on much older foundations, with its lures the rather eccentric collections—Japanese and Egyptian art objects among them—of the most recent owner. Concentrate on fine paintings in the

Great Hall, including work by Sir Peter Lely. And in two additional rooms, examine the paintings, drawings, miniatures, medals, letters, and whatnot from kings and queens in the drama-packed centuries of the Stuart dynasty.

Chilam has its fair share of half-timbered Tudor and brick-walled Jacobean houses. See, also, the handsome church, mostly constructed in the fourteenth and fifteenth centuries and, like its counterpart at Chiddingstone, graced with a superb square tower, but a much larger interior, principal treasures of which include a series of fine carved-wood figures—corbels—supporting the ceiling.

Chartwell (two miles south of Westerham), for some 40 years the country home of Sir Winston Churchill and his family, is not, I should make immediately clear, a great country house like, for example, Blenheim Palace (Chapter 17), where Churchill was born. Quite the contrary; Chartwell is a modest Victorian mansion that the Churchills rebuilt—altering the facade and adding a wing—when they bought it in 1922. You go if you admire Churchill or lived through the World War II period when he led Britain to victory against overwhelming odds.

The quiet taste of the house—drawing rooms, dining room, hall, and the like—is solid British upper class. Grounds, gardens, and setting are bucolic in the best sense. But it is Churchilliana that stands out. Paintings by Churchill are all about. The study—beamed and capacious but not ostentatious—has his books and many mementos. The Museum Room contains more personal objects—including a photo of his beautiful mother, who had been New York's Jennie Jerome; gold cups, a gift of King George VI and the present Queen Mother; an antique Persian bowl from President Franklin D. Roosevelt; his Nobel Prize and Honorary American Citizen certificates. In an adjoining room are still more memorabilia, one of which is, for me, the most memorable and moving of the lot: a letter from Roosevelt, addressed in code to "A Certain Naval Person" and hand-delivered by unsuccessful presidential candidate Wendell Wilkie, in which FDR extends support to his friend at a time—June 1941—when Britain was still fighting alone, half a year before the U.S. entered the war. National Trust.

Knole (Sevenoaks) could well be—indeed, has been—the textbook prototype of the early English stately home. Few houses have as exalted a pedigree, for Knole has been both seat of an archbishop (Canterbury's Thomas Bourchier, who built it in the mid-fifteenth century) and a royal palace (it came into Henry VIII's hands and was inherited by his daughter Elizabeth I). Elizabeth awarded it to Thomas

Sackville, and it remained a Sackville seat over the centuries. Knole sprawls over a multiacre tract, a maze of vast courts, steep-chimneyed roofs, towers, gables, turrets. Its Great Staircase was the first of the showcase stairways. Its Great Hall has a carved-oak screen, above which—from a balcony—bands of musicians played for Tudor balls. Its Brown Gallery, with Jacobean paneling, is a repository of match-less paintings (Lely, Kneller, Vigée-Lebrun, Van Dyck, Reynolds, Gains-borough, Romney, and Hoppner are among the artists) and equally precious furniture. And the Venetian Ambassador's bedroom—slept in by the Doge's envoy to the Court of James I—has tapestry-covered walls, with a canopied bed and gilded blue chairs. Knole's is one of the kingdom's celebrated interiors. National Trust.

Ightham Mote (Ivy Hatch, near Sevenoaks): Chief reason for a visit to Ightham Mote is its moat. This is one of the rare remaining English houses surrounded by a water-filled, swan-populated channel. The facade of this relatively small, relatively simple house, originally four-teenth century, appeals too, part Kentish stone, part half-timbered. Once inside, ignore the mostly undistinguished furniture and concen-trate on the exceptional timbered ceiling and the stained glass win-dows of the nicely proportioned Great Hall and the paneling of the larger, or Tudor, chapel. National Trust.

Penshurst Place (Penshurst) ranks close to Knole among the impor-tant Kentish houses. A dazzler from without as one approaches, it is a veritable Tudor castle, elongated, turreted, and multiwinged, with a formal garden to set it off and a church-centered village adjacent. Penshurst Place dates to 1340. There have been changes and addi-tions, but wisely the Great Hall—with its original tile floor, A-frame roof of wood, and later minstrels' gallery—have been left intact. There is, as well, a Long Gallery, Jacobean, meticulously furnished, and hung with paintings of the scions of the long-resident Sidney family, currently represented by Viscount de l'Isle, the fourteenth-generation landlord. Restaurant.

Hever Castle (near Edenbridge) has royal associations. It was the girlhood home of Anne Boleyn, Henry VIII's ill-fated second consort (Henry courted Anne at Hever) and the mother of Queen Elizabeth I. Smallish, moated, crenellated, and originally thirteenth century, it was rebuilt in the fifteenth century and saw lean centuries thereafter, until wealthy William Waldorf Astor bought it in the early twentieth, restored it extensively, furnished it expensively, and created formal gardens—both flower and topiary and including a maze—punctuated with sculptures. Cafeteria.

Leeds Castle (near Maidstone), not unlike Hever Castle (above) in that it has associations with Henry VIII, was, before Henry's time, home of Dowager Queen Catherine, widow of Henry V and a daughter of France's King Charles VI. You want to see it, first, for its utterly romantic setting amidst a finger of a lake flanked by a verdant park and, second, for its medieval interiors, most especially the relatively recently reconstructed bedroom of Queen Catherine, with emerald-green wall coverings embellished with gold crowns and the royal initials *HC*, a foil for scarlet draperies and two scarlet-canopied beds— one, the quite literally queen-size state bed; the other, a couch-like *sparver*, typical of the period.

SETTLING IN

County Hotel (High Street, Canterbury): The point about the County is continuity. It has been on scene since the early seventeenth century, retaining its traditional ambience, the while keeping pace with the times. By that, I mean all 70 of its rooms have not only baths but showers. Would that countless other British hotels followed suit in both these regards! The lobby is big and beamed, and there are two restaurants and a clublike bar-lounge, with open fire roaring in cool weather. Lovely. *First Class.*

Chaucer Hotel (Ivy Lane, Canterbury) occupies a handsome brick mansion dating to the Regency, with gracious public spaces, including a fine restaurant and popular bar. Location is central. And the bedrooms are attractive. All that's missing is private baths in nearly a score of a total of 51 rooms. Come on, Trusthouse Forte, put your plumbers to work! *Moderate-First Class.*

Slatters Hotel (St. Margaret's Street, Canterbury) is proud of the remnant of Roman wall in its nether reaches. Its main building is considerably newer—beamed Tudor. And there is a contemporary wing. Restaurant and bar are atmospheric, and more than 20 of the 30 rooms have bath. *Moderate-First Class.*

Falstaff Hotel (St. Dunstan's Street, Canterbury): Smallest of our Canterbury group, the Falstaff holds its own with respect to age: fifteenth century. And it has original timbers to show for it. Restaurant and bar are a pleasure. Two-thirds of the 16 rooms—some in a modern addition—have baths. *Moderate.*

Eastwell Manor Hotel (Eastwell Park, Ashford) is splendidly set in an enormous park of its own, occupying an extraordinarily handsome and capacious Tudor mansion. There are just a score of well-equipped rooms and suites. No two are quite alike, and alas, none has the style or good looks that are, more often than not, a hallmark of interiors in hotels of this category; nor do all of the baths have showers. Public rooms are spacious but mundanely furnished, even though the magnificent ceilings and wall paneling have been retained. Eastwell Manor's forte is food; its restaurant warrants additional space on a later page. Member, Prestige Hotels. *Luxury*.

Rose & Crown Hotel (High Street, Tonbridge) is brought to your attention because of its strategic situation in a nondescript Kentish town convenient to much that is worth exploring in the region. The main building was an old coaching inn, bits and pieces of which remain. There are just over 50 adequate-for-overnight rooms. Reliable restaurant, bar. Trusthouse Forte. *Moderate*.

Holiday Inn (Townwall Street, Dover): Well, you can't have everything. In the case of most of Britain's Holiday Inns, that means sacrificing esthetics for good beds and good plumbing. This garish hotel comes through with 83 rooms, each with two double beds and a good bath-cum-shower, as well as a restaurant, off-lobby swimming pool, and—its sole attractive interior—a pub that serves casual lunches. Central. *First Class*.

White Cliffs Hotel (Seafront, Dover): Almost half of this nicely situated hotel's rooms have baths, and the front ones have super views of the Channel. Restaurant. Bar. *Moderate*.

Imperial Hotel (Seafront, Hythe): This excellently equipped hotel is well situated for Kentish travels, even if Hythe, the coastal resort in which it's located —just a few miles west of Dover—holds no interest for you. The Imperial is a century old and has been sensibly modernized, with paneled public spaces; agreeable, spacious bedrooms, with showers in some of the baths; and amenities including indoor and outdoor pools, tennis courts, and nine holes of golf. Restaurant, lounge-bar, in which is served casual lunches. *Luxury*.

Stade Court Hotel (West Parade, Hythe) is just inland from the sea, and though less grand than its sister-hotel, the Imperial (above), offers comfortable rooms (not all have bath), restaurant, bar, and use of the Imperial's facilities, including its golf course. *First Class*.

Victoria & Bull Hotel (High Street, Rochester) compensates with atmosphere for what it lacks in such amenities as private baths; I wish more of its 31 rooms had them. But this hotel is seventeenth century, and Dickens set scenes of *Pickwick Papers* in it. Restaurant and a super bar. *Moderate-First Class.*

DAILY BREAD
Sully's (County Hotel, High Street, Canterbury) represents Canterbury dining at its most festive. Order à la carte—an assortment of *pâtés* or smoked salmon, with grilled lobster or a brace of quail and dessert from the trolley. Or select the excellent-value table d'hôte lunch or dinner. Extensive wine list. *First Class-Luxury.*

Beehive (Dover Street, Canterbury) has a nice buzz to it, with locals and visitors equally evident. Order beef and kidney pie or something with a Continental flair to it. Super sweets. *First Class.*

Caesar's (St. Peter's Street, Canterbury): Crave a hamburger? Canterbury's Caesar's is a reliable source. *Moderate.*

Max Keel Wine Bar (St. Margaret's Street, Canterbury) is reputed for its buffet lunch—salads, cold meats, a hot dish or two. Tasty, with a glass of the house wine, and *Moderate.*

Millers Arms (Mill Lane, Canterbury), dating to the eighteenth century and—happily—looking it, is ideal for a pub lunch or a French-accented table d'hôte. *Moderate-First Class.*

Burgate (Burgate, Canterbury) is a welcoming, old-fashioned coffee shop-tearoom, indicated for a sandwich or salad lunch; daily hot specials, too. *Moderate.*

Weavers (Kings Bridge, Canterbury) is a half-timbered house offering demonstrations of hand weaving and doubling as a restaurant: morning coffee, lunch—served in the garden on fine days—or afternoon tea with delicious cakes. *Moderate.*

King's Head (High Street, Rochester) presents solid victuals—roasts, seafood, specials of the day—in a four-century-old environment. Order the house wine. *First Class.*

Castle Tea Rooms (High Street, Rochester): At lunch, have the beef and kidney pie. Baked-on-premises cakes accompany morning coffee and afternoon tea. Setting is ancient. *Moderate.*

Eastwell Manor Hotel Restaurant (Eastwell Park, Ashford): The Elizabethan paneled walls are original, staff mostly French, fare likewise, and *nouvelle-cuisine*-influenced. Start with turbot terrine or arti-choke with sherry sauce. Soups—especially the crab, spiked with the sauce called *rouille*—are superb. Sole from nearby Dover, scallops, or fresh salmon: Fish are skillfully prepared. And so are meat entrées like chicken braised with endive, roast saddle of lamb, beef tournedos with a truffled sauce. The cheese platter is exceptional in a country where cheese is honored. Well-selected, well-priced wines, mostly French, are offered. In my experience, one of Britain's best restaurants. *Luxury*.

Castle Inn (High Street, Chiddingstone): I don't know what the food was like when this pub-restaurant opened in 1420, but I can vouch for it today. Eat casually, but well, in the wood-beamed bar; or more formally—and more expensively—in the restaurant, whose specialties are rack of lamb and roast beef, with pheasant, venison, and hare. *Moderate-Luxury*.

White Horse Inn (High Street, Chilam) is roughly the same age as the Castle Inn (above). This is a handsome white-brick pub that makes an ideal lunch stop—salads, sausages, the day's hot special—in the course of a Chilam layover. *Moderate*.

Monte Bianco (Townwall Street, Dover): Italian-accented seafood—fried scampi, for example—is a wise choice in this attractive restaurant, and so is pasta. There are good-value three-course lunches and dinners. *First Class*.

Brittania (Wall Street, Dover) is a core-of-town pub-restaurant, packed with locals and visitors alike, especially at lunch, when there's always a hot special. *Moderate*.

AFTER DARK

Marlowe Theatre (St. Margaret's Street, Canterbury) offers plays presented by its own repertory troupe, not to mention prior-to-London dramas, touring orchestras, and the esteemed Kent Opera.

Gulbenkian Theatre (University of Kent, Canterbury) offers plays by university and visiting groups—the range is Kafka through Tennessee Williams—musical, and dance events.

INCIDENTAL INTELLIGENCE

It's from the modern Car Ferry Terminal at Dover's Eastern Docks that ships make the shortest crossing between England and France

(Calais is 22 miles). There is service, as well, to France's Dunkirk and Holland's Zeebrugge. *Further information:* Canterbury Tourist Information Centre, St. Peter's Street; Rochester Tourist Information Centre, High Street; Dover Tourist Information Centre, Town Hall.

9

Channel Islands
Bailiwicks of Jersey and Guernsey

BACKGROUND BRIEFING

Closer geographically to France than England; part of the British Isles, but not part of the United Kingdom; owing allegiance to the Queen as members of the Commonwealth, but self-governing; the Channel Islands are riddled with anomalies.

French—as a written language, designating towns, parishes, and streets (and, on Jersey, in the law courts)—is a commonplace of these islands. As well it might be. They are an anachronism dating to the period following the Norman Conquest in 1066. Two centuries later, when continental Normandy—of which they were a part—was politically detached from England, the islands chose to remain with the English crown; and so they did, by means of constitutions granted by King John still in effect.

Each major island—bigger Jersey and Guernsey—is self-governing in every respect (save defense and foreign affairs, which are controlled by Britain). And each has its own small parliament—called the States—and crown-appointed head of state, or Bailiff. Blessed with a milder climate than that to the north (variously called the Mainland and the U.K.) and with duty-free shopping without the 15 percent VAT tax imposed in the U.K. (so that watches, gold jewelry, appliances, and liquor are good buys), the islands draw masses of British vacationers, with the high season spring through autumn. (Jersey, the more popular, has an area of but 45 square miles and a population of but 75,000, but there are more than 500 hotels and guest houses.) Transatlantic visitors go less for sun and sand than to explore a bit. Which island, you ask? Both of the majors have a principal town-cum-picturesque harbor. Beyond—in the attractive countryside (yes, you *will* see Jersey cows on Jersey, Guernsey cows on Guernsey)— produce farms supplement dairy farms, and white-sand beaches lie beneath rocky cliffs or tuck themselves into neat coves. Each island is divided into a number of administrative districts called parishes, each with a Church of England parish church—invariably Gothic in origin—under the jurisdiction of the Mainland Diocese of Winchester (Chapter 21), there being no bishoprics (and, therefore, no cathedrals) in the islands.

Jersey, where mass-market package tourism is developed, offers a wider choice of hotels, restaurants, shops, and after-dark diversion. Quieter Guernsey concentrates, appreciably, on the more affluent visitor, has the prettier capital, and is the gateway point for its dependency-islands, little Sark and Alderney. Why not spend a couple of days on each of the Big Two islands? A quarter-hour flight on the quaint little aircraft of the local airline whose route links the islands is a requisite Channel Islands adventure.

ON SCENE

JERSEY

Lay of the Land: Nine miles long by five miles wide and ringed by a scenic coastal highway, Jersey's capital, St. Helier, flanks a natural harbor near the center of the south coast. Visitors stay in town, on its outskirts, and at points dotted about the compact island.

St. Helier bases itself on *Royal Square*, which is flanked by the elegant little *States*, or Parliament, open to visitors when in session (there are 51 legislators); and the also-impressive *Royal Court* (where trials are conducted in the French language, the very same used in notices you will observe on the bulletin boards as you make your way to the second-floor courtrooms). King Street, leading from the square, is pedestrians-only and one of the main shopping streets, along with neighboring Halkett Street, Halkett Place, Queen Street, and Bath Street. Pop into the *St. Helier Parish Church* (Mulcaster Street), established some nine hundred years back as La Chapelle de Saint-Helier, with fine Gothic windows and a fat square tower. The *Jersey Museum* (Pier Road) is at its most interesting in the street-floor room devoted to locally born actress Lillie Langtry—"The Jersey Lily" and a mistress of King Edward VII—which brims with amusing Langtry memorabilia. Period rooms and Jersey silver are upstairs. *Fort Regent* (Pier Road) is a huge leisure complex taking up 22 acres of an early nineteenth-century fortress, with swimming pools, mini-golf, the Jersey Aquarium, and 2,000-seat Gloucester Hall with live entertainment on its stage—among much else.

Mont Orgueil (Gorey) is a picture-book fortress going back seven centuries, with a museum recounting its history. It's fabulously flood-lit at night.

German Military Underground Hospital (St. Lawrence): The Chan-nel Islands were German-occupied during World War II, and this onetime hospital is chock-full of mementos of the occupation. Still another occupation-related museum is at *St. Peter's Bunker* (St. Peter).

Jersey Wildlife Preservation Trust (Trinity) is a remarkable zoo founded by wildlife author Gerald Durrell for endangered species—gorillas, orangutans, lemurs, hedgehogs, and snow leopards—to name some; birds, too.

St. Matthew's Church (Millbrook) is prosaic of facade. The kicker is the interior; it was decorated by the celebrated French glass designer, Rene Lalique, in the early 1930s. Vestibule, high altar, lady chapel, font, parts of ceiling, and windows are original Lalique.

Elizabeth Castle (St. Aubin's Bay) dates to the Elizabethan era, and straddles a massive offshore rock connected to the shore by a cause-way that is above water at low tide; several museums are inside, but the castle itself is the star of the show.

La Mare Vineyards (St. Mary): Jersey wine? This is its source. The "château" is a venerable farmhouse, with exhibits telling La Mare's story, and a shop, so that you can buy both the wine and made-on-site cider, too.

GUERNSEY

Lay of the Land: Nearly triangular-shaped and as much as eight miles wide and ten miles long, Guernsey's capital, handsome little St. Peter Port, is midpoint on the east coast. The satellite islands of Sark and Herm (and smaller Jethou and Brechou) are to the east, while larger Alderney is far enough north to be linked with Guernsey by air; it and Sark make for pleasant excursions. The latter has, these many centuries, been ruled by successive generations of the same family, with the ruler called Seigneur, if male, and Dame, if female. Motor transport is *verboten*, which makes Sark ideal for utter relaxa-tion and bracing walks (although passenger transport on farm tractors is allowed).

St. Peter Port—a mix of Georgian, Regency, and Victorian architecture—straddles a horseshoe of a hill that encloses a boat-dotted harbor flanked by the somber stone tower of the Gothic *Town Church*, at the foot of Fountain Street, as it leads into the *High Street*—principal shopping thoroughfare and parallel with the port. *Royal Court* (Smith Street) is the name of the eighteenth-century granite structure housing both the States, or Parliament (open to the public when in session), and the Courts of Justice, with documents in the files dating to the fourteenth century.

Maison Hugo (a.k.a. Hauteville House, Hauteville Road) is the four-story mansion where French author Victor Hugo lived during the middle of the last century; France's President Mitterrand made a surprise journey to Guernsey in 1985 to visit it; elaborately furnished, and unusual in that it is operated by the museums administration of the city of Paris.

Castle Cornet, guarding St. Peter Port harbor, is a dazzler (especially at night when floodlit) of an early thirteenth-century fortress put to contemporary service as the venue of several museums, one depicting the island's maritime history; another, the World War II German occupation.

Guernsey Museum and Art Gallery (Candie Gardens, overlooking St. Peter Port) is at its best in the section exhibiting charming watercolors by a gifted nineteenth-century Guernsey artist named Peter Le Lievre, many depicting solitary island life. Mascot of the gallery is a solitary Le Lievre cat, sound asleep.

Guernsey Folk Museum (Saumarez Park) brings to life the island's rural life of yore; setting is an old stable housing such exhibits as a farmhouse kitchen and bedroom, carts and carriages, costumes and dolls.

SETTLING IN

JERSEY

L'Horizon Hotel (St. Brelade's Bay)—low-slung and contemporary with traditional touches—is a 100-room-and-suite house of no little charm, just outside of St. Helier and with an extraordinary range of facilities. By that, I mean swimming in the indoor pool (with leisure center/sauna/solarium in conjunction) or at the beach; a pair of restaurants, one of which, the Grill, is an all-island leader and the subject of further comment; a trio of bars; dinner dancing; and a lounge made to order for afternoon tea-cum-music. Rooms vary with respect to decor and situation, but those I have inspected are attractive and have excellent shower-equipped baths. To my mind, this hotel is Jersey's finest. Member, Prestige Hotels. *First Class.*

La Place Hotel (St. Brelade) has as its nucleus an ivy-covered stone farmhouse dating to 1640, with beamed public spaces and a commendable restaurant (detailed on a later page) giving onto a flowered courtyard, with the bar attractively cane-furnished. Bedrooms to aim for are those with French windows opening onto the swimming-pool-centered patio. Very nice, indeed. *First Class.*

Grand Hotel (Esplanade, St. Helier) is the capital's old reliable, with nearly 120 rooms of varying design; you want specifically to ask for the most recently refurbished, seafront. There are an indoor pool and sauna and dinner dancing in the immense main dining room, with still another restaurant worthy of comment in a later paragraph and a handsome bar. *First Class.*

Old Court House Inn (St. Aubin's Harbor) is seventeenth century at its oldest, with marvelously atmospheric public spaces—several beamed and stone-walled bars, a restaurant that is one of the best on the island (later detailed), ten rooms (not all with bath, so specify), and owner-management by the Sharp family—as proficient and professional as it's warm and welcoming. *Moderate.*

Longueville Manor (St. Saviour) is respectfully venerable—parts of it are thirteenth century, and one of the dining rooms, superbly oak-paneled, is a principal Jersey attraction. There's a swimming pool in the garden, and there are 33 rooms. Trick is to avoid one of the small doubles—a third of the rooms are this size—which seem more appropriate for Britons down for a night or two, for whom the hotel seems geared, than for transatlantic travelers with appreciable baggage. Service, in my experience, has ranged from cooly correct to abrupt. Member, Relais et Châteaux. *First Class.*

GUERNSEY

St. Pierre Park Hotel (just outside St. Peter Port) takes the name of the pretty park in which it is situated. To call this hotel—the only luxury-category house in the Channel Islands—full-facility is to understate. There are 135 traditionally furnished rooms—not over-large, to be sure, but well designed and with good baths—which are complemented by rambling public spaces, including a trio of restaurants (the casual coffee shop that spills onto a terrace in summer is delightful, and I write in a later paragraph about the Victor Hugo), an indoor pool, a leisure center, a late-hours disco, a nine-hole-par-3 golf course, and a trio of tennis courts. Management is cordial and super-sharp; staff is friendly. A pleasure. *Luxury.*

Old Government House Hotel (St. Peter Port) began life as the official residence of Guernsey's Lieutenant Governor—the Crown's representative. But since it turned hotel in 1858, several additions have been made to it, and getting to certain of the rooms can mean negotiating a seemingly interminable series of stairways and corridors. If you insist upon—and are successful in obtaining—a room within easy walking distance of the lobby, you can be very happy, indeed, in this charmer of an old-school house. Restaurant is handsome and well operated, bar the ideal place to meet Guernseymen, lounge lovely for tea, swimming pool in the garden, staff crackerjack, and location heart of town. *First Class.*

Hogue du Pommier Hotel (Castel), on the island's west coast, is an inordinately handsome, early eighteenth-century farmhouse—the name translates as Apple Tree Hill—in a 10-acre garden. This hotel offers well-equipped bedrooms, essentially contemporary; a Tudor-look bar-lounge; and a restaurant embracing half a dozen joined rooms, with a French-accented menu and no less than 85 wines on its list. *First Class.*

Le Frégate Hotel (St. Peter Port) is a small treasure of a 13-room house on a hill overlooking the town's harbor. All of the doubles have balconies (for breakfast), the bar is amusing, and the restaurant outstanding enough to warrant later comment. *First Class.*

DAILY BREAD

JERSEY

Old Court House Inn Restaurant (St. Aubin's Harbor) has the high decibel count at dinner that only a really popular restaurant can achieve. Lures are super service and super seafood—mussels prepared a variety of ways, lobster and fish of the day cooked as requested, and veal and beef, too. A delight. *First Class.*

Victoria's (Grand Hotel, St. Helier) is, indeed, Victorian with respect to decor, but very French with respect to fare, selected from an à la carte menu. A meal might embrace snails Burgundy-style or caviar-stuffed hard-cooked eggs to start; medallions of beef sautéed with cream and Pernod, grilled lamb chops, scented with tarragon, or steak Diane prepared at table; and *crêpes Suzette*—the choicest sweet. *Luxury.*

Star Grill (L'Horizon Hotel, St. Brelade's Bay): Every visitor to Jersey seems to want to try the Star Grill. Menu is à la carte and French. Open with the celebrated artichoke appetizer. Consider frogs' legs sautéed in white wine or *steak au poivre* as entrées. A chocolate-sauced banana dessert is indicated to conclude. Fine wines. *First Class.*

La Bastille Taverne (St. Helier) is wine-bar-casual, with good things to eat, the range oysters and smoked salmon through fresh fish and roast beef. *Moderate.*

Apple Cottage (Rozel) makes for a nice excursion on a sunny day. It occupies an eighteenth-century house in a fishing village, with steak and lobster—order yours thermidor-style—the Big Two entrées and made-on-premises sweets like apple pie with thick Jersey cream. Fun. *Moderate.*

GUERNSEY

Victor Hugo (St. Pierre Park Hotel) is Guernsey dining at its most stylish: a period-piece of a room, with a tuxedoed staff skilled at serving up French food. You might open with a duck terrine or local shrimp in a blanket of sliced smoked salmon. The lobster bisque is authentic. Seafood entrées are numerous, grilled sole a ranker. And how about chicken Kiev or a veal chop sautéed in a white-wine/butter/rosemary sauce? Flambéed desserts. Fine wines. *Luxury.*

Le Frégate Hotel Restaurant (St. Peter Port) pleases with its mauve-and-pink ambience and picture windows overlooking the town harbor. Try smoked scallops or the house's mushroom specialty to start and *goujons*—finger-like bits—of the day's fish catch, with sauce *rémoulade*, or roast chicken as an entrée. Desserts are old-fashioned—rice pudding and banana splits are but two. *First Class.*

Admiral's Restaurant (Idlerocks Hotel, St. Martin's): Talk about perching a hotel atop a mini-mountain! The situation and views of the south coast alone make this spot visit-worthy. Sustenance? Seafood simply grilled is counseled. Or move over for a casual bar lunch in the hotel's Raffles Pavilion. *Moderate-First Class.*

Friends Bistro (St. Peter Port): You've shopped the morning away and you're famished. How about a really super cheeseburger with a glass of wine? More elaborate meals, as well. Lots of locals. *Moderate.*

SHOPPER'S CHANNEL ISLANDS

Unless regulations change, visitors to the Channel Islands may take back to Britain (where you go through the same kind of customs as you do when entering Britain from across the Atlantic—through the green line if you've nothing to declare; otherwise, red) a bottle of spirits, a carton of cigarettes, eight ounces of cologne or a small bottle of perfume, and—in addition—£28 worth of other merchandise. Best buys on both islands are watches, gold jewelry, Scottish cashmere sweaters, perfume and cologne, tobacco, and alcohol. In all cases, you save the 15 percent VAT tax imposed on the Mainland and perhaps even more, depending upon your purchase. On *Jersey*, leading shops— in and about pedestrians-only King Street, include *Voisin* (pronounced Voy-zen), a nice old-fashioned department store; *De Gruchy*, still another department store; *Elegance* and *Au Caprice* (reliable perfume shops); *Ricki* and *Hettich* (good jewelry stores); *Beau Monde* (clothing); *Jersey Post Office* (stamps for collectors). On *Guernsey*, shops center in and around High Street and include *Creasey's* department store, *A. P. Rogers* (with what has to be the biggest watch selection on the island), *The Jewelers & Silversmiths Co.* (watches and travel alarms), *Le Riche* (liquor), *Vanity Box* (perfumes), *P. W. Kimber* (jewelry), *Béghin's* (Church's shoes for men); and the *Guernsey Post Office* (stamps for collectors).

AFTER DARK

Gloucester Hall (Fort Regent, Jersey) offers variety shows and concerts.

St. James Hall (Guernsey) is an eighteenth-century church deftly converted into a concert hall.

INCIDENTAL INTELLIGENCE

British Airways flies from London and a number of other U.K. cities to Jersey; other airlines do, too. Guernsey Airlines flies from London (Gatwick) to Guernsey; other airlines also serve Guernsey from London (Heathrow) and other U.K. points. Channel Island Ferries sail from Portsmouth to both Jersey and Guernsey; Sealink British Ferries sail from both Portsmouth and Weymouth. Aurigny Air Services link Jersey and Guernsey (flights take a quarter-hour and depart frequently) and fly also to the Channel Island of Alderney, Southampton, and

Cherbourg (in France). Other airlines also link the islands to French points, as do ferries. *Further information:* States of Jersey Tourism Committee, Weighbridge, St. Helier; Jersey Tourism Office, 35 Albemarle Street, London; States of Guernsey Tourist Information Bureau, Crown Pier, St. Peter Port.

10

Exeter

And the Shores of Devon

BACKGROUND BRIEFING

Lay bets with Britons, and I wager you find few who are indifferent about the southwestern county of Devon. Neighboring Cornwall, going toward the Atlantic, can be faulted, perhaps, with respect to its towns, rarely as interest-packed as its shore. But Devon pleases, as much for the mix of rock and sand and verdant elevation on its coast as for its urban portions, not the least of which is its cathedral city: Exeter.

Smallish though it remains, Exeter's role in Britain's evolution is out of proportion to its size. Not unlike so much else of the country, its antecedents are Roman. They came in the first century—the setting at the head of the River Exe near the coast appealed—and, calling their settlement *Isca Dumnoniorum*, made of it the administrative core of the southwest. Later, Saxons took it in hand as their regional town. Aggressive Danes invaded at the start of the eleventh century. Only decades later, the town attempted to fight off William the Conqueror, but without success. Three later kings—John, Richard I, Henry II— honored Exeter with still extant charters. Edward I held a Parliament in Exeter; Edward IV gave the mayor his sword (you may see it proudly displayed today at Guildhall). Elizabeth I's derring-do sea captains—Drake, Hawkins, Raleigh—frequented the still-standing Mol's Coffee House on the Cathedral Close. Charles I stayed for a time in a house on Bedford Street, now the main post office. After the Restoration, his son, Charles II, went to Exeter to knight the then-mayor and give the town a painting of his Exeter-born daughter, on view in Guildhall. World War II bombings, while severe, were not as serious as those suffered by neighboring—and more strategically important—Plymouth. Today's Exeter is among Britain's most immediately likeable, easily explorable small cities.

ON SCENE

Lay of the Land: Exeter's High Street cuts through the heart of town diagonally, northeast to southwest. At midpoint, it passes two landmarks, Guildhall and the Cathedral, the latter in its own pretty park, bordered on the north by Cathedral Close—a history-drenched thoroughfare flanked by historic monuments, the earlier-mentioned Mol's Coffee House, and thousand-year-old St. Martin's Church among them. Nearby streets—Southernhay East and Southernhay West—are rich with houses of the Georgian era. Bedford, Princeshay, and Paul streets, in the core, evoke Exeter's past, with the pedestrian mall of High Street a distinct contrast.

Exeter Cathedral (Cathedral Close) can be ranked with the great ones in the European spectrum, and it's easily among a handful of the finest in Britain. It is felicitously placed—the central, verdant, historic, and very peaceful Cathedral Close is an inspired setting. Exeter is a prime example of English Decorated—the middle category of the three subdivisions of Gothic in Britain. It was in 1050 that Edward the Confessor designated a Saxon church on the site the seat of a new bishopric for the region. Within three centuries after King Edward's decree, the cathedral—by and large as one sees it contemporarily—had been built.

The nave, for me, is one of Britain's monumental esthetic experiences. The complexity of the rib vaulting extending 300 unbroken feet, with multishafted pillars supporting it, is in and of itself reason for an Exeter visit. Then you notice details. Exeter's bosses—the small sculptures punctuating the vaulting—number some 500. There are still another 500 corbels, the term given to similar sculptures affixed to walls rather than ceilings. Look about, taking care to note the misericords—carved folding wooden seats—of the choir; the East Window, a jumbo of a stained glass masterwork; and the Chapter House, restored in recent years and the site of concerts.

Guildhall (High Street) is one of Britain's oldest seats of municipal government, dating to the twelfth century, with additions through the sixteenth. Step in to have a look at the glorious, eight-arched ceiling of its Main Hall. Pause before the paintings, eighteenth and seventeenth century, and assorted treasures—swords through silver, maces through mayor's chains.

Royal Albert Museum and Art Gallery (Queen Street) occupies mock-Gothic quarters. Have a look at the English paintings (Reynolds is among those present), prints, and watercolors; locally produced silver; and—biggest treat of the collection for New Worlders—the

American Gallery: stuffed fauna including both bison and moose, if you please; assorted crafts of various American Indian tribes; and some live species, a South American piranha surely the most memorable, if not the most endearing.

Rougement House Museum (Castle Street) is an elegant Georgian mansion. Its mission is to impart Exeter's past, along with that of surrounding Devon, and it is most successful, in my view, when it moves beyond the Roman and Saxon eras into recent epochs.

St. Nicholas Priory (Fore Street): All that's left of a medieval Benedictine monastery. Which is hardly to carp, given the smashing great hall, not to mention a meticulously equipped kitchen and a vaulted undercroft, or subterranean chamber.

Exeter Maritime Museum (The Quay): Simply walk downhill from Palace Gate (starting at the Cathedral) and in five minutes you'll have reached what has to be the most distinctive of maritime museums in a nation full of same. Setting is the town's old port; subject matter is boats. More than a hundred, with the range sail-powered Arabian dhows and Congo dugouts through a steam tug from Denmark and a mini-fleet for you to row yourself. Fun!

Dartmoor National Park (15 miles west of Exeter) makes for a diverting day's outing. Begin in *Moretonhampstead*, a time-passed-by hamlet with narrow streets flanked by centuries-old houses, a pretty core—church, parish hall, principal square—and an inn-restaurant later recommended. Dartmoor National Park headquarters, in the village of *Bovey Tracey*, operates walking tours of the moor, Easter through September, almost daily, and of half-hour, three-hour, and six-hour durations. Or simply explore on your own. The park embraces serene valleys, trout-filled streams, rugged mountains, delightful villages (do try to take in *Buckfastleigh* and Gothic-era *Buckfast Abbey*, *Dydford* and its fairy-tale castle, and the thatch-house-lined streets of *Dunsford*).

Torquay likes to regard itself as Britain's Riviera. It is not about to put France's Côte d'Azur or resorts just over the frontier on Italy's Mediterranean out of business. But there is no denying that palm trees do indeed thrive, that the coastline—into which are indented crescent-shaped beaches—is agreeable, and that the center-of-town horseshoe of a harbor is eye-filling, hotels comfortable, and ambience relaxing. Torquay—unlike Brighton, with its onetime royal residence and fine art gallery, or Bournemouth, with its network of municipal mini-museums—is purely and simply a good-time town. Pause for lunch

or tea (see Daily Bread) in the course of exploring Devon. Or bed
down (see Settling In) for a night or two.

Plymouth: World War II bombing of this vital port was devastating.
Only remnants of the old remain, but in their stead is a functionally
designed core area. Broad thoroughfares lead from the commercial
zone to a green, plateau-like eminence known as the Hoe, overlooking immense Plymouth Sound. The harbor-bordering, well-restored
Barbican is Plymouth of yore—evoking the Elizabethan Golden Age
when Drake, Hawkins, and Raleigh sailed from it during the wars
with Spain's Philip II and from which, even earlier, the Pilgrim Fathers sailed to the new Plymouth across the Atlantic, from a point
marked now by the *Mayflower Stone*. Pop into this quarter's pair of
old-house museums—*Elizabethan House* (New Street) and somewhat
later *Merchant's House* (St. Andrews Street). Look at portraits of the
family of painter Sir Joshua Reynolds and at the silver and Plymouth
porcelain at the *City Museum and Art Gallery* (Drake Circus). Continue
along Drake Circus and the adjacent City Centre streets to department stores and other shops, allowing time for the antiques shops
along Southside Street in the Barbican area.

Saltram House (two miles west of Plymouth) is an originally Tudor
country house converted during the eighteenth century into a treasure of the Georgian period, with two of its rooms the work of Robert
Adam. One, the saloon, is among Adam's finest achievements, with
a plasterwork ceiling whose design is matched by a specially woven
Axminster carpet on the floor and with works by Rubens, Murillo,
and Reynolds on the walls; in all the house has fourteen Reynolds
portraits. Restaurant. National Trust.

Buckland Abbey (11 miles north of Plymouth), dominated by a
crenellated square tower, went up as a medieval Cistercian monastery, but was turned into a house, to become the home, two centuries
later, of Sir Francis Drake. It is today more a museum—the theme is
Devon's naval past—than a mansion. Go if only for the house's
architecture and Drake mementos. Café. National Trust.

Ugbrooke (eight miles south of Exeter) is one of Britain's underappreciated Robert Adam-designed houses, oddly uncelebrated in contrast to, say, not-far-distant Saltram (above), Scotland's Mellerstain,
or, for that matter, Osterly Park, near London, parts of which were
inspired by Adam's earlier Ugbrooke work. Library and chapel are
among the grander of the state rooms. Concentrate, as well, on furniture, much of it of the same eighteenth-century period as the house;

master paintings; and a surprise: a cache of needlework from the sixteenth century onward. With grounds designed by Capability Brown. Lord Clifford of Chudleigh is your host. Café.

Dartmouth, a few miles south along the coast from Torquay, could not contrast more with its big neighbor. If Torquay is the epitome of the contemporary hotel-dotted resort, Dartmouth is its opposite, a tranquil seaside town—the kind of place Stevenson portrayed in *Treasure Island*. Plan to overnight (see Settling In), to lunch, or to have tea (Daily Bread), walking about the waterfront, detouring to *Butterwalk* to see the seventeenth-century houses, one of which houses the delightful maritime-motif *Borough Museum*, with its stock in trade ship models and mementos of the Devon coast's sailor-heroes. Look up as you walk about Dartmouth. The low-slung, palace-like structure on the horizon is the *Royal Naval College*, which looks elaborately Edwardian because it is: Edward VII opened it in 1905. And it has other royal associations; Kings Edward VIII and George VI were students, as was the current heir to the throne, Prince Charles.

SETTLING IN
Royal Clarence Hotel (Cathedral Close, Exeter) is a onetime Georgian mansion on the street overlooking Exeter Cathedral and its grounds. The public rooms—beamed-ceiling lounge, cozy bar, chandeliered restaurant—are quietly attractive. Bedrooms with Cathedral views are the ones to aim for. Though no two are quite alike, they're all nicely equipped. A pleasure. *First Class.*

Rougemont Hotel (Queen Street, Exeter) typifies Victorian Exeter, with a wrought-iron stairway the focal point of its lobby, off which lead handsome spaces, including a commendable restaurant and a pair of bars, one public, and a source of bar lunches. Rooms are bright. The Railway Station is opposite. *First Class.*

White Hart Hotel (South Street, Exeter) is nothing if not atmospheric. It dates to the fifteenth century, when it was a monk's hostel. This house is at its most winning in the pair of ancient bars, lounges, and restaurant. Fifty-five of the 65 rooms (some in a newer wing) have baths or showers. *Moderate-First Class.*

White Hart Hotel (Moretonhampstead) is no relation to the Exeter White Hart, although, like its Exeter counterpart, it can boast considerable age—in this case some three centuries. A neat, white Georgian house—long ago a layover point for mail coaches—it contains a nifty bar, restaurant, and 16 rooms, 10 with baths. *Moderate.*

Gidleigh Park Hotel (Chagford, a few miles west of Moretonhampstead) in its own garden, is a country house, relatively contemporary
but with a half-timbered facade. It shelters just under a dozen comfortable rooms, with lounges antiques-accented, bar congenial, and
restaurant exceptional enough to warrant comment on a later page.
Member, Relais et Châteaux. *Luxury.*

Imperial Hotel (Parkhill Road, Torquay) is the premium hotel of the
Devon-Cornwall coast; a discreetly luxurious, 177-room-and-suite
house on a garden-surfaced eminence overlooking town and harbor.
Facilities are superb—outdoor and indoor pools, tennis, croquet, putting links, squash courts. Dine in the smart—and dressy—restaurant,
or lunch casually on a seaside terrace, with an adjacent chaise-lounge-
equipped sundeck. There are two cocktail lounges, as many settings
for dancing and entertainment, a sauna-health club, and nearby golf.
Trusthouse Forte. *Luxury.*

Grand Hotel (Seafront, Torquay): If the Grand is not quite as grand
as the Imperial (above), it comes close and is less expensive. Situation—at the other end of town from the Imperial—is seaview and
ambience tastefully traditional; 108 rooms and suites, excellent restaurant and bar-lounges, and facilities ranging from tennis to a sauna,
with an outdoor pool and the beach but yards distant. *Luxury.*

Corbyn Head Hotel (Torbay Road, Torquay) is an agreeable modern
house, seafront, with private baths in most of its 56 rooms, restaurant-
cum-view, capacious bar-lounge with dancing and entertainment,
and swimming pool-sundeck. *First Class.*

Livermead House Hotel (Torbay Road, Torquay) straddles the sea.
Within, it is low slung, perky-modern in look, with a buzzy bar,
attractive dining room, nice lounges. Sixty of the 72 bedrooms have
baths. Swimming pool-sundeck, tennis court, sauna. A Best Western
hotel. *Moderate-First Class.*

Gleneagles Hotel (Asheldon Road, Torquay): Expect nothing like the
opulence of this hotel's namesake hotel in the Scottish Highlands.
Torquay's Gleneagles is relatively modest and away from the beach.
Withal, the garden setting is pleasant. There are 40 functional rooms.
Restaurant, bar. *Moderate.*

Mayflower Post House Hotel (The Hoe, Plymouth) has remained
a Plymouth leader in the decade-plus since I first knew it, the year
it opened—1970—when I was in Plymouth covering festivities

commemorating the 350th anniversary of the Pilgrims' sailing to America. This is a ten-story block embracing a hundred-plus rooms and a pair of bars and restaurants, one named for Boston, with the eighteenth-century Tea Party in that New World city its theme. Outdoor pool-terrace-café. Trusthouse Forte. *First Class.*

Continental Hotel (Millbay Road, Plymouth) has the virtues of a core-of-town situation, along with a convenient restaurant and bar and baths in 29 of its 68 rooms. *Moderate.*

Royal Castle Hotel (The Quay, Dartmouth) is the traditional seaside inn of old that New Worlders cross the Atlantic to experience. It has seventeenth-century origins, claims seven British monarchs have been guests, and is situated directly on the waterfront, with a honey of a beamed bar-lounge and a charming restaurant. Just under half of the 20 rooms have baths. *Moderate-First Class.*

Combe House Hotel (near the village of Gittisham, Devon) is a rambling Elizabethan pile set in its own vast—and ravishingly beautiful—park just outside an idyllic village on the scenic Devon coast that is admirable not only for its movie-set situation, but because of the friendliness and hospitality of its owners, John and Therese Boswell and their family. The paneled walls and stuccowork of the high ceilings in the public rooms are eye-filling, even though they—and some of the bedrooms and vividly papered baths—could do with the ministrations of a good interior designer. The kitchen, at least in my experience, is uneven. *First Class.*

DAILY BREAD

Ship Inn (Martin's Lane, Exeter) leads off my select group if only because of its advanced age (sixteenth century) and historic associations (Drake and fellow Elizabethan sea captains were customers). Have a bar lunch downstairs or a proper meal—grilled local sole, steaks, and chops—in the upstairs dining room. *Moderate.*

White Hart Hotel (South Street, Exeter): Choose the restaurant proper or either of two bars, each ancient and atmospheric. To order: roast beef, and local seafood; sole, trout, salmon, scallops. Study the wine list with care; it's exceptional. *First Class.*

Cooling's Wine Bar (Gandy Street, Exeter): Lunch or dine either main floor or cellar, selecting from the buffet's hot (baked ham, shepherd's pie) and cold dishes—good salads among these. Wine by glass or bottle. *Moderate.*

Chapter's (Cathedral Close, Exeter), a venerable house, is now a source of sustenance—morning coffee, casual lunches, afternoon tea—with a view of the Cathedral as a bonus. *Moderate.*

Turk's Head (High Street, Exeter) is a next-door neighbor to Guildhall. Help yourself to all the roast beef and roast pork you like; accompany with salads. *First Class.*

White Hart Hotel (Moretonhampstead): The cozy restaurant of this village hotel, at the entrance to Dartmoor National Park, does well by traditional English dishes—roast beef and roast pork, beefsteak and kidney pie, lamb chops, and desserts, including treacle tart with Devon's super clotted cream and Dartmoor apple cake. Dinner only. Lunch is served casually in the bar. *Moderate-First Class.*

Gidleigh Park Hotel (Chagford) has a distinguished restaurant, with fare essentially *nouvelle cuisine,* felicitously English-accented. Dinner is a four-course table d'hôte and might begin with a mousse of scallops in shrimp sauce; continue with a main course of beef, duck, or fresh salmon; follow with a platter of a dozen cheeses; and conclude with created-on-premises cakes, ice creams, and puddings. The cellar is well stocked with California, as well as French, wines, should you be homesick for the former. Dinner only, unless you arrange lunch in advance with the American proprietors, Kay and Paul Henderson. *Luxury.*

Grand Hotel (Seafront, Torquay): The chandeliered, traditional-decor, seaview restaurant of this century-old hotel is worth knowing about for its excellent-value three-course-cum-coffee lunches and dinners. Begin with crab salad, continuing with roast duckling, escalope of veal, or a fish dish, and winding up with a choice of desserts or cheeses. Stick to the table d'hôte, and, though the restaurant is *Luxury* category, the price is then down a peg to *First Class.*

John Dory (Lisburne Square, Torquay) is named for the English fish that was named for a chap called Dory. Seafood is the specialty in this attractive onetime residence. *First Class.*

Epicure (Torwood Road, Torquay) is a centrally located old-timer, with a conventional but reliable menu embracing steaks, chops, and local seafood. *Moderate.*

Williams and Cox (Strand, Torquay) is a department store, whose Pantry restaurant is worth noting for solid-value lunches—roasts through salads—or afternoon tea. *Moderate.*

Chez Nous (13 Frankfort Gate, Plymouth): *Vive la France*—and in the core of Plymouth. Solid fare is the specialty—onion soup, country *pâté, steak au poivre vert.* Dinner only. *First Class.*

Beeton's (14 Athenaeum Street, Plymouth): The three-course lunch is a buy. English favorites—beef, hot pies, lamb chops—are the basis of the menu. *Moderate.*

Green Dragon Inn (Stoke Fleming, Dartmouth): Order the fried shrimp for lunch in this mellow pub; dinner offers a wide choice. Drinkers at the bar are likely to include midshipmen from the nearby Royal Naval College. *Moderate.*

Fosse's (Fosse Street, Dartmouth) is heart-of-town and welcoming, with a wide range of edibles—sandwiches through steaks. *Moderate.*

AFTER DARK
Northcott Theatre (Stocker Road, Exeter) presents plays by its repertory company and by visiting troupes, as well. Handsome and modern. Bar, café.

Athenaeum (The Hoe, Plymouth) is a multipurpose hall, with a full program of theater, ballet, and concerts.

INCIDENTAL INTELLIGENCE

There are airports at Exeter and Plymouth; you can fly to the Channel Islands, Scilly Isles, and points in northern France from the latter. *Further information:* Exeter Tourist Information Centre, Civic Centre, Dix's Field; Torquay Tourist Information Centre, Vaughan Parade; Plymouth Tourist Information Centre, The Barbican; Darmouth Tourist Information Centre, The Quay.

11

Lake District
Windermere to Carlisle

BACKGROUND BRIEFING

> *I wander'd lonely as a cloud*
> *That floats on high o'er vales and hills,*
> *When all at once I saw a crowd,*
> *A host, of golden daffodils;*
> *Beside the lake, beneath the trees,*
> *Fluttering and dancing in the breeze.*
> —William Wordsworth

Look up Wordsworth in your *Oxford Book of English Verse*, as I have in mine, and you find according to my count, no less than seventeen of his considerable output of poems anthologized. But who today quotes "Lucy" or "Valedictory Sonnet to the River Duddon" or, for that matter, "On the Extinction of the Venetian Republic, 1802"? No, it's "Daffodils" that sticks in our minds, and it's "Daffodils" that takes us to Wordsworth's lovely lakes.

It's their relatively remote situation—a patch of northwest England near the Scottish border, with nary a solitary industrial city in their confines—that has kept the lakes lovely. And the mountains—still unobstructed—that dip down to their shores. And the resident wild-life. Indeed, no other substantial English region—the Lakes constitute the contemporarily created county of Cumbria and have protection as a National Park, as well—remains in quite so pristine a state. Even the innkeepers do their bit: there's not a vertical shoebox of a hotel in the entire neighborhood.

ON SCENE

Lay of the Land: North Americans, whose own lands are not lacking in areas of natural beauty, tend to bypass the Lakes en route between England and Scotland. They shouldn't. Except in July and August—when vacationing Britons arrive in packs—there is not a region anywhere in the kingdom that is more relaxing, more beautiful, more comfortable, nor—cuisine-conscious London and Edinburgh excepted—more delicious. For it is a fact hardly to be overlooked: The better Lakes hoteliers present in their dining rooms the most interesting cuisine in provincial Britain.

But geography first: The district extends, more or less, from a trio of lakes on its southern fringe—Coniston Water, Esthwaite Water, and Lake Windermere—some 35 miles north through central lakes like Ennerdale Water, Rydal Water, and Haweswater, to northern lakes such as Derwentwater and Bassenthwaite Lake. Carlisle, some 30 miles north of Bassenthwaite and a bordertown with both a cathedral and castle, is the district's major city.

The resort clusters: Key lake is Windermere. Measuring ten miles in length and a mile in width, it's England's largest, and it attracts the lion's share of Lakes vacationers, headquartering at hotels in and about the villages of Windermere, Bowness, and Ambleside, each in and of itself delightful venues for people-watching walks and inconsequential shopping, interspersed with bouts of exploration, to destinations like these:

Brockhole is the name of the onetime country house—a nondescript, turn-of-century dwelling—that serves as the Lake District National Park Visitor Centre. It shows a film that provides background on the lakes, and there are orientation talks by English counterparts of what we call rangers in the American and Canadian national parks, on the flora and fauna. But the major reason for a Brockhole visit is a walk about its extraordinarily beautiful 30-acre gardens, verdant and impeccably tended, with the blue waters of Lake Windermere as backdrop. Cafeteria.

Grasmere, to Wordsworth fans, means two things: the churchyard where he's buried and *Dove Cottage* where he lived between 1799 and 1808. Of course, you want to have a look at this unpretentious two-story house and little next-door museum wherein are displayed some Wordsworth first editions, original manuscripts, and other mementos. For me, though, *Grasmere Church,* amidships in the village, and built between the thirteenth and seventeenth centuries, is more affecting. Wordsworth wrote of it: "Not raised in proportion was the pile, But large and massy; for duration built." And out back, in the churchyard, is the poet's grave, marked by a simple stone commemorating his wife's death as well: "William Wordsworth, 1850. Mary Wordsworth, 1859."

Belle Isle on Lake Windermere: A good excuse for a boat ride is this remarkable circle of a house, pure Georgian and fronted by a quartet of Ionic columns supporting its portico. Situation is an island in Lake Windermere. You board at Bowness Bay, and, once arrived, make sure you don't miss the Romney portrait of a onetime owner, Isabella Curwen.

Rydal Mount (Ambleside): If I had to make a choice, it would be Rydal Mount over Dove Cottage, hands down. This gracious villa was home to the Wordsworths from 1813 until the poet died in 1850. The garden setting is no less charming than the still-inhabited house, where you're welcome to see bedrooms above and drawing and dining rooms below, noting portraits of the Wordsworths on the walls. Many visitors have preceded you; one such was Dowager Queen Adelaide, widow of William IV and aunt of the then-young Victoria. She was shown about by Mr. and Mrs. Wordsworth on a summer day in 1840, with fifty local schoolchildren serving as an auxiliary reception committee.

Kendal, an attractive town ten miles east of Windermere, has two requisite side-by-side museums, one of which, *Abbot Hall Art Gallery,* has the distinction of being unsurpassed among Britain's small museums. It occupies a jewel of a modest-sized manor house dating to the eighteenth century, which has in recent years been superbly restored and meticulously furnished. You are happy enough approaching it from this aspect—colonnaded entrance hall, paneled drawing room, intimately scaled breakfast room, gracious dining room, and library. As you walk about, you realize that you are in a fine-arts gallery of no little distinction, as well as a house-museum. Works of which the museum is justifiably proudest are early paintings by the neighborhood's own George Romney, among all-Britain greats of the eighteenth century. Look for the mother and four children of the Gower Family among a number of Romneys. Along with portraits by Reynolds and Turner, out of the past, there are works of more recent vintage, such as those by Ben Nicholson and André Derain. Just across the lawn from Abbot Hall is the *Museum of Lakeland Life and Industry,* with well-created Victorian rooms and objects—agricultural through educational—interpreting the way Lakes people have lived the last few centuries.

Levens Hall and Sizergh Castle (near neighbors, several miles south of Kendal) are country houses of consequence. If limited time dictates that you choose but one, make it Levens Hall, nicely operated by its young owners, Mr. and Mrs. Hal Bagot. Its surprise is a formal topiary garden—and an extensive one at that—still maintained to the designs of the seventeenth-century French designer. The house itself is essentially Tudor—and terrific. Plasterwork of the ceilings and the oak paneling—especially that of the drawing room—alone make a visit exciting. But there is museum-caliber seventeenth-century furniture and paintings by masters, Rubens through Constable. Sizergh, a mile distant, is somber, lacking the spontaneity and charm of its neighbor, but it has as compensation a formidable towered and crenellated facade behind which there are a number of state rooms with splendidly carved sixteenth-century paneling, furniture—French as well as English—from the eighteenth century, and some very good paintings, including an unexpected Rigaud of a young Stuart prince. National Trust.

Carlisle, what with its razor's-edge situation—straddling the border with Scotland—has known many moments of turbulence during a long history. Allot yourself a day to explore this conveniently compact town, with the Railway Station at the southern edge of its core, centered by Town Hall Square. Adjacent, pedestrians-only English Street leads south, with the circular bastions of the ancient Citadel just beyond. Castle Street leads north, toward *Carlisle Castle* (Ring Road). Set in its own park, behind a high wall that looks, from a distance at least, impregnable, the nearly 900-year-old castle is testament to the Anglo-Scots conflict spanning much of that period. You want to go not so much for the uniforms and battle regalia of the Regimental Museum within, but for the complex: what remains of the keep and the onetime royal residence within the walls. *Carlisle Cathedral* (Castle Street) is heart-of-town, as likable for the handsome ancillary buildings of the parklike precinct that surrounds it as for its sturdy, compact construction, at once Romanesque, Early English, and later Decorated Gothic. There is esthetic excitement here—the choir is a riot of exuberantly carved wood, from the misericords of the seats to exquisitely sculpted capitals of surrounding columns, each a graphic scene of deeply religious or markedly secular life. *Guildhall Museum* (Fisher Street): One of Carlisle's oldest buildings—this half-timbered house dates to 1407—is its newest museum (1978), with each of its eight medieval trade guilds' rooms appropriately restored, the range Butchers and Shoemakers to Tanners and Weavers. With ancient city treasures—silver especially—also on view. *Carlisle Museum* (Castle Street) occupies a winsome Jacobean house—you enter from its capacious garden—and is a likable, if unexceptional, mélange of paintings (Raeburn and Romney stand out, along with two gifted locals from the last century: Sam Bough and W. J. Blacklock), English china, and fragments of really historic Carlisle—from the Roman occupation.

SETTLING IN

Miller Howe Hotel (Windermere) is the Lakes' most celebrated, Britain-wide and abroad, thanks to its creative owner-manager-chef, John Tovey. A cookbook author of repute, Tovey travels widely promoting tourism to his region and, when in America, to his country. His hotel is small—a baker's dozen distinctively Tovey-decorated rooms, the nicest ones those in front facing the garden that slopes down to Lake Windermere; no Lakes hotel affords more sublime vistas. Tovey himself presides over dinner each evening; it's a one-sitting, no-choice presentation about which I comment on a later page. Eccentric, to be sure. But so is the hotel in other respects. There is no reception area, only an office adjacent to the kitchen that is not always attended. There are no room telephones, only an intercom system connecting to the not-always-manned office. Early morning tea—or, if you are departing early, continental breakfast, when ordered the night before—is available. But a proper breakfast—and I pay tribute to Tovey's scrambled eggs, the best I know in the kingdom—is not available until 9:00 A.M., the latest hotel starting-hour of which I'm aware, anywhere in Britain, for the first meal of the day. Withal, Miller Howe is congenial; everyone has a good time. *Luxury.*

Belsfield Hotel (Bowness-on-Windermere) hugs the lakeshore, or at least its pretty lawns do. This is a nineteenth-century mansion nicely transformed to hotel use, with its high-ceilinged, chandeliered restaurant and sliding-roofed swimming pool both standouts. Views from lakeside bedrooms are memorable. Not all rooms have baths. Trusthouse Forte. *Moderate-First Class.*

Windermere Hydro Hotel (Bowness-on-Windermere): The Hydro is a rambling elderly house, nicely—but not overly—modernized with spaciousness prevalent throughout in lobbies and lounges, handsome restaurant, and rooms, too—nearly a hundred—all of which have showers in their baths. *First Class.*

Old England Hotel (Bowness-on-Windermere) hugs the shore of the lake, gray with a white trim and a multiplicity of gables, behind which the look is delightfully traditional, with gracious public spaces and a pool on the lawn. Trusthouse Forte. *First Class.*

Wild Boar Hotel (Crook, near Windermere) is just inland from the lake, an originally seventeenth-century roadside inn, with atmospherically beamed public rooms, a clublike lounge for tea and drinks, a super restaurant, and charming bedrooms with considerable panache. *First Class.*

Ellerthwaite Lodge Hotel (New Road, Windermere) is a find for the budget traveler; all 12 of its pert and pretty rooms have showers in their baths, and there are both restaurant and up-a-flight bar-lounge, each attractive. *Moderate.*

Michael's Nook Hotel (Grasmere) went up in the middle of the last century as a squire's retreat. It is a gem of a house, put together with style by owner-manager Reg Clifford. The drawing room-cum-view charms and the bar welcomes; each of the 10 rooms is different from its neighbor, and the restaurant is exceptional. *Luxury.*

Wordsworth Hotel (Grasmere): Built as a hotel in 1840 and stripped— to become another hotel—a century and a half later, the in-village Wordsworth pleases with its solid good looks and its sensibly equipped bedrooms, all 35 of which have showers in their baths. Restaurant, bar. *Moderate-First Class.*

Swan Hotel (Grasmere): I don't know of any of the many old inns operated, kingdom-wide, by Trusthouse Forte with more unaffected charm than the seventeenth-century Swan. Antique accents are dotted about to good advantage—in dining room, lobby, and bars. There are super views from the lakeside rooms, although, please note, only about half of the 31 rooms have baths. *Moderate-First Class.*

Rothay Manor Hotel (Ambleside): Merchant princes from the South built well when they went north. Rothay Manor went up in the early nineteenth century. Family-run now, it remains eye-filling, with perfectly lovely lounges, a high-caliber restaurant, and a dozen generous-size, handsomely decorated rooms, all of whose baths have showers. Order tea served on the lawn. *First Class.*

Langdale Chase Hotel (Ambleside): This Victorian mansion fronts a brilliant garden, with the lake and a boathouse (its stonework matches the hotel's) just beyond. There are dark-paneled lounges, restaurant and bar both with fine views, and bedrooms—not all with bath—with a light country look. *Moderate-First Class.*

Temple Sowerby House Hotel (Temple Sowerby near Penrith, north of Kendal) began life as a farmhouse, saw later additions during the Georgian era, and, happily, became a hotel in the mid-1980s, with decor essentially Georgian. The red-walled drawing room appeals, bar-lounge is cozy, and restaurant is wood-paneled. There are just a dozen comfortable, no-two-quite-alike rooms. *First Class.*

Cumbrian Hotel (Court Square, Carlisle) is strategically situated, with the Railway Station in one direction and the core of town in the other, easily walkable. This is a handsome, early Victorian house—the original facade has been well preserved—with a nice hum to its lobby, gracious main restaurant, coffee shop, trio of bars, and nearly 70 neatly furnished rooms. *First Class.*

Crown & Mitre Hotel (English Street, Carlisle) is long on the scene, an across-the-street neighbor of Guildhall Museum (above) in the historic heart of Carlisle. There are convenient spots for dining and drinking. Rooms in the modern addition are the preferred ones. *First Class.*

DAILY BREAD

Miller Howe Hotel Restaurant (Windermere): The Lakes' most publicized source of sustenance requires advance orientation. Proprietor-chef John Tovey has carefully orchestrated dinner for you, asking that you be seated just before 8:30 P.M., so that you may order wine from his excellent cellar. And then: Poof! Serving staff comes forward with a five-course-and-coffee repast, neither traditional English, old-school French, nor *nouvelle cuisine*, but a combination thereof, with original—sometimes ingenious—Tovey touches. Mind, now, you have no choice in what's presented, until it's time for dessert. Before then, the meal might run like this: a terrine or *pâté*, followed by apple, celery, and walnut salad served with Cumberland sauce and pickled kumquat. Next, consommé, fennel-seasoned and Marsala-laced. Time, then, for the fish course: filet of sole in coconut, with banana and sweet and sour mayonnaise. Entrée might be boned local quail stuffed with spinach and veal, with wine sauce, and never less than half a dozen fresh vegetables accompanying. There are always eight sweets—tipsy trifle, banana cream ice, black currant pie with cream, chocolate rum squidgy cake, to name some; as well as cheese. Dinner only. *Luxury.*

Michael's Nook Hotel Restaurant (Grasmere): Reg Clifford's dinners are Anglo-French—and delicious. Openers run to hot spiced eggplant or a hot shrimp *soufflé*, with onion soup following, preparatory to an entrée that could be game pie (embracing wild duck, venison, and guinea fowl), or poached trout. Desserts are limited but special. Fine wines. Dinner only. *Luxury.*

Rothay Manor Hotel Restaurant (Ambleside): Setting is superb and cooking is skilled, with first courses invariably imaginative. They might include asparagus tartlets with Parma ham, fried *goujons* of plaice with the house's tartar sauce, or *pâté* of duck liver. Entrées include stick-to-the-ribs *boeuf à la mode*, laced with brandy, as well as white wine; chicken roasted with a thyme and lemon stuffing, and interestingly accompanied; lamb chops baked in a cream-and-onion sauce. Sweets run Sacher torte to carrot cake. *Luxury.*

Langdale Chase Hotel Restaurant (Ambleside): Views of the lake are a bonus with dinners, with such entrées as casserole of pheasant and roast veal. Vegetables are pleasers, too: *ratatouille* and braised celery might be one evening's offerings. *First Class.*

Swan Hotel (Grasmere): This ancient hotel serves lunch in both bar and restaurant and a four-course dinner. *Moderate.*

Old England Hotel Restaurant (Bowness-on-Windermere): Not unlike the Swan (above), a prudent choice for a well-priced, multi-course dinner or, for that matter, lunch, with entrées including roasts and hot meat pies. *Moderate-First Class.*

Wild Boar Hotel Restaurant (Crook, near Windermere): A handsome restaurant in a handsome hotel, and yes, you may indeed have wild boar—at a price. More prosaic entrées—roast beef, baked plaice, chicken à la king—are less costly. *First Class.*

Blue Bell (Heversham, six miles south of Kendal) is indicated for a lunch pause in the course of an expedition to museums and country houses in and about Kendal. Order casually from the bar of this half-timbered inn, or try the temptingly priced table d'hôte entrées, which might include *coq au vin* and roast beef—in the restaurant. *Moderate.*

Coffee Pot (High Street, Windermere): Have quiche or an open-faced Danish-style sandwich for lunch or scones for afternoon tea. The women who own the place prepare what they serve. *Moderate.*

Coxswain's Cabin (High Street, Windermere): A wine-bar. Order a glass or a carafe with the hot special of the day. *Moderate.*

Porthole (Ash Street, Bowness-on-Windermere) looks typically English, but is Italian-owned, with pasta suggested for lunch or dinner. *Moderate-First Class.*

Sheila's Cottage (High Street, Ambleside) is at once attractive and attractively priced. You'll be happy with a shrimp salad at lunch, Swiss fondue at dinner. *Moderate.*

København (Castle Street, Carlisle) offers Danish specialties—open-faced sandwiches and hot dishes, as well. *Moderate-First Class.*

INCIDENTAL INTELLIGENCE

Going north from London by train (or, for that matter, coming south from Scotland), bear in mind that it's necessary to change trains at Oxenholme, proceeding then to Windermere station. Once arrived, do budget time for a steamer ride on the lake. Sealink, a subsidiary of British Rail, operates a four-vessel fleet between Bowness, midpoint on the lake, to Ambleside at its northern tip and Lakeside on its southern flank; departures take place regularly throughout each day, mid-May–mid-September. There are sailboats and rowboats for hire, too. If you're a couple or, better yet, two couples traveling together, consider hiring a private-car service to get you around the Lakes. The charge is generally an hourly one, for as many as four passengers, in which case it can be inexpensive. One such is Windermere Taxi & Private Hire; telephone Windermere 2355. *Further information:* Windermere Tourist Information Centre, Victoria Street; Bowness-on-Windermere Tourist Information Centre, Bowness Bay; Ambleside Tourist Information Centre, Old Courthouse, Church Street; Carlisle Tourist Information Centre, Old Town Hall, Greenmarket.

12

Lincoln
And a Midlands Miscellany

BACKGROUND BRIEFING

Americans, asked to comment on the etymology of the name, would go back as far as the great Civil War President. Cross transatlantic to England's Lincoln and back you go, some nineteen hundred years, to the colonizing Romans who came to settle in—and defend—a region of east-central England where they built a fort atop a hill and dubbed it *Lindum*. The name stuck. Or almost. Over the centuries the "dum" became "on." But today's Lincoln is not without a still-in-use Roman monument. Modern cars drive through the intact Newport Arch, albeit perhaps with less clatter than horse-powered Roman chariots of yore.

Lincoln, though still a small city, respects tradition at least as much as any of its East Midlands neighbors to the west and south. And it is used to company. Saxons, and later Danes, replaced the early Romans, leaving still-sanctified churches with memorable names like St. Peter-at-Gowts and St. Mary-le-Wigford. Then, nearly a thousand years later, after King William crossed the Channel to become The Conqueror, he sent his deputies north to build both castle and cathedral on the hill that had been the Romans' Lindum. So singled out by William I, Lincoln became a city of no little importance over the centuries. Kings honored it with royal gifts (it retains a sword believed presented by Richard II) and royal visits (Charles I's was one such). Cromwell's forces singled it out for damage in battle. Charles II, as if in restitution, gave it a mace after his Restoration. Like any modern city, it has not completely escaped the dubious distinctions of progress; half of the forty churches it knew in the Middle Ages are no longer on scene. Enough else of its past remains, though, to make of Lincoln an absorbing focal point of East Midlands exploration.

ON SCENE

Lay of the Land: Lincoln is an upstairs-downstairs town, with the former the area where you want to headquarter and center your exploration. Upper Lincoln is bisected by a north-south street called Bailgate. As it progresses southward and downward, it passes Castle Square and cross-streets called Westgate and Eastgate—with two flanking landmarks, what remains of Lincoln Castle and, more to the point, Lincoln Cathedral. Continuing south, its name changes—any walker perceives why without being told—to Steep Hill. And, as if to slow one's pace, a plethora of smart shops and boutiques present themselves to right and left in the course of one's descent. Below lies more prosaic Lincoln, the biggest emporia—department stores like Littlewoods of High Street, most especially—and, at the southern edge of town, the Railway Station.

Lincoln Cathedral (Eastgate): Some cathedrals are at their best in the early morning, just after opening, before even the first worshipers have arrived; Winchester, for me, is one such. Other cathedrals make their best impression after dark; Lincoln is one such. The city fathers illuminate it most nights of the year, and that's when one wants to walk past the extraordinary West Front. There is nothing else like it in Britain; that of Peterborough Cathedral, about which I write on a later page of this chapter, comes close in certain respects. So, in a lesser way, does the same side of the cathedral at Wells (Chapter 3).

But Lincoln's West Front—a four-level screen, superimposed in the twelfth century to strengthen the facade erected in the eleventh—is what one most remembers. Several hundred niches frame sculpted scenes from both Old and New Testaments, surrounding and surmounting the immense main portal. And it's free. By that, I mean to say that the interior is, to all intents and purposes, not. Lincoln Cathedral, like Salisbury Cathedral (Chapter 19), stations a cashier at the door and you are expected to cough up a "voluntary" contribution, with the amount specified, again as at Salisbury. However, it must be added, in Lincoln's favor, that its ticket seller is seated at a table, rather than standing behind a theater-style wicket, as in Salisbury. Do pay, though. One can understand why the chief builder of the early Norman bishops, Hugh by name, was sainted for his work. The high, long nave of this mostly Early English Gothic complex is affecting. The windows at either end of the wide transept are beautiful. And there are other attributes—octagonal chapter house built around a single central pillar, tranquil cloisters, one of the four originals of *Magna Carta*, William the Conqueror's charter ordering the original cathedral built, the treasury, and—surprise, these—two Sir Christopher Wren additions of the seventeenth century: screen backing the high altar and recognizably Wren-paneled library. Not to mention surrounding precincts: Houses, medieval through Georgian, many still sheltering Cathedral officials, border the building on all four sides.

Lincoln Castle (Castle Square) is more a case of fragments than a cohesive whole. The Eastern Gateway, in what remains of the Norman Wall, still is in use—and impresses. Within, surrounding well-tended lawns, are onetime battlements that housed a prison, the chapel and cells of which are visitable.

Usher Art Gallery (Lincoln Road), in a mock-Classic pavilion, is more a case of charming mementos than a cache of great art. Not that one wants to skip its collection of antique watches, seventeenth- and eighteenth-century silver and porcelain, and some paintings, watercolors, and drawings, including two Turners—one of Lincoln and its Cathedral, another, later and finer, of the Lincolnshire town of Stamford. Note, too, delightful interpretations of nineteenth-century Lincoln by native-born painter Peter De Wint.

Museum of Lincolnshire Life (Burton Road): A mid-nineteenth-century barracks has been put to good use for a series of lifelike settings of the Lincoln of this century and the last one—early drugstore, doctor's and dentist's offices, clothing and hardware shops, the rooms—nursery through parlor—of a middle-class Edwardian house with an amusing outdoors appendage: local cows, sheep, and pigs in a mock-up of a farmyard.

Guildhall (Saltergate) houses Lincoln's town council and has since the fifteenth century. This is a looker of a half-timbered house that you want to wander about in if the council is not in session. Ask if you may be permitted a peek at the city's official insignia—a historic cache of mayors' chains, processional maces, and ceremonial swords, sometime gifts of royalty over the centuries.

Jews House (Steep Hill): You may or may not be interested in contemporary handicrafts, on display here. But this stone house out of the Middle Ages is of architectural importance, and it's a good spot for a mid-morning cup of coffee or afternoon tea in its café.

City and County Museum (Greyfriars Pathway) is, not unlike Jews House, an architectural treasure: It goes back to the thirteenth century, when Franciscans built it as a focal point of a monastery, which remained active until the Reformation. Today it's a repository for Lincoln—and Lincolnshire—archeology: Roman pottery, Saxon swords, medieval armor.

Belton House (20 miles south of Lincoln), handsomely scaled—not too large and not intimidating—is in the Baroque style of the seventeenth century's Sir Christopher Wren. Within, much of it was decorated in the eighteenth century by James Wyatt. State rooms are handsome: splendid plasterwork in the boudoir; smashing bedrooms, one with the canopy bed installed for a visit of Queen Adelaide in 1844; an oak-paneled saloon; brocaded drawing room with paintings by Titian, Rubens, Raphael, Rembrandt, and Van Dyck; and a sumptuous chapel hung with a Tintoretto. Note the portrait of King Edward VIII in the library; he was godfather to the current master of Belton, the seventh Baron Brownlow. Café.

Boston (32 miles southwest of Lincoln): This little Lincolnshire city, on the banks of the River Witham, grew rich in the medieval centuries as an export center for wool and hides. Its merchants manifested their wealth in the building of a Gothic church, *St. Botolph's*, with a tower so soaring—it exceeds 272 feet—that the church is known the length and breadth of Britain simply and not disrespectfully, as "The Stump." St. Botolph's tower was illuminated in centuries past to serve as a lighthouse for mariners at sea. Even today, if you climb it on a fine day, you may see Lincoln Cathedral more than 30 miles away. Bostonians from the New World subsidized a major restoration of the church six centuries after it went up—in 1931. As well they might.

The new Boston owes its name to the old. For it was in 1607 that a band of Puritans converged upon Boston and boarded a ship bound for voluntary exile in Holland, only to be betrayed by the ship's Dutch master. They were turned over to local authorities, who imprisoned seven of their leaders. Your first stop in Boston should be redbrick *Guildhall*, already two centuries old when its cells—still visitable—were used to incarcerate the Pilgrim leaders prior to a trial in Lincoln.

The Pilgrims sailed 13 years later, first from Southampton, ultimately from Plymouth (Chapter 10), to establish a settlement at the New World's Plymouth. Ten years after that, in 1630, a group set out successfully from England's Boston, and, with an offshoot group from the Massachusetts Plymouth, established a new settlement, at first called Trimountain, with its name later changed—by the Massachusetts Bay Company—to Boston. Today, in St. Botolph's Church, you'll find tablets honoring five English Bostonians who became Massachusetts Governors and a chapel honoring the Rev. John Cotton, who quit the rectorship of St. Botolph's to become minister of a Boston (Massachusetts) congregation.

Compact Boston is easily walkable. From St. Botolph's at its northern end, stroll south along Church Street, to South Square, dominated by Guildhall and adjacent *Fydell House*. An eighteenth-century mansion, now a school, it is open to the public, with Americans welcome to visit the American Room, dedicated in 1938 for the use of visiting Yanks by the then-ambassador to the Court of St. James, Joseph P. Kennedy, President Kennedy's father.

Nottingham (30 miles southwest of Lincoln): Shades of Robin Hood to be sure. But just. Nottingham is a bustling, medium-size city, far too preoccupied with the present to be much concerned with the mythical Robin. It makes for an agreeable layover in the course of an East Midlands journey, as much for creature comforts (later detailed) as for monuments to a not inconsequential past. The city bases itself on a fine square, *Old Market*, by name, dominated by a domed and colonnaded Council House—the city hall—that went up in the 1920s in the style of Sir Christopher Wren. Mercantile Nottingham is in this square's precincts—pedestrians-only Albert Street, with its Marks & Spencer; Victoria Centre, with its massive Boots; Friar Lane, with its Littlewoods; and pricey boutiques on Angel Row. *Nottingham Castle* (Castle Road): Pay your respects to Robin Hood at the statue of him, bow and arrow at the ready, below the Castle walls, with reliefs in the background into which are worked familiar figures, including Maid Marian, Friar Tuck, and Little John. Then go inside to the city's *Museum of Fine and Decorative Arts.* There is glass; silver and pottery of the eighteenth and nineteenth centuries; and a sprinkling of fine paintings, with Rubens, Teniers, a number of Frenchmen (Nattier, Delacroix, Boudin), and, most interesting among the English, the last century's Richard Bonington. *Brewhouse Yard*, at the foot of the Castle, houses the city's folk museum in a clutch of Jacobean houses: mock-up shops, period rooms, tools and costumes, maps and murals, with displays extending into the unusual caves of Castle Hill. *Castle Gate Museum*, also part of the Castle complex, occupies houses a century newer than those of Brewhouse Yard. A charming environment for the municipal collection of costumes, early eighteenth through late nineteenth century, cleverly reposing in a range of meticulously furnished and accessorized rooms of those periods.

Newstead Abbey (nine miles north of Nottingham) went up in the twelfth century as a monastery and was updated over the centuries, especially the seventeenth, when it was taken over by the fourth Lord Byron, and ancestor of the poet George Gordon, who became the sixth Lord Byron and lived at Newstead intermittently between 1798 and 1814. Its *Byron Museum*—manuscripts, first editions, letters, portraits, and even the shoe-last device used to correct his deformed right foot—is a major lure, along with Byron's bedroom, furnished as it was during his residence, and other fine interiors.

D. H. Lawrence Museum (Victoria Street, Eastwood, nine miles northwest of Nottingham): The working-class house in which novelist Lawrence was born, the son of a coal miner, in 1885, is operated as a museum of Lawrence mementos—manuscripts, letters, and personal effects. Lawrence used this district—and his family—as models for the Morel family in *Sons and Lovers*, the autobiographical novel published in 1913, for which he is best remembered.

Kedleston Hall (15 miles west of Nottingham) is a masterwork of the eighteenth-century Scottish architect-designer, Robert Adam. Adam's Marble Hall is a ceremonial salon that could have been transported by him from the Rome of his Grand Tour: 40 feet high, 67 feet long, 42 feet wide, in tones of bronze and ringed by Corinthian columns, with a plasterwork ceiling—Adam is known for these—that is no less splendid. Each of the state rooms—in symmetrical wings flanking the Marble Hall—is a work of genius, filled with fine paintings, mostly Italian, collected by the first Baron Scarsdale, who commissioned Adam. A descendant, generations removed—Viscount Scarsdale—is the current landlord.

The Music Room is hung with works by Bassano, Giordano, and Guercino and filled with furniture designed not only by Adam but by his distinguished contemporary, William Kent. Note Adam's gilt sofas in the state drawing room, with two paintings by Veronese. The library has Adam's original bookcases; Rembrandt and Van Dyck are among the painters. Knellers and Lelys fill the state boudoir. The cupola-topped saloon is in the manner of Rome's Pantheon. And the dining room has Adam-designed, semidomed apsidal ends and the curved tables he created for them. Café.

Hardwick Hall (30 miles northwest of Nottingham): You'll recognize the name; this Tudor mansion is called after the very same Bess of Hardwick whose third husband, the sixth Earl of Shrewsbury, was custodian of the imprisoned Mary Queen of Scots for fifteen years— not at Hardwick, but at other houses in the region, including nearby Chatsworth (below), which was constructed by Bess with her second husband, Sir William Cavendish. Strong-willed Bess—at first friendly with Mary and a collaborator with her on embroideries—later accused Lord Shrewsbury of having an affair with Mary, to the point where they were estranged, after which Bess—a born builder of houses—rebuilt Hardwick. It was completed in 1597, and it is the Hardwick, by and large, which the visitor sees today, remarkable in that it is of a single era, with few additions. Carved-wood paneling combines with tapestries to surface the walls. The great chamber is, despite its decorations, stunningly severe. The long gallery, with a pair of superb fireplaces, a fine ceiling, and choice paintings, is the house at its handsomest. There are beautifully canopied bedrooms; that called the Blue Room, with its alabaster fireplace, is the finest. Café. National Trust.

Chatsworth (33 miles northwest of Nottingham, near Bakewell): Only a handful of country houses, anywhere in Europe, are in a league with Chatsworth: Blenheim and, to a lesser extent, Knole, in England; Vaux le Vicomte, in France; Drottningholm, in Sweden; Beloeil, in Belgium; Nymphenburg, in Germany. Chatsworth's builders (see Hardwick Hall, above) were much-married Bess of Hardwick and her second husband, Sir William Cavendish. Sir William's successor became the first of four Earls of Devonshire; the fourth, in the seventeenth century, was upgraded to duke—highest of peerage titles in Britain. His descendant, nearly three hundred years later, is the eleventh Duke, who, with his talented Duchess and their son, the Marquess of Hartington, operates Chatsworth with a deft touch.

The Chatsworth of Bess and Sir William—where Mary Queen of Scots endured part of her long captivity—was replaced in the late seventeenth and early eighteenth century by a then-new Chatsworth, the work of the fourth Earl of Devonshire; he and the nineteenth century's sixth Duke were the great Chatsworth builders. The first room visitors see, the painted hall with its ceiling fresco portraying the assassination of Julius Caesar, by Laguerre, is a tough act to follow. But not an impossible one. Consider the frescoes by the same Laguerre and by Verrio in the chapel; masterful paneling in the oak room; additional Laguerre ceilings and opulently treated walls and fireplaces in the state bedroom and music room; a drawing room with eighteenth-century English furniture, much of it by William Kent; and the extraordinary art in the library, dining room, sculpture gallery, and bedrooms. Chatsworth paintings are a glory of the house: Van Dyck and Sir Godfrey Kneller in abundance; Veronese and Ricci, Rembrandt and Murillo, Reynolds and Zoffany, Sargent and Landseer, to name only some.

The 100-acre gardens—largely the work of Joseph Paxton, a gardener employed by the sixth Duke and later knighted by Queen Victoria for his design of the London Great Exhibition's Crystal Palace—are a destination in and of themselves, with towering fountains and formal topiary through natural parklands. Chatsworth's own village of *Edensor* is picture-postcard, with a nineteenth-century church in which is buried Kathleen Kennedy, a sister of President Kennedy who had been married to an earlier Marquess of Hartington and who died in a 1948 air crash. Although I don't write of country-house shops in this book, Chatsworth's—operated by the Duchess of

Devonshire—is unusually tasteful and offers the works of author Nancy Mitford, the Duchess's late sister. Restaurant.

Sudbury Hall (33 miles west of Nottingham) is a onetime royal residence that is a richly decorated specimen of the late seventeenth-century period called after Charles II. One could wish for more furniture, but the beauty of Sudbury—aside from an exuberant Baroque facade, which includes an intricate X-pattern in the brickwork—is in the detailing of the state rooms: plasterwork in the entrance hall (with a pair of Sir Thomas Lawrence portraits); high and wide central staircase; Grinling Gibbons wood-carving over the John Hoppner portrait topping the mantel; canopied bed used by Dowager Queen Adelaide, widow of William IV, during her three-year residence (1840–43); and—most striking—the long gallery, whose masterwork is a portrait by Kneller of Louise de Keroualle, whom Charles II made Duchess of Portsmouth—and a royal mistress. Café. National Trust.

Peterborough (50 miles southeast of Lincoln), though larger than Lincoln, has much less remaining from a past dating to the Roman period. The principal exception, *Peterborough Cathedral* (Cathedral Square) is extraordinary enough to make a Peterborough visit worthwhile. Heart of town—its square gives on to shop-lined Bridge Street and its northerly extension, Long Causeway, with the Queensgate Shopping Centre nearby—the Cathedral, not unlike that of Lincoln, is at its most brilliant from without. The West Facade—Early English Gothic from the thirteenth century—is considered one of the great cathedral porticos of Europe. Its glory is a trio of deeply recessed arches, each 82 feet high, surmounted by a stone, cross-topped gable enclosing a rose window and, going from right to left, statues of the saints—Peter (whose name the city also takes), Paul, and Andrew—after whom the cathedral is called. The main entrance is built into the central arch and, passing through, one makes a leap backward to the earlier Romanesque era. Peterborough's nave—covered by a thirteenth-century wooden ceiling whose lozenge-shaped compartments contain likenesses running a gamut of saints through monsters—is an all-Europe standout. Walk back to that area—erected in the fifteenth century in Perpendicular—with fan vaulting of the caliber to be seen in Westminster Abbey.

Noteworthy, too: a plaque marking the spot where Mary Queen of Scots was buried for a quarter-century until, in 1612, her son James I of England and VI of Scotland, ordered her remains removed to Westminster Abbey; and the tomb of still another queen, Spanish-born Catherine of Aragón, the first of Henry VIII's eight wives, under sixteenth-century flags of England and Spain. Then look for a

Peterborough curiosity: a painting, on the west wall, of a gravedigger named Robert Scarlett, who in the course of his ninety-eight years had the dubious distinction of burying both queens.

Peterborough's *City Museum and Art Gallery* (Priestgate) has a dubious distinction, as well. It is, in my experience, not inconsiderable—the only museum in the United Kingdom without a public men's room. (Ladies, worry not: you are provided for.) Most curious of its exhibits is a collection of carved bone and straw objects made by French prisoners in a nearby camp during the Napoleonic wars of the early nineteenth century. There are some period rooms and shops, mostly of the last century; Peterborough historical lore; and the work of local painters, past and contemporary.

Burghley House (just outside Stamford, 10 miles west of Peterborough) is an all-Britain standout, as much for its pedigree (its builder was the first Lord Burghley, Elizabeth I's treasurer) as for its architecture (it is a Tudor palace, rated that era's biggest and grandest) and its art (Italian especially). (The Marquess of Exeter, its owner, publishes a catalog of paintings and furniture, in addition to the usual picture-booklet.) Opulence here can dazzle. Consider works by Reni, Domenichino, Bassano, Titian, Veronese, and Van Dyck in the antechapel; a clutch of Knellers, with Gainsborough and Lawrence, in the billiard room; the very bed—with original coverings and hangings—in which Elizabeth I, the first owner's sovereign, slept, in the bedroom named for her; three Rembrandts, a Velásquez, a Van Dyck, and a Tintoretto in the Pagoda Room; suites of rooms in which royal guests—George IV, Victoria, and Albert among them—stayed; and the most spectacular sections of the house—grand staircase, great hall, and not inappropriately named Heaven Room, its walls and ceiling a single fresco—the seventeenth-century painter Verrio's interpretation of a mythological heaven. Restaurant.

Oakham (midway between Peterborough, above, and Leicester, the city to follow) is the kind of small, uncelebrated—and beguiling—country town North Americans want so much to sample in Britain. Before the ancient county of Rutland was done away with as a political entity, some years back, Oakham was the county town. High Street is flanked on its north side by Market Place, site of *Oakham Castle*, which has to be Britain's tiniest such building so named. It's twelfth century and within is an oddball display of ceremonial horseshoes, gifts in centuries past of peers of the realm, given in the course of official visits to ancient lords of Oakham. Have a look in *Rutland County Museum* (Catmos Street), a onetime riding school out of the eighteenth century, now filled with exhibits explaining how the region made its living over the centuries—blacksmith's bellows and kitchen implements, carriages and churns. Take a look at the lovely stained glass in *All Saints Church* (Church Street), mostly Gothic, with Romanesque origins and a slim steeple. *Oakham School*, a venerable public school, occupies a clutch of historic structures dotted about town. Quite as pretty, in its way, is *Uppingham*, Oakham's neighbor-town a few miles south, the handsome and ancient buildings of its public school dating to the Middle Ages. The somberly black-suited boys you see are Uppingham students in uniform.

Hunt country: You are in an area of Britain that fox-hunters consider one of the kingdom's finest and in which there are a number of venerable hunt clubs; the Cottesmore Hunt, established in the eighteenth century, is one such. Season is September through March. Headed by masters, one of whom, the field master, always with a brass horn, leads, hunts embrace a clutch of the membership—the Cottesmore Hunt has 250 members, male and female, who wear traditional dress when riding—and between thirty and fifty hounds. It is, of course, the hounds, with the riders in pursuit, who seek out—and kill—the fox.

Leicester (40 miles south of Lincoln): If Leicester's *Cathedral of St. Martin* (Guildhall Lane) is no match for those in nearby Lincoln and Peterborough (it was originally a Gothic parish church, now heavily Victorian, which did not achieve cathedral status until 1926), this busy city has other attributes. Choicest bit of urban Leicester is New Walk, so named when it opened as a pedestrian promenade—original trees still border it—in 1785; it leads to what I consider the No. 1 reason for a Leicester visit: *Leicester Museum and Art Gallery* (New Walk) is right up there with the top-rankers of medium-size provincial cities like those of Southampton and Aberdeen. To start is a cache of English paintings by the likes of Gainsborough, Hogarth, Joseph Wright of Derby, and Constable. French representation is good, too—Sisley and Pissarro, Boudin and Degas. Then you come across the surprise package, an extraordinary collection of German Expressionists, the likes of which not many galleries outside Germany can match: a woman's head by Emil Nolde, a sailor-suited boy by Lovis Corinth, Franz Marc's *Woman in Red*, a geometric-lined church by Lionel Feininger, and other striking works by Beckmann, Kirchener, Grosz, and Liebermann. The rest, all of it handsomely displayed, includes English silver glass and English and foreign ceramics. *Newarke Houses* (The Newarke) is a cluster of venerable dwellings put to use as a museum of old Leicestershire, with period rooms, simulated street scenes, a pretty garden, and Leicester's best known painting: an early nineteenth-century portrait by Benjamin Marshall of a young man named Daniel Lambert—red-coated and white-vested—who weighed in at 52 stone 11 pounds, which translates, at 14 pounds to a stone, as 739 pounds! *Guildhall* (Guildhall Lane) is a near-neighbor to the Cathedral (above) and a looker of a half-timbered house that was the Town Hall until as recently as 1876. Have a look at the mayor's reception room and—for contrast—the jail cells. *Wygston's House* (St. Nicholas Circle), a step or two from Guildhall, is worth seeing for its architecture—medieval without, eighteenth-century within—and its contents: clothes of the last three centuries. *University of Leicester* (University Road) is for contemporary architecture buffs. Ask to see the boldly asymmetrical, glass-sheathed Engineering Building by award-winning architect James Stirling.

Belgrave Hall (Church Road, Belgrave/Leicester) is among the best of the country houses operated by Britain's city museums. Named for the suburb of Belgrave, once an independent village, it is a medium-size manor house out of the eighteenth century, each room of which—drawing, dining, bed-, and music—is treasure filled, with a super kitchen and stable house, as well. And thirteenth-century *Belgrave St. Peter's Church*—with graveyard adjoining—is next door.

Kirby Hall (five miles south of Leicester) is a spectacular ruin: a sixteenth-century house that was designed in a transitional manner—Tudor leading into Jacobean—and was reportedly grand enough in the eighteenth century to have been suggested as a retreat for King George III's court in the event of invasion. Its nineteenth-century owners neglected it to the point where much of it, strangely and tragically, was in ruins by the turn of the present century. Parts—the Great Hall especially—still are roofed; others are not. A lesson—bittersweet, to be sure—in architecture, if not history. Department of the Environment.

Althorp (25 miles south of Leicester, five miles north of Northampton): When a house has been home for centuries to a line of nobles related to the Royal Family by marriage to the heir to the throne, it need have minimal esthetic appeal to draw visitors. Althorp, however, has been considered—and rightly so—one of the great English country houses since it went up in 1508, a Tudor brick mansion ringed by a moat, its owner Sir John Spencer. Sir John was an ancestor of the present landlord, the eighth Earl of Spencer, whose third and youngest daughter, Lady Diana, became Princess of Wales when she married Queen Elizabeth II's eldest son, Prince Charles, in a 1981 ceremony televised around the world.

This late twentieth-century association with the Royal Family is not a first for the family. The first Lord Spencer was ambassador to a German court under James I, whose wife, Queen Anne of Denmark, was one of a long line of royal visitors to Althorp. Another Lord Spencer, First Lord of the Treasury under George I, married an heiress of the Duke of Marlborough, effecting a liaison with that noble clan. And so it has gone over the centuries—a Viscount Althorp as Chancellor of the Exchequer; the red-headed, so-called Red Earl, Lord Lieutenant of Ireland; his successor, First Lord of the Admiralty. More of them than not were well-traveled, knowledgeable collectors. A consequence is that Althorp, remodeled in the seventeenth and again—most significantly—in the eighteenth century, emerges as one of the most treasure-filled of English houses. And, as a result of a redecoration as recently as 1976—when the current earl married his second wife, who had been, successively, Lady Lewisham and the Countess of Dartmouth and who is a daughter of pulp-romance novelist Barbara Cartland—it is also among the most handsome and most livable of English country houses.

Every Althorp room warrants the visitor's eye, beginning with the high-ceilinged entrance hall, through corridors lined with exquisite French and English porcelain, to and through the state rooms. The South Drawing Room has furniture by the same Weisweiler who made Marie Antoinette's and, indeed, a Marie Antoinette chocolate set. The Rubens Room is not misnamed; Rubens paintings cover its yellow brocade walls. John Singer Sargent drawings of Spencers—and Royal Family photos—grace the Long Library. The Marlborough Room is a veritable gallery of portraits by Reynolds and Gainsborough, mostly of family members. Angelica Kaufmann was among the painters who decorated the Sunderland Room. The dining room's 54 matching chairs date to 1800. Among the bedrooms are chambers named for visits by William III and George V. A Titian hangs in the Great Room, and the Long Gallery's paintings include a series by Lely of Charles II's female courtiers, a Kneller of Sarah, Duchess of Marlborough, and superb Van Dycks. Café.

Boughton House (26 miles southwest of Leicester) began as a monastery in the fifteenth century and became a manor house in the sixteenth, a great country seat in the seventeenth, and, happily for today's visitor, is little altered since then. This is a big place, with a dozen entrances, more than half a dozen courtyards, and a window for each day of the year. Don't worry, you will not be shown all of it, just the most treasure-filled state rooms—little hall with an El Greco; yellow-paneled drawing room with Van Dyck sketches; Mortlake tapestries in the Rainbow Room; Lelys and Knellers in the audit room; and the frescoed barrel ceiling, tapestries on the walls, and a painting of Elizabeth I by Gheeraerts in the spectacular Great Hall. Your host is the Duke of Buccleuch and Queensbury. Café.

SETTLING IN

Eastgate Hotel (Eastgate, Lincoln): The beautiful part of a stay at the Eastgate—assuming you insist on a front room—is waking up and going to sleep with picture-window views of Lincoln Cathedral, just opposite, and, as a bonus, Roman ruins in the hotel's front yard. This is a modern 71-room house (with a few super suites), with good-value restaurant, coffee shop, bar. Trusthouse Forte. *First Class.*

White Hart Hotel (Bailgate, Lincoln) exudes all of the patina of age absent in the contemporary Eastgate (above). It is an eighteenth-century successor to an originally fourteenth-century inn. And it's a charmer, with nearly 70 rooms, some traditional-style (my preference), some contemporary in look, some with Cathedral views (try for one of these), and most with baths. Have tea in the lovely lounge, lunch in the Orangery, and dinner in the restaurant. *First Class.*

D'Isney Place Hotel (Eastgate, Lincoln) is a handsome brick mansion, early eighteenth century in origin, that has been converted into a hotel. There are just a dozen rooms, each attractive. A full English breakfast served on Minton china and part of the room rate is brought to your room, when you call for it. Lounge, but no bar or restaurant. *Moderate.*

Duke William Hotel (Bailgate, Lincoln) is as much a pub-cum-restaurant as a hotel. Not quite half of the dozen rooms have baths. Neat and economical. *Moderate.*

Victoria Hotel (Milton Street, Nottingham) could not be more aptly named. This is a lovely elderly house, Nottingham's favorite old-timer. The 167 rooms and suites, no two quite alike, are comfortable; there is a pair of restaurants, one of which is carvery-style (all you want of roast beef and lamb), and two bars. *First Class.*

Albany Hotel (St. James's Street, Nottingham) is a charmless modern house, with the distinct advantages of showers in the baths of all 160 rooms and a well-priced carvery with all the roast beef you can eat. Trusthouse Forte. *First Class.*

Strathdon Hotel (Derby Road, Nottingham) is modern and functional, with showers in most of the 67 rooms, a restaurant, and two bars. *Moderate.*

George Hotel (George Street, Nottingham) occupies updated Georgian quarters—it dates to the days of stagecoaches—with baths in 44 of the 72 comfortable rooms, convenient restaurant and bar-lounge, and souvenirs of its past on display, including the check with which Charles Dickens paid a bill. *Moderate.*

Cavendish Hotel (Baslow, Bakewell) is a low-slung country house with precisely a baker's dozen rooms—each handsome, each with a shower in its bath, and each overlooking Chatsworth, the country house (above), in whose estate it is situated. Decor and furnishings (some from Chatsworth itself) were supervised by the Duchess of Devonshire, when the hotel—long on the scene—was refurbished in the early 1970s. Excellent restaurant, amusing bar, and lounge for morning coffee or afternoon tea. I don't know of a lovelier headquarters for touring the country houses in the neighborhood. *Luxury.*

Great Northern Hotel (Station Approach, Peterborough) is a substantial Georgian pile opposite the station. Look is agreeably old-school on the main floors, although rooms are modern, many in a new wing; about half of the 50 have baths. Attractive restaurant serving good-value table d'hôte lunches and dinners. Congenial bar. *Moderate-First Class.*

Hambleton Hall Hotel (Hambleton, near Oakham) went up a century ago as the country seat of a wealthy squire. Handsome and half-timbered, in the style of the Middle Ages, it was purchased relatively recently by a creative young couple, Tim and Stefa Hart, who, with the aid of London interior designer Nina Campbell, converted it into a smart and stunning 15-room inn (with showers in all the rooms' baths) that ranks, at least in my view, in the very top country-hotels category. This is a house with a sense of style—traditional (antique accents, good paintings), albeit with contemporary touches as manifested in the use of color and textiles. Have morning coffee or afternoon tea in the main lounge overlooking the lake called Rutland Water. Enjoy a drink in the amusing red-walled bar. And in no event leave without sampling the excellent restaurant, later reviewed. Member, Relais et Châteaux. *Luxury.*

Grand Hotel (Granby Street, Leicester): The look of the last century—from which it dates—has wisely been retained in the lobby (note the elaborate staircase), restaurant, and bar-lounge. Upstairs, the 93 bedrooms have been deftly updated. *First Class.*

Holiday Inn (St. Nicholas Circle, Leicester) is among the better-looking of this chain in Britain, with 190 rooms and showers in all their baths; restaurant, bar-lounge, swimming pool. *First Class.*

Leicester Centre Hotel (Humberstone Gate, Leicester): I wish rooms were larger, but the baths of all 220 of them have showers. There are two bars and both a proper restaurant and a coffee shop, with the look throughout contemporary. *Moderate-First Class.*

DAILY BREAD

White Hart Hotel Restaurant (Bailgate, Lincoln): This high-ceilinged, chandelier-hung room sets an exceptionally tasty table. Order from the à la carte—smoked Scotch salmon or potted shrimps, grilled Dover sole or steak Diane, roast lamb or roast beef carved from a silver trolley. Or select the good-value table d'hôte. Excellent wines. *First Class-Luxury.*

Harvey's (Castle Square, Lincoln) occupies an ancient house and draws locals, as well as visitors, with good-value, nicely presented lunches and dinners the lure, with simpler specialties—chicken and mushroom pie, lamb stew—the best bets. *First Class.*

Wig & Mitre (Steep Hill, Lincoln) is a pleasing blend of atmosphere (setting is a very old house), congeniality (locals pack the place and have a good time), and hearty fare, daily hot specials through salads and cold meats from the buffet. *Moderate-First Class.*

Spinning Wheel (Steep Hill, Lincoln): Go in for morning coffee or afternoon tea if only as an excuse to sample the pastries. Not that a soup and sandwich/salad lunch is a bad idea, either. *Moderate.*

White's (Jews House, Steep Hill, Lincoln): Setting is a twelfth-century landmark building (above), and specialty is authentic French fare—*coq au vin*, say. French wines, too. *First Class.*

Cheltenham Arms (Guildhall Street, Lincoln): A good bet, this wine bar, for a lunch composed of selections—salads, cold meats—from the buffet or a hot special. With a glass of wine. *Moderate.*

Britannia (Church Street, Boston): A super spot for a casual lunch is this atmospheric pub, reputedly the oldest in town. *Moderate.*

Le Bistro (St. James's Street, Nottingham) has an agreeable bistro ambience, with the more Gallic of its offerings à la carte, but with temptingly tabbed—albeit not necessarily French—table d'hôte meals, too. *Moderate-First Class.*

Flying Horse (Poultry, Nottingham): Why not a pub lunch in this half-timbered establishment, on hand since the thirteenth century? Attractive. *Moderate.*

Old Castle Inn (Castle Place, Nottingham) serves tasty bar fare on tables fashioned of barrels. Walls are paneled. *Moderate.*

Ye Olde Trip to Jerusalem (Castle Gate, Nottingham) not immodestly bills itself as "the oldest inn in England," which it well may be. The name is believed to have come from Crusaders, pausing centuries ago, for refreshment en route to the east. *Moderate.*

Ye Olde Salutation Inn (St. Nicholas Street, Nottingham), built into caves below Nottingham Castle, dates to the Middle Ages. Go for lunch or in the evening and ask for a tour of the cellars. *Moderate.*

Maid Marian (Friar Lane, Nottingham) combines two Robin Hood characters in a single stop (assuming, as I do, that the street is named for Friar Tuck). Stop in for afternoon tea. *Moderate.*

Paxton Room (Cavendish Hotel, Baslow, Bakewell): The restaurant in this hotel on the Chatsworth estate (above) sports double rows of interesting prints on its trendy gray-hued walls. There are delicious things to eat—duck *pâté* or cheese and onion tart; Chatsworth game (venison, grouse, pheasant, hare) in season or the chef's veal, pork, or poultry specialties; smashing sweets, including rum chocolate sponge cake topped with hot cocoa sauce and thick cream. Need I say more? *Luxury.*

Stables (Edensor Village, Chatsworth estate, near Bakewell): Old, unpretentious, and friendly, this is a sensible choice for a simple lunch, mid-morning coffee, or afternoon tea, in connection with a tour of Chatsworth and its village. Opposite the church. *Moderate.*

Hambleton Hall Hotel Restaurant (Hambleton, near Oakham) draws discerning diners from nearby Leicester and Peterborough, as well as touring visitors, as much for its well-priced four-course-and-coffee lunches as its costlier—and more elaborate—dinners. The latter might run to the house's own "three terrines"—a sampling of a trio of the chef's *pâtés*—or snails in a sauce of Pernod and garlic; with entrées like grilled Guinea fowl, stuffed breast of chicken, noisettes of local lamb; ending with both cheese and dessert courses. These last include superb *soufflés*, mince pie with brandy butter, and the Hambleton Pancake—a *crêpe* enveloping made-on-premises ice cream. The wine cellar is outstanding, not unlike the restaurant itself. In my experience, one of Britain's best restaurants. *Luxury.*

Lake Isle (High Street, Uppingham): If it lacks the elegance of Hambleton Hall (above), this restaurant compensates with delicious French-accented cuisine, packaged into an excellent-value four-course dinner (lunch is not served) that changes nightly and is prepared by the talented owner-chef. *First Class.*

Crown Hotel (High Street, Oakham) is Oakham's principal pub. It's a congenial place to meet the locals over, say, a ploughwman's lunch with a half-pint of lager to accompany. *Moderate.*

Du Cann's (Market Street, Leicester) is a wine bar that serves up a perfectly delicious lunch, mostly from a groaning buffet that includes meat sliced from what must be the planet's most gargantuan turkeys. With other good things, soups through sweets. And wine by the glass or bottle. *Moderate.*

Swiss Cottage (Charles Street, Leicester) is attractive, and, although the food is not necessarily Swiss, it is invariably tasty. Steak and kidney pie is a good choice. *Moderate.*

AFTER DARK

Theatre Royal (Clasketgate, Lincoln) is a late-Victorian house, with a schedule presented by visiting troupes, as well as its own.

Theatre Royal (Theatre Square, Nottingham) is a Nottingham landmark, handsome and colonnaded. It went up in 1865. Programs range from the Royal Ballet to the Glyndbourne Opera. The restaurant is open to nonticket-holders.

Royal Concert Hall (Theatre Square, Nottingham) is ultramodern, embracing five striking levels, two of which link it to next-door Theatre Royal. Symphonies, massed choirs, rock groups.

Nottingham Playhouse (Wellington Circus, Nottingham) is still another architecturally significant Nottingham theater, with its own esteemed repertory company presenting plays fall through spring, with summer reserved for visiting troupes. Restaurant.

The Cresset (Bretton, Peterborough) is a modern concert hall, two miles from the center of town, that's known for its music—the Midlands Philharmonic, perhaps, with opera, as well.

Haymarket Theatre (Haymarket, Leicester) is a long-established, well-reputed venue for theater, its own presentations, as well as touring companies.

INCIDENTAL INTELLIGENCE

The region is served by East Midlands Airport at Castle Donington; domestic flights. Additionally, Lincoln is 30 miles south of Humberside Airport at Kirmington; also with domestic flights. *Further information:* Lincoln Tourist Information Centre, Bailgate; Nottingham Tourist Information Centre, Milton Street; Peterborough Tourist Information Centre, Town Hall, Bridge Street; Oakham Tourist Information Centre, Oakham Library, Catmos Street; Leicester Tourist Information Centre, Bishop Street.

13

Liverpool
And the Contrasts of Chester

BACKGROUND BRIEFING
Of course, there is no gainsaying Liverpool's economic decline. It is not the rich and powerful port, the humming center of commerce that achieved global respect under the Victorians. It is even arguable whether it is quite the city that it was a couple of decades back, when four of its native sons—banded together as the Beatles—brought it an unlikely contemporary spurt of celebrity. But it is hardly to be tossed aside, given up on, or, in the case of the curious traveler to Britain, ignored.

Irrespective of its problems, this city—which was granted its first charter by King John, of Magna Carta immortality, in the year 1207—is not without staying power. Half a million Britons call Liverpool, the kingdom's sixth-largest city, home; scores of additional thousands make its metropolitan area—the recently created County of Merseyside, named for the river flowing from the city into the Irish Sea—one to be reckoned with. And, if my Liverpool experience is any indication, to be thoroughly enjoyed. It could not be otherwise, given the Liverpudlian, with distinctive Liverpudlian accent—as hospitable a British city dweller as one will find—and the bracing maritime flavor of the port, which blend well with cultural infusions accumulated over the centuries by farsighted mercantile princes.

ON SCENE
Lay of the Land: Liverpool—world port that it remains, with some seven miles of docks lining the Mersey—bases itself on the nerve center it calls Pierheads. This quarter, flanking the river, is dominated by a trio of gracious office towers—Liver, Cunard, and Dock Company—and fronts a park and piers, from which ships depart for Irish and Isle of Man ports. Ideally, you start your Liverpool explorations at this

point, taking the brief, round-trip ferry ride across the Mersey to the neighboring town of Birkenhead (with which, incidentally, it's also connected by tunnel).

Head east, inland from the river, to central Liverpool, along Water Street, lined with fine buildings—Victorian through Art Deco—attesting to the earlier eras of commercial eminence. Water Street becomes Dale Street as it merges with the shopping area, flanked on the north by a cluster of elegant, classic-style civic buildings and embracing St. John's Shopping Centre (topped off by a revolving restaurant and observation deck, 450 feet skyward); smart smaller shops on Bold Street, leading into Church Street; and contiguous Lord Street. There are abundant department-store choices: Lewis's (inexplicably with a statue of a nude male over its entrance), Marks & Spencer, and Littlewoods.

Lime Street Station, the main railway terminal—and a veritable Edwardian palace—is just east of the shopping district, and not far distant are still other Liverpool thoroughfares of interest. Mount and Hope streets are Beatles' territory: the late John Lennon studied at Liverpool Polytechnic, while Paul McCartney and George Harrison were students at nearby Liverpool Institute of Art—colonnaded and with a semicircular hall in which Dickens lectured.

Cambier Terrace, in the shadow of landmark Liverpool Cathedral, is a row of still-handsome Regency houses. Nearby Rodney Street—even older, with its facades Georgian—is physicians' row. Still another Georgian street—Nelson, by name—embraces Chinatown.

Liverpool Cathedral (St. James Road) vies, in my opinion, with Walker Art Gallery as the chief reason for a Liverpool visit. I lead off with it instead of the long-established, long-reputed Walker, because—being so relatively new (it opened in late 1978)—it is still not as well known as it should be. It is the largest Anglican cathedral in the world. But size is not necessarily greatness. Nor does its architectural motif—overscaled Gothic—alone provide reason for distinction. (Alas, also-big, also-Gothic Guildford Cathedral [Chapter 5] falls completely flat, esthetically.) I suspect it is the scale of architect Sir Giles Gilbert Scott's building that works most in its favor. Scott, taking advantage of the technology of our century—as contrasted with that of the medieval centuries' Gothic builders—opted to exaggerate the Gothic line, lengthen the Gothic column, heighten the Gothic arch, widen the Gothic vault, magnify the Gothic altar, and enlarge the Gothic window. He had a genius for proportion. By that, I mean you do not feel overpowered when you look to the top of the 331-foot-high tower that divides a transept into which three or four ordinary-size churches could fit. Liverpool Cathedral was three-quarters of a century in the building. The Royal Institute of British Architects, when they awarded it their prize in 1979, termed it "a major Cathedral of international rank." A visit is a profound experience.

Walker Art Gallery (William Brown Street): Queen Victoria sent her son, the then-Duke of Edinburgh, to lay the cornerstone for the Walker a little more than a century ago. Named for the wealthy Liverpool alderman who paid for its construction, it cannot claim bigness, like Liverpool Cathedral (above), but it can claim international rank. The Walker's collection is among the great eclectic ones, with the extraordinary range medieval Italians (a *Pietà*—Christ descended from the cross in the Virgin Mary's arms—by Ercole de'Roberti is its trademark masterwork) through to a contemporary California swimming-pool scene by England's David Hockney.

In between? Consider Veronese's *The Finding of Moses*, a sculpted head of Christ by Della Robbia, a Cranach nymph, and Low Countries representation by the likes of Rubens, Rembrandt, van Ruisdael, and van Cleve, as well as Poussin and Guardi, Murillo and Mengs. English greats are especially strong: Liverpudlian George Stubbs's famous eighteenth-century horses, portraits of royals and aristocrats by Lely and Kneller, Hogarth and Zoffany, Hoppner and Ramsay, Raeburn and Lawrence. Benjamin West portrays the death of Lord Nelson, while Sir Edwin Landseer paints Sir Walter Scott. There are Constable landscapes, works by mid-nineteenth-century pre-Raphaelites, including Millais and Ford Madox Brown, and lovely paintings of Liverpool—mostly from the last century. And there are Impressionist treats including Manet, Seurat, Cézanne, and Degas, and post-Impressionists, including Matisse and Vuillard.

Merseyside Maritime Museum (Pierhead) could not be more appropriately situated: on the water at Pierhead, for so long center of Liverpool maritime activity. Opened in 1980, this newest of Europe's maritime museums occupies a refurbished dockside building, along with onetime drydocks. The idea is to re-create the Liverpool age of sail. You not only see vessels—there's a big hall of boats—and equipment of old. You watch sails being made, rope being knotted, barrels being created by coopers. Cafeteria.

Liverpool Town Hall (Water Street) is one of Britain's most beautiful. And that is saying a lot in a country where those buildings are invariably more elaborate and multipurpose than North American counterparts. Liverpool's was originally designed by the same John Wood responsible for Bath's Royal Crescent. Destroyed by fire, it was rebuilt in the same classic style by another famous architect of the eighteenth century—London's James Wyatt. The staircase beneath the central dome is superb, and so are the three chandeliered reception rooms, not to mention the Merseyside County Council Chamber. Caveat: Open hours have been traditionally limited to two summer weeks. But try taking a peek.

Bluecoat Chambers (School Lane) represents early eighteenth-century Liverpool. It is a honey of a Queen Anne pavilion, whose three wings give onto a courtyard and are put to appropriate use for temporary art exhibitions and as well, for a permanent collection of ceramics, jewelry, and textiles.

Merseyside County Museum (William Brown Street): The bulk of exhibits here are your usual schoolkids' stuff—even including an aquarium and planetarium. What you want to head for is the spiffy display of Liverpool pottery, mostly eighteenth- and nineteenth-century, with Liverpool scenes decorating it, along with glass, furniture, and other decorative arts of the city's earlier eras. Café.

Metropolitan Cathedral (Mount Pleasant) is the seat of the Roman Catholic archbishop of Liverpool. It opened in 1967—five years after it was begun—to nothing like the virtually universal design approval accorded its Anglican counterpart (Liverpool Cathedral, above). Locals not happy with the esthetics of the Metropolitan call it "Paddy's Wigwam." And wigwam-like it is, in general contour; circular, with a central stained glass tower framing the high altar (a nineteen-ton slab of white marble), around which are pews seating 2,300 and a ring of chapels.

Beatle City (Seel Street) is, not surprisingly, given its name, for Beatle buffs—an exhibition of original Beatle-owned musical instruments, costumes, and assorted other memorabilia, as well as archive film and videos of John Lennon, Paul McCartney, George Harrison, and Ringo Starr.

Speke Hall (The Walk, off Speke Road, eight miles south of Liverpool) is a half-timbered mansion, whose fifteenth-century facade—based on cloverleaf and herringbone motifs—is among the more sophisticated of its genre. And interiors do not disappoint, especially the carved-wood overmantel and plasterwork of the ceiling in the Great Parlour; the four-poster in the main bedroom; and the "priest holes"—escape tunnels that priests saying illegal Masses during the Reformation used for quick getaways. Café. National Trust.

Lady Lever Art Gallery (in Port Sunlight, a few miles southeast of Liverpool, across the River Mersey) is housed in a domed, colonnaded palazzo that is the landmark of a planned village embracing late nineteenth-century adaptations of English, French, and German designs—erected by Lord Leverhulme, the soap tycoon. The gallery, full of paintings and furniture collected by Leverhulme, is a memorial to his wife. You are not as surprised at the multitude of paintings—Reynolds, Gainsborough, Constable, Turner, and the pre-Raphaelites are among the English artists—as you are at the immense collection of Wedgwood porcelain; period rooms illustrating decoration of the Tudor, Stuart, William and Mary, and other eras; and the quantity—not to mention quality—of the eighteenth-century English furniture.

Chester (22 miles southeast of Liverpool) is a proper city in its own right, to be sure, but conveniently combined with Liverpool. Chester is small, relatively tranquil, and not without the sense of place in history that comes with a core still noticeably medieval and a properly mellow cathedral. If your stay is a long enough one, take a mini-cruise on the Dee, Chester's river (the Romans built a fort alongside it (2,000 years ago), or a walk along at least part of the incredible, two-mile-long city wall (part Roman, part medieval) still encircling the inner city, pausing in two wall-attached towers now municipal museums—the *Water Tower* (exhibits delineate Chester in the Middle Ages) and the *King Charles Tower* (named for a visit by King Charles I and with its subject the city's role in the seventeenth-century's Civil War).

The shorter-term visitor will beeline for the Cross, at the intersection of the main street, Eastgate, and three other ancient thoroughfares—splendid half-timbered houses line the lot of them—Northgate Street, Bridge Street, and Watergate Street. This area is *The Rows*—a unique-to-Chester complex of raised sidewalks and double-tiered shopfronts that are historically documented as having originated in the Middle Ages, probably a consequence of the residue of walls and other structures inherited from the Roman period. Browse its shops, but not at the expense of a visit to *Chester Cathedral*, of special interest because it was a Benedictine monastery for hundreds of years before it was made the seat of an Anglican bishop. Still to be seen are the pre-Cathedral cloister, with recesses in its walls where the monks studied; the monks' refectory, still with the stone pulpit from which one of their number read to them while they ate in silence; and the stone basins at which they washed. Within, the cathedral is a fine Gothic church, as much as a millennium in age, with the carving of its choir stalls dating back almost 800 years. There are two larger museums, each with some noteworthy exhibits.

Guildhall (Watergate Street) documents the city's ancient guilds—23 all told—and *Grosvenor Museum* (Grosvenor Street) is at its best in a series of eighteenth- and nineteenth-century period rooms.

Tatton Park (near Knutsford, 11 miles east of Chester) is a jewel of a smaller Georgian mansion, carefully crafted (each of the four columns supporting its portico is made of a single piece of stone). The architects, building upon an older seventeenth-century house, were Samuel Wyatt, a brother of the celebrated James Wyatt, and a nephew, Lewis. The interior has a sense of style, with paintings by Van Dyck and Canaletto, among others. Allow time for a hike through the gardens. Café. National Trust.

SETTLING IN

Atlantic Tower Thistle Hotel (Chapel Street, Liverpool) is shipshape in two ways: spruced up and neat as a pin, for one; shaped like the prow of a ship, for another. Appropriately enough, for this sleekly contemporary house overlooks Pierhead and the Mersey. Not to be overlooked: all 226 rooms—including some elevated suites—have showers in their baths. Restaurant-cum-views, congenial off-lobby bar-lounge. *First Class.*

St. George's Hotel (Lime Street, Liverpool) is one of a number of modern British hotels plopped unceremoniously atop a shopping complex. As in most cases of this graceless, 1960s architecture, the shops come ahead of the guest, who must wind his way through assortments of passageways to gain lobby access. Ultimately arrived at, however, the St. George's pleases with 155 agreeable bedrooms, a first-class restaurant, a well-priced coffee shop, and a bar-lounge. Trusthouse Forte. *First Class.*

Britannia Adelphi Hotel (Ranelagh Place, Liverpool) reflected the wealth and prestige of maritime and mercantile Liverpool when it went up in the 1920s. Alas, recent years saw deterioration set in during the waning ownership of now-defunct British Transport Hotels. Happily, new owners have righted matters by means of a thorough face-lift. This graceful whitestone pile—whose heroically proportioned main lounge has always reminded me of the first-class lounge of the old Cunarder, *Queen Mary*—sparkles again, as do other public spaces. There's a new leisure center to complement the indoor pool, and rooms—there are 360, all told—have been brightened, too. *First Class.*

Holiday Inn (Paradise Street, Liverpool): Don't let the name of the street lead you to great expectations. Liverpool's Holiday Inn is no handsomer than most of its sister-HIs in Britain. To understate. What saves it is facilities—two double beds in most rooms, showers in the modern baths, a restaurant, and a pair of pubby bars that serve casual meals. *First Class.*

Liverpool Centre Hotel (Lord Nelson Street, Liverpool) lacks charm but compensates with 170 modern, albeit compact, rooms, all with showers in their baths. Carvery-type restaurant (help yourself to roast beef and lamb) and two bars, one traditional pub-type. *Moderate.*

Feathers Hotel (Mount Pleasant, Liverpool) is a bit away from the center, near Metropolitan Cathedral, but it's a good value. Most of its 100 rooms have bath; two restaurants, as many bars. Setting is a cluster of joined Regency houses. *Moderate.*

Chester Grosvenor Hotel (Eastgate Street, Chester): Behind a gabled, half-timbered facade on Chester's ancient and atmospheric main street, the Grosvenor is a 100-room-and-suite house dating back more than a century and an all-Britain hotel leader. Start with a dignified, marble-accented lobby; go on to the restaurants, one of exceptional rank on a national scale, the other with smorgasbord a specialty; and to the bars, one the Grosvenor bar, with casual lunches its forte, the other leading from a lounge where the afternoon tea is Chester's most elegant. That leaves the traditional-style accommodations, no two alike; all that I have seen are delightful. Member, Prestige Hotels. *Luxury.*

Blossoms Hotel (St. John Street, Chester), dating to the seventeenth century, admits to a rebuilding in the nineteenth. Which is not to say it has lost the patina of considerable age—and charm. Bedrooms, 75 in toto, are agreeable, likewise the smart restaurant and pubby Snooty Fox, with its good-value victuals. *First Class.*

Queen Hotel (City Road, Chester), attractively elderly, is a bit away from the core, with the Railway Station a next-door neighbor. Ninety rooms, restaurant, bars. Trusthouse Forte. *First Class.*

DAILY BREAD
Philharmonic (Hope Street, Liverpool): Named for neighboring Philharmonic Hall. "The Phil"—to use Liverpudlians' abbreviation—is a requisite, mock-Baroque palace out of the last century, even to an opulent, marble-walled men's room that women are shown upon

request, after closing. Have a pub lunch—soups, salads, cold meats, hot specials, and a glass of lager—in the pub downstairs or ascend the spiral staircase to the restaurant above, where the options are game soup with Port, through a clutch of fish and seafood specialties, on to steaks. *First Class.*

Beaujolais (Seel Street, Liverpool) is French owned and French in spirit, with noted desserts and appropriate wines. Dinner only. *First Class.*

Italian Bistro (Hardman Street, Liverpool) is a neat-as-a-pin trattoria of the kind that would appeal in Rome or Milan. Try the minestrone followed by an order of pasta. Italian wines. *Moderate.*

Kirklands (Hardman Street, Liverpool): What lures you in is the "By Appointment to the Queen" sign in the window; the monarch referred to is Victoria. Never mind. Kirklands is a looker, with good short-order specialties, including baked—"jacket" is the British term—potatoes with a variety of toppings and super sweets. Fun for lunch. *Moderate.*

The Vines (Lime Street, Liverpool) is one of a number of central pubs dating back to the last century and quite marvelous-looking. Pop in for a bar lunch and/or a beer. *Moderate.*

Jung Wah (Nelson Street, Liverpool): Chinese restaurants are worth knowing about in provincial British cities, because they keep the longest hours. Jung Wah, on the street that constitutes the heart of Liverpool's Chinatown, is a no-frills source of Cantonese specialties. *Moderate.*

Tabac (Bold Street, Liverpool) is a cheery tearoom on Liverpool's smartest shopping street. Drop in for a cup and something to eat with it. *Moderate.*

Chester Grosvenor Hotel Restaurant (Eastgate Street, Chester): Hotel guest (see above) or not, this is a restaurant to be reckoned with. The look is chandeliered and paneled, in earth tones, with Louis XVI-style seating. Cooking is French—with the tastiest kind of English overtones. (Trifle, for dessert, is one such.) Order from the à la carte—caviar, smoked salmon, boned quail cooked in Calvados, asparagus with mousseline sauce, snails in garlicky butter, beef, veal, or lamb. Or select the three-course-and-coffee table d'hôte, an incredibly good value. Distinguished wines. In my view, one of England's best restaurants. *First Class* if you order table d'hôte; *Luxury* if you order à la carte.

Ye Olde King's Head (Lower Bridge Street, Chester) is at once a venerable half-timbered inn (not recommended, as none of its rooms have bath) and a restaurant of consequence—essentially seventeenth-century, with original woodwork and stick-to-the-ribs fare that is an exceptional value when ordered table d'hôte at either lunch or dinner. Friendly. *Moderate.*

Claverton's Wine Bar (Lower Bridge Street, Chester) is just the ticket for a satisfying lunch or dinner—day's specials, roast beef, or beef and kidney pie—with a glass or carafe of the house wine. Attractive. *Moderate.*

Quaintways (Northgate Street, Chester): The good self-service restaurant is not all that easily come by in Britain. Quaintways is an exception—soups, appetizing entrées, nice desserts. *Moderate.*

Great American Disaster (Lower Bridge Street, Chester): That alarming title is a come-on. Go into this tongue-in-cheek spot, red-and-white checked cloths on the tables in its booths, for a decent hamburger and, if you're really homesick, a milk shake. *Moderate.*

AFTER DARK
St. George's Hall (Lime Street, Liverpool) is one of Britain's great concert halls. Built in 1854, it is quite possibly the definitive Victorian adaptation of the classic Roman pavilion, colonnaded on three of its exterior sides, with its elongated interior space elaborately marble-floored, coffered-ceilinged, chandelier-illumined. Go for whatever is on.

Philharmonic Hall (Hope Street, Liverpool) is a winning 1930s auditorium—red-bricked and plain-lined without, with an immense stage the striking part of its interior, which serves as home for the internationally esteemed Royal Liverpool Philharmonic.

Liverpool Playhouse (Williamson Square, Liverpool): A two-theater house with a diverting range of dramas—Harold Pinter through Neil Simon. And, please note: three eateries—restaurant, wine bar, coffee shop—open to nontheatergoers, as well as ticket-holders. Plays also at the *Everyman* (Hope Street), *Royal Court* (Roe Street), and *Empire* (Lime Street) theaters.

Stanley Theatre (University of Liverpool, Mount Pleasant): As good as way as any to become acquainted with the university—concerts, theater, dance.

Gateway Theatre (Hamilton Place, Chester) surprises, in this ancient city so proud of tradition, with its modernity. Range of plays is Shakespeare through, say, the latest stunner by Peter Shaffer. Daytime-through-evening coffee shop.

INCIDENTAL INTELLIGENCE

Liverpool Airport is six miles south, and Manchester Airport, with transatlantic service, is not far distant, either from Liverpool or from Chester. You may depart from Liverpool by ferry for Ireland and the Isle of Man. *Further information:* Liverpool Tourist Information Centre, St. John's Centre; Chester Tourist Information Centre, Town Hall.

14

Manchester
Textiles to Tourism

BACKGROUND BRIEFING

Firsts. Manchester is a city of firsts. It has retained all these centuries the Anglicization of its Roman-bestowed name—*Mancunium.* (Residents, borrowing on the ancient name, are to this day Mancunians.) It began making cloth as long ago as the fourteenth century. Four centuries later—America had just won the Revolution—it was in Manchester that initial application of steam was made to power machines spinning cotton, and so began the mass production of textiles in the Industrial Revolution to follow.

The first English passenger railroad had its terminus in Manchester—on a run from Liverpool, back in 1830. The ingenious 35-mile-long Manchester Ship Canal was begun in 1887, and when it opened in 1894 the city was linked with the River Mersey's estuary at Eastham, and Manchester, for centuries a river port—it straddles no fewer than four rivers—became a leading British seaport.

By that time, the city's liberal political bent had manifested itself. Early nineteenth-century Manchester—when government troops killed and injured citizens peaceably demonstrating for Parliamentary reform—spearheaded national progress in that direction. *The Guardian*—a national publication now, but founded in 1821 as the *Manchester Guardian*—pioneered as a progressive, intellectual newspaper. Later in the nineteenth century, the city was the birthplace of something else again, the so-called Manchester school, which fostered—with widespread effect—the policy of laissez-faire, or minimal governmental participation in economic matters.

Our century saw Manchester pioneer with the airplane, as it had with the train, when it opened Britain's first municipal airport. That was in 1929. During World War II, this center of industry and commerce was a major Nazi bomb target. Recovered and rebuilt not long after the war's end, it became England's second transatlantic air-gateway after London, and, as such, the first bit of Britain to be experienced by many North American visitors, who, if they are sensible, settle in and discover that a major provincial city like this one, not content to be overshadowed by southerly London, is at once stimulating, attractive, and fun.

ON SCENE

Lay of the Land: The wealth that Manchester's canny industrialists, shippers, and entrepreneurs accumulated during the significant Victorian decades manifests itself in the look of this city, than which none in Britain save parts of London and Glasgow has a handsomer nineteenth-century veneer.

Central Manchester is eminently walkable, and for a city of its size—in the neighborhood of half a million—reasonably compact. Consider Deansgate the major north-south thoroughfare, with Victoria, the major railway station, to its north. The heart of the town lies in and about east-west Market Street, flanked at its western end by St. Anne's Square (lovely shops, a lovely church) and at its eastern end by modern Piccadilly Gardens. In between is Arndale Market—"The Market" to Mancunians—a two-level complex of commercial enterprises numbering in the hundreds, from department stores like Littlewoods and Debenhams, to smaller specialty shops, with restaurants and cafés dotted conveniently about; and still other emporia of consequence on Market Street (Burton's department store) and Deansgate (Kendall's department store).

Manchester Cathedral (Cathedral Street) is an originally Gothic parish church begun in the fifteenth century, mostly completed in the sixteenth, and not raised to Cathedral status until the nineteenth. Uncelebrated as English cathedrals go, it is not to be lightly dismissed: gracefully Perpendicular—last and lightest in look of the three English Gothic periods. The nave is the biggest surprise—among the widest in the kingdom and covered by an oaken roof studded with splendidly carved bosses. The Lady Chapel in the apse is visit-worthy, but only after one has looked up into the lining of the square main tower, studied the misericords of the choir, and noted the cathedral's charters, each from a monarch of consequence: Henry V, Elizabeth I, Charles I.

Chetham's Library (Victoria Street) is the Cathedral's (above) next-door neighbor and, not inappropriately, from the same Gothic era. Surrounding a vast courtyard, this medieval complex is purported to be Europe's oldest public library in continuous operation—over a span of seven centuries.

Architectural Manchester, beyond Manchester Cathedral (above), is at its most stunning on central *Albert Square,* dominated by the mock-Gothic *Town Hall,* whose magnificent clock tower is a major city landmark; this is the city's principal monument to the power and wealth it amassed in the nineteenth century. It's worth fitting one of the twice-a-day weekday tours of the interior into your schedule—to see the Council Chamber, reception rooms, and other opulent spaces. Have a look at *Barton Arcade* (off St. Ann's Square), a fine Victorian souvenir, elegantly glass-domed; and at the *Central Library* (St. Peter's Square), with a colonnaded circular upper portion over its portico, below which is a huge stone marking the dedication during the 1920s by George V, with all of his titles, Emperor of India among them, duly chiseled into the granite.

Manchester City Art Gallery (Mosley Street) is at its most special in a main-floor suite of rooms devoted to small-size, seventeenth-century Dutch paintings: the greats, whose work you know well, are represented—Rembrandt and Hals, Steen and de Hooch, van Ruisdael and Hobbema. But so are van Ostade and Goyen, Avercamp and Cuyp, Brouer and Ter Borch, Metsu and Teniers. Look, then, at extraordinary caches of silver (have you ever seen an entire tea service, dollhouse size, in sterling?) and English porcelain (Wedgwood, Staffordshire, Whieldon especially). Then ascend to the floor above. The English work is strong indeed: pre-Raphaelites of the last century including Millais, Ford Madox Brown, and Dante Gabriel Rossetti; Turner and Constable from earlier in that century, and choice works of Hogarth, Gainsborough, Zoffany, Reynolds, Romney, and Raeburn. End with the French: from Corot and Courbet on into the Impressionists—Pissarro, Sisley, Gauguin, among them. And a painting that will stay with you: Frenchman Adolph Valette's impressionistic portrayal of a foggy day on Manchester's Albert Square; you'll recognize Town Hall in the background.

Manchester Gallery of Modern Art (Princess Street) is just around the corner from the Art Gallery (above), and its emphasis is on British modernists—with sculpture by Dame Barbara Hepworth, Sir Jacob Epstein, and Henry Moore, among much else, including work by contemporary Manchester painters.

John Ryland's Library (Deansgate) delights bibliophiles with its displays of antique Bibles, first editions of a variety of titles from a span of centuries, and manuscripts in a plethora of languages.

North Western Museum of Science and Industry's (Grosvenor Street) role is to interpret the technology behind Manchester's evolution as a major manufacturing center. Here is how textiles are machine-spun and dyed, how paper is made, how cameras are created, with sections devoted to steam power, printing, electricity.

Whitworth Art Gallery and Manchester Museum (Oxford Road) are University of Manchester-operated and nicely explored in tandem. Both are smashers. The Whitworth, occupying a modern pavilion, bright and airy, has sections devoted to textiles and wallpapers, but it is, for me at least, at its strongest in its British art sections— sculpture by Hepworth, Epstein, Moore, Kenneth Armitage; drawings by Ben Nicholson and John Piper; and a Constable landscape, watercolors by Turner, a Lawrence portrait, and deliciously satiric Rowlandson cartoons. The Manchester Museum is old-fashioned in contrast to the Whitworth, rich in archeological and ethnological collections— African sculpture, Egyptian tomb treasures, ancient coins, and even an aquarium with endless arrays of well-mannered schoolkids in attendance.

Gallery of English Costume (Platt Hall, in the Rusholme quarter, away from the center): Americans are startled, before even entering, to see a statue of none other than Abraham Lincoln in the garden. It was, one learns, a 1919 gift to the City of Manchester from the Taft family of Cincinnati, and it is very well executed. Platt Hall, just beyond, is still another treat: a severe, though pleasing, Georgian mansion, pedimented and flanked by lower wings, which has been sensibly—and imaginatively—transformed by the City Art Gallery into its repository of English clothes, seventeenth-century to this very season. They are displayed on rakish mannequins in two felicitous floors of galleries.

Heaton Hall (Heaton Park, away from the center): Thank eighteenth-century architect James Wyatt, and the builders working with him, for Heaton Hall's staying power. What appears to be a congenial staff of one—ticket-seller, postcard-vendor, guide, and guard—is on duty in the massive and magnificent interior of this onetime country mansion, while without, hordes of scruffy kids gambol on a littered lawn, stuffing themselves with ice cream. The Hall, fortunately, holds no interest for them. But you want to go in. The City Art Gallery, its landlord, apparently has little budget, for there is not much furniture, but the proportions of the rooms—above all the saloon—are splendid. No less so are Wyatt's designs—on a Pompeian theme—on the walls and ceilings. Forlornly lovely.

Lyme Park (15 miles south of Manchester, near Disley): I don't know of a better excuse to enjoy the rolling hills of Cheshire than to earmark half a day for an excursion to this originally fourteenth-century country seat of generations of the Legh family. Lyme Park has had extensive embellishments, and is now dominantly Palladian without, Jacobean within, albeit with parts of it earlier Tudor. It all comes together surpassingly well; neoclassic courtyard, entrance hall, and a very grand staircase, intricately carved paneling by Grinling Gibbons in the Saloon, formally furnished dining room, tapestry-walled morning room, and—grandest of the lot—drawing room with Queen Elizabeth I's arms over the fireplace. Save time for the topiary gardens, a deer park, and vast stretches of landscape (bikes are for hire). Café. National Trust.

SETTLING IN

Midland Hotel (Peter Street, Manchester): Post-World War II refurbishers attempted to mar the Midland's brilliant Victorian facade—a carved-stone masterwork—by replacing the original entranceway and reception area with a graceless, tasteless environment. But, despite recently commenced, ongoing updating by new owners, the rest of this onetime railway hotel has, mercifully, been left as it was constructed, including a high-ceilinged lounge—super for tea or a drink; three restaurants (an intimate, elaborately decorated one with French-inspired cuisine, another all-purpose, a third the recommended—and handsome—coffee shop); bars aplenty (one a wine bar with good-value lunches); and just over 300 rooms and suites, many extra-large, and some with showers in their baths. And what a looker: even the black-and-white brickwork design of the enormous inner courtyard is handsome. *First Class.*

Piccadilly Hotel (Piccadilly, Manchester) is one of a number of provincial British hotels that went up a decade or so back smack atop shopping centers and their garages. Getting into and out of the Piccadilly is hardly pleasurable. But it *is* confusing. The up-a-flight lobby is a functional but nondescript contemporary, with a coffee shop worth knowing about, in that it is open round the clock, and other facilities, including a rooftop restaurant, range of bars, and 250 rooms, a virtue of which is that all of their baths have showers. *First Class.*

Grand Hotel (Aytoun Street, Manchester): A comfortable oldie, nicely brought up to the present day, with 146 functional rooms, a pair of restaurants (the Templars has good-value table d'hôte lunches and dinners), and as many bars. Trusthouse Forte. *First Class.*

Portland Thistle Hotel (Portland Street, Manchester) has such a splendid turn-of-century facade that you're surprised that its 221 rooms are so small—bright and well-equipped though they are. Public spaces are likewise and include a restaurant and two bars. *First Class.*

Mitre Hotel (Cathedral Gates, Manchester) is as good a budget bet as is to be found in the center of town; only some of the rooms have baths. Restaurant. Bar. *Moderate.*

DAILY BREAD

Isola Bella (6 Booth Street, Manchester) tries hard to be grander than it is, which is not at all necessary, for this is an attractive enough basement spot serving excellent Italian fare—soups, antipasti, veal specialties, Italian wines. *First Class.*

Blinkers French (Princess Street, Manchester) and *Blinkers Bijou,* (Clarence Street, Manchester) are a pair of catchily titled, Gallic-flavored bistros, with popular standbys—onion soup and snails, through *coq au vin* and *entrecôte grillée,* and on to sweets including *mousse au chocolat.* Excellent-value table d'hôte lunches and dinners. Attractive. *First Class.*

Copenhagen Room (Cross Street, Manchester) embraces a series of eateries, with red and white—the Danish colors—as the motif. Choose the stand-in-line cafeteria or the bar-cum-snacks. Everything is delicious, *smørrebrod* (open-faced sandwiches) through *Wienerbrod* (Danish pastry). *Moderate-First Class.*

Shambles (The Shambles, Market Place, Manchester) is an Elizabethan half-timbered house sheltering a two-story pub-restaurant that has been around these many centuries, updating itself as time has passed. Have a casual bar-lunch downstairs or a proper meal, noon or evening, upstairs. *Moderate-First Class.*

Farmhouse (Blackfriars Street, Manchester): A cafeteria, to be sure, but a very good one, brick-walled, and offering appetizing victuals, morning coffee through lunch and tea into dinner. *Moderate.*

Old Wellington Inn (Market Street, Manchester): Handsomely medieval, this pub makes good sense for a casual lunch with half a pint of lager. *Moderate.*

Carving Corner (Crown Square, Manchester): Visit the counter for all you want of roast beef, lamb, or pork, with potatoes and vegetables and a first-course preceding. *Moderate-First Class.*

Charlie Chan (George Street, Manchester) is, alas, without photos of Warner Oland, Sydney Toler, or any of the other silver-screen Charlies. It's a simple upstairs place, with the lure straightforward Cantonese cooking, temptingly tabbed. *Moderate.*

Rajdoot (South King Street, Manchester) is one of a number of Indian restaurants in town that specialize in clay-oven-roasted tandoori chicken, along, of course, with curries. The table d'hôte lunch is well priced. Decor is very Indian, indeed. *Moderate-First Class.*

Bella Napoli (Kennedy Street, Manchester) may or may not recall Naples, but the pizza is good and a good buy. *Moderate.*

AFTER DARK
Free Trade Hall (Peter Street, Manchester) takes its unusual name from a mid-nineteenth-century political movement. It dates to that times, as does the *Halle Orchestra*, the internationally reputed Manchester symphony, still called after Sir Charles Halle, who founded it in 1857. Other musical events, as well.

Royal Exchange Theatre (St. Mary's Gate, Manchester): Go to a play in the evening, Shakespeare and Molière through Emlyn Williams and this season's most talked about new playwright. Go for a Sunday afternoon concert. Or a midday lecture. Or, for that matter, lunch or dinner at Le Stage d'Or, with super steaks and pasta.

Palace Theatre (Oxford Street, Manchester) is an eye-filling old-timer where the ticket might be the Royal Opera, up from Covent Garden, a drama, or a musical; watch, too, for what's on at other theaters, such as the *Library* (St. Peter's Square), and *University* (Devas Street).

INCIDENTAL INTELLIGENCE

Manchester International Airport links the region nonstop, via British Airways, with New York; domestic service and flights to Ireland and the Continent, as well. *Further information:* Manchester Tourist Information Centre, Town Hall, Albert Square.

15

Newcastle and Durham
Core of Northeast England

BACKGROUND BRIEFING

It is no longer a case of "carrying coals to Newcastle." That household adage—long inappropriate to a city that is now more manufacturing and transport terminus than mining depot—appears to have made its point. The pleasure visitor, as a consequence of the association with sooty coal, tends to keep his distance from Newcastle and neighborhood when, actually, this region of Britain deserves acquaintance. It is at once history-rich, abundant in cultural treats, and hardly lacking in natural endowments.

The "new" in Newcastle—to give you an idea of its age—is relatively recent, if one considers that it began life as a northern outpost of the Roman Empire—*Pons Aelii*—nearly two millennia back. Angles had long since succeeded Romans as residents when—as a defense against incursions by not always cordial Scots just over the frontier, due north—a son of William the Conqueror built a fortified castle in 1080, which became a landmark of the city (a visitable segment of it remains) and gave it a name that stuck.

Strategically situated—on the River Tyne near where it flows into the North Sea—Newcastle upon Tyne grew rich as a coal-shipping center within a couple of centuries of the building of its "new" castle. A brisk trade in wool added to its eminence as the Middle Ages became the Renaissance. With the advent of the Industrial Revolution, the city had become a multi-industry center.

While Newcastle thrived on mercantile agglomeration, its near-neighbor, Durham, followed another path: At about the same time that Newcastle's castle went up, Benedictine monks there were building not only their own castle, but a cathedral on the site of an earlier church that had long been celebrated as the shrine of a locally beloved saint. William the Conqueror took advantage of its situation near the Scottish border and very sensibly placed Durham Castle's fortifications and next-door Durham Cathedral in the charge of a bishop, Walcher by name. He was the first of a long line of Prince Bishops, who, for seven and a half centuries, ruled the area temporally, as well as in matters of the faith. The last Prince Bishop died in 1836, and, not long after, Durham's university was founded in the castle no longer needed as the Prince Bishop's seat.

ON SCENE

NEWCASTLE

Lay of the Land: Newcastle descends a hill to the River Tyne. Arrive by train and you alight at Central Station, not far from the half-dozen landmark bridges spanning the river. The Keep—open to visitors—is all that remains of the castle from which the city takes its name. New Newcastle is typified by Eldon Square, one of Europe's biggest shopping centers, extending through to the city's main business thoroughfare, Northumberland Street, and the Newcastle outpost of Selfridges department-store chain. Shorter than Northumberland Street, but of far more architectural significance, is nearby Grey Street, the bend of which presents an array of facades dating to the early nineteenth century. Theatre Royal, its pediment supported by columns topped by Corinthian capitals, is the standout of the lot.

St. Nicholas Cathedral (Mosley Street) went up in the fifteenth century but wasn't elevated to cathedral status until 1882. Even a century later, "Geordies," as natives of the city are called, refer to it as "St. Nicholas's." What you want particularly to notice is the crownlike tower, believed to be even older than the similar—and better known—spire of St. Giles's Cathedral in Edinburgh. Local forces saved it from destruction by Scottish forces in the course of the seventeenth-century siege, by the simple ploy of placing Scottish prisoners of war in the tower. Within, note the Ascension Chapel's stained glass, fine scale of the nave, and chapel in the crypt.

Laing Art Gallery (New Bridge Street) was a benefaction—at the turn of the century—of a local boy who made good. Its Renaissance-style building is a repository of British paintings, eighteenth-century through to this very month. Have a look at portraits by Allan Ramsay, Sir Joshua Reynolds, and Sir Thomas Lawrence; and landscapes by the likes of Richard Wilson and John Constable. Nineteenth-century greats are represented by works of the Victorian favorite, Sir Edwin Landseer; pre-Raphaelites like Rossetti, Hunt, and Burne-Jones; and later painters like Augustus John and Richard Sickert. There is a superb showing of British watercolors and—to impart local flavor—a gallery of paintings, mostly of the last century, which interpret Newcastle's emergence as a city of consequence; porcelain, silver, and glass, too.

John George Joicey Museum (City Road) is housed in what had been Holy Jesus Hospital—a municipal almshouse from the late seventeenth century until the early decades of the twentieth. Idea of the museum is to portray the city's social history. Concentrate on a dozen furnished-in-period rooms on the second floor—Early Stuart through Art Nouveau. The Joicey is a joy.

Blackfriars (Friars Street) is a Middle Ages Dominican monastery that has been deftly restored as a museum of local lore.

Old Assembly Rooms (Westgate Road): A charming bit of the eighteenth century—Ionic columns support a classical pediment—the Old Assembly Rooms were designed in the style of Robert Adam, even to the elaborate plasterwork.

Hancock Museum (Claremont Road) is a bit away from the center, and its mixed-bag collections—stuffed birds and Egyptian mummies, geology and an aquarium, the ethnology of Africa and the South Seas—may not necessarily tempt you.

Hadrian's Wall: A glance at a portion of what is generally agreed to be the greatest of the Roman monuments in Britain may or may not be your idea of amusement. Still, Hadrian's Wall goes back some eighteen centuries, was built of turf, as well as stone (as high as 20 feet), is named for the Emperor who ordered it as a barrier to Celtic invasions from the north, extends some 70 miles, and was punctuated by a network of forts. A good way to gain the wall is to proceed a dozen miles west from Newcastle to little Hexham; the wall is to its immediate north.

Alnwick Castle (Alnwick), a 25-mile hop north toward the Scottish border, is one of the storybook castles, right up there with Arundel and Warwick in the South. You know, as you approach the turreted, gray-stone facade, that twelfth-century Alnwick is history-laden. Inside, you are overwhelmed with surprises: Resident Dukes of Northumberland made major improvements in both the eighteenth and nineteenth centuries. To see: superb furniture; paintings by such masters as Titian, Canaletto, and Van Dyck; even a museum of regional Roman antiquities.

Washington Old Hall (Washington) was home to ancestors of President George Washington as long ago as 1183, when it was built by the de Wessyngton family—the Anglo-Saxon spelling of Washington. (Washington was descended from Walter de Wessyngton, who lived in the fourteenth century.) The line continued all the way into the seventeenth century, by which time the family had moved south to Sulgrave Manor (Chapter 17). John Washington, who emigrated to Virginia, was George Washington's great grandfather. Washington Hall is one of the least grand of the important British country houses. It is a felicitous restoration—mostly paid for during the years before World War II by an Anglo-American Preservation Committee with funds from both sides of the Atlantic. Old Glory flies in the Great Hall. To see as well: wood-paneled reception room, kitchen, and bedrooms. President Carter paid a visit in 1977; you'll see his signature in the visitors' book. National Trust.

DURHAM

They are separated by only 13 miles, but Durham and Newcastle could not be less alike. Replace the latter city's bustle with an almost bucolic calm in pretty riverside Durham, whose side-by-side ancient monuments—Cathedral and Castle (core of the University of Durham) are its principal raisons d'être.

Lay of the Land: Thank the river for making Durham's geography distinctive. Like the crook of a shepherd's staff, it winds around the city's core. Palace Green, almost dead center, is flanked to the south by the Cathedral and to the north by the Castle, with ancient houses of no little architectural distinction flanking equally ancient streets— North Bailey, Saddler Street, and Silver Street, among them.

Additional landmarks are Guildhall (the originally fourteenth-century Town Hall) and St. Nicholas Church, which edges the Castle to its north. Mercantile Durham lies both to the east and the west of the river. It's at its best in Millburngate Shopping Center, adjudged, in a recent competition, as one of Europe's handsomest.

Durham Cathedral (Palace Green): Look, first, from across Prebends' Bridge, spanning the River Wear. No cathedral in Britain is quite so idyllically situated, on a green eminence above water. An eleventh-century outgrowth of the Benedictine monastery with the tomb of northern England's most revered saint—Cuthbert—Durham embodies architecture (it is considered England's premier Romanesque church) and art (no cathedral's treasury is richer), creating an environment that few of its fellow cathedrals can match. Every visitor to

Britain compiles his own Favorite Cathedrals List; my Big Three are Exeter, Winchester, and Durham. To note: carving of the Romanesque arches flanking the nave; misericords, or seats, of the carved-wood choir; elegant Nevile Screen of the high altar; 155-foot-high tower at the center of the transept; delicately arched Galilee Chapel; and—on display in the onetime monks' dormitory—jeweled crosses, candlesticks of silver, golden altar plates, seals of the prince bishops, illuminated Bibles, embroidered stoles, and brocaded copes.

Durham Castle (Palace Green): Credit University College of the University of Durham—whose home the castle has been since 1837—for retaining the essentially medieval ambience of this nine-century-old complex, for long, the seat of the Prince Bishops of Durham. The courtyard, where tours begin, is a mix of coats of arms embedded in stone walls, crenellated towers, and Romanesque arches. The three vast fireplaces of the high-walled kitchen go back five centuries. And there are two chapels, the earlier Romanesque one an all-Britain standout.

Gulbenkian Museum (Elvet Hill Road) occupies quarters on the modern University of Durham campus, a five-minute drive from the center. Lure is an absolutely fabulous collection—world-class—of Asian art and artifacts. Chinese objects—cloisonné vases, T'ang horses, figures of ivory and jade—dominate, but there are scrolls and pottery from Japan, miniature paintings from India, ancient Persian silver, and—exceptional treat, this—Egyptian treasures: mummies, mini-sculptures, papyrus rolls, vases of alabaster, and striking sculpture. Special.

Bowes Museum (Barnard Castle): Terminology first: Barnard Castle is the name of the village—about 20 miles southwest of Durham—wherein are located the ruins of a medieval castle, Barnard by name; a High Street flanked by atmospheric old houses, in one of which Dickens set *Nicholas Nickleby*; and—the subject of this paragraph—a mock-French château out of the late nineteenth century, set in a 20-acre garden and built by a local aristocrat expressly to house an extraordinary museum of the fine and decorative arts. Schoolkids—who go in droves—adore a mechanical silver swan whose articulated neck lowers to pick up a fish, to musical accompaniment. But there are paintings by El Greco, Goya, Tiepolo, and Courbet—among many others; tapestries and porcelain; enamelware and dolls; and period rooms in which valuable furniture, much of it French (Louis XV and XVI), is presented.

SETTLING IN

County Thistle Hotel (Neville Street, Newcastle) is an unabashed old-timer, smartly updated, the while retaining its Victorian ambience. There are a capacious lobby; a pair of restaurants (including good-value Conservatory); and two bar-lounges, one named Platform 1, with a rail motif as a tribute to the across-the-road Central Station. A hundred and fifteen rooms of varying shapes and sizes. *First Class.*

Royal Station Hotel (Neville Street, Newcastle) is, like the County (above), a neighbor of Central Station and similarly traditional, with not a few architectural features to note—a century-old grand stairway and porte cochère, most especially. Most of the 115 rooms and suites have baths, and some have showers. Main and less pricey restaurants, bar-lounge. *First Class.*

Swallow Hotel (Newgate Hotel, Newcastle), if unexceptional as regards esthetics, has the advantages of a central situation, 60-plus well-equipped rooms, rooftop restaurant affording fine views, and a bar-lounge. *Moderate.*

Crest Hotel (New Bridge Street, Newcastle) occupies a contemporary tower. The 180 bedrooms tend to be small, and beds are narrow. Pair of restaurants, trio of bars. *Moderate.*

Royal Turk's Head Hotel (Grey Street, Newcastle): Admirably situated on Newcastle's grandest street; some 90 rooms, not all with bath; restaurant-bar. *Moderate.*

Royal County Hotel (Old Elvet, Durham) is Durham's leader: a smartly contemporary environment with Old Durham touches in the main restaurant and bar-lounge. A hundred and thirty pleasant rooms. Coffee shop. Central. *First Class.*

Three Tuns Hotel (New Elvet, Durham) is a deft updating of a cluster of old houses. Half a hundred comfortable rooms, delightfully old-style restaurant, and bar-lounge. *Moderate-First Class.*

Bowburn Hall Hotel (Coxhoe, Durham) is agreeably small: 20 functional bedrooms, restaurant, bar; near the center. *Moderate.*

DAILY BREAD

Jim and Carol's Kitchen (Blenheim Street, Newcastle) is at once handsome, festive, tasty, and indicated for your splurge Newcastle dinner. Specialty is game—partridge, pheasant, grouse pie. With delicious sweets. *Luxury.*

Italian Job (Dean Street, Newcastle): Blue-and-white check cloths complement the red-sauced pasta in this bright, amusing, and delicious spot. *First Class.*

Oscar's Viking (Royal Station Hotel, Neville Street, Newcastle): You could be across the North Sea in Scandinavia, but the menu has traditional favorites, including hamburgers. *Moderate.*

Reno's Wine Bar (Great Market, Newcastle): Solid value—roast beef, lamb chops, daily specials—accompanied by the house wine, glass or bottle. *Moderate.*

Theatre Royal Buffet Bar (Theatre Royal, Grey Street, Newcastle) has its own entrance and is open for weekday lunches, as well as on performance evenings. Daily specials. *Moderate.*

Royal County Hotel Restaurant (Old Elvet, Durham) draws locals, as well as visitors, for, say, roast beef from the trolley, steak and kidney pie, and French-accented specialties, too. Handsome. *First Class.*

Tudor Restaurant (Three Tuns Hotel, New Elvet, Durham): Go for the excellent-value table d'hôte. *Moderate-First Class.*

Denhoffer's Wine Bar (Handyside Arcade, Durham) is indicated for a salad or daily-special lunch, with a glass of wine. *Moderate.*

Undercroft Restaurant (Durham Cathedral, Durham): A handsome environment, just off the cloister, for a lunch of, say, soup, salad, or the day's special, with exceptional sweets. *Moderate.*

Market Tavern (Market Place, Durham): A core-of-Durham pub that's just the ticket for an unpretentious but satisfying lunch—pork pie, perhaps, and a pint of lager. *Moderate.*

AFTER DARK
Theatre Royal (Grey Street, Newcastle), classic-style and one of the most beautiful theaters in the north, presents entertainments the year round—plays by major companies, seasons of the English National Opera North and the Northern Opera, ballet, and concerts. Other theaters: *Newcastle Playhouse, Gulbenkian Studio.*

INCIDENTAL INTELLIGENCE

You may fly to Newcastle from throughout Britain, as well as from a number of points in Scandinavia and Continental Europe. Newcastle is linked by ship—from nearby North Sea Ferry Terminal—to Denmark, Norway, and Sweden. From Hull to the South, there is passenger-ship service to Holland. *Further information:* Newcastle Tourist Information Centre, Blackfriars, Friar Street; Durham Tourist Information Centre, Claypath, Durham.

16

Norwich and East Anglia

"Ye Olde" in England

BACKGROUND BRIEFING

The first point worth making about East Anglia is that there's no West Anglia, let alone North or South. Its name derives from the Angles, North German immigrants who settled this region of northeast England, bordering the North Sea, fifteen centuries back.

The second point to make is that, with the Renaissance a millennium later, East Anglia became one of the great wool-producing centers of Europe. With wool came wealth, manifestations of which—a still elegant cathedral city and cathedral-size parish churches in still tranquil villages of half-timbered houses—make East Anglia as authentic a souvenir of Ye Olde England as is to be found in today's United Kingdom, with the Cotswold villages (Chapter 17) offering perhaps the stiffest competition.

Ideally, an East Anglian visit begins in Norwich, traditional "capital" of the ancient region and continues south to a cluster of time-stood-still towns, several associated with the early nineteenth-century painter John Constable and still another with the late eighteenth-century painter Thomas Gainsborough, with a history-rich royal residence among the preeminent country houses.

ON SCENE

Lay of the Land: Norwich goes back a thousand years, to the time when its Castle (still a landmark, although altered over the centuries) and its Cathedral (still a landmark and—happily—virtually unaltered over the centuries) were built, in the company of a substantial sprinkling of parish churches—run by pioneering bands of Augustinian, Dominican, and Franciscan friars—a number of which still stand.

The high-on-a-hill Castle and the single spire of the wall-enclosed Cathedral are to this day this city's major monuments and aid in geographic orientation to one of Britain's most underappreciated city centers. The Cathedral, in its parklike Close, fronts a uniquely named street called Tombland. From that major north-south thoroughfare, the direction is westerly to the core, past boutiques and cafés occupying medieval houses on the street called Elm Hill, combining department stores like Jarrolds and Bonds with ancient Guildhall and modern City Hall.

Norwich Cathedral (Tombland) stuns with the startling severity of its essentially Romanesque construction. The nave—flanked by three levels of subtly decorated arches and surmounted by a high stone roof, with the heads of the extraordinary bosses sculpted of wood—is spectacular. (Look up at details of the bosses through the wheeled mirrors thoughtfully provided.) Misericords—carved-wood folding-seats of the fifteenth-century choir—warrant detailed inspection, too. Stroll the cloister, largest such of any English cathedral, with some 400 bosses on its roofs, and the *lavatorium*—stone-carved basins where medieval monks washed themselves before dining, so very long ago. Edith Cavell, the locally born and far-famed World War I nurse whom the Germans executed in Belgium is buried in the churchyard. Walk Cathedral Close, dotted with aged buildings, including those of a public school, Norwich by name.

Norwich Castle Museum (Castle Meadow): A visit to this municipally operated hodgepodge of a repository is a good excuse to have a close-up look at the castle, today more nineteenth- and twentieth-century than medieval, its basic boxy contour excepted. The museum is based on a high-ceilinged rotunda, around which galleries display a variety of Norwich-origin objects: a helmet from Norwich-based Romans, a thousand-year-old penny, unsophisticated pottery, rare porcelain, and, most interesting, a presentation of Norfolk drawn and painted works, Georgian through our own day. What remains of the old battlements are shown on guided tours. Café.

Strangers Hall (Charing Cross), named either for foreigners who came from Flanders half a millennium back to staff the wool industry or for refugee priests from Revolutionary France, is a treasure of a town house, its oldest parts fourteenth-century. There are a score of rooms starting with the sixteenth-century Great Hall, with a number of interiors from the decoratively important seventeenth century, as well as later representation—Georgian dining room, Regency music room, Victorian dining room. And don't neglect the Tudor courtyard. Lovely.

Bridewell Museum (Bridewell Alley) is an ancient dwelling—the onetime home of a medieval merchant—later used as a "Bridewell," or vagrants' shelter—now a museum of Norfolk crafts and as interesting for its architecture as its exhibits: spinning wheels, a blacksmith's forge, early machinery, shawls, clocks, shoes, and bicycles. Have a look at adjacent *St. Andrew's Church*—late Gothic.

St. Peter Hungate Museum (Princes Street): Desanctified churches operating as museums of ecclesiastical art are not as common in Britain as on the Continent. St. Peter Hungate, a Gothic gem on a charming street near the Cathedral, is one such. You like it as much for itself—wood-beamed roof, tile floor, arched windows—as for its treasures: bosses (wood-carvings from vaults of churches) through stained glass, with the sculpture choice.

Guildhall (Market): You may or may not be able to have a look, but it is worth my noting that this early fifteenth-century structure was Norwich's City Hall for five hundred years, until a successor opened nearby, just before World War II. A succession of 529 mayors made it their seat. Now a courthouse, its guards may let you peep at the onetime council chamber and other nooks and crannies.

St. Peter Mancroft Church (Bethel Street), a near-neighbor to the square called Market, is Perpendicular—third and latest of the English Gothic periods—generously scaled, with a fine roof, good stained glass, and no less than a dozen bells, which you'll perceive without difficulty if you're nearby when they are rung.

Blickling Hall (14 miles north of Norwich) was built in the early seventeenth century by the same talented architect responsible for Hatfield House (Chapter 2). This outstanding Jacobean mansion— with not infelicitous eighteenth-century embellishments—is at its most spectacular in its 130-foot Long Hall. But there are other features— grand stairway and tapestries of the state rooms, among them. Stroll the garden. Café. National Trust.

Holkham Hall (38 miles northwest of Norwich) straddles the north coast of the Norfolk peninsula, a Palladian monument with a pair of semidetached pavilions framing a colonnaded main house—and positively stunning interiors. Builder was a local aristocrat home from a Grand Tour and hooked on classic architecture. Holkham Hall was designed by William Kent. Its 50-foot-high Marble Hall is only the beginning. The Saloon, with matchless furniture, paintings, and proportions; and the tapestry-walled state bedroom—centered on a canopied bed—are memorable, too.

Sandringham House (42 miles northwest of Norwich and ideally visited in tandem with Holkham Hall, above) is, except for Windsor Castle (Chapter 2), the only one of the Queen's houses open to visitors. (Unless you count the gardens—only—of Balmoral Castle, in Scotland [Chapter 27], the Queen's Gallery and Royal Mews of Buckingham Palace [Chapter 2], or Holyrood House [Chapter 24], which is the Queen's residence when she is in Edinburgh.) So that you should not be surprised to be in the company of hordes of fellow-visitors; most are Britons old enough to remember when Sandringham was used more often than it is now, especially at Christmas, when monarchs George V on through a young Elizabeth II used it as the venue for Christmas broadcasts to the Empire, and its successor, the Commonwealth. Edward VII, when he was Prince of Wales, built Sandringham—long and rambling, in the center of a vast, still very much in business royal estate—on the site of an older house that was razed. Edward VII's son and successor, George V, and George V's son and ultimate successor, George VI, were born in York Cottage, a house on the grounds that now serves as offices. Nearby, *Sandringham Church*—typically Norfolk Gothic, with it chunky entrance tower—has known royal worshipers over the years. Sandringham gardens, with a pair of lakes centering them—are far-flung. But it is the interior of Sandringham House that is the big draw. So long as you don't expect the opulence—fine art and fine furniture—of Windsor, or, for that matter, Holyrood, you won't be disappointed. Only a few state rooms are open (crowds are such that the dining table has been removed from the dining room). They are of interest primarily for portraits of former occupants—Edward VII's consort, magazine cover-beautiful, Danish-born Queen Alexandra, is the subject of more than one—and absorbing exhibits of photos of the Royal Family, from Edward and Alexandra all the way through to the current occupant of the throne and her kin.

The onetime coach house, fire station, and assorted other outbuildings comprise *Sandringham Museum;* with royal cars, game trophies, equestrian gear, and even gifts presented to Queen Elizabeth II while on her world tours. Cafeteria.

Villages of John Constable country: Though better known for his much-reproduced paintings of southerly Salisbury Cathedral, John Constable was born and bred in East Anglia—and painted it. It is possible to headquarter for a visit to this village-cluster either at bigger *Ipswich*, a few miles to the north (and with four Constable paintings in its *Christchurch Mansion Museum*, Bolton Lane), or at *Colchester* (with Constable portraits and drawings, as well, in the *Minories Museum*, an eighteenth-century house-museum on High

Street). But the charm of this Stour River Valley region lies in its villages.

The son of a miller, Constable was born in 1776 in *East Bergholt*, whose major monument from his time is *St. Mary's Church*, which he painted often and where there are family tombstones. The nearby *Old Rectory* is where he met his wife, subject of a portrait you may recall in London's Tate Gallery. The mill in *Flatford*, another painting at the Tate, still is to be seen in that village. You'll want to visit *Stoke-by-Nayland*, with a church that Constable used as a subject for a number of drawings.

Then comes *Dedham*, loveliest of the region's villages to this day and the subject of Constable paintings in London's Victoria and Albert Museum and Edinburgh's National Gallery. It is agreeable to look first at the village from on high, as one approaches. You could do worse than to begin at the general store-cum-post office on the High Street, where the postmistress-proprietress will provide directions for a self-guided tour. Start in *St. Mary's Church*, a great Gothic beauty that went up in 1492. Walk through its yard to the quarter of half-timbered houses called *Flemish Cottages* after their initial tenants, weavers from Flanders. It's a brisk walk, then, just outside the village, to *Castle House*, a Tudor-Georgian mansion where a much later artist than Constable—this century's Sir Alfred Munnings—painted pictures that brought him fame, the presidency of the Royal Academy, and a knighthood.

Lavenham and Sudbury, two villages a short distance northwest of Constable Country, warrant attention. Lavenham's *SS. Peter and Paul's Church*—with a 141-foot-high square tower—is among England's great parish churches, a remarkable specimen of Late Perpendicular, last of the three English Gothic styles, essentially sixteenth-century and with typically immense windows flanking the nave. The National Trust operates the sixteenth-century *Guildhall* fronting a central square—Market Place—as a museum, whose exhibits explain how this and other villages in the region became rich as a consequence of the medieval wool trade. As in Dedham, you want to walk about, making sure not to miss architecturally distinctive Water and Prentice streets.

It's time then for *Sudbury*, still another painter's town, and this the most universally known of the trio: Thomas Gainsborough. Gainsborough was one of nine children, the lot born and raised in a brick dwelling *(Gainsborough House*, Gainsborough Street) with a Georgian front and a Regency rear. Unlike homes of other great painters—Rembrandt's in Amsterdam, Hogarth's in London—it is not without representation of the master's paintings, including several painted in

Bath and one of the then-Countess of Dartmouth. In his 61 years—he died of cancer in 1788—the prolific Gainsborough painted 800 elegant portraits, not to mention 300 of his less well-known landscapes.

Bury St. Edmunds, a smallish, albeit ancient town some 20 miles north of Lavenham, is an East Anglian charmer—just plain "Bury" to its friends. You want first, though, to know about that odd name. Edmund, a ninth-century king killed by marauding Danes and later sainted, was buried in the town's abbey, now a ruin at the town's eastern end. Have a look and then walk east to Crown Street, to *St. Mary's Church,* one of two exemplary Perpendicular Gothic churches at the Abbey's edge, and the tomb of Henry VIII's sister, Mary Tudor. (Look up at the huge, carved-wood angels supporting the ceiling.) Then walk north a bit to the other church: St. James's is its original name. It has two special attributes. The first is that the Romanesque tower that was part of the ruined abbey is now its belfry. And the second is that since as relatively recently as 1914 it became Bury St. Edmunds' Cathedral.

Take time for Bury's two museums. Twelfth-century *Moyses Hall* (Cornhill) is chock-filled with local lore. But *Angel Corner* (Angel Hill) is the name of an eighteenth-century house, operated by the National Trust as a museum of clocks, watches, and other antique time-telling devices, the lot of them old and beautiful. And peep into another National Trust property, the Regency-period *Theatre Royal* (Westgate Street); its architect was William Wilkins, designer of London's National Gallery, and its four-level auditorium—red and gold and green under a painted, cloud-filled blue sky—is so special that it is traditionally open for daily inspection.

Ickworth (three miles southwest of Bury St. Edmunds) is one-of-a-kind among country houses—an early nineteenth-century conceit that consists of a 600-foot-long rotunda whose center is taken up with a 104-foot-high dome, with curved wings on either side the setting for a series of state rooms, filled with fine furniture, silver, porcelain, and paintings. Hoppners and Lawrences look down on an almost interminably long dining table. Hogarth graces the library. There are Gainsboroughs of early Earls of Bristol—the building family—in the Drawing Room, along with works by Romney, Reynolds, and the eighteenth century's two ranking female portraitists, Angelica Kauffmann and Elisabeth Vigée-Lebrun—rarely seen together in the same room. The pillared library is the showplace, with a dazzler of a painting by Velásquez. Café. National Trust.

SETTLING IN

Maid's Head Hotel (Tombland, Norwich): Happiness in Norwich is a room with a view in the original building—the pedigree is respectable, totaling seven centuries—of the Maid's Head. (Location is just opposite the Cathedral.) If you really want to feel special, ask for the four-poster chamber in which Queen Elizabeth I is reputed to have slept, albeit in another bed. Not all singles have baths, but the rest of the rooms do, some with showers. Two bars, a fine restaurant, and a lounge for snacks day-long and for afternoon tea that is one of Britain's most delicious. *First Class.*

Nelson Hotel (Prince of Wales Road, Norwich) is a contemporary rectangle, deftly tucked into a spit of land flanking the River Wensum. The look in the lobby is severe, but bedrooms are a pleasure, with showers in every bath. Some bedrooms have river views, which is the case, as well, with the main restaurant and bar-lounge. Coffee shop, too. *First Class.*

Castle Hotel (Castle Meadow, Norwich): An adequate elderly house without any special charm, the Castle—neighbor of Norwich Castle—has been updated. I wish more than a third of the 77 rooms had baths. Restaurant, two bars. *Moderate.*

Lansdowne Hotel (Thorp Road, Norwich): You're seeking budget accommodations in a restaurant-and-bar-equipped hotel? The Lansdowne makes it; 18 of its 44 rooms have baths, and a few of these have showers. Nothing fancy. *Moderate.*

Dedham Vale Hotel (Stratford Road, Dedham) is an agreeably elderly house, half of whose dozen bedrooms have baths. Restaurant, bar. *Moderate.*

Swan Hotel (High Street, Lavenham) is the kind of inn we cross the Atlantic to experience in Britain. At its oldest, it is fourteenth-century, with a half-timbered facade, plop in the heart of the village. Perfectly lovely public areas include a good restaurant and two bars, one atmospherically wood-beamed, and a lounge where tea is a pleasure. There are 42 comfortable rooms. Trusthouse Forte. *First Class.*

Mill Hotel (Walnut Tree Lane, Sudbury) is aptly named. It's a three-century-old mill house, alongside the River Stour, with the wheel still operative. Observe it while having a drink in the adjacent bar. Restaurant, half a hundred rooms. *Moderate-First Class.*

Angel Hotel (Angel Hill, Bury St. Edmunds): I can't imagine staying anywhere else in the course of a Bury visit. The Angel is eighteenth-century, with a mix of decors in the 44 bedrooms, not all of which have bath. Some, though, have four-posters. The room in which Charles Dickens lived (he lectured in the Robert Adam-designed Athenaeum just next door) is named in his memory. Restaurant, one bar called Dickens, the other Pickwick. *First Class.*

Suffolk Hotel (Buttermarket, Bury St. Edmunds): About a third of the approximately 40 rooms in this centrally situated house have baths, and there's a mod-look restaurant and bar. *Moderate.*

DAILY BREAD

Minstrel Room (Maid's Head Hotel, Tombland, Norwich): Setting is a Georgian room hung with crystal chandeliers. Fare embraces excellent-value table d'hôte lunches and dinners, but there is an exceptional à la carte, as well—lobster or crab bisque; entrées—tournedos Rossini, noisette of lamb estragon, escalope of veal—prepared with a deft Franco-Italian touch; and superb sweets, especially the cakes. *First Class.*

Tatler's (Tombland, Norwich): My preference, along with the Minstrel Room (above), for a festive Norwich dinner is this Georgian house, a hop-and-a-skip from the Cathedral, a source of atmospherically presented English (roast beef, grilled lamb chops) and French-accented (*steak au poivre*, chicken tarragon) dishes, with rich desserts and interesting wines. Dinner only. *First Class.*

Assembly House (Theatre Street, Norwich): This landmark eighteenth-century structure now sees service as a cinema, meeting hall, and restaurant. Go in, mid-morning, for coffee, through dinner. Fare is English, environment handsome. *Moderate.*

Winkles (Old Post Office Yard, Norwich) shares a welcoming eighteenth-century house, heart of town, with *Parson Woodforde:* the former is for grilled trout, fish pie, and other seafood treats; the latter specializes in venerable favorites like Elizabethan pork stew, with prepared-on-premises sweets. *Moderate-First Class.*

Princes Inn (Princes Street, Norwich): Handsome and half-timbered, the inn specializes in the local Norfolk duckling at dinner, while a wise lunch choice might be the sautéed trout platter. *Moderate-First Class.*

Spinning Wheel (Steep Hill, Norwich): Each of the two ancient rooms of this snack-lunch-tea-dinner spot is snug. There are tasty daily specials, salads made just for you, super cakes. *Moderate.*

Swan Hotel Restaurant (High Street, Lavenham): Why not a festive dinner in a medieval setting—wood-beamed ceiling, minstrel gallery, the lighting softened by silk shades? With good-value table d'hôte menus featuring solid fare, roast beef invariably included. *Moderate-First Class.*

Angel Hotel (Market Place, Lavenham): More pub than hotel, the ancient Angel, exquisitely wood-paneled, beckons when it's an unpretentious lunch you fancy—grilled sausages, cold meats with salad, a glass of beer. *Moderate.*

Sun Hotel (Hotel Street, Dedham): A five-century-old source of bar lunches or more formal dinners in the half-timbered, split-level dining room, with daily specials good bets. *Moderate-First Class.*

Rose (Thorrington Street, Stoke-by-Nayland): You're touring Constable Country and you're hungry: The Rose is a venerable pub that serves up a cheese-centered ploughman's lunch. *Moderate.*

Bowman's (Market Square, Sudbury): An agreeable spot for a lunch break in Gainsborough's home town. Mostly English favorites, based on beef and lamb; accompany with a glass or carafe of the house wine. *Moderate.*

Peggoty's (Guildhall Street, Bury St. Edmunds): A restaurant named for a lovable Dickens character—in a town with Dickens associations—has to have something going for it. Peggoty's does: roast beef carved for you at a counter, as part of ample—and tasty—three-course lunches or dinners. *Moderate.*

Greene King (Angel Hill, Bury St. Edmunds): Established in 1799—and still with a nifty Georgian look to it—this busy pub is indicated for lunch, centered on the hot plate of the day. *Moderate.*

AFTER DARK
Theatre Royal (Theatre Street, Norwich) is a modern, municipally operated house, wherein are presented its own dramatic and musical productions, as well as those of touring companies out of London, opera and ballet included.

Maddermarket Theatre (Maddermarket, Norwich) is a reconstruction of an Elizabethan theater in a former church that is home base for the Norwich Players, a repertory company that goes back more than half a century.

Theatre Royal (Westgate Street, Bury St. Edmunds) is a Regency landmark, relatively recently restored, and so visitworthy that it's open days for inspection (above). At this point, I recommend a performance, be it a locally produced play or a touring musical, and dining, if you like, in the *Dress Circle Bar*.

INCIDENTAL INTELLIGENCE

The East Anglian port of Harwich is a terminus for modern passenger ships, linking Britain with Hook of Holland in the Netherlands; Esbjerg in Denmark; Bremerhaven and Hamburg in Germany; and Kristiansand in Norway, with additional service from the nearby port of Felixstowe to Gothenburg, Sweden. There are international airports (with domestic services, as well) at Norwich and Stansted. *Further information:* Norwich Tourist Information Centre, Tombland; Bury St. Edmunds Tourist Information Centre, Abbey Gardens, Angel Hill.

17

Oxford
Stratford and the Cotswold Villages

BACKGROUND BRIEFING

If it's slower to charm than Cambridge, less well manicured, faster-paced, and more urban, if you will, well, Oxford has its reasons. It compensates with more advanced age (Cambridge [Chapter 7] is an offshoot—clone would be too strong a word); more than its share of distinction—historic, architectural, intellectual; and a situation that encourages the visitor to link it with exploration of Stratford, William Shakespeare's natal town, and still unspoiled villages of the Cotswold Hills.

Today's Oxford is an unlikely meld of higher education and auto manufacture. Neither early Romans, nor slightly less early Saxons, nor even friars of the abbey whose church now doubles as a college chapel and cathedral of the regional diocese, made of Oxford an especially distinctive town.

A trickle of students, come from Paris of all places, made the difference. What happened was that Anglo-French politics of the early twelfth century were such that England's King Henry II considered it expedient to recall those of his countrymen studying in France. Probably because it was at once easy of access and politically insignificant, they resumed their studies in Oxford. Early on, they had no formal organization, living in local inns and studying with masters where they could.

Given the English penchant for organization, it is not surprising that before long they set up a system of halls—centers for both teaching and boarding—each directed by an alumnus. And so the Oxford system of the residential college—emulated later by Cambridge, with modifications by New World universities like Harvard and Yale—evolved. Pioneering colleges—University, Balliol, Merton—remain very much a part of the Oxford scene. But those thirteenth-century colleges are now part of a confederation of twenty-eight undergraduate colleges and seven postgraduate colleges, each with its own enclosed campus, library, dorms, dining halls, and resident tutors, which share common university facilities—museums, science labs, major libraries, and the like—and are united under a broad university umbrella.

Until the last century, Oxford and Cambridge had no British competition, save the three senior Scottish universities (St. Andrew's, founded in 1410; Glasgow, dating to 1451; and Edinburgh, which opened in 1583). Not only were their student bodies elitist (this is less the case today), but they attracted the nation's cream-of-the-crop intellectuals to teach and undertake research and the nation's leading architects, painters, landscapists, and interior designers to create their facilities. I try to make clear how important this heritage is for the visitor to Cambridge in Chapter 7. Herewith, the case for bigger and more senior Oxford.

ON SCENE

Lay of the Land: Oxford the city and Oxford the university blend—if not always felicitously with respect to town-gown relationships over the centuries, at least geographically. By that, I mean central Oxford is at once the city's business quarter (allow yourself time for the excellent shopping) and is interspersed with complexes of the various colleges.

Carfax Tower—all that remains of a medieval church and ascendable for a bird's-eye view—is at the intersection of the principal thoroughfares. Cornmarket Street, coming from the north (and with big outlets of such chain stores as Debenhams, Littlewoods, Edinburgh Woolen Mills, Boots, and London's Reject China Shops), becomes St. Aldate's Street as it passes Carfax to go south. Queen Street, west of Carfax (with branches of London's Selfridges department store and Marks & Spencer), becomes High Street as it proceeds east, passing the university-associated, Gothic-era St. Mary's Church, to become the core of a major concentration of Oxford colleges and, as such, one of Britain's best-looking principal thoroughfares. Not as central as Cambridge's Cam, Oxford's River Cherwell flanks it on the east. The Railway Station is west of center.

Visiting the colleges: Pick up a map of town from your hotel or the Oxford Tourist Information Centre and set off, allowing a pair of half-days for the colleges and—important, this—another day for a remarkable library and two art museums, one of which is among Britain's best. Order of the colleges I have herein selected—a representative group—is geographical, south to north. Start with triplethreat, admission-charging (college, chapel-cathedral, art gallery) *Christ College* (St. Aldate's Street). Landmark Tom Tower, over its main gate, was designed by Sir Christopher Wren. Walk through it to the immense dining hall, its walls lined with fine paintings. Proceed, then, to the college chapel that is, as well, *Oxford Cathedral* (the dean of the cathedral serves also as head of Christ College), like no other in Britain, with its nave lined by chunky columns that are Romanesque at their base, but with Corinthian capitals, and with its choir covered by a later ceiling, the ribs of whose vaults are bold and star-shaped. End in Christ's sleeper of a *Picture Gallery*, surely the least publicized of any such of its importance in Britain, traditionally open only in the afternoon and worthy of a return visit, if you happen to be touring the college in the morning. On display are a relatively small but rich collection, mostly of Italian masters, including Lippi, Tintoretto, Veronese, Carracci, Strozzi, Rosa—to give you an idea— along with a brilliant bonus of drawings and prints by the likes of Lorrain, Raphael, Titian, and Dürer. *Pembroke College* (St. Aldate's Street), founded in the sixteenth century by King James I, warrants a visit, if only because of its art-filled chapel (eighteenth-century) and dining hall (nineteenth-century). *Merton College* (Merton Street)— one of the pioneering early colleges, dating to the thirteenth century—has a dining hall, part of which is that old, and a library only a century newer and of even more interest; ask if you may see its antique manuscripts. And don't miss the gargoyles of the chapel or, beyond, the lawn of the Warden's House. *Oriel College* (Oriel Square) is another royal-founded college; the king was Edward II, in the fourteenth century. Look at the paneling in the sixteenth-century chapel and the high, wood-beamed roof of the dining hall. *All Souls College* (High Street) had Henry VI as a cofounder six centuries ago. Given its opulence—the twin towers are an Oxford landmark—it is hard to believe that this graduate school has an enrollment under sixty. Nicholas Hawksmoor, a protegé of alumnus Sir Christopher Wren, designed the main quadrangle. The library has a Wren sundial. And the chapel—soaring Perpendicular Gothic—is notable for both its carved-stone reredos backing the high altar and the misericords, carved-wood folding seats of the choir. *Queen's College's* (High Street) pair of classical porticos stand out, on "the High"—as Oxonians call High Street. Notice stained-glass likenesses in the Dining Hall of Charles I and other sovereigns. Visit the chapel, noting the fresco covering the ceiling. *New College* (New College Lane) was new in 1379, when William of Wykeham, bishop of Winchester Cathedral and founder of Winchester College (Chapter 21), established it. Aside from a Sir Jacob Epstein sculpture of Lazarus at the chapel entrance, it is almost completely the Gothic college of Wykeham's day, with linenfold wood paneling (characterized by a pattern of close-together vertical slits) in its dining hall and—aside from the Epstein—chapel art that includes windows painted by Reynolds and an El Greco near the altar. Wow! *Jesus College* (Turl Street) had as its founder Queen Elizabeth I. Beeline to the Dining Hall to see paintings of royals lining its walls, including the founding Elizabeth, Charles II, and a Van Dyck portrait of his father, Charles I. You'll recognize a sculpted T. E. Lawrence (he studied at Jesus) in the chapel. *Balliol College* (Broad Street): Ask if you may be shown some of the medieval illuminated manuscripts in the library. Peek into the eye-filling Dining Hall. End in the Victorian chapel, impressively paneled. And walk the quadrangle. *Trinity College* (Broad Street): Stroll the broad quadrangle to the chapel; carving on the altar of this paneled and stuccoed room is believed to be Grinling Gibbons. The library, older, is atmospheric. *St. John's College* (St. Giles Street): Allow time for the gardens; they're the work of eighteenth-century landscapist Capability Brown. The Dining Hall is big and art-filled, and there is a fine reredos in the chapel from the late years of the last century. *Wadham College* (Parks Road) pleases on all counts—a medieval quadrangle, paneled Dining Hall busy with paintings and coats of arms, serene chapel.

Ashmolean Museum (Beaumont Street): Oxford's Ashmolean (based on a collection given to the university by Elias Ashmole, a seventeenth-century graduate) ranks with Cambridge's Fitzwilliam and, like it, is sadly neglected by visitors, in favor of the colleges. This is an all-Europe top-ranker, occupying a handsome, classic-design building, with paintings upstairs and the other departments—a fascinating mixed bag—on the main floor, where I suggest you start. Amble about through the subcategories of the vast Antiquities Department, with such treasures as a prehistoric dagger carved of flint; jewelry fashioned of gold; pottery from the Romans' occupation of Britain; medieval swords; Egyptian ivory; Persian bronze; Minoan sculpture; Greek terra-cottas. Even nonnumismatists like me are intrigued with the coins, not only out of ancient Greece and Rome, but of earlier British centuries. The Eastern Art section is a stunner, with stellar specimens—sculpture, scrolls, porcelain, and paintings—from India, China, Japan.

That leaves the second and third floors' paintings, reason enough in and of themselves for an Oxford visit. Start with Italians—Michelangelo, Bellini, Veronese, Della Robbia, Raphael, Lippi, Bronzino, to give you an idea. Go on to the Low Countries—Van Dyck, Rubens, Rembrandt, van Ruisdael, among others. Lorrain, Watteau, and Chardinare are among the earlier French. British representation is extraordinary—Hogarth, Richard Wilson, Constable, Joseph Wright of Derby,

Gainsborough, and Reynolds. French Impressionists and post-Impressionists fairly dazzle—Cézanne, Monet, Van Gogh, Renoir, Manet, Pissarro, Toulouse-Lautrec, Sisley, Marquet, Fantin-Latour, Daubigny, and Derain, and on to Bonnard and Picasso. With special treats as you wander—a room filled with Old Master drawings, for example; another gallery exclusively of seventeenth-century Dutch still-lifes; and a whole case full of Rubens sketches.

Bodleian Library (Broad Street): If the Ashmolean (above) is called after a chap named Ashmole, the Bodleian—with its priceless painted ceiling—just has to be named for a Bodley. And it is: Sir Thomas, to be precise. And its ravishing collections date to 1602, with illuminated manuscripts stars of the show. They are so exquisite—Alexander the Great at a banquet, *The Last Judgment*, a sainted monk teaching in a monastery, an angel hovering over St. Joseph—that you find yourself recklessly buying color postcard reproductions in the library's shop.

Other Oxford destinations of significance include the Sir Christopher Wren-designed *Sheldonian Theatre* (Broad Street), used for university convocations and concerts, whose painted ceiling you don't want to miss; *Radcliffe Camera* (Radcliffe Square), marvelous circular building in neoclassic Baroque style, now a library; *Museum of Oxford* (Town Hall, St. Aldate's Street), a small, relatively recent municipal museum of the town's history; and other university-operated museums, including *University Museum* (Parks Road), an ebullient glass-roofed Victorian pavilion, packed with immense prehistoric animals' skeletons and geological exhibits; *Pitt Rivers Museum* (Parks Road), with treasures brought back home by Captain Cook—and other explorers; *Museum of the History of Science* (Pembroke Street), with its scope scientific instruments, sundials to microscopes.

Blenheim Palace (Woodstock, seven miles northwest of Oxford) is the only nonroyal house in Britain with the appellation "palace." Blenheim was given by Queen Anne, in the early eighteenth century, as a gift from her countrymen to John Churchill, the first Duke of Marlborough, to thank him for winning the battle with the French for which the house is named. One expects Blenheim to be monumental, but for architect John Vanbrugh and landscapist Capability Brown to have created a place of such style and beauty, well, these are bonuses. One look at the high-arched Long Library, the Salon's Laguerre frescoes, and the three State Rooms' paintings (by the likes of Reynolds, Van Dyck, and Kneller) and tapestries, and you're willing to buck the long queues (mostly of Britons come to see the bedroom in which Sir Winston Churchill—part of the Marlborough clan—was born) all

over again. And note the Thornhill ceiling fresco in the Great Hall.
Restaurants.

Waddesdon Manor (near Aylesbury, 20 miles east of Oxford) is a
French Renaissance-style château in its own 125-acre park, built by
Baron Ferdinand de Rothschild in the 1880s and filled by him with
priceless French antiques and even more valuable paintings and other
art objects, whose inspectors have included Queen Victoria and Kings
Edward VII and George V. Today's visitor sees not only a spectacular
Victorian interpretation of a French castle, from without, but inside,
a series of gracefully proportioned rooms, almost every feature of
which is aged. Wall paneling is mostly from ancient Paris town houses.
Some of the furniture was made for France's King Louis XVI and his
wife, Marie Antoinette. Paintings are by England's Gainsborough,
Reynolds, and Romney; France's Fragonard, Boucher, and Watteau;
and Rubens, Guardi, Metsu, and de Hooch. To see, too: Sèvres and
Meissen china, rare books, silver, carpets, glass, and enamels.
Café. National Trust.

Stonor (near Henley, 12 miles southeast of Oxford) is an essentially
Tudor house, of special interest because it was a center of Catholic
resistance to the Reformation, during which time St. Thomas Campi-
on operated a secret printing press only to be arrested and executed
for so doing. Mass still is said in the fourteenth-century chapel, in
which members of the owning Stonor family are buried and which
contains a contemporary *Stations of the Cross*, a gift of author Graham
Greene. The first picture painted of Mary I, as Queen, is in the library,
and the dining room is charming, with Regency wallpaper and chairs.
Café.

Stratford-upon-Avon's sole industry is trading upon its having been—
some four centuries back—the town in which William Shakespeare
was born. Countless visitors, Britons and foreigners alike, many of
whom have doubtless never read Shakespeare nor seen his works
performed, stream into this riverside town some 80 miles northwest
of London and half that distance from Oxford, to pay—quite literally—their respects to the Bard's memory. They stream in and out of
a handful of restored Tudor houses with Shakespeare associations,
usually leaving at the end of the day, too early to take in a performance of the theater where his works are performed and which, when
all is said and done, is Stratford at its most worthwhile.

  If you're going to go at all to what is, as far as I can tell from my
explorations, Britain's only tourist-trap town (even the church in which
Shakespeare is buried charges a fee to see his tomb), do book a hotel

room (the choice is wide and excellent in Stratford) so that you can see a performance at Royal Shakespeare Theatre. The second theater on the site (you'll see a plaque at the entrance indicating that it was opened by Edward VIII while he was Prince of Wales, in 1922, with his father, George V, its royal patron) overlooks the swan-populated Avon, as it flows through the heart of town, constituting Stratford's only concession to charm. The main street—running the same east-west direction as the river—is called, variously, High Street, Chapel Street, and Church Street and is some distance from the Railway Station on the northern edge of town.

The so-called Shakespearian properties are operated by an enterprise called the Shakespeare Birthplace Trust. *New Place* (Chapel Street), the most central, deceives with its name. It is not New Place, the house in which Shakespeare lived his last years (and died), but rather a house next door to New Place, whose foundation can be seen in the adjacent, very handsome, and—wonder of wonders in Stratford—open-for-free garden. The structure now identified as New Place is actually a museum of Stratford history (ideally, that is what it should be called), with some excellent Elizabethan furniture on the ground floor and, upstairs, exhibits of documents and small objects pertaining to the town's past. *Shakespeare's Birthplace* (Henley Street) embraces a living room, kitchen, and bedrooms—including the room in which the playwright was born—with the only original piece the desk he is believed to have used at school. Another part of the house—used by his father, John, a leather worker—is a little museum of Shakespeariana. *Hall's Croft* (Old Town) is the onetime residence of the physician who married Shakespeare's daughter Susanna; its rooms include a dispensary, and the garden is stroll-worthy. *Anne Hathaway's Cottage* (a mile to the west of Shottery) is thatched-roofed, its carved four-poster bed the standout in its interior. You do not need to be reminded that Anne (eight years her husband's senior) became Mrs. Shakespeare; the year was 1582. *Holy Trinity Church* (Trinity Street) lies alongside the Avon, south of the center. Its huge Perpendicular Gothic windows impress, as does its beamed ceiling. A verger, sitting at a cash desk at the high altar and selling tickets to see Shakespeare's tomb, is something else again.

Ragley Hall (eight miles west of Stratford) is a beautifully proportioned, beautifully furnished eighteenth-century mansion, treasure-filled and the home of Marquesses of Hertford since it was built. Its 70-foot-long Great Hall, created by James Gibbs, is not misnamed; with Gibbs's plaster decorations picked out in pale gray against a salmon background. Furniture throughout—in the study, 10,000-volume library, blue room, yellow dining room, red saloon, and green drawing room—is museum-caliber. And paintings! Reynolds, Ramsay, Hoppner, Kneller, and Lawrence are just a handful of the artists. Café.

Warwick Castle (10 miles north of Stratford), though no longer inhabited by Earls of Warwick, is a monument to them: a thousand-year-old medieval fortress, surrounding a keep and dwarfing little Warwick town, below. Towers, dungeon, and armory—armor-filled— are inspectable, but it's the state rooms that most impress: Gothic chapel; dining room with its Van Dyck portrait of an equestrian Charles I; stone-walled, tapestry-lined Great Hall; trio of drawing rooms, with furnishings of the seventeenth and eighteenth centuries; and a bedroom named for Queen Anne, with the bed she slept in at Windsor Castle and a Kneller portrait of her. Café.

Sulgrave Manor (28 miles southeast of Stratford, near Banbury) is at once a charming, not overlarge country house dating to 1500, *and* the home of ancestors of George Washington. The first American President had even earlier ancestors—they spelled their name Wessington or Wessyngton—at Washington Old Hall in County Durham (Chapter 15). But Sulgrave's Washingtons are traced from Laurence Washington—a mayor of Northampton—from whom the manor went to descendants, one of whom, John by name, emigrated to Virginia. His great-grandson, George, was born there in 1732. Sulgrave was opened to the public in 1921 by the late Queen Mary's brother, the Marquess of Cambridge, with restoration funds from a British campaign that had King George V as a patron. Later, the Colonial Dames of America endowed the house and continue as its operators. Americans are proud to see the Stars and Stripes flying out front and an original Gilbert Stuart portrait of President Washington in the Great Hall, along with a room full of Washingtoniana. The rest of the house is a joy—Oak Parlour, paneled, with Queen Anne furniture; three four-poster bedrooms, one with a Hepplewhite chair that was owned by Washington; and a kitchen equipped with shining copper utensils. Adjacent is the hamlet of *Sulgrave*, in whose fourteenth-century church there is a Washington family pew. Have lunch or tea in the village's Thatched House Hotel.

The Cotswolds are a cluster of too-good-to-be-true villages that constitute a southwest-to-northeast diagonal between Bath and Stratford. Their name comes from the network of gently rolling hills in which they are set. They're built, by and large, of beige sandstone, locally quarried, and quite obviously of considerable staying power.
One does not look for intellectual stimulation in the Cotswolds any

more than is the case—the Shakespeare theater aside—in Stratford. They are for relaxation, and they serve as excellent bedroom communities for exploration of this region of England.

Specifics? Well, they are, by and large, one-street affairs, invariably with a charming church of respectable vintage (not always open), an inn or two or three, a choice of places of sustenance, and, it should go without saying, a plethora of shops. Along with the occasional, unassuming little museum of local lore.

I am partial to the villages in the northern part of the region— *Broadway, Chipping Campden, Moreton-in-Marsh,* specifically—not only because of their smashing good looks (each could be a Ye Olde England movie set), but for strategic considerations. You reach them easily by train from London (board at Paddington Station, exit at Moreton-in-Marsh). They are close enough to Stratford to make evening performances at its theater convenient. And they are exceptionally well equipped with respect to creature comforts. Though tiny, *Broadway* is not without monuments. The tower that takes its name— early nineteenth-century, free-standing, mock-Gothic—affords smashing views from its summit. St. Edburghas Church dates back a thousand years. The adjacent village of Stanton is a Cotswolds microcosm: stone farmhouses and barns in sheep-populated meadows edging it, with a stunner of a Gothic church in its center. Still another near-to-Broadway village, Stowshill, boasts Stowshill Manor, a National Trust-operated Tudor-era house. *Chipping Campden's* Woolstaplers Hall Museum dates to 1340, but I have the feeling that its staff is spoiled by mobs of customers over the years, and its admission fee is steepish. More to the point is the village's architecture. A row of severe stone almshouses leads to the dramatically high Perpendicular Gothic tower of the exceptionally capacious parish church, with a splendidly vaulted nave. The fifteenth-century Market Hall is National Trust-protected. *Moreton-in-Marsh's* Market Hall is its High Street landmark. There's an oddball Curfew Tower topped with a four-century-old Curfew Bell and a gracefully steepled parish church.

Other Cotswold villages warrant exploration, too. *Ablington* is entered over a typically Cotswold stone bridge spanning the River Coln and past beautiful specimens of the region's so-called dry walls—in which pieces of stone are fitted together so precisely that there's no need for mortar. It is architecturally rich, cottages through barns, with a pair of mansions, for good measure. *Bibury's* Parish Church is part Saxon, part Norman, part Perpendicular Gothic. There's a stone mill and a clutch of National Trust-operated row-cottages. *Blockley* is delightfully devoid of anything newer than the middle of the last century, with a honey of a church (you see its Perpendicular Gothic tower for miles around, but parts of the building are much older Norman).

Bourton-on-the-Water's prettiest quarter is that flanking the River Windrush, in and about the eighteenth-century Old Manse Hotel. The parish church is an architectural hybrid, but why not pop in? *Burford's* high point is its High Street, descending a hill, wide and shop-flanked, with a Norman-origin church, a somewhat newer almshouse-school complex at its base, and, on adjacent Sheep Street, a hotel—the Bay Tree—built by one of Elizabeth I's courtiers and just the ticket for lunch or tea. *Chipping Norton* is a perky market town with a broad main square and, beyond, its major monuments: a row of four-century-old almshouses on Church Street and a big Perpendicular Gothic parish church. *Cirencester*—quite as important as London in Roman times—grew rich during the Golden Age of the medieval Cotswold wool barons and is proud of its parish church, one of the ranking Perpendicular Gothic structures of the kingdom—with a dazzling tower, striking nave, and beautifully carved ceilings. The core of town is strollable—its buildings span the centuries—and a pause for lunch or tea is indicated at its King's Head Inn. There is a pair of tiny villages named Coln. *Coln Rogers* edges a stone bridge spanning the River Coln, and its little parish church has a rare 800-year-old Saxon chancel. Neighboring *Coln St. Denis* straddles the same River Coln, and its Norman-era church is a treasure. *Northleach* asks that you climb a hill, past centuries-old gravestones, to reach its stunning parish church, an all-England standout of Perpendicular Gothic style immodestly dubbed "The Cathedral of the Cotswolds" by locals—and with reason, not least of which is staggering size. Nearby is the Cotswold Countryside Collection, a museum of regional life. The memorably named Slaughters—Lower and Upper—attract with good looks. *Lower Slaughter's* chief lure is a venerable brick mill, but its chief charm is Slaughter Brook, flanked by stone houses. *Upper Slaughter* straddles a hill, with a Norman church its showpiece and Slaughter Brook a core-of-village waterway. *Stow-on-the-Wold* draws antiques collectors to its Market Square and adjacent streets; quality—for both British and foreign furniture, porcelain, and silver—is invariably high, and Stow Lodge is ideal for lunch or tea. *Winchcombe* embodies half-timbered Tudor, as well as typically Cotswolds stone architecture, with a landmark Perpendicular Gothic church and a choice of centuries-old inns for refreshment, one of which, the George, dates back 700 years.

Sudeley Castle (at the edge of the Cotswold village of Winchcombe) is an originally twelfth-century mansion—the facade remains crenellated in the manner of the Middle Ages—that has seen changes over the centuries, none, that I can perceive, for the worse. Bearing the name of a line of Barons Sudeley, the Castle interior is Jacobite and

Tudor. Paintings by the likes of Constable, Turner, Rubens, and Van Dyck line the walls, and there are super four-poster bedrooms, including one with a bed on which Charles I overnighted. Walk through the beautifully tended gardens to the Gothic chapel, proceeding to the rear where you'll see the tomb of Henry VIII's sixth wife, Queen Catherine Parr; she survived her royal husband to marry Thomas Seymour and make Sudeley her final home. Café.

SETTLING IN

Randolph Hotel (Beaumont Street, Oxford) wisely retains its mellow Victorian facade (it went up in 1864) and the Victorian look of its interior, including a very grand central staircase and a lovely lobby lounge that's Oxford's top tea locale. Bedrooms vary in size; ideally, you want one in the front, facing the Ashmolean Museum. Locals like both main floor restaurant and basement Buttery—and with good reason. Busy bar. Trusthouse Forte. *First Class.*

Eastgate Hotel (High Street, Oxford) is an elderly house with little of esthetic value to show for its age and a central situation its major attribute. Twenty of the 44 adequate rooms have baths. Restaurant, bar that serves pub lunches. *Moderate.*

Royal Oxford Hotel (Park End Street, Oxford) is unpretentious and fairly central and has baths in 10 of its 23 neat rooms. Restaurant, bar that serves pub lunches. *Moderate.*

Cotswold Lodge Hotel (Banbury Road, Oxford) would follow the Randolph in my Oxford grouping if only it were central; still, there is frequent bus service to town. This is a pleasant place, occupying elderly, tastefully updated quarters in a capacious garden, with gracious public spaces, including a worth-knowing-about restaurant that serves top-value table d'hôte lunches and dinners. Almost half of the 45 rooms have showers in their baths. *First Class.*

Linton Lodge Hotel (Linton Road, Oxford): An agreeable low-slung complex—albeit away from the center—with good facilities that include a restaurant and a bar that obliges with casual lunches. Most of the 73 cheery rooms have baths with showers. *First Class.*

Isis Hotel (Iffley Road, Oxford): A budget house, but with some bath-equipped rooms, restaurant, bar. Not central. *Moderate.*

Cliveden Hotel (near Taplow, southeast of Oxford, and pronounced *Clihvden*, as in *lived*) is the originally seventeenth-century mansion of the then-Duke of Buckingham—largely rebuilt in the mid-nineteenth century by the then-Duke of Sutherland—that was sold to the Astor family at the turn of the present century, to become the seat of the much-chronicled "Cliveden Set," literary and political figures hosted between World Wars I and II by Viscount and Viscountess Astor (the latter, Virginia-born Nancy Langhorne, who became the first female member of Parliament). The mid-eighties saw this sumptuously furnished historic house—its formal gardens, on the banks of the Thames, are among Britain's finest—converted into a hotel by the same firm owning Brighton's Royal Crescent Hotel. Ordinary bedrooms are esthetic experience enough, but there are, as well, half a dozen suites named for distinguished occupants of Cliveden over the centuries; restaurant, bar-lounge, heated pool in a walled garden, tennis, and squash. *Luxury.*

The Feathers Hotel (Market Street, Woodstock) is nothing less than an utterly charming inn with seventeenth-century origins, which is a kind of country-house hotel, albeit in the heart of the village whose principal claim to fame is Blenheim Palace (above). Proprietor-manager Gordon Campbell Gray has deftly converted the venerable premises into an intimate fifteen-room house. Each room is individually decorated in traditional style with antique accents. The lounges are cozy, the staff cordial, and the restaurant so good that I accord it space in a later paragraph. *First Class.*

Bear Hotel (Park Street, Woodstock) is four centuries old with attractive public spaces that include a good restaurant and bar-lounge. There are 40-plus comfortable rooms, most (but not all) with bath. *First Class.*

Moat House International Hotel (Bridgefoot, Stratford-upon-Avon): The former Hilton International Stratford is a four-story complex centered in a five-acre garden at the Avon's edge, just opposite the Shakespeare Theatre, and a five-minute walk to the center of town. The 250 rooms and suites brightly blend contemporary with traditional, and baths are luxurious—all with showers, as well as tubs, and sinks with taps that mix hot and cold water, U.S.-style, praise be. There are restaurants—one luxurious, the other casual and a bar-lounge. *Luxury.*

Shakespeare Hotel (Chapel Street, Stratford-upon-Avon) may well be proud of its nine-gable Tudor facade. This half-timbered house has been a hotel at least since the mid-eighteenth century. All 66 nicely updated rooms are named for the Bard's plays or their characters, and there are showers in about half of their baths. Restaurant, pair of chatty bars. Trusthouse Forte. *Luxury.*

Alveston Manor Hotel (Clopton Bridge, Stratford-upon-Avon) is senior even to its sister hotel, the hardly young Shakespeare (above). The Alveston Manor's origins precede the Norman Conquest, but the present cluster of buildings are later and an interesting mix: core of the main house and the bar-paneling is Elizabethan; gables without, William and Mary; center windows, Queen Anne. Stay either in the wonderful main building or the contemporary wing across the garden, all of whose baths have showers. Beautiful restaurant, beautiful lobby, beautiful bar. Near the theater. Trusthouse Forte. *First Class.*

Falcon Hotel's (Chapel Street, Stratford-upon-Avon) ace in the hole is an Elizabethan main building whose bedrooms—limited in number—are not easy to come by. Bulk of accommodations are in a modern wing *way* to the rear. Restaurant, bar. Groups are a specialty. *First Class.*

Grosvenor House Hotel (Warwick Road, Stratford-upon-Avon) occupies a cluster of joined Regency houses on a central street. Convenient restaurant, bar-lounge, baths in most of the 61 pleasant rooms. *Moderate-First Class.*

Swan's Nest Hotel (Bridgefoot, Stratford-upon-Avon): In a garden of its own, opposite the theater, the attractive Swan's Nest has baths in 52 of its 70 smallish rooms. It also has a restaurant and bar. Trusthouse Forte. *Moderate.*

Stratford House (Sheep Street, Stratford-upon-Avon): This ex-Georgian town house's principal attribute is baths: seven of its ten small but nice rooms have them. Breakfast only. Friendly. *Moderate.*

Welcombe Hotel (Warwick Road, Stratford-upon-Avon): This mock-Tudor mansion of a hotel, set in its own park a couple of miles from Stratford, is of interest primarily, it would seem to me, to golfers, drawn to its 18-hole, par-70 course, for which hotel guests pay lower greens fees than outsiders. Look is Victorian country-house, with generous public spaces, a restaurant giving onto the garden, bar-lounge, big bedrooms in the main building, and a modern wing whose baths are shower equipped. If stairs are not for you, specify a ground-floor room when booking; there's no elevator. An Orient Express hotel. *Luxury.*

Lygon Arms Hotel (in the village called Broadway, in the Cotswolds): Britain abounds in coaching inns seeing service, contemporarily, as hotels. But none has a more distinguished pedigree than Douglas Barrington's Lygon Arms, which, though named for an eighteenth-century general, has origins in the sixteenth century. Visitors over the years have included both King Charles I and the very same under whose orders he was beheaded, Oliver Cromwell. The main Lygon building shelters cozy lounges and a snug bar—at their best when log fires are lit over tea on nippy afternoons and in the company of a drink on cool evenings. The distinguished restaurant, about which I write more in a later paragraph, occupies an appended Great Hall with a dramatic arched ceiling; wine bar-café, too. There are 67 rooms, with no two alike in the original ancient building—one has a priceless 1620 four-poster bed—the ones to aim for; the baths of most have showers. To sum up: the Cotswolds' best; and, for that matter, one of Britain's best. Not for nothing is the Lygon honored by membership in Leading Hotels of the World, Relais et Châteaux, and Prestige Hotels. *Luxury.*

Dormy House (Broadway, Cotswolds) is high atop Willersley Hill and isolated from the life of the village—restaurants, shops, and the like; it went up as a stone-walled farmhouse some three centuries ago. There are half a hundred full-facility bedrooms of varying design, attractive restaurant, and pleasant bar. But I prefer being down in Broadway proper. *First Class.*

Broadway Hotel (Broadway, Cotswolds) is a smaller, down-the-road neighbor of the Lygon Arms (above), occupying a half-timbered Elizabethan house, nicely modernized, with baths in virtually all of its two dozen rooms; dining room, bar. *Moderate-First Class.*

Swan Hotel (Bibury, Cotswolds) is a Cotswolds charmer: venerable with beamed and paneled public rooms, an adjacent river (the Coln) for atmosphere, and a couple of dozen comfortable rooms, with a proper restaurant and a bar whose buffet lunches are tasty. *Moderate.*

Old Manse Hotel (Bourton-on-the-Water, Cotswolds) is indeed aged: a mid-eighteenth-century structure in the prettiest part of a popular Cotswolds village—on the banks of the River Windrush. There are just eight traditional-style rooms, a locally reputed restaurant, and a lively bar-lounge. *Moderate.*

Cotswold House Hotel (Chipping Campden, Cotswolds): This classy Regency mansion is a charmer, from the colonnaded and chandeliered restaurant through to the two dozen rooms, many with bath, and one of which—old-movie fans, please note—is named for Sir C. Aubrey Smith, who was born on the premises. Cozy bar that's ideal for a snack lunch. Pretty garden, too. *Moderate-First Class.*

Noël Arms Hotel (Chipping Campden, Cotswolds) dates to the seventeenth century. It's warm and welcoming, and if you can manage it, snag Room 14, with a hand-carved four-poster that's as old as the hotel. Most of the 19 rooms have baths. The stone-walled restaurant is handsome, and the beamed bar (where casual lunches are served) is no less so. *Moderate-First Class.*

Manor House Hotel (Moreton-in-Marsh, Cotswolds) is a low-slung house that was originally built of local Cotswold stone in the seventeenth century. You feel at home immediately when you step into the lobby-lounge, as nice a spot for morning coffee or afternoon tea as you'll find in the area. The restaurant is good, and the white-walled bar friendly. Most of the 30 rooms—the more interesting are those of the original building, with others in a modern wing—have their own baths. Those in the back look over the hotel's garden, with the village church beyond. *Moderate-First Class.*

Redesdale Arms Hotel (Moreton-in-Marsh, Cotswolds): I wish that more than just under half of this inn's 13 rooms had baths. This is a onetime coaching inn out of the eighteenth century that retains its traditional ambience. Restaurant, two bars. *Moderate.*

Lords of the Manor Hotel (Upper Slaughter, Cotswolds): The name alone was enough to lure me. But the house, dating to the seventeenth century, is special, too, with a felicitous range of public rooms that include a competent restaurant and bar-lounge. There are 15 agreeable rooms, and the back yard has its own trout stream, wherein management invites you to try your luck as an angler. *First Class.*

DAILY BREAD
Wrens (Castle Street, Oxford): Thrust is French fare, and very tasty, too; interesting soups through grills (including steaks) and seafood, with the pastries deliciously Gallic, too. *First Class.*

Randolph Hotel Restaurants (Beaumont Street, Oxford): The Randolph is so central and its dining rooms (the main floor restaurant and the basement Buttery) so reliable, that I call them to your attention;

the former for its excellent-value, well-prepared lunches and dinners, the latter for hot plates and short orders. *Moderate-First Class.*

Elizabeth (St. Aldate's Street, Oxford) sounds considerably more British than it turns out to be, with the menu essentially Gallic. Try the poultry and seafood specialties—delicious. *First Class.*

Nosebag (St. Michael's Street, Oxford): The name is a bit off-putting, to be sure, but the cooking is much better than you would expect in a cafeteria-style operation, with all points of the Continent of Europe contributing dishes. Lunch through tea. *Moderate.*

Burlington Bertie's (High Street, Oxford): You mount the stairs for this rambling eatery, unexceptional as regards looks, but with well-priced daily specials, salads, and the variously stuffed baked—or jacket—potatoes that are so popular in Britain. Go up still another flight and you're in the same management's *Bogie's Pizza Parlour.* *Moderate.*

La Sorbonne (High Street, Oxford) has sensibly taken an academic name from the country of origin, in this academic city. The menu is bourgeois bistro; by that, I mean favorites like onion soup, *entrecôte grillée, coq au vin.* (There is a separately entered snack bar that accepts no credit cards, and is *Moderate.*) The restaurant proper is *First Class.*

Selfridges (Queen Street, Oxford) has not nearly the selection of restaurants as its Mother House in London; still, this department store offers the self-service Grosvenor Room and the café-like Bistro. Both are reliable and *Moderate.*

Head of the River (St. Aldate's Street at the River Isis, Oxford): Walk to the far end of Christ College and you nearly collide with this nineteenth-century structure, originally a warehouse and now embracing a restaurant with well-priced table d'hôte lunches and a pub-cum-terrace with hot and cold dishes, with a tearoom, as well, and—in summer—an ice cream parlor. *Moderate.*

Grapes (George Street, Oxford): A looker of a Victorian pub, at once central and congenial, with generous cold buffets at lunch; hot dishes, as well. *Moderate.*

Golden Cross (Cornmarket Street, Oxford): Half-timbered and medieval, this atmospheric pub serves up traditional English fare, lunch through dinner. *Moderate.*

Turf Tavern (Bath Place, Oxford)—a marvelously atmospheric pub dating to the thirteenth century; go for lunch. *Moderate.*

Feathers Hotel Restaurant (Market Street, Woodstock) is at once intimate (there are a dozen tables) and eye-filling (high-backed, deep-blue, upholstered chairs complement pale walls) and delicious, with Anglo-French specialties like hot leek *soufflé*, cream of pea and pear soup, and a venison/grouse terrine, among starters; and breast of duck in a honey sauce, whole lemon sole stuffed with a salmon mousse, and veal sweetbreads on a bed of spinach, among entrées. Desserts? I'm not going to divulge the ingredients of the Feathers's Highland Dream; you'll enjoy finding out for yourself. Order à la carte or from good-value prix-fixe lunch and dinner menus. *First Class.*

Bear Hotel (Park Street, Woodstock): Have an aperitif in the beamed bar and then—unless you're in the chips—the good-value table d'hôte lunch. *First Class.*

Warwick Grill (Moat House International Hotel, Bridgefoot, Stratford-upon-Avon): At once festive and friendly, Stratford's premier restaurant presents, artfully, a well-rounded choice of international specialties—smoked Scotch salmon, sautéed frogs' legs, or onion soup to start; panfried or grilled Dover sole, roast beef carved from a copper trolley, Scotch sirloin steak, or veal escallop, among the entrées; sweets flambéed at your table, if you like. Wine list is special. Dinner only. *Luxury.* (The same hotel's *Tavern* has a super hot-and-cold buffet— including roast beef or another hot dish—at lunch; other choices, too. *Moderate-First Class.*)

Alveston Manor Hotel Restaurant (Clopton Bridge, Stratford-upon-Avon): This perfectly beautiful restaurant, with its extraordinary ancient paneling, is the source of excellent-value table d'hôte lunches and (slightly pricier) dinners, with roasts—chicken, lamb, beef, duck— among the entrées. *First Class.*

Box Tree and River Terrace (Royal Shakespeare Theatre, Stratford-upon-Avon): Ideal for preperformance, the River Terrace, at ground level, affords river views, serves up surprisingly good pasta and other short orders, and is *Moderate.* Grander, upstairs, and a proper restaurant, the Box Tree features three-course dinners—game *pâté*, roast duck with sauce Grand Marnier, *crème brullée* or syllabub—at tabs that average out *First Class.*

Cobweb (Sheep Street, Stratford-upon-Avon): The two-floor Cobweb is a morning-coffee through afternoon-tea operation, with its table d'hôte lunches (as well as à la carte omelets, fish, and roasts), tasty. And see if you can pass by the bakery department; never less that 70 varieties of cakes and pastries. *Moderate.*

Marlowe's (High Street, Stratford-upon-Avon): The house special—steak, a baked potato, and trifle for dessert—is a winner in this attractive Elizabethan-era restaurant. *First Class.*

Opposition (Sheep Street, Stratford-upon-Avon) may not sound Italian, but its fare runs to spaghetti, cannelloni, and pizza. Italian wines. Brown and white checked cloths. *Moderate.*

Vintner (Sheep Street, Stratford-upon-Avon): Order a glass of the house wine, along with something substantial to eat; quiche and turkey pie are good choices. *Moderate.*

Pargetter's (Bridge Street, Stratford-upon-Avon) is the Stratford standby for afternoon tea—good cakes and sandwiches—or a snack. *Moderate.*

Thatch (Cottage Lane, Shattery, near Stratford-upon-Avon): Anne Hathaway's cottage took more of the morning than you anticipated and you want lunch? Thatch is, not surprisingly, thatched and, again not surprisingly, with English specialties. *Moderate.*

Lygon Arms Hotel Restaurant (Broadway, Cotswolds): The three-course table d'hôte lunches in this handsome environment—the room is a long gallery with a superbly arched ceiling—are at once delicious and reasonably priced; there is generally a roast—beef, lamb, pork, chicken, duck—among the entrées, with a choice of appetizers and one of the house's reputed desserts. Dinner is a good time for a splurge with the French-influenced à la carte. Wines are a Lygon specialty. In my experience, the Cotswolds' best restaurant—and one of Britain's best. *First Class-Luxury.*

Goblins Wine Bar (Lygon Arms Hotel, Broadway, Cotswolds): With its own entrance next door to the hotel's, Goblins is a sensible choice for a casual meal—soups, omelets, pizza. Wine by the glass or bottle. *Moderate.*

Hunters Lodge (Broadway, Cotswolds) is an impressive stone-walled house set back from the main Broadway street. The Swiss owner-chef's veal specialties are tasty, and the whole-wheat bread, served one-slice-per-diner at a time, is excellent. But illumination is by candlelight only—one lighted candle per occupied table, so that your dinner can be dark and gloomy, if business is not brisk. *First Class*.

Gallery (Broadway, Cotswolds): The three-course table d'hôte lunch is the buy, roast beef the entrée. Dinner is à la carte, with wide-ranging choices, grilled trout among them. *Moderate*.

Cotswold Café (Broadway, Cotswolds): A good bet for a luncheon is steak (they're the specialty) or bacon and eggs, served all day long. Dinner Saturday and Sunday only. *Moderate*.

Redesdale Arms Hotel Restaurant (Moreton-in-Marsh, Cotswolds) is handsomely traditional and especially tempting at dinner, when there is a three-course table d'hôte that might include avocado vinaigrette or baked mushrooms, followed by chicken Maryland or a veal cutlet, with sweets from a stacked trolley. Lunch is less elaborate in the restaurant and is also served, pub style, in the bar. *First Class-Moderate*.

Cotswold House Hotel (Chipping Campden, Cotswolds): Lovely things to eat in this lovely hotel. At dinner, roast beef is invariably on well-tabbed table d'hôte. Order lunch in the bar, à la carte, with choices including *pâté maison, coq au vin,* or bacon and cheese flan. *Moderate-First Class*.

Bakers Arms (Broad Campden, adjacent to Chipping Campden, Cotswolds): This formidable stone house in its own garden has been a pub for 200 years, although it's questionable if the food was so good early on as is now the case—homemade soups, quiche, and stuffed tomatoes, among the salads, and always the house special, smoked mackerel. *Moderate-First Class*.

George Inn (Winchcombe, Cotswolds): A capacious dormitory with a splendid beamed ceiling, used by religious pilgrims in the fifteenth century, is now the restaurant of this charming inn, at its best when candles light each table at dinner—a temptingly tabbed three-course table d'hôte. At midday, stop for a pub lunch in one of the two bars. *Moderate-First Class*.

AFTER DARK
Oxford Playhouse (Beaumont Street, Oxford) is the University-operated theater, with university productions and those of outside troupes, too.

New Theatre (George Street, Oxford) is another venue for plays and for seasons of visiting companies, English National Opera North among them.

Sheldonian Theatre (Broad Street, Oxford): Sir Christopher Wren designed the Sheldonian; it's used for concerts by such organizations as the Oxford University Orchestra, Oxford Orchestral Society, and Oxford Bach Choir. Still other concerts take place in Oxford's *Town Hall* (St. Aldate's Street).

Royal Shakespeare Theatre (Stratford-upon-Avon): The grand-daddy of the world's Shakespeare theaters—it goes back a century—the Royal Shakespeare Theatre, it should be pointed out, performs in London at the Barbican Centre for Arts and Conferences, as well as at its home base. Traditionally, there is a three-month spring Stratford season—April through June—and a summer season of several months' duration, starting in July. It should be made clear, too, that in Stratford there are performances both at the main theater, on the Avon, and in the company's little theater, called *The Other Place*, where non-Shakespeare (O'Casey's *Shadow of a Gunman*, for example) is performed, as well as works of the Bard. Caliber of the productions—invariably original, often bold, daring, and unconventional—is unsurpassed, and if you've the least interest in the theater or Shakespeare, you want to experience this company. If you can, book before arriving in Stratford; you may do so by telephone, using your American Express Card—from across the Atlantic. Call 0789-297129. Note, too, that there are one-night packages out of London for Stratford theatergoers; ask your travel agent.

INCIDENTAL INTELLIGENCE

Getting to Stratford by train from London, you must change at a town called Watford. If you're concentrating on the Big Two universities, note that there is daily Oxford-Cambridge/Cambridge-Oxford bus service; worth knowing about, as train connections between these two points are, to understate, inconvenient. *Further information:* Oxford Tourist Information Centre, St. Aldate's Chamber, St. Aldate's Street; Stratford-upon-Avon Tourist Information Centre, Judith Shakespeare's House, High Street.

18

St. Ives

And the Cornwall Peninsula

BACKGROUND BRIEFING

Cornwall's inadvertent publicists have, perhaps, done too good a job. By that, I mean even though the southwestern peninsula of Cornwall reads beautifully in novels—and even though there can be no denying the splendor of its rockbound, cliff-backed, cove-tucked, beach-bordered coasts—the fact remains that this most exotic of England's counties is not necessarily the stuff of which overseas visitors' vacations are made.

The preoccupation of writers as disparate as, say, Daphne du Maurier and Virginia Woolf with Cornwall is understandable. Within half a day out of London, one is able to experience the kind of almost foreign remoteness that, elsewhere in Britain, can be likened to the considerably more distant Highlands of Scotland. Not even Wales, with its still-spoken native language, connotes any more sense of distance from the heartland of the kingdom.

Cornwall's geographic and cultural distinctiveness are its pluses. Ancient Greeks traded for its tin. And Cornishmen, with the Celtic language (akin to languages of Brittany and Wales) they spoke well into the eighteenth century, fought off Saxon settlement longer than their neighbors to the east. Converted early on to Catholicism, they resisted, as well, Henry VIII's Reformation.

They are, of course, Britons, like their countrymen today (tradition has long had it that the eldest son of the monarch has among his titles Duke of Cornwall), but it is to their credit that they remain essentially Cornish—farmers and miners and villagers, by and large deeply religious, albeit, to use the British term, nonconformist. For although they did not welcome with open arms the sixteenth-century's Church of England, they accepted, in the eighteenth century, the less ritualistic preaching of John Wesley.

Wesley traveled the duchy—it is to this day called by that term—more extensively than did most contemporary tourists; it is today more Methodist than Anglican. And it is a warm and friendly part of the world. But tourism is geared to the Briton from harsher climes in search of a bit of sunshine. By and large, the visitor's Cornwall is a network of coastal resorts equipped for vacationers in the mass, which means—given the persistent aversion among working-class Britons to the private bath—hotels that do not, for the most part, meet the needs of the international traveler. A major exception is the resort that has more than facilities to recommend it. St. Ives could win—not without fierce competition, to be sure—the Cornwall Natural Beauty Sweepstakes.

ON SCENE
Lay of the Land: Look at a map of this westernmost part of England. St. Ives's convenient situation is at once apparent. It is on the rock-bound—and more magnificent—north shore of Cornwall (the south coast terrain is less elevated and more tranquil), but it is, at the same time, westerly enough to be close to landmark Land's End and south shore towns like Penzance and Falmouth, with the airport at Newquay (the north coast resort that's Cornwall's biggest), the ruins of King Arthur's castle at Tintagel, and the interior town of Truro (the closest Cornwall comes to having a metropolis) within easy driving distance.

St. Ives quite literally—and stunningly—descends a mountain (the longtime leader of a hotel is at the summit) to a jumble of narrow commercial streets fronting its central quay (the railway station is in this area). You take your choice from among three popular beaches: central Porthminster, a honey of a natural crescent, rarely tranquil in summer, but not uninteresting, with cruise boats that take passengers on tours of adjacent waters; Porthgwidden, to the east; and westerly Porthmeor, directly on the Atlantic, with strong surf its draw.

Barbara Hepworth Memorial Museum (Fore Street): Writers who frequented St. Ives in the past—D. H. Lawrence and Virginia Woolf, for two—have left nothing tangible as reminders. But contemporary sculptor Dame Barbara Hepworth, who settled in St. Ives just before World War II (at first with her husband, painter Ben Nicholson), remained until she died in a 1975 fire in the home that is now a museum of internationally acclaimed work. Art and design greats like Alexander Calder, Marcel Breuer, and Walter Gropius were frequent visitors to the Hepworth house and garden. Now admirers beeline to see not only personal memorabilia, but a generous sampling of the Hepworth oeuvre—a score of starkly nonobjective monoliths, most

with the trademark Hepworth hole in their centers—grace the ver-
dantly foliaged garden. (And yes, you *will* recognize other Hepworths
as you amble about town; the artist's works—her own personal gifts—
pop up at Guildhall, at the bus terminal, and in the Parish Church,
among other places.)

New Gallery (Norway Square) is a desanctified church housing the
elder of the two principal St. Ives artists' outlets, wherein you'll find
representational works; on scene for about half a century.

Penwith Gallery (Back Road West) is the showplace for contemporary art created by St. Ives-based painters and sculptors.

St. Ives Museum (Street-an-Pol) conveys a nice bit of background on
the town and on Cornwall's tin miners, fishermen, smugglers, and
farmers—maps and documents, drawings and photos, and assorted
bits and pieces, many of considerable age.

St. Ives Parish Church (Fore Street) is the town's most elaborate—
and most venerable—interior, fifteenth-century Gothic with a granite
tower, flanked by the kind of carved stone cross seen often in Ireland.
Within, you want to see the Hepworth *Madonna and Child*—very
much of this century—and contrast it with the dissimilar sculpture in
the ancient choir. (The Parish Church is Anglican. There are, however, nearly a score of nonconformist churches—or chapels, as they are
called in Britain—Methodist and otherwise. That named for John
Wesley, Methodism's founder and a frequent eighteenth-century visitor to St. Ives, is on Chapel Street.)

Land's End (an 18-mile drive—through countryside strangely similar
to the bleak terrain of Ireland's Connemara—southwest along the
coast from St. Ives) is where England stops. By that, I mean its westernmost point—as far as you can go. Gift shops and snack bars
provide not necessarily welcome clutter. But the views along this
rocky eminence are so striking that you forgive them their trespasses.

Penzance (15 miles south of St. Ives) has nary a trace of either Gilbert
or Sullivan, much less their pirates. Though hardly a beautiful town,
it's strikingly situated, with waterfront Penzance Promenade affording views, seaward, of towering St. Michael's Mount (below) and, in
the opposite direction, of the substantial Gothic tower of *St. Mary the
Virgin Church*, on a hillside, surrounded by its own immense graveyard and somber stone houses.
A domed temple—you are surprised to see it is the local Lloyds

Bank branch—dominates shop-lined Market Jew Street. The *Egyptian House* (Chapel Street) boasts an elegant 1830 facade, recently restored and fronting a National Trust shop and information center. And *Penlee House* (Penlee Park) is inspectable if only for the graphic—and artistic—way in which it portrays Penzance's past. Signs along Penzance Promenade make it easy to find the pier from which ships sail to the *Scilly Isles* (below).

Scilly Isles, a cluster 25 miles off the coast, of which *St. Mary's* (to which there is helicopter service from Penzance) is the largest and best equipped for visitors. An island one and a half miles wide by two and a half miles long is hardly giant, but St. Mary's is the site of the Scillys' "capital," tiny *Hugh Town,* a lovely beach, the islands' best hotels, golf links, and excursion boats to others of the Scilly group.

St. Michael's Mount (just off the coast from Penzance) is a translation—not only in words, but physically as well—of Brittany's Mont Saint-Michel, a medieval castle perched atop a mini-mountain on a mini-island. Originally a monastery—for a period it was actually owned by monks of France's Mont Saint-Michel—it eventually became a residence. When the tide is out, you walk over, across a causeway, from the mainland; when it's in, you go by ferry. (Is there another British country house to which access is by boat?) The best parts of the interior are the monks' chapel and refectory. But it's the setting—no less romantic than its French counterpart's—that makes St. Michael's Mount special. National Trust.

Tintagel, the Cornish north coast's most romantic destination, straddles the summit of an extraordinary seaside cliff. There are good beaches. But you go because of the legendary association with King Arthur. There are remains—just barely—of an early Celtic monastery. The fifteenth-century castle is also in a ruined state. But what ruins! Setting is a headland high above the spray of waves beating against a rocky shore. As you look about—recognizing outlines of a great hall and chapel—you find yourself believing the Arthur legend, quite convinced that the Round Table now on display in Winchester (Chapter 21) was originally in this spot. Down below, on the town's High Street, pay your respects at *King Arthur Hall,* where the legends come to life in a series of exhibits. End at the National Trust-operated *Old Post Office,* which was a medieval manor house before it entered the postal service.

Truro is a lively, albeit ancient, community that, about a century back, decided it was disgraceful that neither it nor any town in

Cornwall had a Church of England cathedral. The cornerstone for *Truro Cathedral* (St. Mary's Street) was laid by Edward VII while he was Prince of Wales, and the nave was blessed by his son before he became George V. The style is a nineteenth-century adaptation—and very creditable—of the first of this country's three Gothic styles, Early English, with a touch of the later Decorated and Perpendicular, as well. The cathedral—with two front towers and a higher rear one—towers over Truro. Within, you want to notice the lovely detail of the carved-stone screen at the high altar and the bishop's throne, one of the most elaborate in the kingdom. The *County Museum and Art Gallery* (River Street) goes back to the early nineteenth century, and its painting collection—most especially works by English artists, including Lely, Kneller, Hogarth, Gainsborough, Constable, and Millais—is remarkable. Do have a look at Cornishman John Opie's eighteenth-century portraits and at exhibits having to do with matters Cornish—a dazzling display of local minerals, most especially.

SETTLING IN

Treganna Castle Hotel, located in its own park high atop St. Ives, is King of the Mountain—and has been since it went up, originally as a private home. But it's been a hotel for more than a century. Crenellated mock-Gothic, it is among Britain's more sublimely situated hotels, surrounded by broad lawns that make a very gradual descent to town and sea. One ample-size, traditional-style lounge leads into another; there's a commendable restaurant and a congenial bar. Rooms are bright and airy, but not necessarily overlarge. You want to insist on a front one, so that you're not denied the sublime view. Outdoor pool, nine-hole golf course, tennis, squash, badminton, croquet. *First Class.*

Porthminster Hotel overlooks St. Ives's Porthminster Beach. This is a gracious old house modernized with good taste and good sense, with 52 pleasant rooms, the front ones with smashing views. A congenial cocktail lounge leads from the lobby, and there is a pleasant restaurant, too. *First Class.*

Chy-An-Drea Hotel lies just above St. Ives's Porthminster Beach and nicely mixes elderly with contemporary. Some rooms have modern seaview balconies; most have baths. There's a cozy bar-lounge, and the restaurant is special. *Moderate-First Class.*

Garrack Hotel (Higher Ayr, St. Ives): Just under half of the 18 rooms in this agreeable budget hotel have baths. Choose the main house or the newer annex. Restaurant, bar. *Moderate.*

Queen's Hotel (The Promenade, Penzance): Nicely located, seaside, this is a traditional-style house, 50 of whose 70 rooms have baths. (Ask for a front one, to see the sea!) Restaurant, bar. *First Class.*

Lamorna Cove Hotel (Lamorna Cove, Penzance): You're out of town at the Lamorna Cove, but the setting is easy to take—a five-acre garden with the cove of the title down below. Seafood is the restaurant specialty. Swim in the outdoor pool. Play golf nearby. Fish, if you like. *Moderate-First Class.*

Meudon Hotel (Mawnan Smith, just south of Falmouth): This relaxing, garden-encircled country house of a hotel overlooks a secluded white-sand beach. The picture-window restaurant is excellent—local lobsters, oysters, and other seafood are its pride. Thirty of the 38 rooms have baths. Golf nearby. *First Class.*

Green Bank Hotel (Harbourside, Falmouth) is as good a reason as any for overnighting in the heart of this well-situated south coast resort. Rooms are updated and tasteful, and so are the restaurant and bars at water's edge. *Moderate.*

Bell Rock Hotel (St. Mary's, Scilly Isles) leads the pack on pretty St. Mary's: an elderly house, 15 of whose 17 rooms have baths. Restaurant, bar. Swimming pool. *Moderate-First Class.*

DAILY BREAD
Treganna Castle Hotel Restaurant (St. Ives): Even if you're not staying here, this historic hotel—high above St. Ives—warrants a visit for a meal, preferably dinner, following drinks in the bar. Stick to unsauced dishes—roast beef, lamb chops, and the like—and you'll be pleased. *First Class.*

Chy-An-Drea Hotel Restaurant (St. Ives): The Chy-An-Drea is nothing like as atmospheric as the Treganna (above). Lure in this attractive room is the excellent-value table d'hôte. Very pleasant. *Moderate-First Class.*

Outrigger (Street-an-Pol, St. Ives) is intimate in size—and look— with a nicely French-influenced bill of fare, the range guinea fowl in port through seafood *crêpes* and *steak au poivre*. Interesting wines. Dinner only. *First Class.*

Le Matou (St. Andrew's Street, St. Ives) translates as The Tomcat. Never mind, it's the authentic French cooking that interests you, as well it might, with the *boeuf bourguinonne* among the entrées, along with well-prepared fish. Dinner only. *First Class.*

Blue Haven (overlooking Porthminster Beach, St. Ives) is a reliable— and agreeable—source of sustenance, breakfast through casual lunch, through afternoon tea. *Moderate.*

Red Lion (Fore Street, St. Ives) is an unassuming, stone-walled, centrally situated pub. Go for a bar lunch or a beer. *Moderate.*

Admiral Benbow (Chapel Street, Penzance): Shades of *Treasure Island* and the inn of that name in the Stevenson novel! This Benbow drew local smugglers when it opened two centuries back. Now, clientele is more respectable, drawn by solid English fare—including seafood. *Moderate.*

Penzance Buttery (Modrab Street, Penzance): A bright-look, scrubby-upped source of good-value lunches, snacks, and afternoon tea. *Moderate.*

Gorton's (Pydar Street, Truro): Just the ticket for lunch in conjunction with a visit to Truro Cathedral (nearby) and the County Museum. To order: the reasonably tabbed table d'hôte built around solid entrées. *Moderate.*

INCIDENTAL INTELLIGENCE

The regional airport is at Newquay. *Further information:* St. Ives Tourist Information Centre, Guildhall, Street-an-Pol; Penzance Tourist Information Centre, Alvert Street; Truro Tourist Information Centre, Municipal Building, Boscawen Street.

19

Salisbury
And the Mansions of Wiltshire

BACKGROUND BRIEFING
There are others which would fill the bill as well—nearby Winchester, undervisited Worcester in the west Midlands, or northerly Durham. But if a single place name conjures up the prototype of the English cathedral town it is Salisbury. An early nineteenth-century painter who wandered south from East Anglia—John Constable by name—to paint Salisbury Cathedral, is largely responsible for this state of affairs. All the world appears to know the Constable oils of the single-pinnacle church, cows grazing contentedly on the banks of the River Avon, out back.

But credit first where it is due: To its great credit, the south-of-England town has not let its universal celebrity spoil it. Salisbury was my first English Cathedral town; I first knew it more than a quarter century back. The chaps who run the cathedral have, to be sure, become more money-conscious over the years. (You line up to buy a ticket now, as for a movie or a circus.) And the proportion of private baths has increased somewhat in the hotels. But, otherwise, Salisbury remains a good-looking, essentially ancient, nonintellectual market town, with only the Cathedral spire creating any semblance of a skyline.

Salisbury came about solely as a consequence of its cathedral, and only after a site a few miles away was found wanting. It happened long ago. A cathedral to serve the region had been built in a settlement called Old Sarum in the eleventh century. But by the early thirteenth, clerics in charge were unhappy. There was not enough water to create a plentiful supply. Winds appeared to blow ceaselessly (Old Sarum, now a flat mound of ruins, but still visitable, is elevated and exposed), and soldiers in the adjacent garrison were bothersome, even insolent. An appeal went out to the Pope in Rome for permission to build anew, nearby. It was granted. The site selected—New Sarum—is today's Salisbury, with the River Avon at the Cathedral's side and waters of three other rivers converging nearby.

Few English cathedrals were built so quickly. Foundation stones were laid in 1220, and, in 1225, services were being conducted in what is now the cathedral apse, in the Lady Chapel. Little more than half a century later, the building was complete, unique in pre-Reformation England in that it is essentially of a single style—Early English Gothic—and the result of a solitary building project, not a detached series of stops and starts over a period of centuries.

ON SCENE

Lay of the Land: The grid design of Salisbury's medieval planners remains today the core of town. Check into a central hotel and you may walk all about, effortlessly and pleasantly, utilizing as a landmark the spire of the Cathedral. It is surrounded by the partially walled, parklike Cathedral Close, dotted with historic buildings and flanked by a ring of streets—Bishop's Walk on the east, Broad and West walks on the west, De Vaux Place on the south, and North Walk. From this last, north-south High Street is but steps distant. Midpoint of the grid is Market Square, for centuries the site every Tuesday and Saturday of one of England's most color-drenched public markets.

Salisbury Cathedral (West Walk): Cows no longer graze the banks of the Avon, but if Constable were to return today he could paint the Cathedral quite as he had in the early nineteenth century. Its 404-foot spire—loftiest such in England—has no vertical competition. And from every direction—looking east from the square of emerald lawn in the massive cloister, north from the bucolic banks of the Avon, west from across the expanse of the Close—the Cathedral is serenely beautiful.

Entering it is something else again: very much in the pattern of the late twentieth century. You queue up to pay what is technically a "voluntary contribution," but what amounts—unless you resist, which, of course, most people do not—to an admission fee. The cashier expects you to fork over the "suggested" amount, which is higher here than anywhere else in Britain, except London's Westminster Abbey. (Of the provincial cathedrals, the only other one I know that has a cashier at the door to take "voluntary contributions" is Lincoln, where, however, the procedure appears far less commercial—and more personable—than at Salisbury.) Awarded a ticket by the cashier, you pass by unattractively lettered signs indicating a restaurant, shops, and rest rooms, following a route that leads you—finally—into the cathedral proper.

Your first impression—looking down the very long, unobstructed nave—is of architecture that is immediately understandable. Because it was erected almost entirely in a six-decade span to Early English Gothic designs, it comes together effortlessly, and it functions well—in the shape of a double cross (there is a main transept where the choir begins and still another transept in the midst of the choir). Highlights present themselves as one walks about: bishops' tombs in the side aisles; bishop's throne dominating the dark wood of the choir; delicate marble pillars supporting vaults of the Lady Chapel; one of four surviving copies of the original *Magna Carta* signed by King John in 1215, in the Morning Chapel; and—leading from the unusually large cloister—the octagonal Chapter House, built as the meeting place of the Dean and Canons who operate the cathedral, with fan vaulting surrounding a single central column and Old Testament scenes depicted in an extraordinary group of eight-century-old sculptures forming a frieze.

Salisbury and South Wiltshire Museum (The Close): After more than a century in an aged, though undistinguished, onetime residence in another part of town, the museum moved, in 1981, into a superb stone mansion just opposite the Cathedral. Though with medieval origins—the porch dates to 1450—King's House is essentially Jacobean. Indeed, its name comes from two visits paid by James I in the early seventeenth century. There's a lot here. Concentrate on the section having to do with Stonehenge before you visit that near-Salisbury prehistoric ruin (below). There are objects from Old Sarum as well: excellent glass and ceramics, seventeenth- through nineteenth-century, and—most delightful—paintings and drawings, including a not-to-be-missed pair of views of the interior of the Cathedral just across the way, by Turner.

Mompesson House (The Close): Queen Anne was in the second year of her reign when, in 1701, the Mompesson family, grown rich as merchants, built their house just opposite the Cathedral. Mompesson delights for two reasons. First is its livable scale—arched entrance hall, trio of downstairs reception rooms, and handsome east bedroom. Second is the plasterwork, exuberant and original, in every room of the house. There's also a collection—numbering more than 300—of English eighteenth-century drinking glasses. National Trust.

Malmesbury House (The Close) has, like Mompesson, a Queen Anne facade, although parts of it are considerably older. The stairwell leading from the entrance hall appears quite literally to float to the floor above. The library is fanciful Gothic Revival out of the mid-eighteenth century. And, throughout, as in Mompesson, the plasterwork is extraordinary. Traditionally limited opening-hours.

Sarum St. Thomas Church (St. Thomas Street) is the fifteenth-century successor to a thirteenth-century frame structure, erected to serve as a place of worship for builders of Salisbury Cathedral. The present Sarum St. Thomas is not without attributes: dramatically high beamed ceiling, elaborate Lady Chapel, organ that was originally a gift of King George III to the nearby cathedral.

Trinity Hospital (Trinity Street) is Salisbury's least-touted beauty spot. A plaque explains that it was founded in 1370, built as we see it in 1702, and restored in 1909. Note the ancient sundial over the front door as you move along inside to the chapel—tiny, square, exquisite—at the far end of a dollhouse-size courtyard.

Wilton House (three miles west of Salisbury): Ancestors of the occupant, No. 17 in a long line of Earls of Pembroke, entertained guests (George II was one such) in half a dozen state rooms designed in the seventeenth century by the school of Inigo Jones. They are all brilliant: Corner Room, with its Rubens and Lotto paintings; Colonnade Room, with works by Reynolds and Lawrence; and the chunky gilded furniture, a collaborative effort of William Kent and Thomas Chippendale, in the Double Cube Room—one of the most famous interiors in Britain. It is so named because it is exactly twice as long as it is wide. Paintings lining its walls are mostly by Van Dyck. And its gilded ceiling is no less notable. If you have time for but one country house near Salisbury, it should be Wilton. Restaurants.

Stonehenge (10 miles north of Salisbury): It may leave you cold, but as long as you're in the neighborhood, pay your respects at this most significant monument of antiquity in Britain; some three quarters of a million visitors are curious enough to make the pilgrimage annually. Here's what they see: an outer ditch, dating to 2,000 years before Christ, surrounding a circle of stone slabs—as high as 20 feet—and within that circle a horseshoe-shaped group of additional stones, the lot going back to 1650 B.C. In the center, lying flat, is the Altar Stone, and surrounding that monument is a series of fifty-six holes, called after their seventeenth-century discoverer, John Aubrey. They are believed to go back to 2400 B.C.: human remains were found in some thirty-odd of them, as recently as 1926. Experts believe the pattern of their spacing indicates that Stonehenge had an early function as a sundial, and it is further believed that it was the site of sun worshiping ceremonies in what was essentially a religious center. Excavations have continued at Stonehenge regularly. Department of the Environment.

Braemore House (nine miles east of Salisbury): There are bigger and better-known Elizabethan country houses, to be sure, but none with which I am familiar with a more consistently high standard of furnishings. Take your time as you go through a dozen main floor and upstairs rooms. Each—great hall, blue and west drawing room, dining room, bedrooms—is treasure-filled, as regards furniture (sixteenth- and seventeenth-century but some eighteenth, as well), paintings (Van Dyck and Teniers are among the artists), Brussels tapestries, on through to what has to be one of the great collections of antique copper utensils—beautifully polished!—in the kitchen. Chances are, your guide will be Braemore's knowledgeable owner, Sir Hamilton Westrow, Bart.

Stourhead (about 27 miles west of Salisbury) is, I should point out, as requisite for garden buffs as for aficionados of architecture and interiors. The seventeenth-century landscape paintings of France's Claude Lorrain inspired Stourhead's eighteenth-century designers. Recall Greek temples perched atop hills, with well-placed lakes in the foreground? Builder Henry Hoare scattered Stourhead's gardens with monuments of interest—ancient grotto, medieval cross, slender tower, domed temple. He created a lake, crossed it with a stone bridge, and bordered its shores with flowers. If you walk the gardens first, the Palladian house on high can seem anticlimactic—until you step inside, and see who had a hand in the interiors: Angelica Kauffman was among the painters. There is woodwork carved by Grinling Gibbons. And the younger Chippendale designed much of the furniture. National Trust.

Longleat House (25 miles west of Salisbury and nicely combined with Stourhead, above) is—along with Woburn Abbey (Chapter 2)—about as unabashedly commercial an operation as is to be found among country houses in Britain. Still, if you concentrate on the Marquess of Bath's sixteenth-century house alone, the only thing you will regret about your visit is the way groups are rushed—in the company of a guide—from room to room, rarely with enough time to savor the contents. Longleat is palatially scaled, with its full share of fine furniture and paintings, the range of artists Titian and Van Dyck to Sargent and Graham Sutherland. Few rooms are without interest, but some hold excitement—the tapestry-hung saloon and the leather-walled state dining room, especially. Restaurants include one with a hardly discreet exterior sign of an ice-cream manufacturer that I could do without.

SETTLING IN

White Hart Hotel (St. John Street, Salisbury) is a welcoming eighteenth-century inn, not as grand as its colonnaded facade suggests, but still the best in town. Fifty of the 70 rooms have baths (15 of those with showers, as well). Prettiest views of the Cathedral are from front rooms in the main building, but the nicest rooms are in the relatively recent addition. The restaurant is attractive and reliable, but the bar's lunches (not cooked in the hotel kitchen, but sent in) are to be avoided. Trusthouse Forte. *First Class.*

Red Lion Hotel (Guilford Street, Salisbury): If its facade is elegantly Georgian, still other parts of this charming hotel date to the Middle Ages, including half-timbering in the restaurant and some of the bedrooms. Thirty of the 55 rooms have baths, 15 of these with showers. The bar is atmospheric, and tea in the lounge is a treat. *First Class.*

Rose & Crown Hotel (Harnham Road, Salisbury) is half-timbered— and enviably situated, with views of the Avon and the Cathedral. There are a popular restaurant, a cozy bar, and antiques-accented rooms in the lovely antique of a main building; rooms with more modern baths are in the new wing. *Moderate.*

Cathedral Hotel (Milford Street, Salisbury) is an across-the-street neighbor of the Red Lion (above), albeit without its patina or, for that matter, its facilities. Still, rooms are comfortable, a number have baths, and casual lunches are served in the bar. *Moderate.*

County Hotel (Bridge Street, Salisbury) lies alongside the River Avon, embraces no less than five bars—no one goes thirsty at the County— and two restaurants. Not all rooms have baths. *Moderate.*

DAILY BREAD

Haunch of Venison (Minster Street, Salisbury): Allow enough time at the Haunch for a premeal libation in one of the bars on the ground floor of this restaurant, whose records indicate it has been on the scene since about 1320. Soak in the atmosphere before you go up the stairs for lunch or dinner, à la carte. Of course, you may have haunch of venison, but consider Scotch salmon, roast lamb, beef, or other English standbys. Good wines. *First Class.*

Provençal (Market Place, Salisbury) offers no-nonsense bistro cooking, with the flavor of the country south of La Manche—snails or onion soup, *coq au vin* or *boeuf bourguinonne*. Sensibly priced wines. *First Class.*

Burke's Bar & Buttery (New Street, Salisbury) may not sound like a source of creditable lasagna or cannelloni. But it is. Setting is a fine old house, and there are non-Italian options, too. *Moderate.*

New Inn (New Street, Salisbury) is a neighbor of Burke's (above), and it, too, occupies attractively ancient quarters. It was new in the thirteenth century, according to management. Solid English fare, nicely presented. *Moderate.*

House of Steps (High Street, Salisbury) is indicated for a cream tea, morning coffee cake, or a soup-and-salad lunch. *Moderate.*

Market Inn (Market Place, Salisbury): Just the ticket for a satisfying pub lunch—say, ploughman's or cold meats and salad, with beer to accompany. Long established. *Moderate.*

AFTER DARK
Salisbury Playhouse (Fisherton Street, Salisbury) is, unlike so much else in Salisbury, strikingly contemporary—with a full program of plays and other entertainment, including pantomime. Both restaurant and bar are open to the public for lunch and dinner on performance nights.

INCIDENTAL INTELLIGENCE

Further information: Salisbury Tourist Information Centre, Endless Street.

20

Southampton
And the South Coast

BACKGROUND BRIEFING
My first visit to Southampton was pretty much door-to-door, from the creaky old Cunard pier in New York to then-busy docks in the city that had for long been Europe's premier passenger port. My destination was the University of Southampton. From the ship, I simply taxied to Highfield Hall on the campus and unpacked.

It would not be that direct today. The jet has replaced the luxury liner as the major means of access to Britain for North Americans. (Only the *Queen Elizabeth 2* [Chapter1] maintains a proper schedule of transatlantic crossings, when it's not off cruising in other oceans and climes.)

Still, even during its Golden Age of steam, the pity of Southampton was that not all that many arriving passengers gave it even 24 hours of their time. They went from the pier to a special boat train and then immediately north to not-far-distant London. Take it from a former student at the local university: This major Hampshire city warrants attention.

Given its situation—on the body of water called the Solent, facing into the English Channel, but with the Isle of Wight positioned before it as a welcome natural obstruction against nasty weather—it is hardly surprising that Southampton was singled out for maritime prowess (and accompanying urban eminence) as early as the start of the Christian era, when the Romans came to Britain. Their settlement—*Clausentum*—evolved by the eighth century into the Saxons' *Hamtun;* two centuries later "Suth"—or South—was added as a prefix to distinguish the southerly city from another Hampton to the north.

The basic town plan developed after William the Conqueror landed. His successors developed a port of consequence, with merchant princes following to make additional contributions to it. Although nearby

Portsmouth thrived during this period essentially as a naval base, Southampton played its full share in the Hundred Years War and ancillary Anglo-French conflicts. As Plantagenet kings were succeeded by those of the houses of Lancaster (a treason trial in Shakespeare's *Henry V* is believed to have taken place in Southampton's still-functioning Red Lion pub), York, and Tudor, the city grew richer. And New World visitors want to remember that the Pilgrims first set sail from Southampton (a monument commemorates the event) in April 1620, with their intermediary stop in Plymouth necessitated because the *Mayflower's* then-sister ship needed repairs. A nearby plaque honors the two million U.S. troops who sailed from Southampton after D-Day, 1944.

Only when international trade patterns changed, with the entry of Continental Europeans into New World colonization, did Southampton's fortunes begin to suffer. But they revived. The late eighteenth and early nineteenth centuries saw the town vie with Brighton as a fashionable resort. The still-top-class Dolphin Hotel dates from that period, and Jane Austen lived for a period in Castle Square. By 1840, there was rail service linking London with the port of Southampton, increasingly expanded as the Royal Family (beginning with Queens Victoria and Alexandra while they were princesses) went down to dedicate new piers.

The marvel of the city is its felicitous rebuilding, following extraordinary devastation by World War II bombing. Miraculously, enough ancient monuments remained, so that planners were able to use them as a nucleus for refashioning the city center much more successfully than was the case in also-damaged Portsmouth. Southampton serves well as a focal point for exploration of other noteworthy South Coast points—Portsmouth, the Isle of Wight, Bournemouth, Dorchester, and the Channel Islands—all but the last included in this chapter.

ON SCENE

Lay of the Land: Southampton's High Street, running north from the waters of the Solent, is the street with which to orient yourself. At its southern tip, it leads to waterfront monuments—the Pilgrim Monument in West Gate at Mayflower Park; ancient structures with contemporary functions, including the Wool House and God's House Tower; and, of course, the docks, for sailings transatlantic, to the Continent, and to the Isle of Wight. Modern Southampton is to High Street's north. At venerable Bargate, it becomes a perky, department-store-filled pedestrian shopping area, gradually changing its name to Above Bar Street, where it leads to the Civic Centre complex, with the Railroad Station due west and the University of Southampton in a modern northern quarter.

Southampton Art Gallery (Civic Centre) ranks, in my estimation, with those of Aberdeen and Leicester in the top rank of art museums in medium-size British cities. The setting—vast and starkly arched— is a stunner, but it's the paintings you go for: a cluster of luminous Italian Renaissance masterworks, including an altarpiece, *The Coronation of the Virgin*, by Allegretto Nuzi, and a *Madonna and Child* from the Venetian studio of Giovanni Bellini; Britons, Lely through Romney, Turner, and Constable; pre-Raphaelites like Burne-Jones on to the very contemporary David Hockney; Low Countries representation from Ruisdael and Jordaens; and—ranking with the early Italians—the later French, David, Corot, Sisley, Pissarro, Monet, Renoir, Rouault, and Vuillard.

Tudor House (St. Michael's Square) is ancient Southampton at its most evocative: a half-timbered structure, originally—in the fourteenth century—three separate houses. You enter a Great Hall and go on to what has been a dining room, with minstrel's gallery and original carved-stone fireplace. Exhibits bring to life Southampton's past—paintings, furniture, even musical instruments. Early occupants? Legend says Henry VIII accompanied one of his six queens— Anne Boleyn—to Tudor House and that Philip II lodged in the house en route from Spain for his ill-fated 1554 marriage, in nearby Winchester Cathedral (Chapter 21), to Henry's daughter Queen Mary I, just a quarter-century before Philip's Armada was defeated by the fleet of Mary's half-sister, Elizabeth I. Philip II is believed to have attended High Street's *Holy Bond Church*, bombed in 1940, and in its ruined state a World War II memorial to Britain's Merchant Marine.

St. Michael's Church (St. Michael's Square) is, at its oldest, eleventh-century. It went up shortly after the Norman Conquest, but is now mostly somewhat younger, with thirteenth-century chapels and much fifteenth-century work. To note: the font, dating to 1170, of limestone from Tournai, in Belgium.

Wool House (Bugle Street) is so called because medieval merchants stored English wool under its roof in anticipation of export to the Continent. It has been restored and converted into the city's Maritime Museum. There are models of the port's ships over the centuries. Having made my first two transatlantic crossings on the old Cunarder, *Queen Mary*, you can understand that my favorite is the miniature of that Art Deco masterwork.

Bargate Museum (High Street): The city's north gate in the Middle Ages (Elizabeth I was greeted there by the mayor in 1591), Bargate now sees service as a repository of municipal historic lore, armor, pottery, and documents—medieval through World War II. The arched Gothic windows are beauties.

Portsmouth (15 miles southeast of Southampton) is Southampton's major urban Hampshire rival. They are both maritime cities, about the same size (in the 200,000 population category), and rebuilt after dreadful World War II devastation by German bombers. I am happier with the geography of Southampton; it is more cohesive, with a concentrated, easy-to-comprehend central area. Portsmouth spreads itself out, not only within its own boundaries, but to an adjacent resort, Southsea, with its myriad hotels and bed-and-breakfast houses.

There are three principal areas. First, the northeast part of Portsmouth, near Portsmouth Southsea Railway Station, includes the Guildhall civic center complex, Her Majesty's Naval Base, and the Commercial Road shopping area, with solid department store representation. Second is to the southwest, edges the sea, and embraces Old Portsmouth, with Portsmouth Cathedral and High and Broad streets its focal points. (If you are able, allow time for a stroll along atmospheric old Broad Street to Portsmouth Point Promenade, at its northern tip, for a panorama of the shipping in the harbor.) Third is Southsea, south of Old Portsmouth, with its principal artery Clarence Esplanade, flanking a long stretch of wide, white-sand beach.

H.M.S. Victory (Her Majesty's Naval Base): You don't need to be as enthusiastic a Lord Nelson buff as most Britons are (the hero of the Battle of Trafalgar—wherein the fleets of France and Spain were vanquished and Napoleon along with them—remains a British national idol two centuries after his death) to find a tour of the 226-foot *Victory* rewarding. Guides are sailors and Marines who take you about, stem to stern. What you don't forget are the cavernous crews' quarters (a single compartment wherein lived 800 enlisted men); the personal suite of Admiral Horatio Lord Nelson (with replicas of the draperies over his cot made by his mistress, later his wife, Lady Hamilton); and—on the quarterdeck—a plaque indicating where Nelson fell—fatally wounded—on October 21, 1805. Just across the way is the *Royal Naval Museum*, repository not only of fascinating Nelsoniana, but of a wide range of exhibits—mastheads and china, model ships and battle maps, furniture and flags, uniforms and paintings—that bring to life the British Navy's distinguished history.

Adjacent, also, is the *Mary Rose Exhibition*, occupying an eighteenth-century boathouse, with more than 6,000 objects recovered only in recent years from the long-wrecked *Mary Rose*, a warship commissioned by Henry VIII and lying on the seabed of the Solent since 1545. Taken together—bows and arrows, a barber-surgeon's chest, a ship's compass, musical instruments, clothing, eating utensils, carpenter's tools—they offer an extraordinary picture of maritime life in the Tudor era. But it's not only the contents of the ship that are on show. Preserved by the sediment of the seabed after it was sunk in a battle with the French, while, presumably, King Henry looked on, is the vessel's starboard hull. The exhibition was opened by Prince Charles, who served as president of the organization that raised the remains of the ship from the briny depths and organized the new museum; Prince Charles himself made nine dives to the site of the excavations.

There are skippable destinations in what remains of the visitor's Portsmouth. *Dickens's Birthplace* (Old Commercial Road), the small, two-story, red-brick house in which Charles Dickens was born is one such, except for the most compulsive Dickens' fans. Virtually nothing in its simple interior connotes an association with the author or his family. (Dickens's London house [Chapter 2] is more interesting.) Also dispensable is the *Portsmouth City Museum* (Museum Road); you'll have seen at least as good-caliber antique furniture, glass, ceramics, and fine paintings elsewhere. *Portsmouth Cathedral* (High Street) was a parish church until it became seat of the bishop of a diocese created as recently as 1927; it rather successfully melds architecture running a gamut between twelfth and twentieth centuries, with the bulk lying somewhere in between. Look for a model sailing ship made of gold; it had been the church's weathervane from 1710 until it was brought inside for safekeeping in 1954 and mounted on a plank of oak from *H.M.S. Victory.*

That leaves *Southsea Castle* (Clarence Esplanade)—a sixteenth-century fortification out of a history book—seaside, of course (climb to the roof for views of town, water, and—on a clear day—the Isle of Wight), with displays explaining Portsmouth's role as a coastal fortress. Near the castle is the relatively recent *D-Day Museum*, which relates the unfolding of World War II from its origins to the aftermath of the 1944 Normandy invasion. Principal exhibit is the 272-foot-long Overlord Embroidery, tracing the planning of Operation Overlord, as D-Day was called, from 1940 to 1944.

The Isle of Wight, among the most romantic-sounding of British points, is actually nothing of the sort. Its main business is catering, on a mass basis, to Britons who settle for it, come summer holiday time, rather than more distant destinations on the Continent. Which is hardly to imply that you should keep your distance; a boat ride to and from the island—from Southampton, Plymouth, or Lymington— is short and agreeable. The island's countryside is rolling and, at times, pretty. (It is as wide as 23 miles, as long as 13.) And if its principal towns—Newport, the inland "capital"; Cowes, the principal port whose harbor on the Solent is busy every August with Cowes Week yacht competitions; and the west coast's Yarmouth—are without major monuments, there are lures of consequence.

Osborne House (a mile south of East Cowes) is the principal reason for the sea voyage to Wight. Prince Albert, Queen Victoria's talented consort, had a major hand in its design—it evokes a multitowered Italian Renaissance villa with much charm. Because Victoria's son and successor, Edward VII, did not much care for it, its interiors—quite literally Victorian—are just as Her Majesty left them when she died in her Cowes bedroom. The setting, elevated, amidst a brilliant park of a garden sweeping down to the sea, is idyllic. And the Department of the Environment, which looks after the place, lets you walk about at your speed to and through delightfully sculpture-cluttered corridors; the Queen's sitting room, with family pictures nearly engulfing it; dining room heavy with mahogany; Durbar Room, a mock-up of the Imperial India, which the Queen adored but never visited; state drawing room, its ceiling supported by Corinthian pillars, its floor embedded with a brass plaque bearing the legend: "Here in Peace Queen Victoria Lay in State Awaiting Burial at Windsor, 1 February 1901"; and—upstairs—the Queen's bedroom, with a photo, on the headboard of her bed, of the deceased Albert—who died many years before she did—lying in state.

Osborne House's major visitor-competition is *Carisbrooke Castle* (a mile south of Newport). Charles I stayed there for a year, in the course of what was intended as his escape from Hampton Court Palace (Chapter 2). In fact, his Wight sojourn was a term of imprisonment, terminated only when Charles was returned to London for beheading in 1649. But Carisbrooke long predates him. It is medieval, even to moat and drawbridge. There are two chapels, a museum devoted to Isle of Wight history, and—unusual, these—a contingent of five donkeys who take turns working one-hour shifts drawing the castle's water supply up to its well house by the bucketful, with an ancient windlass. Department of the Environment.

Bournemouth (20 miles southwest of Southampton): Unlike Brighton (Chapter 5), Bournemouth has little of historic or architectural import, and it never had a patron with anything like the charisma of George IV. The rugged and rockbound look of the coast surrounding the Cornish resort of St. Ives (Chapter 18) is missing, too. Bournemouth—hardly everyone's cup of tea, but popular with countless thousands of vacationers, the overwhelming bulk British—is neither unattractive nor unwelcoming. Its ace-in-the-hole is beach, beach, beach: seven miles of unbroken white sands, backed by high cliffs.

Central Bournemouth is cut through by pedestrians-only Westover Road. The clock tower of a landmark circle called—inaccurately but affectionately—The Square and a public bandstand plop in the center of the Lower Gardens dominate an area that forms part of a roadlike system of parks extending from the sea.

Bournemouth is not entirely culturally barren (its symphony is distinguished), but there are no requisite recommendations in this respect. *Natural Science Museum* (Christchurch Road); *Rothesay Museum* (Bath Road)—with its range Nepalese knives to Victorian shirt studs; and *Typewriter Museum* (in the Rothesay's building, with some 300 elderly machines) are all easily skippable, if not to say forgettable. *Russell Cotes Museum* (Russell Cotes Road) occupies the late nineteenth-century home—the entire lower floor is the main gallery, with upstairs rooms containing overflow—of a onetime Bournemouth mayor and his wife, who bequeathed the catchall they collected on a series of world tours to the city, along with their house—a weirdo of a mock-Moorish mansion—as the site of the museum taking their name. Contents are nothing if not eclectic, not to say eccentric—German vases, a bust of Florence Nightingale, Buddhist shrines, a children's sled, Japanese bells. Best part is the setting, with fine views of the sea below.

Dorchester (25 miles west of Bournemouth) holds interest for devotees of Thomas Hardy, whose nineteenth-century novels had recently enjoyed renewed popularity as a result of a dramatization in film of *Tess of the d'Urbervilles* and television's *The Mayor of Casterbridge*. Hardy was born nearby, in Bockhampton, and the Wessex of his writings is his native Dorset, with Dorchester not only the Casterbridge of *The Mayor of Casterbridge*, but figuring as well in *The Return of the Native*, *Far from the Madding Crowd*, and *Under the Greenwood Tree*. A reconstruction of the study in Hardy's Dorchester house is the core of the Thomas Hardy Collection—with some 700 volumes of his manuscripts and other Hardiana—in the *Dorset County Museum* (High Street). The thatched-roofed cottage—set in a lovely garden and dating to 1800—in which Hardy was born in 1840, is at Higher Bockhampton, a few miles east of Dorchester; note, though, that even though it's owned by the National Trust, you can go inside only with the tenant's permission.

SETTLING IN
Polygon Hotel (Cumberland Place, Southampton) has been Southampton's No. 1 as long as I can remember. It's not beautiful, but it is substantial and full-facility, with 120 pleasant rooms, good—and good-value—restaurant, and two bars. Trusthouse Forte. *First Class.*

Southampton Park Hotel (Cumberland Place, Southampton) is newer and smaller than the Polygon (above), but quite as well situated; restaurant, pair of bars. *First Class.*

Dolphin Hotel (High Street, Southampton), as we see it today, is essentially eighteenth-century. Look up as you enter; the arms above the Palladian window are those of Queen Victoria's uncle and predecessor, William IV, given as a token of his appreciation while a guest. There are a Georgian-style lobby-lounge, attractive restaurant, and bar. And 72 pleasant rooms. Trusthouse Forte. *First Class.*

Star Hotel (High Street, Southampton): The Dolphin's High Street neighbor is late eighteenth-century, with its lovely original facade. I wish more than a third of the 32 rooms had baths. Restaurant and four—yes, four—bars. *Moderate.*

Berkeley Hotel (Cranbury Terrace, Southampton): Not in, but near the center, the Berkeley occupies Georgian quarters functionally updated; more than half its 40 rooms have baths. Nice restaurant, bar. *Moderate.*

Portsmouth Centre Hotel (Pembroke Road, Portsmouth) is in Old Portsmouth. It is inelegant, but well equipped, with two restaurants, two bars, and 169 comfortable bedrooms, all of whose baths have showers. *Moderate-First Class.*

Pendragon Hotel (Clarence Parade, Portsmouth/Southsea): You'll like this house, which is old, but updated in traditional style, with a restaurant, cozy bar-lounge, and baths in 35 of its 55 rooms; front rooms overlook the Solent. Trusthouse Forte. *Moderate-First Class.*

Queens Hotel (Clarence Parade, Portsmouth/Southsea): Ask for a seafront room in this house; they cost no more. But not all of the nearly 90 rooms have bath. There is nothing subtle about the look of the Queens—lounges, restaurant, and bars are vibrant, but not unwelcoming; swimming pool in the garden. *Moderate.*

Peacock Vane Hotel (Bonchurch, Ventnor, Isle of Wight): This is a jewel, a rambling Regency house in its own wooded grounds in the prettiest—and most historic—part of Ventnor. There's a lounge on the ground floor, but the drawing room—all antiques and chintz and with the makings of a bar set out atop the grand piano—is up a flight. That's where you enjoy premeal libations and postmeal coffee or just plain relax. The restaurant is similarly atmospheric. There are only six rooms, each with showerless bath—whose fixtures are ready for replacement. But that is my only criticism of John and Rosalind Wolfenden's lovely hotel. *First Class.*

Winterbourne Hotel (Bonchurch, a mile east of Ventnor, Isle of Wight) is a veritable giant compared to Peacock Vane (above): a country house with all of 19 rooms, along with the patina that comes of age—Charles Dickens worked on *David Copperfield* while in residence—and set atop a gardened slope, with views of the sea from its excellent restaurant and garden-side rooms. *First Class.*

Royal Hotel (Belgrave Road, Ventnor, Isle of Wight): The Royal goes back to Victorian times, but has kept pace at least to the point where about half of its rooms have baths. The dining room is chandeliered and reliable, and there's a cocktail lounge, as well as a pub, which serves lunch. Outdoor pool, elevated garden setting, vistas of the sea. Trusthouse Forte. *First Class.*

Royal Bath Hotel (Bath Road, Bournemouth): Twin towers, in the manner of a French château, flank the facade of the Royal Bath, set way back in a three-acre garden, cliff-top, alongside the sea. A big lobby is supported by Corinthian columns. Also: restaurant, three bars, bedrooms really generous in size, pool, and sauna. *Luxury.*

Carlton Hotel (East Overcliff, Bournemouth) is elderly, but with a decidedly contemporary flair blended into attractive bedrooms, public spaces embracing two restaurants, as many bars, lobby-lounge where tea is served, rooms for billiards and cards, and outdoor pool, with the beach just beyond. *Luxury.*

Marsham Court Hotel (Russell Cotes Road, Bournemouth) understates with taste, offering subtly attractive lobby-lounge, low-slung restaurant in blues and grays, monotone bedrooms, and pool in the garden, with the sea below and the center of town minutes away. *First Class.*

Savoy Hotel (West Hill Road, Bournemouth) is open to a garden-cum-pool, seaside. Almost all of the 90 bedrooms have baths; some, balconies. Restaurant, bar. *Moderate.*

Cliff End Hotel (Manor Road, Bournemouth) is good value, functional, sensibly updated, and small enough to be friendly. Restaurant, bar, pool, beach nearby. *Moderate.*

King's Arms Hotel (High East Street, Dorchester): Hardy buffs, you'll recognize the King's Arms from Hardy's works. This graceful, modernized eighteenth-century house retains its traditional ambience. Restaurant, bar. *First Class.*

Plumber Manor Hotel (near Sturminster Newton, Dorset) is a much-restored, originally seventeenth-century house that bills itself as a "restaurant with bedrooms," and with good reason: It does not offer full hotel service. Guests must go elsewhere for lunch on any day and for dinner on Monday; and breakfast does not begin until 8:30 A.M., a latish hour for many travelers. Rooms, though, in the contemporary annex building are large and have excellent baths, and there is no denying that chef and co-owner Brian Prideaux-Brune turns out a tasty meal on those six evenings when his kitchen is operating. *First Class.*

DAILY BREAD

Hamtun Restaurant (Polygon Hotel, Cumberland Place, Southampton): Establishment Southampton continues to rely on the Polygon's Hamtun, but the visitor benefits, as well, with a wide-ranging à la carte and good-value table d'hôte, with fare basic English—count always on good beef—albeit with Continental influences. *First Class-Luxury.*

Simon's Wine Bar (Vernon Walk, Southampton) comes through as an engaging source of hot meat pies, bracing soups, interesting daily specials, and, among the desserts, a trifle by no means trifling. Wine by glass or carafe. *Moderate.*

Vegia Zena (Bedford Place, Southampton): As is generally the case in Britain, Italian restaurants satisfy. Vegia Zena's expertly sauced pastas are a case in point, but the seafood dishes, Mediterranean-style, are good, too. *First Class.*

Duke of Wellington (Bugle Street, Southampton) has origins half a millennium back, but the beat remains lively, with locals and visitors alike popping in for a drink or, at midday, a bar lunch. Atmospheric. *Moderate.*

Red Lion (High Street, Southampton) complements the Duke of Wellington (above) for core-of-town pub atmosphere. Order casually in this Tudor-origin establishment. *Moderate.*

Seagull (Broad Street, Portsmouth) is appropriately named. Its half-timbered facade edges the water and, again appropriately, concentrates on seafood; fish simply grilled or more complex dishes. Congenial. Dinner only. *First Class.*

Still & West (Broad Street, Portsmouth) is indicated for a pub lunch-cum-panorama in Old Portsmouth. On a sunny day, gain the view from the outerdeck; at other times, be glad of the picture windows giving on to the port. Daily specials. *Moderate.*

Coal Exchange (Broad Street, Portsmouth), though without the perspective afforded by a table at Still & West (above), is a good alternative lunch spot in Old Portsmouth. Baked potatoes with a variety of stuffings are the specialty. *Moderate.*

Dickens Restaurant (Pendragon Hotel, Clarence Parade, Portsmouth/ Southsea): Named for the little house in which the author was born, not far distant, this attractive room—positioned for a view of the Parade and sea beyond—is a winner, especially if you take advantage of the well-priced table d'hôte. Delicious roasts are a staple. *Moderate-First Class.*

Peacock Vane Hotel Restaurant (Bonchurch, Ventnor, Isle of Wight): Mr. and Mrs. John Wolfenden carry on the tradition of Mrs. Wolfenden's mother, Joan, who with her husband founded the Peacock Vane and was its initial chef. There are table d'hôte menus at lunch or dinner, with a wider choice of entrées at the latter meal. Lunch might be noisette of pork with fresh broccoli and leeks or a seafood casserole with a salad. Casserole of pigeon, tarragon-accented roast lamb, or the Wolfendens' special *coq au vin* are other possibilities. Their soups—you've never tasted a richer tomato—make good starters, and sweets—pies, cakes, puddings—are of their own creation. Precede your meal with a sherry in the antiques-furnished drawing room, the setting, as well, for coffee. On sale: Joan Wolfenden's honey of a cookbook, *Recipes to Relish.* In my view, one of Britain's best restaurants. *First Class.*

Winterbourne Hotel Restaurant (Bonchurch, Ventnor, Isle of Wight): This gracious hotel's gracious restaurant, old-fashioned in the nicest sense, presents bountiful table d'hôte lunches and dinners, with solid standbys, like beef and lamb roasts, among the entrées and delightful desserts. *First Class.*

Hare & Hounds (Downend, near Newport, Isle of Wight) is indicated for a bar lunch, should you be en route to or from, say, Carisbrooke Castle, at midday. Nicely elderly. *Moderate.*

Causerie (Carlton Hotel, East Overcliff, Bournemouth) is the ideal choice for a festive Bournemouth evening—dressy, lively, and with a wide-ranging, Continental-influenced menu, including steaks. *First Class-Luxury.*

San Marco (Holdenhurst Road, Bournemouth): Locals and visitors keep San Marco lively. Well-prepared, well-priced pastas and other Italian specialties are the reasons. *Moderate-First Class.*

Long's (Old Christchurch Road, Bournemouth) is a mixed bag, embracing a trio of bars and an upstairs restaurant, with food available in all subdivisions—well-priced hot plates in the bars and a table d'hôte in the restaurant. *Moderate.*

AFTER DARK
Guildhall (Civic Centre, Southampton) makes an impressive setting for concerts (the estimable Bournemouth Symphony performs often) and other cultural events.

Gaumont Theatre (Commercial Road, Southampton) draws such troupes as the Royal Shakespeare Company, Royal and Festival Ballets, Glyndebourne Touring Opera.

Turner Sims Concert Hall and Nuffield Theatre (University of Southampton) are the university's principal venues for music (the former) and theater (the latter).

Guildhall (Park Road, Portsmouth) is at once the name of the Civic Centre complex and of its handsome 2,000-seat hall, where entertainment ranges from, say, the Moscow Philharmonic on tour through to the Portsmouth Choral Union.

Rings Theatre (Albert Road, Portsmouth/Southsea) offers plays, both locally produced and as performed by national touring companies.

Shanklin Theatre (Shanklin, Isle of Wight) is booked throughout the warm weather months with plays and musicals. Gilbert & Sullivan included, produced by Island troupes. Variety shows are the summer specialty at not-far-distant *Sandown Pavilion.*

Winter Garden Theatre (Priory Road, Bournemouth): The range is diverse—plays and musicals, opera, and the celebrated Bournemouth Symphony. (With comedies summer-long at Bournemouth's amusement pier.)

INCIDENTAL INTELLIGENCE

Southampton is linked by ship with New York (Chapter 1); Le Havre and Cherbourg, across the English Channel in France; and the Isle of Wight. Portsmouth is also connected by sea with the Isle of Wight, Le Havre, Cherbourg, and St. Malo in France, as well as the Channel Islands. Southampton's Eastleigh Airport serves the region, with flights to and from Belgium, France, and the Netherlands. *Further information:* Southampton Tourist Information Centre, Above Bar Precinct; Portsmouth Tourist Information Centre, Civic Offices, Guildhall Square; Ventnor Tourist Information Centre, High Street; Bournemouth Tourist Information Centre, Westover Road; Dorchester Tourist Information Centre, Antelope Yard, South Street.

21

Winchester

And the New Forest

BACKGROUND BRIEFING

Wait until dark before you stroll Winchester's High Street. The Market Cross reveals itself, under strong light, as more elongated than most, a veritable Gothic spire rising from the pavement. Boots the Chemist occupies a brilliantly illuminated half-timbered—and ancient—palace. And the Lloyds Bank branch is the onetime Guildhall, where one legend indicates a 1711 rebuilding and another—beneath a niche framing a little statue of Queen Anne—solemnly and in Latin identifies the sovereign and the peaceful year in which her image was created: *Anna Regina Anno Pacifico 1713.*

Not, in other words, your run-of-the-mill High Street. But then, Winchester is not your run-of-the-mill provincial town. In the days when Alfred was king—a long time before Queen Anne reigned from London—Winchester was capital of England.

Or, to term it by its then-name, Wessex. This Hampshire town—at the northeast corner of southern England's still intact anachronism, the New Forest—began life as the early Britons' *Caer Owent,* was next termed *Venta Belgarum* by Roman settlers, and finally *Wintanceastre* by the Saxons. The last appellation took hold during a period when the Saxons—beginning in the seventh century, not long after the pope had sent St. Augustine to nearby Canterbury (Chapter 8)—became Christian. Alfred became king in the ninth century, and Wessex—by then ecclesiastical as well as political center—remained capital until after the Norman Conquest in the eleventh century, vying with London in the post-Norman period.

Although wool played a role in its early mercantile development, Winchester's role has always been as a religious center and focal point of political struggles, often with far-reaching implications, from battles against Vikings to battles against Cromwell's antimonarchist forces.

Today's Winchester bears witness to its role in England's development. Winchester College was founded by a fourteenth-century bishop, William of Wykeham (the school's alumni to this day are called Old Wykehamists), the very same who was responsible for the rebuilding of the Winchester Cathedral we see when we visit today. Queen Mary I—sadly remembered in history as Bloody Mary—was married in the cathedral to Spain's King Philip II. The ruin of the castle where she stayed is still to be seen.

The medieval castle where Wessex parliaments deliberated and the setting for King Arthur's legendary Round Table is partially intact. Izaak Walton, seventeenth-century author of *The Compleat Angler*, is buried in the Cathedral. So, for that matter, is author Jane Austen, who died in Winchester, after an abortive visit from her nearby Hampshire home for medical treatment. And we may still visit the ancient hostel where Anthony Trollope set his novel, *The Warden*.

All of the smaller British cathedral towns—in contrast to the large cities, which are, among much else, seats of bishops—are invariably winning. There is not, in my view, a loser among the lot, from Carlisle on the border with Scotland, to, say, St. David's, the westernmost point of Wales. But none has quite the cachet of this onetime Saxon stronghold that knew glory a thousand years ago as the kingdom's capital—and hasn't forgotten.

ON SCENE

Lay of the Land: Begin with east-west High Street, a pedestrian precinct in its central portion, with what remains of ancient Winchester Castle at its western end, Winchester Cathedral and its parklike Close (with the ruins of Wolvesey Castle, where Mary I lived, and next-door Wolvesey Palace where Bishops of Winchester live) a block south, and Winchester College at the Cathedral Close's southern extremity. The Railway Station is to the north of High Street. Within this general area, the operative word is: walk. Streets leading toward the Cathedral are early nineteenth-century (Great Minster Street is a good example), eighteenth-century (College Street, with the house in which Jane Austen worked on her novel, *Persuasion*, and died), and seventeenth-century (St. Peter's Street, with a house believed to have been inhabited by the French-born mistress whom Charles II created Duchess of Portsmouth).

Winchester Cathedral (Cathedral Close) is the third on the site. The first was seventh-century, not long after Rome sent its initial missionaries. The second preceded the Norman Conquest by a century, while the present structure opened within decades of William the Conqueror's accession in 1066. That Romanesque structure remains in part, to be sure—three tiers of semicircular arches in the south transept, Epiphany Chapel in the north transept, and a vast subterranean crypt stand out in this respect. But Winchester's glory is with the scale it achieves in the Perpendicular Gothic reconstruction brought to conclusion under the creative bishopric of William of Wykeham (whose tomb you owe it to yourself to see). You want, as well, to inspect the exquisitely illuminated twelfth-century *Winchester Bible* and the charter presented the Cathedral by Henry VIII when it became Anglican, in the library; the Lady Chapel in the apse; and ancient frescoes in little Holy Sepulchre Chapel. Make it a point to return in advance of the first daily service, traditionally at 7:40 A.M. Take a pew—chances are you'll be all alone—and look down Bishop Wykeham's nave—one of the longest and loveliest in Christendom. Dead ahead will be the high altar. It is backed by a reredos in whose niches are a score of sculpted saints, the lot surrounding a sublime *Crucifixion*. For me, there is no more beautiful cathedral.

Great Hall of Winchester Castle (High Street): You can't very well visit Winchester without having a look at what is believed to be King Arthur's Round Table, in the Great Hall—all that remains of the city's medieval castle. It's big, surfaced with pie-shaped wedges in alternating colors, with a statue of Arthur at the top, and his knights' names inscribed around the circumference. Tests indicate the table dates to 1335.

Winchester College (College Street): The marvel of this enchanting medieval complex—built mostly in the fourteenth century by its founder, the cathedral's Bishop William of Wykeham, who also established Oxford's New College, where many Old Wykehamists, alumni of Winchester, continue their studies—is that it remains not only standing, but in splendid shape, despite wear and tear from countless generations of energetic schoolboys. Six hundred-fifty youngsters attend Winchester, and you may see the classrooms where they study; their high-ceilinged dining hall; a twentieth-century cloister honoring the dead of the two World Wars; a charmer of a small, one-room structure, called simply School and believed to have been designed by Sir Christopher Wren; and the college's *chef d'oeuvre*, a Perpendicular Gothic chapel, with a vaulted ceiling that anticipated the later fan vaulting and was the work of the architect of Westminster Hall, in London's Parliament complex.

Hospital of St. Cross and Almshouse of Noble Poverty (St. Cross Road, a 10-minute drive south of the center): One of my fondest memories of a visit to Winchester a quarter-century ago was this extraordinary carryover from the Middle Ages. A bishop of Winchester who was a grandson of William the Conqueror opened St. Cross in 1136 as a residence to house 13 poor men, "feeble and so reduced in strength that they can hardly . . . support themselves." Three centuries later, St. Cross expanded with the addition, by another cardinal, of the Almshouse of Noble Poverty—for a dozen noblemen who had seen better days. There was, to be sure, segregation of the two classes, with the untitled men wearing black and the impoverished peers in red robes. Today, St. Cross operates as it always has, robes and all. Visitors inspect the original dining hall and kitchen and the twelfth-century chapel of the style called Transitional—part Norman, part Early English Gothic—and one of the finest such in the kingdom. When I exited St. Cross on my first visit, I was asked if I wanted the Wayfarers Dole—a wooden plate with St. Cross's distinctively designed cross embedded in it in silver, from which I was served four squares of bread and a small glass of beer. The dole had been given to visitors since the institution was founded, and, when I returned again in the course of researching this book, I learned to my delight that it is, still. There will, indeed, always be an England.

Winchester City Museum (The Square) is at its best in its nether reaches. By that, I mean you should ascend to the third floor to see a perfectly beautiful—and almost perfectly intact—mosaic floor from Roman Winchester; it was excavated in 1965. Then work your way down, past mock-ups of a nineteenth-century pharmacy and tobacco shop; exhibits of early Winchester, most especially iron implements from Saxon times; and Roman glass and pottery.

Westgate Museum (High Street): What better use for the interior of a superb Gothic gate? Westgate evokes old Winchester, and, even if you are not especially into armor and ancient weapons, see it.

Royal Hampshire Regimental Museum (Southgate Street): Britain abounds in museums devoted to paraphernalia—uniforms, decorations, weapons, battle maps—of military units; and because they are of interest principally to locals having association with, or special knowledge of the subject matter, I omit them from this book. But the Royal Hampshire is an exception because of its setting: a gracious eighteenth-century mansion set in its own well-manicured garden, heart of town.

St. Swithin-Upon-Kingsgate Church (College Street, opposite Winchester College) is an enchanter: Gothic, mite-like—cunningly tucked into upper reaches of an ancient city gate and reputed to be one of the kingdom's tiniest ecclesiastical interiors. The beamed, arched ceiling is special.

Jane Austen's Home (Chawton, near Alton, east of Winchester) is requisite for Austen devotees, Jane lived here between 1809 and 1817, the year she died at the College Street house in Winchester (not open to the public), which I mention above. Chawton, a three-story brick house, has first editions of all the Austen novels, two of which, *Emma* and *Persuasion* (on which she also worked in Winchester) were written here, the others revised here. With paintings and letters, and all manner of Austeniana.

The Vyne (near Basingstoke, 18 miles north of Winchester) is oddball, but beautiful: a Tudor mansion to whose front was added a Baroque colonnaded portico and to whose interior—in the eighteenth century—were added such embellishments as a series of damask-walled reception rooms and an elegant staircase. Which is not to say that nothing Tudor remains. The long Oak Gallery is masterfully paneled, and the chapel, constituting a side wing, is Gothic, with stained glass windows brought from Renaissance Flanders. Café. National Trust.

The New Forest was new approximately 900 years ago—when William the Conqueror, within decades after the Norman Conquest, set aside its 93,000 acres as a royal game reserve. To this day, more than 100 of its nearly 150 square miles—lying between Romsey (due south of Winchester) in the northeast and Christchurch in the southwest—are Crown Land administered by the British Government's Forestry Commission, with the official in charge a successor (some centuries removed, to be sure) of the Lord Wardens of the Forest, first appointed during the reign of William I. The forest is an anomaly, with a resident population of some 3,000 ponies, each with its owner's brand, each with the same rights of grazing first guaranteed when the forest was created, many popping up on the streets of the forest's network of venerable villages.

A New Forest visit can be as short as a pleasant day's outing, or a relaxer stretching over a sustained period. Minimally, in my view, it should include the following.

Romsey Abbey: The abbey dominating the storybook village of Romsey is an all-Briton standout. Its chunky exterior is deceptive. Step in and your view is of an extraordinarily high nave, bordered by three levels of splendidly decorated Romanesque arches. A onetime convent—its nuns educated Henry I's consort, Queen Matilda, in the twelfth century—it might well have been razed after Henry VIII dissolved monasteries in the sixteenth century, had not Romsey's citizens banded together and bought it for a hundred pounds. (The deed of sale remains in the Abbey archives.) Romsey's most distinguished citizen of modern times, Earl Mountbatten of Burma—who was killed off the coast of Northern Ireland when his boat was exploded by an IRA bomb in 1979—is buried in the Abbey.

Look at his tomb—severely simple—in the south transept. Then amble through the village, passing Market Place—the main square—and popping into half-timbered *Tudor House* nearby (now, appropriately, the village tourist office), before proceeding a half-mile south to the Mountbatten family's country seat.

Broadlands: If it is not ranked as one of the great country houses—in a class, say, with Chatsworth or Knole or Blenheim—Broadlands is not to be underappreciated. It is the home of a branch of the Royal Family descended from Queen Victoria's daughter Alice, whose daughter Victoria married a Battenburg prince. (The Germanic-sounding *Battenburg* was changed to *Mountbatten* at the time of World War I.) The house is a relatively small-scale Palladian mansion erected by the mid-eighteenth century's Viscount Palmerston to replace a much older antecedent. Capability Brown designed its park, and architects William Kent and Henry Holland the Younger (along with, it is believed, Robert Adam) and portraitist Angelica Kauffmann were involved in the house's creation.

You are shown through a number of rooms behind a colonnaded facade, with the standout features of the interior its paintings—the dining room's four Van Dycks and portraits, as well, by Hoppner, Lawrence, Reynolds, Romney, and Raeburn. Upstairs is the bedroom where Queen Elizabeth II—a cousin of the late Lord Mountbatten—and Prince Philip—a nephew of Mountbatten—spent their honeymoon (the Queen's heir and daughter-in-law, the Prince and Princess of Wales, followed suit and spent the first part of their 1981 honeymoon at Broadlands), a desk in the Chinese Room where the Queen attends to State papers on Broadlands visits, and—so rarely shown in country houses—bathrooms attached to some of the bedrooms. England being England, none has a shower. Lord Romsey, grandson of the late Earl Mountbatten, has set aside part of the house for an exhibit depicting highlights of the career of his grandfather, who was, among much else, last British Viceroy of India. Cafeteria.

Other exploration-worthy New Forest points include a pair of charming churches that time has passed by—that near the village of *Boldre*, with a disproportionately large fourteenth-century-origin tower and an interior several centuries older; and that at *Minstead*, with parts dating to the twelfth century, and with a later, unique-in-England, three-decker pulpit. Take a look at two of the larger Forest towns. North-central *Lyndhurst* calls itself the Forest's "capital," has an architecturally interesting High Street, and offers a parish church out of the last century where the lure is stained glass windows designed by pre-Raphaelite artists, including Burne-Jones. *Lymington*, bordering the waters of the Solent, is a terminus for Isle of Wight ferries, with Georgian and Regency houses on Quay Hill.

Christchurch: Aside from Southampton, which flanks the Forest to its east, and Bournemouth, which lies to its southwest, that leaves— at least among towns of consequence—oddly uncelebrated Christchurch, a few miles northeast of Bournemouth, at the Forest's southern edge. It is called after a nine-century-old Romanesque-Gothic structure that is the longest parish church in England (and larger than some cathedrals). *Christchurch Priory,* in a park of its own flanking the River Avon, warrants concentration, especially in the case of the carved-wood misericords and the carved-stone reredos, or altar screen, of its Lady Chapel. An ancient workhouse, now *Red House Museum,* tells the region's history with wit and style. Save time for a walk along High and Castle streets, to the Norman-era bridge crossing the Avon.

SETTLING IN

Wessex Hotel (Paternoster Row, Winchester): The idea behind the design of the Wessex was contrast—with the cathedral just across the lawns of the Close. It is just possible, though, that its severe, post-World War II architecture is almost too plain. But never mind. Ask for a cathedral-view room—they're all comfortable in this 94-room, full-facility house—and I don't know how you could be unhappy. Two restaurants, bar. Trusthouse Forte. *First Class.*

Royal Hotel (St. Peter's Street, Winchester): This rambling house set in its own pretty garden, heart of town, goes back a century and a half and has aged gracefully, with agreeable public spaces (the restaurant and bar especially) and baths in not quite half of its 36 no-two-alike rooms. Lovely. *Moderate-First Class.*

Lainston House Hotel (Sparsholt, near Winchester) is a Queen Anne mansion in its own park, converted only in the last decade to hotel use. And with panache. A very grand and venerable oak stairway leads from the pillared entrance hall to 30 handsome bedrooms. The bar is paneled and relaxing, and the restaurant, whose French doors give on to the grounds, is tastefully Anglo-Gallic, with a distinguished cellar. Lovely service. Member, Prestige Hotels. *Luxury.*

Red Lion Hotel (London Street, Basingstoke) is ideal if you would tarry north of Winchester, in the neighborhood of The Vyne (above).

This is an updated, traditional-style house, with baths in a majority of its 34 rooms, cozy bar, restaurant. *Moderate-First Class.*

White Horse Hotel (Market Place, Romsey) has been a Romsey landmark since it opened as a coaching inn some four hundred years ago. It's inviting—lobby, bar busy with locals, restaurant, and 41 no-two-quite-alike rooms. Trusthouse Forte. *Moderate-First Class.*

Crown Hotel (High Street, Lyndhurst): You're just about dead center of the New Forest in Lyndhurst. The Crown makes a nice tarrying point, with an ancient half-timbered facade, smartly traditional interior, good restaurant, congenial bar-lounge, and 40 tastefully decorated rooms. *First Class.*

Stanwell House Hotel (High Street, Lymington): The Isle of Wight beckons, just a ferry ride away. But you may want to tarry at Stanwell House, eighteenth-century, with looks and style of that era throughout, including a score of rooms, most with bath, some harbor-view. Restaurant, bar. *Moderate-First Class.*

Kings Arms Hotel (Castle Street, Christchurch): A handsome house, with a seventeenth-century pedigree, two restaurants, and as many bars—atmospheric the lot—and 34 well-equipped rooms. Central. *First Class.*

Avonmouth Hotel (Mudeford, Christchurch) is nothing if not scenic: an elderly house fronting Christchurch's picture-book harbor, with a pool in the garden, good-value dining room, and nicely situated bars. Most of the nearly 50 rooms have baths; ask for one giving on to the water. Trusthouse Forte. *Moderate-First Class.*

Chewton Glen Hotel (New Milton): I save the best hotel in this chapter for last. Indeed, Chewton Glen is one of Britain's preeminent country hotels. In a park of its own, just beyond a village between the New Forest and Christchurch, Chewton Glen's nucleus is a rambling white-frame mansion that has been transformed with warmth and charm into the core of a traditional-style inn, no two of whose 52 stylish rooms are quite alike. Owner Martin Skan's personal touches— mini-bottles of sherry to welcome guests in their rooms, great bouquets of fresh flowers in the public spaces, skilled and smiling staff— are ubiquitous. Relax in either of two bar-lounges. Play tennis or croquet, take a dip in the beautiful pool without, and savor every meal. Chewton Glen's classical French restaurant—later reviewed— would be extraordinary even in France. Member, Leading Hotels of the World, Relais et Châteaux, Prestige Hotels. *Luxury.*

DAILY BREAD

Mr. Pitkin's (Jewry Street, Winchester) occupies two stories of a handsome old core-of-town house. The ground floor is a wine bar, both à la carte and table d'hôte. They're tasty, and daily specials are a sound value. Upstairs, the restaurant is at once small, antiques-accented, and quite grand, albeit with deliciously prepared food in keeping with the ambience. *Moderate-First Class.*

Elizabethan Restaurant (Jewry Street, Winchester) is indeed Elizabethan, a half-timbered, furnished-in-period Tudor house, with delicious, essentially English fare—steaks and roast beef, shepherd's and beef and kidney pies, lamb chops—that is a solid value. Friendly. *Moderate-First Class.*

Alice's (Jewry Street, Winchester): Can't get a table in Mr. Pitkin's? Next-door Alice's is a good substitute, though it's less ambitious, with chili and hamburgers essentially the order of the day. Attractive and congenial. *Moderate.*

Old Market Inn (Market Street, Winchester) is a convivial pub that serves a satisfying meal—chicken and bacon pie and steak and kidney pie are specialties. Accompany with a lager. *Moderate.*

Moles (High Street, Winchester): I don't find the name of this place appetizing, and you must look hard to find it—in a basement beneath the Design and Craft Gift Shop. Select from the buffet: salads and cold meats, hot daily specials, tempting sweets. Wine by the glass or carafe. Lunch through tea only. *Moderate.*

Eclipse Inn (The Square, Winchester): A half-timbered, onetime rectory out of the sixteenth century houses the worthy Eclipse. What you want here, at least at midday, is the cheese-based ploughman's lunch, with beer or a glass of wine. Lots of locals. *Moderate.*

Baker's Arms (Market Lane, Winchester): You're hungry after a morning in the nearby cathedral and the sun shines. Head, then, for a table in the sunny courtyard of the unpretentious Baker's Arms and order a sandwich or salad lunch-cum-beer. *Moderate.*

Wessex Hotel (Paternoster Row, Winchester): It's mid-to-late afternoon and you're exiting the cathedral or City Museum. Walk across the Close for tea in the lounge of this hotel, either the Festive (less pricey and with hot crumpets) or the Wessex Warmer (a festive cream tea). *Moderate.*

Lattimer's (Bell Street, Romsey) is delicious no matter the time of day you go—house-baked cakes with your morning coffee or your afternoon tea; and soup, salads, quiche, or hot pies from the buffet at lunch. Would that it were open for dinner! *Moderate.*

Red Lion (Boldre): Time your visit to Boldre's ancient church (above) so that you'll arrive at the also-ancient Red Lion in time for a casual bar lunch. *Moderate.*

Bow Windows (High Street, Lyndhurst) is at once easy to locate, attractive, and well priced, with reliable choices—roast beef, lamb, and pork are tasty—on the table d'hôte. *Moderate.*

Kings Head (Quay Hill, Lymington): The window panes shine in this whitewashed, black-trimmed old house, on Lymington's handsomest street. Ask for the daily special. *Moderate.*

Chewton Glen Hotel Restaurant (New Milton): As I did with the hotel, so I do with its restaurant: save best for last. Proprietor Martin Skan staffs his intimate Marryat Room with skilled French chefs and dining room staff. The à la carte menu is extraordinary, with the choice wide: clam and mussel soup through lobster mousse in a butter sauce; on to saddle of hare or duck breast sliced *magret*-style; with desserts matchless, including one you might want to remember— *mille feuilles de pommes au coulis d'abricot*—puff pastry layered with a hot-apple filling, blanketed with apricot sauce, and served warm. Remember, too, that Chewton Glen's table d'hôte lunches are excellent buys. And the wine list bears careful scrutiny; it's extensive and extraordinary. In my experience, one of Britain's best restaurants. *Luxury.*

AFTER DARK
Southampton, Portsmouth, and Bournemouth are in the neighborhood; I refer you to the After Dark section of Chapter 20.

INCIDENTAL INTELLIGENCE

The regional airport is Southampton. *Further information:* Winchester Tourist Information Centre, Guildhall; Romsey Tourist Information Centre, King John's House, Church Street; Christchurch Tourist Information Centre, Saxon Square.

22

Worcester

And Two Sister Cathedral Towns

BACKGROUND BRIEFING
It is not in every region of Britain—or in any country in Europe, for that matter—that a trio of superb ancient cathedrals, each dominating a country town, is to be found within 15 to 20 miles of one another, and good friends, at that: the choirs of Worcester, Gloucester, and Hereford cathedrals collaborate in a unique annual festival, each cathedral serving as the site of the performance every third year.

It is, of course, possible to settle in at any or all of these towns, the lot of them just east of Wales (Chapter 28) and just west of the Cotswold villages (Chapter 17) and of the Regency spa-town of Cheltenham, whose attributes I delineate in this chapter. Given a choice, though, I would headquarter in Worcester, reputed as much for a bottled sauce as for pricey porcelain.

The point about Worcester is not so much its plethora of royal charters—Richard I's in the twelfth century, Henry III's less than a hundred years later, and James I's in the seventeenth century. Rome considered Worcester substantial enough as a Christian seat to make of it the seat of a bishop.

It grew not only because of ecclesiastical eminence, but as a market town for the region and as an educational center (the Royal Grammar School opened in the thirteenth century, the King's School in the sixteenth) of kingdom-wide repute.

Then, in the seventeenth century, Worcester became a battleground. The very first encounter of the Civil War, between the royalist forces of Charles I and the Parliamentary troops of Oliver Cromwell, took place in and around the city, and the decisive last battle of the same war—the Battle of Worcester—saw King Charles II's forces defeated on the grounds of a building called the Commandery—a visitable Worcester destination.

ON SCENE

Lay of the Land: The walker does well in Worcester. The commercial core—from southerly Lynchgate through north-south High Street and The Shambles—extends north to Blackfriars Square, and much of it is pedestrians-only. The prettiest part of town is due west—North, South, and Diglis Parades the various names of the thoroughfare that flanks the bucolic banks of the River Severn and its landmark structure, the Cathedral.

Worcester Cathedral: Of the riverbank cathedrals, surely Durham (Chapter 15) is the greatest. But Worcester's situation on the Severn's bank is hardly a mark against it. On the contrary, this originally twelfth-century cathedral—despite the destruction it suffered in the Civil War's Battle of Worcester—is an all-England standout. Look down the long nave, still partly Norman but later Transitional and Decorated Gothic, as well. Take in the well-proportioned choir, noting deftly carved scenes of battle, civil life, ancient mythology—and its folding seats, or misericords. Step into the original Norman crypt. Admire the multiarched Lady Chapel. Visit the circular chapter house and the beautifully vaulted cloister. Don't fail to observe the thirteenth-century tombs of King John, the very same of *Magna Carta* (he liked Worcester and ordered that he be buried there), and Prince Arthur, elder brother of Henry VIII.

Commandery (Sidbury Street) goes back a thousand years, when it opened as a hospital, changing function, and for that matter, form, over the centuries. Since the fifteenth, it has been a half-timbered house, on whose grounds—a century later—Charles II's commander, the Duke of Hamilton, was killed in the Battle of Worcester. Only since the mid-1870s has this historic place been a museum. Its Great Hall has been well restored, and all about, on two floors, are exhibits that tell Worcester's story, from early Romans to later Worcestershire sauce in the familiar Lea and Perrins wrapper.

Tudor House Museum (Friar Street): Another lovely house, another repository of Old Worcester, with period rooms both Tudor and Stuart and, for contrast, an Edwardian bathroom and kitchen from the 1930s.

Dyston Perrins Museum (Severn Street): Subject matter is porcelain, Royal Worcester not surprisingly, from eighteenth-century beginnings onward. Tours of the adjacent factory—at a charge, unconscionable for so commercial a venture, in my view—are available, although entry to the salesroom and the separate Seconds Shop (where good buys can be made) is free, as well it should be.

St. Swithin's Church (St. Swithin Street): There is no more painless way to achieve an understanding of the elegance of Georgian Worcester. This eighteenth-century church, classic-style, is handsome.

Sir Edward Elgar's Birthplace (Broadheath, a mile north of Worcester): Not everyone is a devotee of this Victorian-Edwardian composer. Still, his *Pomp and Circumstance March in D Major* is celebrated. And the red-brick house where he was born—now full of mementos of his career—is attractive.

Gloucester, largest of the towns of this chapter, is also the most contemporary, with a fairly lively—and quite modern—city center, not without pockets of antiquity. The Severn River is at the town's western flank, and the main railway station is at its northeastern edge. The main streets, Southgate, which becomes Northgate, and Westgate, which becomes Eastgate, cross in the center of town, with sleekly modern King's Square shopping center to the east and Gloucester's glory, the Cathedral, to the west. *Gloucester Cathedral* (College Street) is originally eleventh- through thirteenth-century Romanesque and might well still be, had not its administrators, in the fourteenth century, agreed to bury the body of the murdered—and later declared martyred—King Edward II. The crush of pilgrims from all over Britain—as Edward III encouraged development of a cult in his father's memory—to the Royal tomb impelled rebuilding. A consequence was the establishment of England's important contribution to Gothic architecture: its Perpendicular—or latest—style, as exemplified at Gloucester by the extraordinarily beautiful—and extraordinarily large (38 by 72 feet)—east window, still with its original stained glass, and by the fan vaulting—England's first—of surpassing loveliness, in the cloister. Note, as well, the intricately vaulted choir, with its bosses—carved figures—of exceptional quality; the great window of the apse's Lady Chapel; and the long stone washbasin, or *lavatorium*, of early monks. *Gloucester Folk Museum* (Westgate Street) is housed in a half-timbered house, the subject matter working Gloucester over the centuries, handicrafts especially. *Gloucester Museum and Art Gallery* (Brunswick Road) typifies the smaller-city British museum, with varied contents, for me most interesting in sections for furniture, silver, and china.

Hereford: Of course you remember the line from *My Fair Lady,* repeated by Cockney heroine Eliza Doolittle, at the urging of her speech teacher, Professor Henry Higgins: "Hartford, Hereford, Hampshire," with the second word coming out correctly as "hairaford." And so it does, still. Now tranquil, Hereford has known more exciting periods.

It was, back in the seventh century, capital of the Saxon kingdom of Mercia and later focal point of battles between the English and the almost-next-door Welsh. A battle was fought within its precincts in the seventeenth-century Civil War. People come now to buy and sell cattle at Hereford's regional market and to shop in and about the central square called High Town and in the streets—High, Commercial, Widemarsh—leading from it.

They come, too, to visit *Hereford Cathedral*, just south of High Town, in a capacious precinct edging the River Wye. Before going in, I suggest—so that you can see the cathedral from without at its handsomest—crossing the old, triple-arched, stone Wye Bridge and taking in the perspective from the river's far bank, noting how the squat structure is dominated—but not overwhelmed—by its square fourteenth-century tower. Hereford Cathedral is as old as the twelfth century (Cistercian monks were its original constructors) and as recent as the twentieth. It is not big, but it is appealing, beginning with fat columns that support the Romanesque arches lining its nave and concluding with a remarkable map—*Mappa Mundi*—delineating the world as a fourteenth-century cartographer would have it and a clutch of chained books—early manuscripts chained in position to discourage theft—in its library, gained by a steep and ancient flight of stone steps and with knowledgeable volunteer-librarians on hand to explain the extraordinary collection.

Exiting the Cathedral, you want to amble about the grounds—the Bishop's Palace is just out back, and there might be a band concert in adjacent Castle Green. By all means, trek through the first-rate museum called *Old House* on the main square, High Town; it's half-timbered, and furnished in the period of its sixteenth-century construction. And inspect furniture, china, and antique costumes at *Churchill Gardens Museum*, Venn's Lane.

Croft Castle and Berrington Hall are a pair of National Trust-operated houses a few miles north of Hereford, just beyond Leominster, which are close enough to each other for the Trust to sell a specially priced ticket admitting you to both houses, and on sale at each. The former—Croft Castle—is, to me, the more interesting. Home of the family whose name it has had for something like eight of the last ten centuries, it remains medieval from without—there is a crenellated round tower at each of its four corners—but surprises, inside, with the elegance of a Georgian-era refurbishing. The grand staircase, in particular, is a dazzler. Not that Berrington Hall is to be slighted; its architect-designer was a top ranker of the eighteenth century: Henry Holland. Proportions of the squarish structure, fronted by a magnificent portico, are superb; likewise, plasterwork of the state rooms' ceilings, most especially that of the dazzling library; and the surrounding park, created by the redoubtable landscapist, Capability Brown. Café.

Cheltenham owes its original eminence to eighteenth-century visits to its spa by King George III and the first Duke of Wellington. Before long, titled Britons from throughout the kingdom were following. Cheltenham never became as elegant as Bath. But a look at it today and one perceives that it was not overlooked by ailing and fashionable citizens of two centuries back. If its *Museum and Art Gallery* (Clarence Street) is skippable (aside from a handful of seventeenth-century Dutch paintings by such masters as Steen and Hobbema and some good English furniture, porcelain, pewter, and glass), there are other lures. The colonnaded Queens Hotel (see below), facing the *Imperial Gardens*, on the core-of-town Promenade, is positively palatial. One may still taste the waters (I suspect you will prefer Perrier) at lovely, old *Pittville Pump Rooms* (Pittville Park, Evesham Road) or at more central *Town Hall*, giving on to the Imperial Gardens. All of central Cheltenham, especially shop-lined Montpelier Walk and the Promenade, is eminently walkable, and so are Lansdown Crescent and Suffolk Square, a bit more distant. Bonus: The Cotswold villages (Chapter 17) are next door.

SETTLING IN
Giffard Hotel (High Street, Worcester): Worcester's longtime leader has a lot going for it: location near both Cathedral and shops, attractive public spaces that include two good restaurants and a bar, and— not to be taken lightly, especially in an older hotel like this one— showers in all the baths of its 106 rooms, many of which tend to be small. Trusthouse Forte. *First Class.*

Cottage-in-the-Wood Hotel (Holywell Road, Malvern Wells near Worcester): This is a get-away-from-it-all spot: an early nineteenth-century manor (and adjacent coach house) turned country hotel, high on a hill-cum-view in the cluster of Malvern villages, just south of Worcester. Owner Malcolm Ross has put his inn together with a sense of very likable style—exceptional restaurants and lounges: 20 no-two-alike rooms, 17 of which have baths. *Luxury.*

Abbey Hotel (Abbey Road, Great Malvern, near Worcester) occupies an aged building—crenellated like a castle—in grounds opposite Great Malvern's ancient Benedictine Priory Church. Within, it is quite contemporary—from the lobby, restaurant, and bar to the bedrooms, 70 of which have baths. *First Class.*

Green Dragon Hotel (Broad Street, Hereford): A few four-poster suites and rooms excepted, most of the 89 rooms are modern, but the Green Dragon has wisely retained eighteenth-century ambience in the rest of the house, with a congenial bar-lounge patronized by locals and an attractive—and very good—restaurant. Special kudos for the Georgian facade. Trusthouse Forte. *First Class.*

Oaklands Hotel (Bodenham Road, Hereford): Not all 15 rooms have baths at the Oaklands, but you should be comfortable here, and the restaurant is convenient. *Moderate.*

New County Hotel (Southgate Street, Gloucester): The New County's major plus is central location, but I wish more of the 37 otherwise adequate rooms had baths. Restaurant, two bars. *Moderate.*

Crest Hotel (Barnett Way, Gloucester) is Gloucester's newest, with 100 functional rooms, a restaurant, a coffee shop, and a bar popular with the heavily business clientele of the hotel. Away from the center, though. *First Class.*

Queen's Hotel (Promenade, Cheltenham) has one of Britain's superior hotel facades: half a dozen Corinthian columns rise four stories to support a pediment at the center of a gracefully proportioned 1838 building. Chandeliered lobby, cocktail lounge, and restaurant are handsome. And there are 77 rooms and suites, essentially contemporary in look and invariably comfortable. Friendly. Trusthouse Forte. *First Class.*

George Hotel (St. George's Road, Cheltenham) occupies a cluster of contiguous, Regency-era houses in an attractive, reasonably central part of town. Lounge, restaurant, bar—all are comfortable. So, for that matter, are the bedrooms, but I regret that only 7 of the 46 have baths. *Moderate.*

Greenway Hotel (Shurdington, just outside of Cheltenham) is an originally sixteenth-century manor house. Owner-manager Tony Elliott (ex-Savoy Hotel, London) and his wife, Maryan, have retained the period look of the house in smart public spaces and a dozen bedrooms, eight of whose baths have showers. There's a red-walled bar, garden-cum-lily pond (around which summer lunches are served), log fires in winter, and first-rate food served with smiles. Fresh trout, venison, and game birds are among specialties. *First Class.*

Hotel de la Bere (Southam, just outside of Cheltenham to the south): This country hotel, in its own meticulously tended gardens, went up in the sixteenth century as the seat of the family whose name it takes. Original paneling—including carved-wood fireplaces—and ceilings have been retained in public rooms, while bedrooms—no two alike— charm with traditional-style good looks that run to four-poster beds and timbered ceilings. Two atmospheric restaurants and bars, tennis, squash, swimming pool. *First Class.*

DAILY BREAD

Giffard Hotel Restaurant (High Street, Worcester): Up a flight you go to this attractive hotel's dining room. At lunch, there's a two-course-and-coffee table d'hôte—with a roast which is one of the entrées—that's an excellent value. Dinner offers a more extensive table d'hôte, or order à la carte. *Moderate-First Class.*

Bottles (Friar Street, Worcester) is a congenial wine bar with a limited hot menu and a choice of cold meats and salads. Have a glass of the house wine. *Moderate.*

La Roma (Broad Street, Worcester): A restaurant named for the Italian capital shouldn't be ignored: La Roma's pastas do not disappoint. *First Class.*

Hodson's (High Street, Worcester) is an attractive café, busy with locals who pop in for morning coffee (with a jelly doughnut), ploughman's lunch, or afternoon tea. *Moderate.*

Inglenook's (Edgar Street, Worcester): Venerable, brick-walled, and furnished with Windsor chairs. Stop in for a snack, lunch, or, most particularly, afternoon tea. *Moderate.*

Farrier's Arms (Fish Street, Worcester): A half-timbered pub, just off High Street, that's an ideal source of a grilled sausage or quiche lunch-cum-beer. *Moderate.*

Effy's (East Street, Hereford) is the attractive enterprise of a multinational female triumverate—the countries are Australia, England, and Wales—with local lamb and poultry specialties, as well as expertly prepared game (grouse and pheasant in particular) and fish (salmon and trout). *First Class.*

Greyfriars Garden (Greyfriars Avenue, Hereford): Engagingly situated along the banks of the Wye, with a wide-ranging bill of fare, including game in season. Festive. *First Class.*

Saxty's (33 Widemarsh Street, Hereford) is a well-patronized wine bar, with the choice steaks through salads and good-value house wine. *Moderate.*

Don Pasquale (Kingsholm Road, Gloucester) is at once central, welcoming, and tasty, with Italian treats, cannelloni through zabaglione, Italian wines. *First Class.*

Comfy Pew (College Street, Gloucester): Daily hot specials at lunch, sandwiches and pastries the day long, through afternoon tea. Not open for dinner. Near the Cathedral. *Moderate.*

Debenhams (Northgate Street, Gloucester): The Gloucester outlet of a national department-store chain, with a reliable restaurant: table d'hôte lunches are a solid value. A good bet, too, for morning coffee and afternoon tea. *Moderate.*

Queen's Hotel Restaurant (Promenade, Cheltenham): An appealing room in a period-piece of a hotel is worthy of a meal, especially when the table d'hôte is such a good value, with entrées such as ham steak, fish of the day, and roast lamb. *Moderate-First Class.*

Aubergine (Imperial Square, Cheltenham): Solid French fare, authentically prepared, in a fine old house in the heart of town. *First Class.*

Forrest's (Imperial Lane, Cheltenham): Try the daily special, or select from an invariably reliable menu, soups through sweets, in this popular-with-locals wine bar. *Moderate.*

AFTER DARK
Swan Theatre (Pitchcroft, Worcester) offers its own and visiting troupes' plays and other entertainments.

Nell Gwynne Theatre (Edgar Street, Hereford): A modern house bearing the name of the seventeenth-century actress and mistress of Charles II, who is believed to have been a local lass. Local and touring productions.

Everyman Theatre (Regent Street, Cheltenham) presents a full schedule of theater.

Three Choirs Festival: Worcester Cathedral, Hereford Cathedral, and Gloucester Cathedral alternate—every August—as hosts for this annual collaboration, when their choirs perform en masse, along with imported symphonies, and soloists of note.

Cheltenham International Festival of Music is an annual summer event of long standing, with such top-caliber troupes as the Welsh National Opera and the Berlin Symphony performing in historic venues all around town over a two-week period.

INCIDENTAL INTELLIGENCE

The regional airport is Birmingham, with flights both domestic and international. *Further information:* Worcester Tourist Information Centre, Guildhall, High Street; Hereford Tourist Information Centre, Shirehall, St. Owen's Street; Gloucester Tourist Information Centre, College Street; Cheltenham Tourist Information Centre. Municipal Offices, Promenade.

23

York
With Diversions into Yorkshire

BACKGROUND BRIEFING

Northern British cities are built to withstand the elements. When they are beautiful, they are beautiful even in the rain. It was in the rain, teeming and unrelenting, that I first visited York—even walking its encircling walls—and fell head over heels for it. Return exploration, in the sunshine, has not been any less satisfying. On the contrary. A walk through York on a fine day is a walk through much of English history. Never great in size, York, with a population of about 100,000, has always been important, nonetheless, as a principal northern outpost—for church as well as crown. The Romans who called it *Eboracum* had made of it by the fourth century A.D. a major political center, not unlike Germany's Trier and Spain's Tarragona. It had prestige enough to have been selected as the venue for the official proclamation of Constantine the Great as Emperor. (A remarkable smattering of Roman York still is to be seen in the too-often-skipped Yorkshire Museum.)

There were other major moments. In the seventh century, the Saxon king chose York not only as his capital, but as the site of his conversion to Christianity; King Edwin was baptized in the wooden church that anticipated today's great York Minster. Later, with the eleventh-century takeover of England by the Norman-led forces of William the Conqueror, York continued to play a major ecclesiastical role, by which time centuries-old competition with the church brass in Canterbury (Chapter 8) came to a head. York's clerical leaders wanted to be No. 1 among the kingdom's dioceses. The issue went to Pope Innocent VI, and it is interesting that his decision—made in the fourteenth century, when the established church in England was still Catholic—remained in force after Henry VIII's Reformation a century later, and is the case until this day: What the pope decreed was that the Archbishop of York was to be "Primate of England," but that York's Canterbury counterpart was to be "Primate of *All* England." And it is worth observing, too, that Canterbury and York prelates— alone in England—are archbishops; heads of other Church of England dioceses, even in London, are simply bishops.

Medieval York was more than ecclesiastic. The core of town— much of it still intact—became a jumble of half-timbered houses sheltering residences, shops, and offices of prosperous merchants. Guilds became sophisticated. (To see what I mean, visit that of the Merchant Adventurers, who became powerful international explorers.) Wealth bought political clout. Kings visited—Tudor at first (Henry VIII stayed in York with Queen Catherine Howard), Stuart later (Scotland's James VI tarried en route south from Edinburgh to London, where he added a title: James I of England). Charles I was in residence, too.

With the advent of the Georges as monarchs, the eighteenth-century city became England's northern social capital. Gentry in the region built York town houses. There were balls at the Assembly Rooms, plays at the Theatre Royal. But although, in the nineteenth century, York became a major railway depot, it did not become heavily industrial. Enough of its fabric—Victorian and Georgian, medieval and Roman—remains so that this city carries past into present, effortlessly and pleasurably.

ON SCENE

Lay of the Land: York's landmarks are its towering Minster, near the northern edge of its center, and the River Ouse, which runs north to south, flanking the core's western precincts. Petergate, running south from the Minster, changes names at King's Square and becomes the Shambles, whose half-timbered, onetime butchers' houses now constitute a shopping quarter of consequence. Other ancient but busy thoroughfares, lined by antique houses, lead from King's Square. Another important street, Stonegate, leads west, from Petergate to attractive St. Helen's Square. Three bridges cross the Ouse; most important is Lendal Bridge, because it leads to Station Road and the Railway Station.

York Minster (Petergate): This is the largest of the English Gothic cathedrals; the word *minster* was applied, many centuries back, to missionary churches set up in non-Christian territory. It is at its loveliest in the light either of the moon or of electric spots that glorify its architectural detail, as one walks by of an evening. York staggers with its wide nave, enormous central tower, choir (larger than that of many parish churches), and likewise large crypt. The magnitude of the

Minster can make it possible to overlook treasures. York's stained glass is on a par with that of France's Chartres. Concentrate on the Five Sisters window—so called for its five fingerlike panels; Great West Window, noting the heart design of its tracery; and—for me, these are the most beautiful—the vast windows virtually constituting the walls of the octagon-shaped chapter house. Allow time for the undercroft, uncovered in relatively recent excavations and now an important museum of the cathedral's Roman origins, with medieval and later treasures—in ivory, silver, sandalwood, and gold—on display, as well.

Treasurer's House (Minster Yard): Few cities have great mansions the equal of Treasurer's House in their very core. Named for the medieval treasurers of the adjacent Minster—whose official residence it was—Treasurer's House changed hands and styles of architecture frequently over the centuries. It includes Georgian drawing and dining rooms; King's Bedroom—named for Edward VII, who visited in 1900; and Queen's Bedroom—named for Edward VII's consort, Alexandra, each with magnificent canopied beds. The house is bigger than it looks, with a dozen sumptuous rooms on two floors. And do stroll the walled garden, not only for the view it affords of the Minster, opposite, but because there are tombs of two long-dead dogs, beloved pets of Treasurer's House owners in centuries past. National Trust.

Castle Museum (Piccadilly): Take a pair of contiguous eighteenth-century prisons—palatial looking, at least from the outside—and put them to use as a museum of domestic Yorkshire life, using as a nucleus remarkable collections garnered by a local physician. And you have one of Britain's most engaging museums. The prisoners' exercise yards have been turned into cobbled streets of past centuries, shop-lined and authentically so. Elsewhere there are charming rooms furnished—and meticulously—in periods Jacobean through Victorian. Toys and mechanical instruments. Costumes and kitchen gadgets. Farm tools and soldiers' uniforms. Horse drawn carriages and dueling pistols. Dolls' houses and suits of armor.

York Art Gallery (Exhibition Square) is not big, but it is good. The painting collection includes Old Master Italian (Domenichino), Dutch (Van Goyen), Spanish (Valdes Leal), and Flemish (Snyders) works. The super English representation embraces Sir Peter Lely, Sir Godfrey Kneller, and Sir Joshua Reynolds, not to mention York's own talented William Etty; and—star of the show—a portrait of a white-gowned child, Miss Elizabeth Heathcote, who is seated before a lake, with a basket of just-picked flowers, a broad-brimmed bonnet covering her pretty face, and a black spaniel in attendance.

Merchant Adventurers' Hall (Fossgate) is Instant Medieval York: headquarters of fourteenth- through seventeenth-century exporters of north-country textiles to dominions beyond the seas. Two floors of rooms, chapel, and beamed Great Hall are standouts.

Fairfax House (Peasholme Green) is a stunner of a Georgian mansion, relatively recently restored at a cost of nearly three quarters of a million pounds by the York Civic Trust. Viscount Fairfax and an unmarried daughter used it as their town house in the course of a mid-eighteenth-century decade. Highlights are the picture-hung drawing room, exquisitely furnished; four-poster bedrooms; and a kitchen with an authentic range of the period.

Railway Museum (Leeman Road) appears to be the final resting place of Britain's most important locomotives—and other railway impedimenta—from the mid-nineteenth-century period when trains became popular. Dedicated rail buffs go bonkers, but even the rest of us have a good time, especially in the course of inspecting opulent coaches that carried Queen Victoria and her son, Edward VII. Amusing posters, menus, and signs as a bonus.

King's Manor (St. Leonard's Street) constitutes the main campus of the University of York. Go to see the medieval buildings surrounding its courtyard and, most particularly, the oversize coat of arms over the door of the structure known as King's Manor, commemorating 1633 and 1639 visits of Charles I.

Yorkshire Museum (St. Leonard's Street), adjacent to King's Manor, occupies two attractive buildings, a half-timbered structure with remnants of Roman York—the mosaics are dazzlers—and a neoclassic building with less interesting exhibits of later centuries. The backyard bonus is the ravishing ruins of Gothic *St. Mary's Abbey*.

York churches: No provincial city has more architecturally important, mostly Gothic churches, which are noteworthy, as well, for matchless stained glass windows. If you have time—and if they're open, which is not always the case—consider visits to *Holy Trinity* (Goodramgate), with unusual box pews; *St. Crux*, tiny and tucked into the Shambles shopping quarter; *St. Helen's* (Stonegate), with a jewel of an octagonal tower and extraordinary windows; *All Saint's* (North Street), fifteenth-century and with the finest stained glass of any city church; and *St. Mary Castlegate* (Castlegate), desanctified and now seeing service as headquarters of a permanent exhibition, *The York Story*, with paintings, models, mock-ups, and other contemporary artistic representations of city monuments.

Guildhall (St. Helen's Square) dates to the fifteenth century, since when it has been the city government's ceremonial headquarters. I am partial to it because of a bronze wall plaque, whose text I have copied:

"*To the ancient city of York, whose storied monuments and living chronicles enshrine so great a part of the history of the English-speaking race, this tablet is affectionately inscribed as an expression of goodwill from her godchild in America. The City of New York, John F. Hylan, Mayor, July 18, 1924.*"

Who says the New World's York hasn't got a heart?

Beningbrough Hall (five miles northwest of York) is the closest-to-town of open-to-visitors country houses, dating to the early eighteenth century, with an absolutely smashing high-ceilinged Great Hall; state bedroom, with a monumental canopied bed; and the only on-display Victorian-era laundry that I know of. With a surprise collection of a hundred paintings on permanent loan from London's top-rank National Portrait Gallery. Café. National Trust.

Sutton Park (eight miles north of York) is, like Beningbrough, convenient to the city. You go for the gardens (Capability Brown designed them), the handsomely pedimented eighteenth-century house, and a range of state rooms filled with corking good Chippendale, Sheraton, and French furniture. Cafeteria.

Harewood House (25 miles west of York) is—indisputably—one of the preeminent country seats. It was built by the first Lord Harewood in the mid-eighteenth century, to designs by a York architect, John Carr, and the then thirty-year-old Robert Adam. Facade is neoclassic—a central building with two elegant wings. Interiors—beginning with a high-ceilinged entrance hall, with stuccowork picked out in tones of gray, white, and brown—are dazzling, which is hardly surprising: Thomas Chippendale was commissioned to design much of the furniture.

And it is worth your knowing that since 1922, when the sixth Lord Harewood married the only daughter of King George V—Mary, the Princess Royal—the house has had close Royal Family associations. The late Princess Royal's elder son, the seventh earl, is current master of Harewood House. He is, as well, an opera scholar and first member of the Royal Family—he is a first cousin of Queen Elizabeth II—to obtain a divorce; the current Countess of Harewood, whom he married in 1967, is his second wife.

Rooms to note especially: Old Library, with chairs used by family members at recent coronations; East Bedroom's Turner drawings;

positively opulent Spanish Library, its walls covered in Spanish leather, with sculpted heads of notables, William Pitt to George VI, and a superb ceiling; Rose Drawing Room with an Adam-designed carpet complementing the ceiling's design; and the four largest—and most memorable—rooms: Green Drawing Room, Long Gallery, Dining Room, and Music Room, with paintings of major rank by Giovanni Bellini, El Greco, Titian, Veronese, and Angelica Kauffmann, not to mention English portraits by Gainsborough, Hoppner, Lawrence, Romney, and Reynolds. The adjacent *Bird Garden*—professionally operated and with its penguin section captivating—is highly recommended. So is the first-class restaurant; cafeteria.

Castle Howard (14 miles northeast of York, near Malton) ranks with Harewood House as a requisite north-of-England country house. How could it be otherwise, given the architect: the very same Sir John Vanbrugh who created Blenheim Palace (Chapter 17). Castle Howard, designed for the third Earl of Carlisle and lived in by his descendants, is familiar to viewers of the television dramatization of Evelyn Waugh's novel *Brideshead Revisited* as the Brideshead Castle of the title. Castle Howard is in the same heroic Baroque mold as Blenheim, a great central dome—sheltering the 80-foot-high Great Hall—its focal point. You amble about awestruck not only at the proportions, but at the caliber of the decoration. Frescoes and capitals of the columns put one in mind of the churches of Rome. Furniture—mostly eighteenth-century—is no less exquisite than the paintings, with Gainsborough in the music room; Romney in the Tapestry Room; Rubens, Bassano, Veronese, Poussin, and Bourdon in the Orleans Room; a slew of Lelys, along with Van Dyck, Kneller, Holbein, and Sir Thomas Lawrence in the Long Gallery; and Burne-Jones and William Morris, not to mention Sansovino's bas-relief *Madonna and Child*, in the pillared chapel. A fountain-centered reflecting pool highlights the peacock-inhabited formal gardens. Cafeteria.

Ripon (30 miles northwest of York) is among Britain's smaller—and more winning—cathedral towns, as unlike larger, busier, visitor-crammed York as it could be. Main streets—Fishergate, Kirkgate, Westgate—lead into ancient Market Place, whose thirteenth-century, half-timbered *Wakeman's House*—longtime residence of the town's "wakemen," who to this day sound an "All's well!" on a horn nightly at 9:30—contemporarily serves as Ripon's all-purpose museum, chock-filled with historic mementos. Have a look and then walk a couple of blocks east to *Ripon Cathedral*. None in Britain runs a more incredible architectural gamut. The crypt (housing the cathedral's treasury) is early Saxon, and you work your way along to more recent Norman (around the east transept), Transition (the tower), Early English (porch), Decorated (choir), and Perpendicular (nave). Have a look at the choir's misericords; heads carved therein are remarkable.

Newby Hall (three miles southeast of Ripon): Robert Adam was the creative force behind this eighteenth-century country house's ace-in-the-hole: a suite of galleries in the manner of a Roman temple, embracing a pair of low-ceilinged rooms flanking a domed rotunda, with the lot displaying a cache of classical sculpture. State rooms, as well, Chippendale furnished and tapestry embellished. Lovely.

Fountains Abbey, Fountains Hall, and Studbury Royal Garden (four miles southwest of Ripon) constitute a triple treat. The ruined Cistercian abbey (operated by the Department of the Environment) comprises what had been a Romanesque church, with its high tower still standing alongside an extraordinary, 300-foot-long, still-vaulted cellar. Seventeenth-century Fountains Hall edges the abbey ruins, with a fine Jacobean facade and furnished-in-period interiors. Adjacent is Studbury Royal, an extensive eighteenth-century formal garden, punctuated with pools, and highlighted by a colonnaded classic-style temple. Quite a show.

Harrogate (20 miles west of York) is a blandly pretty spa town, jam packed with hotels, the better to serve the conventions on which it thrives and interspersed with a range of meticulously tended formal gardens. Shop in James Street, in the center; take the traditional cure—Turkish baths, massage, sauna—at the cupola-topped *Royal Baths Assembly Rooms* (Victorian in origin) on Parliament Street. And have a look at the older *Royal Pump Room* (Crescent Road), now a museum of local lore and costumes.

SETTLING IN

Judge's Lodging Hotel (Lendal, York) is an early eighteenth-century town house, now a small hostelry of considerable panache, operated by an Anglo-French couple—Mr. and Mrs. G. C. Mason—with style and taste. A honey of a staircase leads from the traditionally furnished lobby floor to 15 no-two-alike rooms; one, a tower chamber with a four-poster bed. All are antiques-accented. There is a restaurant (Madame Mason is the chef) and a basement bar-lounge in which casual but tasty bar lunches are served. *First Class-Luxury.*

Dean Court Hotel (Duncombe Place, York) is enviably well situated—just opposite the Minster. This is a likable hotel—traditional in ambience, with inviting lobby-lounge (ideal for morning coffee or afternoon tea), good-value restaurant, cozy bar, and three dozen rooms, many of them extra-spacious. Ask for Room 27, with its superb Minster view. Friendly. A Best Western Hotel. *First Class.*

Viking Hotel (North Street, York): If it does not reflect Old York in either its modern architecture or decor, the Viking is big (187 rooms and suites) and full-facility, with two restaurants (one a worth-knowing-about carving-style operation, with all you want from the buffet carved to order), bar-lounge, and—hardly to be underappreciated—showers in all baths. *First Class.*

Abbots Mews Hotel (Marygate Lane, York) is a Victorian coachman's cottage and coachhouse converted, relatively recently, into a delightful hotel. The two-dozen-plus brightly wallpapered rooms are no two quite alike, with showers in most of the baths. Congenial bar-lounge, good and good-value restaurant. *First Class.*

Elliotts Hotel (Sycamore Place, York) shows what a hotelier with a sense of style can do, given a century-old mansion that's to be converted into a hotel. Public spaces—including a restaurant and a bar-lounge—are smart; likewise, well-equipped bedrooms. *First Class.*

Royal York Hotel (Station Road, York) opened as the Station Hotel in 1853. A year later, Queen Victoria stopped in for lunch, and it became the *Royal* Station Hotel; again it changed its name with new management in the early 1980s. Actually, the present building is an 1877 replacement for the first. There are a handsome central staircase, lounge for tea, chandeliered restaurant, small coffee shop, pair of bars, and 135 rooms, with those facing the garden and the Minster the nicest. Location is across the River Ouse from the core of town, a ten-minute walk away. An Orient Express hotel. *First Class.*

Friars' Garden Hotel (Station Road, York) is relatively new, occupying a refurbished building adjacent to the Royal York Hotel (above) and charging lower rates. There are two dozen twin-bedded rooms off a little lobby, along with a restaurant and bar. *First Class.*

Jorvik Hotel (Marygate, York) is an agreeable, small house, about half of whose 16 neat rooms have baths. Restaurant and bar are in the basement. Central. *Moderate.*

Middlethorpe Hall Hotel (Bishopthorpe Road, just south of York) is an early eighteenth-century brick mansion, set in a 26-acre park, that has recently been thoroughly refurbished to become a country-house hotel of no little distinction. The original ballroom is now the guests' drawing room, with an adjoining library. Still another ground floor salon is now the restaurant—fare melds English dishes with French—and there are just over 30 rooms, a dozen in the main house, the remainder in deftly converted auxiliary buildings. Same astute management as Bodysgallen Hall Hotel in Wales. *Luxury.*

Ripon Spa Hotel (Park Street, Ripon) is a rambling house of some vintage, attractively updated to the point where all but 2 of its 41 rooms have baths. Lobby-lounge, restaurant, and Turf Tavern Bar (honoring Ripon's racetrack and popular with locals) are inviting, and the rooms comfortable. A Best Western hotel. *First Class.*

Old Swan Hotel (Swan Road, Harrogate) has the virtue of a broad garden setting, but it's right in town. Old-school in ambience, it has 150 bedrooms, some of whose baths have showers, attractively traditional lounges, a reliable restaurant and coffee shop, a pair of congenial bars, and literary eminence: This was where mystery novelist Dame Agatha Christie was found after a mysterious ten-day disappearance in 1926. *First Class.*

Caesars Hotel (Valley Drive, Harrogate), near Harrogate scenic Valley Gardens, is an intimate but well-equipped house, with a cozy bar, attractive restaurant, and well-equipped rooms. *Moderate.*

Devonshire Arms Hotel (Bolton Abbey, near Skipton, 15 miles west of Harrogate) is a venerable coaching inn on land long owned by the Dukes of Devonshire, landlords of Chatsworth, the world-renowned Midlands mansion about which I write in Chapter 12. In 1980, the Duchess of Devonshire (one of the gifted Mitford sisters, which numbered authors Nancy and Jessica) and her husband set about turning the inn into a top-class country-house hotel. Harry Moon undertook the architectural renovations (for which he was later to receive a Royal Institute of Architects award), and the Duchess herself (responsible for decor of the Cavendish Hotel on the Chatsworth grounds) designed the interiors. The result is a charmer of a traditional-style hotel with 38 antiques-accented rooms, a clutch of relaxing lounges, and a restaurant whose cuisine is a deft blend of English and French, with the exceptional wine list compiled by the Marquess of Hartington, the duke's heir. *Luxury.*

DAILY BREAD
Chandelier (Goodramgate, York): One might fault the decor as fussy. But this is a professionally—and cheerfully—operated restaurant, with

Continental-accented fare, especially tasty at dinner. Lobster thermidor, *steak au poivre*, and roast duck are among the à la carte specialties, and a good-value four-course table d'hôte is also available. Lunch is more traditionally English. *First Class.*

Grapevine (Grape Lane, York) occupies two stories of a low-ceilinged, half-timbered medieval house. Dinner might consist of the day's soup or half a canteloupe, grilled pork chop or roast chicken, and a selection of cheese or sweets prepared on premises—from a groaning trolley. Wines are well priced, and the owning-operating family hospitable. Dinner only. *First Class.*

Judge's Lodging Hotel Restaurant (Lendal, York): Madame Mason, French half of the couple who own this small hotel (above), is chef and serves a three-course table d'hôte, with the house's terrine or *potage du jour* among starters; *coq au vin, tournedos béarnaise,* or *veau viennoise* among the entrées; a selection of fresh vegetables; salad and cheese courses if you so request; dessert; and coffee and chocolates to conclude. Dinner only. Pub lunches are served in the bar. Good cellar. *First Class.*

Thomas's Wine Bar (Museum Street, York): This superb Georgian house—King George IV was a guest—offers a tempting selection of salads from the buffet and daily hot plates at lunch, when it's always packed. At dinner, there's a three-course menu with coffee that's a buy; desserts include an estimable bread pudding. Super. *Moderate-First Class.*

Ye Olde Starre Inne (Stonegate, York) dates to 1664, and I doubt that it's had many quiet mealtime moments since. It's a honey of a pub-restaurant, especially good for shepherd's pie, grilled sausages, chicken salad, daily hot specials, and one of the best cheese boards I've come across. Fun. *Moderate.*

Black Swan Inn (Peasholme Green, York) was home to York's Lord Mayor when it was built in the sixteenth century. It's a half-timbered pub in the old tradition, welcoming and multiroomed. Open with a sherry at the bar, and continue with chicken pie and a glass of red wine. *Moderate.*

St. William's College Restaurant (College Street, York): The college is a onetime priests' residence, circa 1461, that's now part York Minster offices (the Minster is just opposite), part self-service restaurant. Lunch embraces soup, cold dishes, and hot specials. Morning coffee and afternoon tea means matchless cakes and pies and good scones. Closed for dinner, more's the pity. *Moderate.*

Plunkett's (Petergate, York): You've an uncontrollable urge for a bowl of chili or a hamburger? Pop into Plunkett's for either or, better yet, both. *Moderate.*

University of York Refectory (King's Manor, St. Leonard's Street, York): This upstairs student eatery welcomes strangers at lunchtime. Cafeteria style, satisfactory, and *Moderate.*

Ristorante Bari (Shambles, York): Pizza and pasta, chicken and steak, well priced and tasty. *Moderate.*

Old Deanery (Minster Road, Ripon): Dinner is a pleasure in this aged house, for long the residence of the deans of the cathedral, just across the way. The Swiss-style veal dishes are special; lunch is less elaborate. *First Class.*

Warehouse (Kirkgate, Ripon): Up a flight you go, for a nourishing lunch of, say, soup, salad, or quiche. *Moderate.*

Betty's (Parliament Street, Harrogate) is ideal for lunch—the table d'hôte is a good buy—or for snacks, morning coffee through afternoon tea. Not open for dinner. Central. *Moderate.*

Oliver (King's Road, Harrogate) is just the spot for a festive dinner. The fare is English, with Continental influence in agreeable doses. Attractive. *First Class.*

AFTER DARK
Theatre Royal (St. Leonard's Place, York)—originally Georgian, later Victorian, with a contemporary updating—presents its own repertory company in plays and visiting troupes, as well. Coffee bar serves snacks, and restaurant is open to nonticket-holders, morning coffee through dinner.

Lyons Concert Hall (University of York) is the site of frequent symphonic and chamber concerts by university and visiting groups.

Harrogate Theatre (Oxford Street, Harrogate) is among the handsomer of the north's traditional-style houses; repertory and visiting troupes' plays.

Royal Hall (King's Road, Harrogate) is still another looker of a Harrogate auditorium, frequently the site of symphonic and other concerts.

INCIDENTAL INTELLIGENCE

The regional airport is Leeds-Bradford, from where there are both international (Scandinavia, the Continent, Ireland) and domestic flights. Ships connect nearby Hull with Holland. *Further information:* York Tourist Information Centre, De Grey Rooms, Exhibition Square; Ripon Tourist Information Centre, Wakeman's House, Market Place; Harrogate Tourist Information Centre, Royal Baths Assembly Rooms.

24

Edinburgh
And the Scottish Borders

BACKGROUND BRIEFING
It does not seem probable, let alone possible, with the twenty-first century approaching. But here is a European capital that is in part a medieval town beneath a castle on a crag—and in part an exquisite Georgian town. Edinburgh has never been ordinary, either architecturally, geographically, or historically.

Glasgow overpowers it today in size and economic importance, and in no way can it compete with the global preeminence of London. Still, Edinburgh is a proud city—proud of beauty so striking that not even rain nor mist diminish it; proud of the stubbornness with which it holds onto the gray stone monuments of its history, in an era when plastic dominates; proud to be governmental seat of a land—275 miles long by 150 miles wide, with a population exceeding five million—that occupies nearly a third of the area of the United Kingdom; and not unmindful that it was the Britons, one of the four major tribes of fifth-century Scotland (then called *Caledonia* by the departing Romans) whose name the current kingdom takes.

I first realized how strong is the sense of history of these people when, some years back, I found myself in a town on the South Island of distant New Zealand. Its first inhabitants, colonists from Scotland, named it Dunedin—"fortress on a ridge." This was the name Edinburgh's first inhabitants gave *their* settlement, only to have the ancient Angles take the "edin" from Dunedin—resembling the "Edwin" of the king at the moment—and add the suffix "burgh." It stuck.

Edinburgh, with its great age and its great castle, figures in Scottish history from the very beginning. (There have been, to capsulize, five principal Scottish dynasties, beginning with Kenneth MacAlpin, in 843; continuing with the houses of Dunkeld, Canmore, and Bruce; and on to the Stewarts (or Stuarts), whose last reigning sovereign,

James VI, left Edinburgh in 1603 to rule England, as well as Scotland, as James I. For a small country, whose monarchs have come from the South for several centuries now, it is even more remarkable than it might otherwise be for the gallery of memorable sovereigns it has produced.

Take Duncan, whom Shakespeare was to write about and who was among the earlier of the kings, reigning almost a thousand years ago. His trusted general, Macbeth, murdered him, took over the kingdom, and himself reigned for seventeen years—ably, according to accounts. But Macbeth paid for his crime when Duncan's son Malcolm killed him and became King Malcolm III. Malcolm's career deserves notice. First, he married a lady named Margaret, sister to the pretender to the throne of England. Second, though he embroiled Scotland in war after war during a reign of nearly four decades, he was able to keep his kingdom independent at a crucial time.

Third, wars or no, his devout, English-speaking wife reorganized the church in Scotland, deemphasizing the major role of the Gaelic-speaking clergy in favor of English-imported priests from the South, who played a not insignificant role in encouraging Scotland's linguistic drift from Gaelic to English. Fourth, Malcolm had the distinction of being husband to a queen who was sainted by the Catholic Church (not for her work in the area of language, but rather for her piety and devotion to the poor), father to four sons who became kings of Scotland, and, as if that were not enough, father to two daughters who became queens in England. Considering the relationship they were to have in ensuing centuries—both warlike and peaceful—it is just as well that St. Margaret helped bring the English language to Scotland; the two peoples have been able to communicate with each other ever since, though not always amicably.

Economic, religious, and political disputes for a long while impelled the Scots to take the French as their allies against the English. France's role in the affairs of the two countries was never more important than when, toward the end of the sixteenth century, James V, a Stuart, was married to the French Mary of Guise, who succeeded him as Queen Regent upon his death and who obtained permission from the Scottish Parliament to have their daughter Mary raised in Catholic France at a time when Protestant Reformers were gaining strength in Scotland. While still a young woman, Mary became the widow of young King François II of France. Upon the death of her mother in Edinburgh Castle, Mary returned to the land of her birth to reign as its queen. She married the Earl of Darnley, an English cousin; saw her Italian secretary, Rizzio, murdered in Holyrood Palace by courtiers presumably working with Darnley; became implicated in the later death of Darnley; and married again (her third and last husband was

the ill-fated Earl of Bothwell), against the advice of her nobles. She then found herself embroiled in a test of wills with her cousin, Elizabeth I of England, only to spend the last two decades of her life a prisoner of Elizabeth in a succession of drafty English castles before losing her head at Fotheringay.

There was, however, more than melodrama in Mary's story. There was much irony, as well. For it developed that Mary's only child—her son by Darnley—succeeded her as James VI of Scotland *and* came to rule as James I of England—the first joint sovereign of the two long-antagonistic kingdoms. It is this same son of the beautiful, but unlucky, Mary Stuart whose name was given to the Protestant Bible in general use today and also to Jamestown, the first English settlement—founded in 1607—in America.

Almost a century elapsed—a century full of animosity—before, in 1707, the Act of Union properly dotted the i's and crossed the t's and gave Scotland the representation that was rightfully hers in the British Parliament (to whose House of Commons she sends seventy-one members). And while not absolutely everyone on both sides of the border has lived happily ever after (battles ensued in the clan-dominated Highlands—by Stuart-descended, so-called Jacobite pretenders to the British throne for another century, and, as recently as 1953, Scottish nationalists made away with the Scots' ancient Stone of Scone from London's Westminster Abbey), the two countries have shared the same monarchs ever since, as well as a number of common government services. A member of the Cabinet in London, the Secretary of State for Scotland, represents the Scots who have, over the years, rightly insisted upon certain institutions of their own. (The Church of Scotland, for example, is Presbyterian, not Anglican—which in Scotland is called the Scottish Episcopal Church—and laws of Scotland, as a result of Scotland's earlier ties with France, are, in certain respects, closer to those of France than to those of England.)

Still, Anglo-Scottish wounds were long in healing, as reflected in the lapse between reigning monarchs' visits north of the Tweed: there were none between Charles II in the seventeenth century and George IV in the nineteenth. Ever since Victoria's time, sovereigns have spent part of every summer at Balmoral Castle (Chapter 27) in the Highlands, while the official Edinburgh residence of the Royal Family is the same Holyrood House—largely rebuilt by Charles II, to be sure—where Mary Stuart saw her secretary murdered.

ON SCENE

Lay of the Land: You can't miss in Edinburgh. Edinburgh Castle is always there as a landmark to guide you. The medieval Old Town extends from Edinburgh Castle down a succession of four streets, one following the other—Castlehill, Lawnmarket, High Street, and Canongate—and collectively known as the Royal Mile, to the Palace of Holyrood House; there is no more romantic a walk in all Europe. Wide and splendid Princes Street—with parklike Princes Street Gardens on the side facing the castle—separates the Old Town from the eighteenth-century New Town. Aside from the Castle, there's one other elevated sector of the town visible from all about. With the structures atop it, you might think it a kind of Acropolis. Actually, it is called Calton Hill.

THE ROYAL MILE

Edinburgh Castle (Royal Mile) straddles an eminence 270 feet above Princes Street. It has been around a long time. That very same King Edwin—earlier mentioned as the king for whom Edinburgh is named—was among early tenants; others of note were the same Malcolm III and his sainted wife Margaret whose contributions to Scottish history are discussed in earlier pages. Indeed, the oldest structure within the castle complex is the lovely little Margaret Chapel, named for the saint-queen and done in Romanesque style. Of more interest, though, is the room where Mary Queen of Scots gave birth to James VI of Scotland and I of England. To be inspected, too, is the big hall that has served variously as banquet room and parliament and that is now a museum of old weapons. The Scottish Regalia is in a room that invariably has a long queue at its door, but the bejeweled crown is spectacular and worth a wait.

Palace of Holyrood House (Royal Mile) is open only when no member of the Royal Family is occupying it. It was first used as a royal residence by Mary Stuart's grandfather, James IV, but after the Restoration (Edinburgh had been rather a busy place during the Charles I–Cromwell period), Charles II largely, but not completely, rebuilt it. The most recent refurbishing was by the reigning sovereign, Elizabeth II, in the 1980s. The state rooms are perfectly beautiful. But there's more. You may see Mary Stuart's supper room, and there is a plaque where the body of David Rizzio, her Italian secretary, was found after his murder in that little chamber by courtiers with whom Mary's second husband, Lord Darnley, was collaborating. Bonnie Prince Charlie, the Stuart prince who cut such a dashing figure when he tried in vain in 1745 to gain the throne with the aid of Highland followers (and who later sadly roamed the Continent a drunk), entertained at Holyrood. King George IV gave a ball on the occasion of his Edinburgh visit in 1822; he delighted his Scottish subjects by wearing full Highland dress.

St. Giles's Cathedral (Royal Mile) is an unusual squarish Gothic structure, distinct from the Gothic one sees in England, whose single tower is topped by an equally unusual, crown-shaped dome; this is believed to be the oldest part of the building—early twelfth-century. St. Giles fascinates with its history; indeed, few churches in all Britain surpass it in this respect. Upon St. Giles's fortunes rested those of Scotland and its ultimate relationship with England, and differences of consequence between the two nations centered on the way people organized systems of worship. St. Giles began as a Catholic parish (ironically, it was not then the seat of a bishop, even in a church organized on episcopal lines), became principal pulpit for the strongly anti-Episcopal Reformation preaching of Presbyterian John Knox in the mid-sixteenth century (the last Catholic mass was said in 1560), and reverted to Episcopacy under the pro-Anglican policy of King James VI and his son, King Charles I. After the Civil War, the episcopate resumed with Charles II and was not abolished until the Act of Union, under Queen Anne, in the early eighteenth century, when St. Giles again became Presbyterian. Ever since George IV worshiped in St. Giles, British monarchs have visited it as heads of the Church of Scotland. And it is today the site of a chapel, called Thistle for the order of Scottish knights who meet in it, built in the early twentieth century and a hop and skip—irony of ironies after centuries of turmoil—from the specially designated Royal Pew.

Parliament House (Royal Mile) is interesting in part because it is no longer a Parliament House and hasn't been since the Act of Union in 1707, when its functions were taken over by Westminster—not always to the satisfaction of the Scots. It is interesting also because it is now a courthouse; Scotland's highest tribunals meet here. Interiors are among Scotland's most sumptuous; by all means, go in and have a look around.

John Knox's House (Royal Mile): Even the most ardent admirers of Mary Queen of Scots will find John Knox's house worthwhile. For one thing, it is not certain that that fanatically anti-Catholic and unrelenting adversary of the Queen actually owned the house, although he is believed to have lived in it. It is, at any rate, late fifteenth-century and typically Edinburgh of the period.

Gladstone's Land (Royal Mile) sounds like the title of a soppy romantic novel, but it's actually the name of a superbly furnished house of an affluent seventeenth-century merchant, still with a street-floor shop area and living quarters—painted-beam bedroom with a giant fireplace and grand green-walled drawing room, most striking—above. National Trust for Scotland.

Lady Stair's House (Royal Mile) pales in contrast to Gladstone's Land, its neighbor. Still, you might pop in for a quick survey of manuscripts, correspondence, and portraits of three major Scottish authors—Stevenson, Burns, and Scott. Seventeenth-century.

Huntly House (Royal Mile) goes back to the sixteenth-century and serves well today as a repository of Edinburgh historical lore—well-furnished rooms of various periods most especially, with lovely old objects in additional galleries, silver and crystal, porcelain and paintings among them. Nice.

Canongate Tollbooth (Royal Mile), about the age of Huntly House, is for tartan buffs: there's a striking display of them and the occasional temporary exhibition, as well.

THE NEW TOWN

The New Town's general grid plan is mostly late eighteenth- and early nineteenth-century, with considerable work by Robert Adam, that era's great architect-designer. With the help of his brother James, Adam drew on the designs of ancient Rome and Greece, eliminating heaviness and pompousness from them, much like the Palladian villas of northwestern Italy. Adam's houses, furniture, decorative objects, and entire areas of towns (as in Bath, for example) are to be found throughout the British Isles. Although the principal architect for New Town was a twenty-three-year-old Scot named James Craig, it was Adam who designed *Charlotte Square* as an integrated unit. Its north facade is considered one of his best pieces of work.

To see what I mean, you have only to buy a ticket at No. 7—now called *Georgian House*—and go right in. This jewel-like Adam work, after a meticulous restoration and furnishing in period, was opened as a museum in 1970 by Queen Elizabeth the Queen Mother. A town house, it is not big, but it is choice; entrance hall, parlor, and drawing room on the ground floor; bedroom and dining room above, with paintings of the same caliber as the furniture by Scottish masters like Ramsay and Raeburn and Europeans like Teniers and Bols. National Trust for Scotland.

George Street—main thoroughfare of the New Town—is a visual delight. Particularly worth viewing are the *Church of St. Andrew and St. George*, a Georgian gem, with superb plasterwork in its oval ceiling; and the *Assembly Rooms*, splendidly proportioned and hung with great crystal chandeliers that serve during the annual Edinburgh festival as headquarters for the Festival Club, which visitors join on a membership basis. *St. Andrew Square* is at the opposite end of George Street from Charlotte Square; most of its handsome houses are now bank-occupied. And there is still another major Robert Adam building: *Register House*, opposite the main post office on Princes Street; both it and Charlotte Square's *West Register House*—by architect Robert Reid, with a dome modeled on St. Paul's in London—welcome visitors and have exhibits relating to their history and design.

PRINCES STREET

Princes Street, which separates medieval Edinburgh from the New Town, lies beneath the summit of the Castle, and with it as a background—and the nineteenth-century Sir Walter Scott Memorial, resembling nothing so much as a detached campanile of a Gothic church, garden encircled—it is one of Europe's major main streets. Hotels and Waverly Railway Station are landmarks.

MAJOR MUSEUMS

Scottish National Portrait Gallery (Queen Street) is the one to begin with. The idea is not unlike that of the National Portrait Gallery in London—to give you an idea of what the country's past was all about by letting you look at pictures of the people who made it, painted by their contemporaries. The early Stuarts—all six Jameses, Mary, Mary's beautiful French mother, Mary of Guise; and later Stuarts, too—Bonnie Prince Charlie as a lad and as a debauched man in his fifties; his common-law wife, Charlotte, Duchess of Albany, and . . . but look yourself; you'll recognize many portraits you've seen reproduced in books. The *National Museum of Antiquities* occupies the ground floor of the building housing the National Portrait Gallery, and is full of surprises—weapons and shields most especially, but more mundane objects, too.

National Gallery of Scotland (Princes Street), along with Glasgow's underappreciated City Art Gallery and that of Aberdeen following—is an all-Scotland leader. It occupies a gracious mock-classic temple, heart of town—precisely where it deserves to be with so luminous a collection. Get to know the Scots first, in a section devoted to the country's own painters of the seventeenth, eighteenth, and nineteenth centuries, with Sir Henry Raeburn, Allan Ramsay, and David Wilkie the standouts. Then concentrate on English and Continental European work. Every major school is represented, from French post-Impressionists like Gauguin and Degas to Spaniards like Goya and

Zurbarán, Italians like Raphael and Tiepolo, and Dutchmen like Rembrandt and Hals. You'll not soon forget blue-gowned *Madame de Pompadour*, by Boucher; lace-collared *Mrs. Graham*, by Gainsborough; Velásquez's *Old Woman Cooking Eggs;* Ramsay's portrait of his beautiful wife; Vuillard's own studio as painted by himself; and Titian's *Three Ages of Man.*

Royal Scottish Museum (Chambers Street) is an old-fashioned hodgepodge from the middle of the last century—with lots of things for the schoolkids in science and technology sections, but with some priceless objects (everything except paintings) from throughout Europe and Asia (Moslem enamels, Meissen porcelain—to give you an idea).

Scottish National Gallery of Modern Art (Royal Botanic Garden) is not central, but it's super—with the bonus of a walk through the lovely Royal Botanic Garden to reach it, in an understatedly eye-filling mansion that's bigger than it looks. The collection surveys the modern art movement from the early part of this century—Italian sculptor Medardo Rosso's head of a boy—to the New York School's Roy Lichtenstein and other Americans, including Duane Hanson, represented by a frightening lifelike sculpted couple called, simply, *Tourists.* And there's much in between, including Switzerland's Klee, Germany's Kirchner, and Britons like Ben Nicholson and Percy Wyndham, with Matisse, Derain, and Braque among the French and lots more, Belgium's Magritte through Spain's Miró.

OTHER EDINBURGH DESTINATIONS

Edinburgh University (Chamber Street), founded by King James VI, is best known abroad for its medical school, but architecture buffs will want to admire its Old College Quadrangle, an early nineteenth-century complex built from designs by Robert Adam.

National Library of Scotland (George IV Bridge) is the Scottish counterpart of London's British Library and the National Library of Wales in Aberswyth and, like them, enjoys the privilege of copyright deposit—entitlement to every book printed—and has since 1710; it houses some four and a half million books, but what you want to see is the exhibit—which changes periodically—of treasures from its collections.

Edinburgh Zoo (Haymarket) is a quarter-hour's drive (why not go by public bus?) west of Princes Street, with its major draw the biggest captive colony of penguins extant. Every afternoon, precisely at 2:30, they leave their enclosure for a walk among their fans; Edinburghers call it the Penguin Parade.

SUBURBAN EXCURSIONS

Hopetoun House (12 miles west of town, near Forth Road Bridge) is one of the top-drawer British country estates, and, if I were you, I would no more miss it than did King George IV, in the course of his historic visit—the first of a British monarch's to Scotland since that of Charles II—in 1822. Named for the first Earl of Hopetoun, for whom it was designed in 1703, it was enlarged later in the century to designs of the Adam family—William Adam, the father, and his sons John and Robert. Superbly symmetrical, in the Palladian manner, it embraces a four-story central house that is flanked by two lower wings, each surmounted with a cupola. Setting is a park at the edge of the Firth of Forth. You tour the house in halves. The so-called Bruce bedchamber, with an incredible early eighteenth-century gilded four-poster, highlights the first half. The second is full of treats—paintings by Rubens, Canaletto, and Teniers in the yellow drawing room; a Robert Adam stucco ceiling of distinction in the red drawing room; and a dining room that is among the grander in a nation of grand country-house dining rooms, with portraits by Gainsborough, Raeburn, and Ramsay. Restaurant.

Lauriston Castle (Davidson's Mains, five miles from town) is late sixteenth-century, with original gables and turrets of its somber stone facade remaining, in a garden setting on the Firth of Forth. Within, there have been changes, not necessarily felicitous. Still, the tapestry-walled dining room, drawing room with eighteenth-century furniture and a graceful domed ceiling remain impressive, and the 1903 copper fixtures of the main bathroom are, to understate, one of a kind.

Cramond is a village on the Firth of Forth, the North Sea estuary that is Edinburgh's outlet to the sea. It is of Roman origin—minor treasures excavated are in Huntly House Museum (above) on the Royal Mile—but the major draws, apart from a sailboat-dotted harbor, are restored eighteenth-century houses and a tower going back to medieval times. Still other area villages that charm effortlessly are *Rosslyn* (with a fifteenth-century chapel), *Swanston* (whitewashed, thatched houses on a traditional green, with a house nearby that was a retreat of Stevenson's), and *South Queensferry*, from which you have a fine view of the two bridges spanning the Firth of Forth; the newer of the two, by far, was opened by Queen Elizabeth II in 1964, and has a central span of 3,300 feet; the oldest—the rail bridge—has been going strong since 1890. And last but hardly least is *Leith*—hardly a village, but rather the bustling seaport of Edinburgh, with its historic core eminently visitable. Beeline for *Lamb's House*, for which Mary Queen of Scots herself beelined, upon landing at Leith in 1561 (National Trust for Scotland), and have a look, as well, at Gothic-origin *St. Mary's Church.*

Vat 69 Distillery may be combined with a visit to Hopetoun (above); it's passed en route to it, and is also taken in as part of organized inspection of the Firth of Forth area—with bus tours memorably named Whisky and Water. If you go on your own, admission is free; no samples.

THE SCOTTISH BORDERS

Aptly named, the undervisited Borders region lies just below Edinburgh, extending some 30 miles south to the English border, with Carlisle (Chapter 11) on the west and Newcastle (Chapter 15) on the east. Because it is so close to Edinburgh, good hotels and restaurants are relatively few and far between, so that you might want to consider exploring the Borders on an excursion or two out of the capital.

Traquair House (Innerleithen, 29 miles south of Edinburgh) is outstanding not because it is beautiful—which it isn't, in the conventional sense—but because it is extraordinarily old and history-rich. By the time of Mary Queen of Scots' mid-sixteenth-century visits to the house (whose museum displays her rosary, crucifix, purse, letters with her signature, a quilt she and her attendants [the "Four Maries"] worked, and a cradle in which she rocked the son who was to be James VI of Scotland and I of England), it was some four centuries old and long associated with the Scottish Royal Family, not to mention English sovereigns from across the nearby frontier. All told, 27 kings visited Traquair. State rooms—drawing room, dining room, so-called still room—are attractive, but you go to Traquair because it breathes Scotland's past. All hail to Peter Maxwell Stuart, its twentieth laird, for operating it so professionally.

Mellerstain (35 miles south of Edinburgh, near Gordon) looks Gothic Revival without, but is Palladian-style Robert Adam within. Set beside formal gardens, Lord and Lady Binning's country seat is nothing like as monumental as bigger Hopetoun House (above), another Adam house. Mellerstain understates. Its major interior is the library. Pompeiian motifs and the busts of Roman emperors surmount its bookcase-lined walls, and the pale-green-and-salmon ceiling plasterwork is among Adam's loveliest. More Adam ceilings are to be seen in the other state rooms, and there are fine paintings, with Ramsay (in abundance), Raeburn, Gainsborough, Constable, and Van Dyck among the artists. With fine furniture, much of it original, by Adam. Café.

Floors Castle (40 miles south of Edinburgh, near Kelso) is fancifully turreted and domed—in the manner of a medieval castle—but is actually a meld of the early eighteenth and early nineteenth centuries, with William Adam (Robert's father) its original designer, for the first in a long line of Dukes of Roxburghe, who still are resident. Pronounced like the first syllable of *flouride* (with an *s* added), it is aptly sited and has gracious interiors, its plastered pink-and-white sitting room perhaps the most important. The art is sumptuous. Raeburn's portrait of an early nineteenth-century Duke of Roxburghe stays with you, and there are paintings by Lely, Reynolds, Gainsborough, Ramsay, and Richard Wilson.

Bowhill (45 miles south of Edinburgh, near Selkirk), backed by a high hill and fronted by a languid lake, was built in 1812 by ancestors of the current occupant, the Duke of Buccleuch and Queensbury. Note imported Chinese papers and silk brocades surfacing the walls, exceptional French furniture and Aubusson tapestries in the state rooms, and priceless paintings, including no less than eight by Guardi, with Canaletto, Holbein, and—special, this—Leonardo da Vinci represented. Café.

Abbotsford (35 miles south of Edinburgh, near Melrose) was erected in 1811 by Sir Walter Scott, in the Romantic style he so espoused in his novels. Its exterior is agreeable enough, but unless you are an absolutely avid Scott buff, the half dozen rooms of the interior open to visitors—including the author's paneled study and quantities of arms, swords, and other Scott-collected memorabilia—may disappoint. What I like best is a portrait of Sir Walter with an adoring wolfhound, by Sir Henry Raeburn. Mrs. Walter Maxwell-Scott, O.B.E., a descendant, is the current occupant.

The Border Abbeys—one each in St. Boswell's, Jedburgh, Kelso, and Melrose—are in ruins and within a compact area that can be likened to a triangle, each side about 12 miles in length. *Dryburgh Abbey*, in bucolic St. Boswell's, is not to be underestimated, as adjacent to it is one of the best hotels in the Borders; the abbey dates to the twelfth century, and the English enemy damaged it on two occasions, with post-Reformation attacks, as well. Monks' living quarters are more intact than the church, and Sir Walter Scott's tomb adds interest.

Melrose Abbey, on Abbey Street in the town that takes its name, must once have been superb. Twelfth-century, it suffered a series of attacks, not unlike Dryburgh; tracery of the Gothic windows of the long chapel and the transept indicate how elaborate it must once have been. *Kelso Abbey*, on Bridge Street in Kelso, remained in good shape longer than the others, into the sixteenth century. The western transept and bits of the cloister are the most impressive remains. Before leaving this town on the River Tweed, have a look at a square called, simply, The Square—eighteenth- and early nineteenth-century, with a cupola-topped Town Hall. *Jedburgh Abbey*, just off Market Place in the center of Jedburgh, looks—if one is far enough away—as if it might be substantially intact. The three tiers of arches of its high and mighty nave survive, and so do enough of the walls to afford the visitor an idea of what this Augustinian monastery was like until its ultimate destruction four and a half centuries ago. Nearby, off High Street, is a stone house where Mary Queen of Scots stayed, recovering from an illness on a 1566 visit; it contains a little exhibit—museum is too grand a term—about Mary, but worry not, if you miss it. Still another little museum of local lore occupies a nineteenth-century building, an ex-jail atop Castlegate Hill.

SETTLING IN

Caledonian Hotel (Princes Street, Edinburgh): If it was never as superior architecturally as its longtime sister-hotel, the North British (below), the "Callie," over the years, became the city's most fashionable. Withal, it was no longer lovely to look upon when Gleneagles Hotels took it over from expiring British Transport Hotels in the early 1980s. They pumped millions of pounds into a stem-to-stern renovation, rooms through restaurants. And they achieved considerable esthetic success. The Callie has become a looker. One of its two restaurants, accorded later space in this chapter, is an all-Britain leader. The lounge is ideal for tea, and there's a congenial bar and a coffee shop, as well. Member, Leading Hotels of the World. *Luxury.*

North British Hotel (Princes Street, Edinburgh) has always, for me at least, been the most romantic of the city's hotels, occupying a Victorian château whose Big Ben-like clock tower is an Edinburgh landmark. Though reasonably well maintained in its last years as a British Transport hotel, the "NB" needed a facelift. Taken over by the crack Gleneagles chain in the early 1980s, it has been subjected to meticulous and costly refurbishing. The glorious public rooms— handsomest of any hotel in town—have been impeccably restored. (One of them is used for the fabulously successful, regularly scheduled "Hail, Caledonia" evenings—featuring a dinner of Scottish specialties, including haggis, preceded by cock-a-leekie soup and followed by roast beef and dessert, traditional entertainment-cum-bagpipers, and a sing-along.) The Palm Court is again a lovely lounge for tea and drinks. The American Bar has never looked spiffier. The Cleikum restaurant (about which more later) is again first-rate. The 200 high-ceilinged suites and rooms—some with vistas of Edinburgh Castle—are being updated as part of a continuing program. And there is a convenient elevator connection with subterranean Waverly Railway Station. *First Class.*

Edinburgh Sheraton Hotel (Lothian Road at Festival Square, Edinburgh): A contemporary hotel in the very core of Edinburgh? The Edinburgh Sheraton—more horizontal than vertical, striking of facade, but at the same time designed with the restraint that becomes a luxury hotel in the conservative Scottish capital—fronts a recently created square opposite circular Usher Hall, the city's principal venue for concerts. The Sheraton's lobby, which doubles as a morning-coffee and afternoon-tea lounge, is pastel hued. Its sole restaurant—generously proportioned Café Beaumont, open nonstop from early breakfast through late supper—is one of the superlative interior spaces in town, with the Atholl Cocktail Bar just opposite. There are just over 260 smartly furnished, chintz-accented suites and rooms, with superb American-style baths. A Fitness Center houses sauna, whirlpool, and plunge pool. Specify a front room, so that your view will be of Edinburgh Castle. *Luxury.*

George Hotel (George Street, Edinburgh) reflects the graciousness of the eighteenth-century New Town, of which it's a part, with a perfectly lovely lobby, high-ceilinged restaurant, pair of delightful bars, coffee shop, and very pleasant rooms in contemporary contrast with traditional-look public spaces. *First Class.*

Roxburghe Hotel (Charlotte Square, Edinburgh) ranks almost with the George (above) as the ideal New Town headquarters, occupying a clutch of eighteenth-century mansions in Robert Adam-designed Charlotte Square. Restaurant and bar have contemporary touches, as do the nearly 80 rooms, just over 60 of which have baths, with showers in some singles. Lovely. *First Class.*

Carlton Hotel (North Bridge, Edinburgh): When I first knew it, the venerable Carlton was part of the Trusthouse Forte group and the only hotel in Edinburgh whose every room had a bath. It has changed hands over the years and relatively recently expanded into the adjacent building, in the course of a thorough and much-needed facelift.

There are now 220 bright, full-facility rooms; a leisure center that includes pool, gym, and sauna; and convenient restaurant and bar-lounge. An enviably central location. *First Class.*

Albany Hotel (Albany Street, Edinburgh) is a New Town house or, I should say, a group of contiguous New Town houses joined and converted with panache into a modern 21-room hotel, with original architectural features—the glass cupola-topped stairwell, for example—remaining. Restaurant, bar. *First Class.*

Howard Hotel (Great King Street, Edinburgh), in an updated trio of joined New Town houses, offers just over two dozen bedrooms, some traditional style (these are attractive—and pricey), some contemporary; single rooms have showers. There are, as well, an excellent restaurant and a bar whose lunches are deservedly popular. *First Class.*

King James Thistle Hotel (Leith Street, Edinburgh) is unexceptional architecturally—a modern box, though well equipped, with 160 full-facility bedrooms (some with showers in their baths), restaurant, and two bars, one of which doubles as a late-hours disco and serves lunches. *First Class.*

Mount Royal Hotel (Princes Street, Edinburgh): Visitors like the Mount Royal's location. It's not fancy but it's full facility: 157 compact rooms, restaurant, bar. *Moderate.*

Royal British Hotel (Princes Street, Edinburgh)—not to be confused with the same street's North British (above)—is a budget-category house, contemporary within, albeit with an imposing facade of old. Most rooms have baths. Restaurant, bar. *Moderate.*

Old Waverly Hotel (Princes Street, Edinburgh) boasts an elaborate turn-of-century facade, but is simpler inside. Most of its 72 rooms have baths, however; restaurant and bar. *Moderate.*

Saint Andrew Hotel (St. Andrew Street, Edinburgh) has an enviable situation, a step from Princes Street. It's agreeably elderly, with a restaurant and bar, but I wish, given the top location, that more than 9 of its 72 rooms had baths. *Moderate.*

Gordon Bruce Hotel (Learmouth Garden South, Edinburgh): You're a wee bit away from the center here, but within walking distance. This is a turn-of-century house turned into a small hotel, most of whose rooms have baths, some with shower. Restaurant and a bar. *Moderate.*

Rothesay Hotel (Rothesay Place, Edinburgh): More than half the 40 rooms in this brightly decorated, if unpretentious, hotel have baths, and you can walk to the center. *Moderate.*

Dalhousie Castle Hotel (Bonnyrigg, eight miles south of Edinburgh): Not many hotels are seven centuries old. Dalhousie has been a proper castle most of that time, with guests ranging from King Edward I to Queen Victoria. The two dozen rooms are large and antiques-accented, some with four-posters and those lovely eighteenth-century chests of drawers called highboys. Bar is congenial, library paneled, restaurant candlelit. *First Class.*

Dryburgh Abbey Hotel (St. Boswell's) takes the name of the ruined abbey (above) that is its immediate neighbor. This is an idyllically situated old house in the Borders country. Sixteen of the 29 rooms have bath. Attractive restaurant, bar, and lounge that's ideal for morning coffee or afternoon tea. *First Class.*

Traquair Arms Hotel (Innerleithen) is an unassuming but welcoming house in the Borders area, about half of whose 10 bedrooms have baths. Restaurant is good, bar congenial. *Moderate.*

Teviotdale Lodge Hotel (Teviotdale) is an unassuming eight-room house—a few rooms have full baths—in the Borders, with a restaurant and bar, wherein are served good-value lunches. *Moderate.*

Cross Keys Hotel (High Street, Kelso) is an impressively facaded, onetime coaching inn: 13 of its 20 rooms have baths. Popular restaurant and two bars, one of which serves lunch. *Moderate.*

George & Abbotsford Hotel (High Street, Melrose) was opened well over a century back and has seen recent refurbishing. Thirteen of its 20 rooms have baths, and there are both restaurant and bar, the latter serving inexpensive lunches. *Moderate.*

DAILY BREAD
Prestonfield House (Priestfield Road, two miles from the center of Edinburgh): I start with this noncentral restaurant because it is exceptional. Prestonfield is a Baroque mansion out of the seventeenth century that is today a small, five-room inn and a restaurant of consequence. Benjamin Franklin scooted up while he was our Ambassador

to France. I don't think I would go quite that distance, but it's surely worth the ride from Princes Street. The architect was the very same who redesigned Holyrood House for Charles II; possibly for that reason there's a portrait of that king on the premises. The ground floor is given over to eating and/or drinking in a pair of bars and pair of dining rooms, each furnished in exquisite pieces of the period. Fare is at once Scottish and Continental, with delicious entrées of beef, lamb, and, in season, game; and a trolley of made-on-the-premises sweets that alone make a pilgrimage worthwhile. *Luxury.*

Pompadour Restaurant (Caledonia Hotel, Princes Street, Edinburgh), restored to its mock-eighteenth-century glory, is at once one of the handsomest rooms in town and a source of extraordinarily good, French-influenced cuisine, with welcome local touches, to be sure. By that, I mean you may open with a nouvelle-style mousse or terrine or, if you prefer, typically Scottish cock-a-leekie soup. Beef is heartily British, but there are veal specialties from south of the Channel. Sweets are superb, wine list exceptional, and service expert. In my view, one of Britain's best restaurants. *Luxury.*

Café Beaumont (Edinburgh Sheraton Hotel, Festival Square, Edinburgh) is a dramatic exercise in low-key pastels, walls lined with banquettes, tables handsomely laid, and picture windows affording views of Usher Hall and, beyond, Edinburgh Castle. The hotel's sole restaurant, it is open from 7:00 A.M. until 11:00 P.M. and is particularly posh when candlelit at dinner. Specialties include lentil salad with smoked eel or *tagliatelli* with caviar and lime cream as openers; venison with *chanterelles* and gooseberries or rock lobster on fresh broccoli as entrées; and a fabulous *Drambuie soufflé* with a poppy-seed *mousseline* as the *dessert-de-résistance.* There's a buffet lunch midday and a between-and-after-meals menu featuring steaks, burgers, salads, and sandwiches. Depending upon when you pop in, *Moderate through Luxury.*

Milano (Victoria Street, Edinburgh): You will have detected in other chapters of this volume my penchant for Italian restaurants in Britain; no foreign cuisine travels to these islands more satisfactorily. Milano is a case in point. It looks good—amply proportioned, beige-walled, chandeliered. And it tastes good. Given its name, it makes a point of serving *risotto ala milanese* to perfection; pasta dishes are cooked *al dente* and are superbly sauced. Chicken specialties—one in a mushroom and pepper sauce—are first rate; likewise, those of veal. And I've had no better poached salmon anywhere in Scotland. In my view, one of Britain's best restaurants. *First Class.*

Cousteaus (Hanover Street, Edinburgh), with its light, bright look, appears upon entering to be more casual an operation than proves to be the case. The name of its game is seafood, prepared as it is in France. By that, I mean very well, indeed, with the range *moules* (mussels) *marinière*, simply grilled salmon, trout *amandine*, and lobster thermidor. *Dauphinois* potatoes accompany entrées at dinner. Lunch—embracing the house's delicious fish soup, entrée, dessert, and coffee—is a solid buy. *First Class.*

Cleikum (North British Hotel, Princes Street, Edinburgh): What's Scottish food all about? A meal or two at Cleikum provides authentic answers. You may have to order haggis—sheep innards, suet, and oatmeal cooked in a sheep's paunch and served with *chappit tatties* (mashed potatoes) and *bashed neeps* (turnips)—in advance. But less bizarre specialties are always available—Scotch broth (made with vegetables and barley), cock-a-leekie soup (based on leeks), potted hough ("frae an auld cottage recipe"—a beef dish), mince and tatties (stewed potatoes and onions), and all the celebrated Scottish fish— salmon, finnan haddock, and kippers; not to mention the good Scottish beef, in steaks and, of course, roasted. Have the sherry trifle to end. *First Class.*

Carvers' Table (George Hotel, George Street, Edinburgh): The George has transformed its domed and colonnaded main restaurant into an eat-all-you-like roast beef, lamb, and pork operation, and I can't think of a better reason to have a meal in the city's handsomest restaurant environment. Hie yourself to the buffet, carve as much as you like of the roasts, and help yourself to vegetables, after being served a first course, with cheese or dessert and coffee to follow. Excellent value. *First Class.*

Number 36 (Howard Hotel, Great King Street, Edinburgh) is the name of the stylish subterranean restaurant of this hotel. Fellow diners are mostly local, drawn by a creative mix of Scottish specialties—a *pâté* of kippers, a Scotch smoked-salmon omelet, and Scotland's own version of Cheddar as a dessert cheese—and other favorites: roast venison through steak-and-mushroom pie. You also can get a lemon pudding with cream and almond filling from the celebrated nineteenth-century cookbook by the legendary Mrs. Beeton. Good-value table d'hôte at lunch and dinner, in addition to à la carte. *First Class.* (With exceptional pub lunches in the *Claret Jug Bar: Moderate.*)

Black's (Jeffrey Street, Edinburgh) is an old-reliable, traditional-decor source of succulent roast beef and other simple but deliciously prepared nourishment. *First Class.*

Café Royal (Register Place, Edinburgh) occupies two floors of respectably aged quarters. Ascend to the restaurant proper, which is elaborate Edwardian, for the good-value buffet lunch—*pâtés*, salads, sweets, with unlimited wine. *First Class.*

Ping On (Deanbaugh Street, Edinburgh): Chinese restaurants are invariably good in Britain, and they keep the longest hours. Go to Ping On for specialties like lemon chicken, beef and black-bean sauce, succulent spare ribs. *Moderate.*

L'Auberge (St. Mary Street, Edinburgh), properly—and pleasantly— Gallic, offers its best value with a table d'hôte lunch on Sundays only. Weekdays at midday, pick the well-priced *plat du jour*; it could be *coq au vin, boeuf bourguinonne* or *navarin*—stew—of lamb. Dinner is à la carte. *Moderate-First Class.*

Refreshers (Hanover Street, Edinburgh) attracts with its nifty Art Deco environment. There is a pair of bars for drinks and casual lunches. The daily special can be good in the restaurant. *Moderate-First Class.*

Black Bull (Strawmarket, Edinburgh) is a solid-value wine bar. Order the day's casserole, a chicken specialty, or a bowl of chili. Wine by glass or bottle. *Moderate.*

Jenners (Princes Street, Edinburgh): Take your choice, in this leading department store, of a snack in the fifth-floor *Coffee Bar*; a good-value lunch at either the *Princes Street Restaurant* on two or the *Rose Street Restaurant* on one; or pizza at the mod-look *Night & Day*, entered from Rose Street. *Moderate.*

Mr. Boni's (Lochrin Buildings, opposite King's Theatre, Edinburgh): There can be times when cravings for gooey ice-cream concoctions overtake the most intrepid of travelers. Repair to Mr. B.'s for a hot fudge sundae or a banana split. *Moderate.*

Hawes Inn (South Queensferry Village, at Forth Road Bridge, Edinburgh) is just the ticket for a pub lunch en route to or from a visit to Hopetoun House (above). Attractive and *Moderate.*

Cramond Inn (Cramond Village, outside Edinburgh): Make a pilgrimage to this charming Old-World hamlet (above) and, ideally, combine it with lunch, a drink, or afternoon tea in this centuries-old restaurant. Scottish specialties. *First Class.*

AFTER DARK

Usher Hall (Lothian Road at Festival Square, Edinburgh) sees performances of the Scottish National Orchestra, not to mention a diverse range of other musical organizations, many from abroad.

Kings Theatre (Leven Street, Edinburgh) is as much for plays (Scottish Theatre Company and other troupes, as well) as for dance (Scottish Ballet—with a diverse repertoire, including *The Nutcracker* and *Les Sylphides*, as well as contemporary works).

Royal Lyceum Theatre (Grindlay Street, Edinburgh): Plays enacted by its own well-regarded repertory; diverse in content, from, say, St. James M. Barrie to Gore Vidal.

Queen's Hall (Clark Street, Edinburgh) presents the Scottish Chamber Orchestra, Scottish Baroque Ensemble, and other events.

Playhouse (Leith Walk, Edinburgh): Hope that the Scottish Opera will be performing during your visit.

Adam House (The Mound, Edinburgh) is a principal University of Edinburgh auditorium for the performing arts.

Traverse Theatre Club (West Bow, Edinburgh) is locally esteemed; plays with contemporary themes. *Note:* Ask your hotel concierge for a free copy of *What's On Across Scotland;* it covers the southern cities and towns.

SHOPPER'S EDINBURGH

Bless Edinburgh for its geographical clarity. By that, I mean the shopper does very well, indeed, by simply traversing beautiful Princes Street and, parallel to it, George Street. Princes Street's mercantile kingpin is architecturally distinguished *Jenners*, the premier department store, with a mock-Tudor atrium that is a principal souvenir of Victorian Edinburgh. Have a look at its tartan shop and big men's and women's clothing and accessories departments, with cashmere sweaters in variety. Amble through *Waverly Market*, a strikingly contemporary shopping mall adjacent to Waverly Station and the North British Hotel, with a range of cafés and shops (many specializing in clothing), including *Gleneagles of Scotland*. Other Princes Street emporia include a branch of bargain-packed *Marks & Spencer*, the *Scotch House* (Scots-created woolens and accessories), and branches of the kingdom-wide *Debenhams* department stores and of London-based *Austin Reed* (clothing). *Frasers* department store is much smaller than its Glasgow counterpart. But hardly to be missed on Princes Street are two outlets of a national chain, *Edinburgh Woolen Mills*, with the best prices I have found anywhere in Britain for Scottish-loomed cashmere sweaters. *Scottish Craft Centre*, on Canongate, is a source of hand-loomed woolen rugs and hand-thrown pottery. Streets connecting Princes with George, like Frederick Street (with an outlet of the trendy *Next* clothing chain) and Hanover Street (with shops like *Connections*, for trendy women's accessories, and *Miss Selfridge*, a national chain) are worth checking out. On George Street, note *Highland Home Industries* (handicrafts, and lovely), *Aitken & Niven* (pricey men's and women's fashions), *Linley's* (china), and *James How* (snazzy men's wear), as well as branches of firms that you know from London and elsewhere, like *Laura Ashley* (clothes, home furnishings, textiles), *Gieves & Hawkes* (custom-made men's suits), *Moss Bros.* (good-looking men's wear), and *Mappin & Webb* (jewelry and crystal).

INCIDENTAL INTELLIGENCE

The Edinburgh Festival, preeminent among those of Europe, takes place for three event-packed summer weeks each year, usually starting in mid-August and—worth noting, this—packing in crowds for its program of music, as well as drama, in a variety of settings all over town. Performing companies are from all over Britain and from continental Europe and North America, as well. At the same time, the Edinburgh Tattoo—massed pipers and drummers—takes place on the esplanade of floodlit Edinburgh Castle; several hundred performing-arts groups perform in a kind of auxiliary festival called The Fringe; and concurrently there is the Edinburgh International Film Festival.

Although Prestwick Airport, just south of Glasgow, is Scotland's transatlantic airport, Edinburgh Airport, adjacent to the capital, is served by frequent British Airways shuttles linking it with London's Heathrow and with flights north to Aberdeen, as well as to several British (including London) and Continental cities. There is crack train service, daytime and sleeper, between Edinburgh and London. Trains depart every half-hour, on the half-hour, until 11:00 P.M., from Edinburgh's Waverly Station for Queen Street Station, Glasgow (and vice versa). There are more excursions to more Scottish points from Edinburgh (including, of course, Loch Lomond [Chapter 25]) than from anywhere else in Scotland. *Further information:* Edinburgh Tourist Information & Accommodation Service, Waverly Bridge, with a branch at Edinburgh Airport.

25

Glasgow

Loch Lomond and Burns Country

BACKGROUND BRIEFING

Poor Glasgow. It is rarely given much credit in the British—or, for that matter, the Scottish—scheme of things. Nearby Edinburgh is the northern Glamour Girl. Glasgow, when non-Scots give it any thought, is appreciated for little more than size (it was, until Birmingham overtook it, the second city of the kingdom), slums (one might think no other British city had counterparts of Glasgow's Gorbals), and an ability to make money (the Clive Shipyards inevitably are given their due).

Well, Glaswegians appreciate their city. And well they might. It is among Britain's more important and—I should like to emphasize, looking in as an outsider—more interesting urban entities, architecturally and artistically, not to mention financially. The fact that many foreign visitors to Britain assiduously avoid it on Scottish forays is a touristic blunder of the first magnitude. This is a city at once culture-laden, full of spirit, with monuments of the Victorian age of building unsurpassed in Britain, and—hardly to be overlooked—home to something like one out of six Scots.

Glasgow is proud enough of Mungo, the sainted sixth-century founder of its cathedral, but it does not, oddly, make much of its advanced age in other respects. Still, its evolution through the centuries was not unlike that of the neighboring Scottish Lowlands. If it was not in the thick of things militarily and politically, Glasgow was never remiss in economic development. Its Clyde River situation—close to the Atlantic and to markets of the New World and southerly enough in Scotland so as to be convenient to England—has always stood it in good stead, through the medieval and Renaissance centuries, when it honed mercantile and manufacturing skills and on into the period leading to the Industrial Revolution. In the eighteenth century, it began to amass wealth trading for American tobacco. In the early nineteenth century, commerce in cotton proved of value, with heavy industry following (nearby coal deposits were valuable) in that century's later decades.

As it grew wealthy, so did Glasgow sharpen its intellect. (St. Andrews and Edinburgh universities may be more fashionable, but Glasgow's was founded as far back as 1451, making it but forty-one years younger than St. Andrews, and more than a century older than the University of Edinburgh.) The last century saw rich Glaswegians put accumulated pounds to good use collecting paintings, building museums, and concerning themselves with the performing arts, the while indigenous movements in these areas (a Glasgow school of representational art, innovative architecture, and interior design of Charles Rennie MacIntosh) flourished, and city planners created a substantial core to rival those of the south.

ON SCENE

Lay of the Land: Glasgow centers itself on George Square, named for the third of the kings by that name and one of the most eye-filling of British plazas for three reasons: flowers and greenery surfacing it, landmark buildings surrounding it, and—give these a bit of study—a remarkable series of statues. Most noticeable is that of novelist Sir Walter Scott surmounting an eighty-foot column in the center of the square, but others line its four sides. They are mostly of distinguished Scots—poet Robert Burns, steam-engine inventor James Watt, India-warrior Lord Clyde among them. But there are, as well, likenesses of Victoria, Albert, and other non-Scots, to provide a bit of balance.

George Street, going west from George Square, cuts through the heart of the business area. Of the streets it intersects, the one to remember is the bench- and flower-lined Buchanan Street, pedestrians-only and leading north from Argyll Street, site of the main railway station, past department stores to Sauchiehall and Renfrew streets and the theater district.

Architectural Glasgow: Start at George Square with extraordinarily grandiose *City Chambers*. Seat of the Glasgow District Council, it is a Victorian conceit based on lines of Renaissance Italian palazzos, with a pair of side towers flanking a central one rising 240 feet; Queen Victoria journeyed north to open the building in 1888. Latch onto one of the two-a-day tours, taking in the marble-pillared lobby, two sumptuous grand staircases, coffered-ceiling banqueting hall, and council chamber. The across-the-square *Merchants House* is of similar age, and only slightly less elaborate; it houses the Glasgow Chamber of Commerce and is usually open weekday afternoons. Head two blocks south, then, to Ingram Street and a clutch of monumental buildings, including the Victorian *Courthouse and City Hall* (site of symphonic concerts and not to be confused with City Chambers above), Robert Adam-designed *Trades House* (1794), *St. David's Church* (1825), and *Sterling's Library* (1775).

Older Glasgow is represented by seventeenth-century *Tolbooth Steeple*, due east near Trongate, and by late eighteenth- and early nineteenth-century structures on Clyde Street, bordering River Clyde, due south, with no less than a trio of churches named for St. Andrew— *Catholic Cathedral* (1816), *Scottish Episcopal Church* (1750), and *Church of Scotland's St. Andrews* (1739).

Newer Glasgow—turn of century—is represented by two buildings associated with architect-designer Charles Rennie MacIntosh, Glasgow native and internationally recognized for his innovative Art Nouveau-style work, as evidenced by the *Glasgow School of Art* (Renfrew Street), with each facade distinctive, and a fascinating open-to-visitors MacIntosh-furnished library within; and *Queen's Cross Church* (Maryhill Road), headquarters of the MacIntosh Society, and with considerable architectural and decorative detail by MacIntosh, which volunteers on duty in the society's shops will point out.

Glasgow Cathedral (Cathedral and Castle streets) is at its Gothic best when taken in from the churchyard to its rear, the better to appreciate the grace of its towering steeple. Note its very long, very high nave and its unusual Lower Church—not actually a crypt because it is above ground—with two features to recommend it: the sixth-century tomb of founding St. Mungo and splendid fan vaulting. See, too, the lovely choir, and the pew especially designed for the reigning sovereign (Queen Elizabeth II worshiped at the cathedral in 1977). Odd, this—a kind of separation of church and state situation whereby there are two booths selling guide books and postcards, one operated by the government's Department of the Environment (which looks after the building physically), the other by the Church of Scotland (which looks after it spiritually). Take your choice as to whose wares you purchase. Or, better yet, sample both!

Burrell Collection (Pollokshaws Road, in Pollok Country Park, five miles southwest of town and ideally combined with a visit to Pollok House [below]): What happened was this. By the time Sir William Burrell, a wealthy Glasgow ship owner, died at the age of 96 in 1958 he had collected—with the aid of dealers, of course, but impelled by his own brilliant taste and his own special interests—more than 8,000 art objects. Having gathered one of the planet's superlative personal collections of this or any age, Sir William presented his treasures to the City of Glasgow in 1944, along with a gift of £450,000 for the construction of a building for their display to the public, stipulating that it be away from the city center, in a country setting without high levels of air pollution that might be damaging. It took nine years to find such a site. In 1971, architect Barry Gasson, trained both at Columbia University in New York and in England, won a competition for the building's design. Unabashedly contemporary—a bold meld of stone and glass, stainless steel and natural timber, with medieval arches and doorways that Sir William had collected put to practical use throughout—it took twelve years to build. Set amid the forest-like growth of Pollok Country Park, it complements both natural setting and, more to the point, the Burrell art.

Operated with flair and distinction by the Glasgow Museums and Art Galleries (whose longtime flagship museum [below] is at Kelvingrove in another part of the city and is but one of half a dozen-plus museums directed by this all-Britain ranker of a museums group), the Burrell wants easily a solid half-day of your time (there is a striking-looking cafeteria for coffee and lunch breaks). And you may well want to return for repeat visits. Only a portion of the collection is on view at any given time. It breaks down into half a dozen sections, reflecting Sir William's expertise in as many areas. Medieval art and artifacts were a Burrell passion; go through the three rooms transplanted in toto from Hutton Castle, the Burrell family seat at Berwick-on-Tweed—entrance hall, dining room with rare so-called linenfold wood-paneled walls, and splendid drawing room. As you walk about, thereafter, special treats are specimens of medieval stained glass embedded in walls and stone-carved portals from similarly aged churches and castles serving as doorways. Tapestries, ivories, sculpture, enamels, and furniture round out this era's treasures. But there's more—contents of Egyptian tombs, Greek pottery, busts from ancient Rome, Chinese ceramics and bronzes and jades, prints from old Japan, tiles from ancient Persia, and carpets from Ottoman Turkey. Paintings include a Memling *Annunciation*, a Cranach *Stag Hunt*, a Giovanni Bellini *Virgin and Child*, a Rembrandt *Self-Portrait*, and a smiling Hals gent, as well as British portraitists like Raeburn and Hogarth and French masters—Chardin, Daumier, Manet, Sisley, Degas, and their fellow Impressionists and post-Impressionists.

Glasgow Art Gallery and Museum (Kelvingrove): First, the building. It is a turn-of-century red sandstone palace on a gargantuan scale based on the architecture of the Renaissance, with an atrium-like main hall that constitutes one of Scotland's most dazzling interiors. You might, in the interest of time, want to skip the natural history sections. Archeology—at least that having to do with Scottish folk life, is absorbing. The decorative arts areas—porcelain, glass, silver, jewelry, furniture, the lot with Scottish concentration—are choice. Then comes one of Europe's superlative caches of paintings, rich with Italian Old Masters (including Giorgione's *Head of a Man*, Guardi's *Santa Maria Maggiore*); Flemish Primitives—such as Van Orley's *Virgin and Child*; and Renaissance Low Countries greats—Rubens, Van Dyck, Hals, and Jordaens. Of course, Scots are present—Ramsay and Raeburn most especially, with English counterparts like Hogarth, Romney, Lawrence, Reynolds, and Gainsborough; Constable and Turner; the pre-Raphaelites (Burne-Jones, Ford Madox Brown); and moderns like Graham Sutherland and Ben Nicholson. And the French! Oudry, Géricault, Delacroix, Millet, Courbet, Corot, Daubigny, Boudin, Daumier, Degas, Van Gogh, Sisley, Gauguin, Signac, Manet, Monet, Utrillo, Seurat, Vuillard, Bonnard, Matisse, and Picasso. Cafeteria.

Hunterian Art Gallery (Hillhead Street at University Avenue on the beautiful University of Glasgow campus) is a ten-minute walk from the Glasgow Art Gallery and Museum (above). In striking modern quarters, it is but one part of the extraordinary collection—the remainder is in the nearby Hunterian Museum—of a handsome and talented eighteenth-century physician-obstetrics teacher-university alumnus who amassed high-caliber holdings in areas ranging from art to zoology. The nucleus of the paintings in this gallery were Dr. Hunter's, including a portrait of himself in powdered wig, which he commissioned Allan Ramsay to execute. Still another Hunter-ordered work is that of a moose—of all animals!—by George Stubbs, who usually painted horses. But these are only the nucleus. The special treat is a group of Whistlers—some eighty paintings and many more prints, drawings, and pastels—on a par with the repository of that late nineteenth-century American's work at Washington's Freer Gallery. You move along, then, to Rembrandt's *Entombment of Christ*, Chardin's *Scullery Maid*, a group by Ramsay and Raeburn, with Lawrence and Reynolds and a choice selection of French masters, Corot through Pissarro. There are some three-score pieces of original furniture of Glasgow's own turn-of-century Charles Rennie MacIntosh to complement that on display at the Glasgow School of Art (above). The *University Library* (just next door) displays rare manuscripts in its Special Collections Department. You may obtain sustenance in the *University Refectory* (just opposite) and take in, as well, Dr. Hunter's archeological and ethnological exhibits at the *Hunterian Museum* in the sprawling main university building—a Victorian masterwork—just off University Avenue, nearby.

Pollok House (Pollokshaws Road in Pollok Country Park, five miles southwest of town) is operated—and well—by the Glasgow Art Gallery and Museum (above). Not that it could go far wrong, given the setting: an eighteenth-century Palladian mansion in its own park, severe without, unrestrained rococo inside, with entrance hall-cum-grand stairway, brilliant blue-and-white-walled dining room, and music and drawing rooms—each with superb stucco decoration—the most spectacular. But the point of Pollok—at least as much as its interior—is paintings. The surprise is Spanish works, with the Big Three of that nation—El Greco, Murillo, and Goya—generously represented. Italians like Del Piombo and Signorelli, Dutchmen like Steen, Germans like Mengs, and Britons like Romney and Hogarth—not to mention William Blake—are also represented. Choice Glasgow-made furniture of the preceding two centuries is displayed, along with fine china and glass, domestic as well as Continental European. End in the amusing Edwardian kitchen, now a welcoming tearoom.

People's Palace Museum (Glasgow Green) opened in 1898 as a recreation center for the city's East End. In recent years, the Glasgow Museum and Art Gallery converted it, with wit and style, into the city's historical museum—medieval sovereigns (yes, there are Mary Queen of Scots mementos), through the prosperous trade with the American colonies, and beyond to the Industrial Revolution and the Glasgow of the Victorians and Edwardians: a portrait of a 1790s shopkeeper, trade union emblems of the 1820s, a poster from a 1910 circus, clay pottery and clay pipes, early sewing machines, and photographed suffragettes. Fun.

Museum of Transport (Albert Drive): Britain abounds in this kind of museum, but I like Glasgow's best, probably because it extends from elegant carriages through early horseless carriages and on to a section of local shipbuilding in the Clyde Room, opened relatively recently by the Prince of Wales, with models of ships of all eras, even including the late *Queen Elizabeth*, the *Queen Mary* (now tied up at Long Beach, California), and Canadian Pacific's *Empress of Scotland*.

Glencoyne Distillery (15 miles north of town): You're taken through and emerge an expert on what malt whisky is all about. Phone before setting out: 332-6361.

Loch Lomond (18 miles north of Glasgow) is the Glaswegian's principal playground. Not that it is neglected by the rest of us. Very few overseas visitors pass the "Bonnie Banks" by, if only on a day-long bus tour from Glasgow and from more distant Edinburgh (Chapter

24), as well. A better way to go, in my view, is by train—again from Edinburgh (you must leave earlier), as well as from closer Glasgow's Queen Street Station (depart about 9:00 A.M.), connecting with the lake's restaurant-equipped steamer, *Maid of the Loch*, for a day-long journey north. You board the vessel at hotel-and-restaurant equipped *Balloch* and stop along the mountain-bordered, island-dotted, 21-mile-long lake (Britain's largest body of inland water) at the lakeside ports of *Luss* (with a Gothic church and roses climbing its High Street houses), *Rowardennan* (in *Queen Elizabeth Forest Park* and adjacent to oft-climbed, 3,192-foot-high *Ben*—or Mount—*Lomond*), and *Innernaid* (with its own waterfalls). Return is via the same route, connecting with a train arriving back in Glasgow (and later Edinburgh) in the evening.

There is, of course, no need to rush things; stay overnight or two or three days. The Lomond area is not without hotels and diversions, from, say, walks along the lake and into the mountains to exploration of villages beyond those on the *Maid's* itinerary (including *Ardem*, whose lure is open-to-visitors, handsome eighteenth-century *Rossdhu House; Tarbet*, with hotels; and *Ardlui*, very pretty and at the north end of the lake). Excursions may also be made from Loch Lomond to neighboring western lakes, including lochs *Long* and *Gare*. And there remains the adjacent Trossachs district, due east.

The Trossachs is that area north of Glasgow roughly between Loch Achray in the south and northerly Loch Katrine, just to the east of Ben Lomond, which has Loch Lomond virtually lapping its western shore. It's agreeable to headquarter in *Callendar* at the eastern end of *Loch Venacher* and tour about Trossachs lakes like Earn, Menteith, Achray, and Ard, taking to the waters aboard the *Sir Walter Scott*, which cruises *Loch Katrine* the summer long.

Stirling, a substantial town overshadowed by Glasgow and Edinburgh—it lies between the two—is 20 miles south of Callendar and visit-worthy if only because of magnificent *Stirling Castle*, high on its own rocky crag—in the manner of Edinburgh's—and visible for miles. Dating mostly to the fifteenth century, it was where both Mary Queen of Scots and her son, James VI, were crowned, with its Chapel Royal and Great Hall the best of the interiors.

Robert Burns country, centering on the town of Ayr and Scotland's transatlantic airport at Prestwick, is about 30 miles southwest of Glasgow, seaside, with good golf among its attributes. Burns—Scotland's premier poet and called Rob, Robbie, Rab, even Robin by the Scots, but never Bobbie—lived a short (1759–1796) but productive life, all of it—Highlands and Edinburgh visits excepted—within this south-west region. Scots know all of Burns's works and know them well. Foreigners tend to remember songs like "Flow Gently Sweet Afton," "My Heart's in the Highlands," "Auld Lang Syne," and "Comin' Through the Rye." Burns's continuing popularity with his country-men is attributed to his portrayal of the country's rural life and his facility with the vernacular unsurpassed before or since. Burns coun-try is compact. In the town of *Ayr*, begin at the seventeenth-century *Auld Kirk* on the street called Common Vennel, off High Street. Burns was baptized by this church's minister, but at nearby Alloway. Move then, to what was *Tam O'Shanter Inn*, named for the hero of one of his poems and now a Burns museum. Continue to the nearby town— a couple of miles south—of *Alloway*. Its pilgrimage points are *Burns Cottage*, the simple thatched house—three rooms and adjacent barn— where the poet was born, and adjacent *Burns Museum*, a three-gallery repository of early Burns editions, the Burns family Bible, Burns let-ters, and other memorabilia. Nearby are *Alloway Kirk*, about which Burns wrote in *Tam O'Shanter* and where his father is buried; the bridge, *Brig O' Doon*, over which the hero of *Tam O'Shanter* ran, with witches in pursuit; and the much painted and photographed, classic-style *Burns Monument*, its nine columns supporting a cupola, at the edge of the River Doon.

Culzean Castle (nine miles south of Ayr) looms large—in formidable Gothic Revival style—over an exquisite garden, in the midst of a public park, with views beyond of the Firth of Clyde. Its designer was Scotland's own Robert Adam (he finished it in 1790), and the most memorable parts of the interior are the saloon, which Adam built into an immense circular tower; and a spectacular spiral staircase, with Adam's celebrated plasterwork decoration throughout. Note of inter-est to Americans: In appreciation of his efforts as Supreme Allied Commander during World War II, an apartment here was reserved for the use, whenever he visited, of General Dwight D. Eisenhower. It is rentable, as hotel rooms might be (see Settling In, below). Restau-rant. National Trust for Scotland.

SETTLING IN

Hospitality Inn (Cambridge Street, Glasgow): You might quarrel with the overbusy decor, but this centrally located, 320-room house has a lot going for it. Deluxe-category rooms, each with two double beds, are the biggest such that I know of in Glasgow. There are proper showers in the baths, ice machines on all floors, a pair of good restau-rants (one of which I recommend on a later page; the other, a late-hours coffee shop) and congenial drinking parlors. High marks. *First Class.*

Diplomat Hotel (George Square, Glasgow): You need not be an old-timer of special vintage to remember Glasgow's beloved North British Hotel, a Victorian railway hostelry facing the city's landmark central square, adjacent to Queen Street Station—the terminus for trains to and from Edinburgh. By that name, it is no more. Under a new guise as the Diplomat, its public spaces have been gutted and both refurbished and refurnished in turn-of-century style. Lobby, restaurant, and bar-café are redolent of the hotel's heyday period. And the 125 suites and rooms above stairs are being thoroughly renewed, as well. (Historical note: On January 18, 1941, Prime Minister Winston Churchill met at the old "N.B." with Harry Hopkins, a top aide of President Franklin D. Roosevelt; they signed an agreement which led to America's vital lend-lease aid to wartime Britain: a plaque in the hotel's Hopkins Room—happily retained by the Diplomat management—tells the story.) *First Class.*

Holiday Inn (Argyle Street, Glasgow): I wish the nearly 300 rooms— at least those I've seen—in this busy, modern house were bigger. Still, in true Holiday Inn style, each has two double beds and a proper shower in the bathroom. Again, in what used to be typical of many Holiday Inns, the restaurant adjoins an indoor swimming pool; unexciting buffets are its specialty. Bar-lounge. Central and *First Class.*

Stakis Grosvenor Hotel (Great Western Road, Glasgow) is, like the White House (below), away from the center in the West End, but it is agreeable enough—the facade is part of a row of Victorian joined houses—for you to consider, if you've a car. There are just over 90 rooms (twins can be small, those with two double beds are larger) whose super baths have proper showers over the tubs. Public spaces are handsome and include a restaurant (later recommended) and a trio of bars. *First Class.*

White House Hotel (Cleveden Crescent, Glasgow), though away from the center (you should have a car), is brought to your attention because it consists of an attractive pair of joined West End town houses, with just over 30 nicely furnished rooms, no two quite alike, but each with kitchen, as well as bath. Although there is no restaurant or bar, management will serve meals via room service. *First Class.*

Crest Hotel (Argyle Street, Glasgow) has the virtues of a central situation and 123 full-facility rooms (including some set aside for nonsmokers) in a contemporary setting that includes a reliable restaurant and a pair of bars. *First Class.*

Albany Hotel (Bothwell Street, Glasgow) is characterless contemporary from without. Besides 250 rooms and suites, there are two restaurants, as well as a pair of bars, one of which serves lunches. Trusthouse Forte. *First Class.*

Central Hotel (Gordon Street, Glasgow) is an oldie of a railway hotel (it adjoins Central Station) that deteriorated in its final British Transport Hotels years and has had a partial facelift, courtesy of the current owners. Most of the 200-plus rooms have baths. Restaurant, bar. *Moderate.*

Ingram Hotel (Ingram Street, Glasgow) is near Glasgow Cathedral. It's full facility—with restaurant and bar—and well priced. *Moderate.*

Royal Stuart Hotel (Clyde Street, Glasgow) flanks the southern edge of central Glasgow near the River Clyde. Seventy of the 112 functional rooms have baths; restaurant, bar. *Moderate.*

Gleddoch House Hotel (Langbank, a 30-minute drive west of Glasgow) is a 1920s mansion turned hotel, high on a hill overlooking the River Clyde and—golfers note—adjacent to 18-hole, par-72 Gleddoch Golf Course, with its café-equipped clubhouse; play on the course is without charge to hotel guests. There are 18 bedrooms, some more luxurious than others; attractive public spaces include an inviting cocktail lounge and a restaurant giving onto a broad terrace, with the garden just beyond. *First Class.*

Buchanan Arms Hotel (Drymen, near Loch Lomond): This is a smallish house, Scots plaid in decor, with pleasant rooms (all but six of the two dozen with baths), restaurant, and bar. *Moderate.*

Winnock Hotel (Drymen, near Loch Lomond) is unpretentious but nicely situated; all 30 rooms have baths, and there are both restaurant and bar. *Moderate.*

Balloch Hotel (Balloch, Loch Lomond) is worth knowing about should you want to overnight at the start or finish of a Loch Lomond steamer journey; Balloch is the chief terminus. A number of rooms have bath; restaurant, bar. *Moderate.*

Tarbet Hotel (Tarbet, Loch Lomond) is an elderly castle of a house, nicely situated, with baths in the majority of its 80 rooms, two restaurants, bar-lounge. *Moderate.*

Lubnaig Hotel (Leny Feus, outside of Callendar) makes for a nice overnight stop in the course of Trossachs touring. Baths of all 10 rooms are shower equipped; restaurant, bar, garden. *Moderate.*

Stakis Station Hotel (Station Road, Stirling) is convenient for layovers en route north or south from the Trossachs. There are 25 comfortable rooms, restaurant, bar-lounge. *Moderate.*

Stakis Station Hotel (Burns Statue Square, Ayr) is a turn-of-century house, adjacent to the station, with 74 pleasant rooms and high-ceilinged public areas that include a pair of restaurants and cozy bar. *First Class.*

Turnberry Hotel (Turnberry, near Ayr) has two 18-hole courses, one of them the championship par-71 Ailsa links; the other, the not-quite-so-difficult Arran links. There are, in addition, a 12-hole pitch-and-putt course and 18 putting holes, not to mention super tennis courts and a croquet court, with the sea just beyond. But we haven't gone indoors, yet. This hotel is a long, low-slung exercise in white, backing its golf links, with not quite 130 rooms and (refurbished stem-to-stern in the mid-eighties, by new owners who took over from the defunct British Transport Hotels), public spaces in the grand manner that include restaurant and bar-lounge. Indoor diversions include swimming, billiards, movies, and dancing. An Orient Express hotel. *Luxury.*

Culzean Castle's National Guest Flat (nine miles south of Ayr): The antique-furnished apartment of the Robert Adam-designed country house (see above) that was given to General Dwight D. Eisenhower (for use during his lifetime) by the National Trust of Scotland in appreciation of his leadership as Supreme Allied Commander during World War II is rentable the year round on a nightly basis. Reached by its own private elevator, it comprises the handsome Round Drawing Room (with views of the rocky coast from its windows), a sumptuous master bedroom with bath, study, and kitchen. The additional bedrooms (four with private baths, two that share a bath) may be booked separately. Breakfast is provided by Culzean's housekeeping staff, and other meals may be ordered. General Eisenhower stayed in the flat several times, once while President of the United States. You can, too. Book through Administrator, Culzean Castle, Maybole, Ayrshire, Scotland. Shared-bath rooms are *First Class;* others, *Luxury.*

Caledonian Hotel (Dalblair Road, Ayr): You're away from the center here, albeit in a well-appointed, 108-room house, with a pair of restaurants and no less than five bars. *First Class.*

Savoy Park Hotel (Racecourse Road, Ayr): A neat house with baths in 13 of the 16 functional rooms. Restaurant, bar. *Moderate.*

DAILY BREAD

Buttery (Argyle Street, Glasgow) could be a private club. Besides dark paneling, it offers starched napery, a solicitous staff, and perfectly delicious things to eat. The fare is mostly Gallic-origin with local overtones, as, for example, a terrine of Scottish seafood with a tomato vinaigrette or venison with a Cumberland sauce. Entrées include roast brace of quail with a port sauce, steak prepared French style, and *pommes dauphinois. Crème brullée* and bread and butter pudding are suggested sweets. And delicious petits fours come with coffee. In my view, one of Britain's best restaurants. *Luxury.*

Ambassador (Blythswood Square, Glasgow) occupies basement quarters on one of the city's finest squares. It is old-fashioned plush in look, and the staff, apparently mostly Italian, is congenial. And the fare—an Italo-British meld—is competent when British and delicious when Italian, as, for example, minestrone soup, authentically sauced pasta, and veal scaloppine Marsala. Well-priced prix fixe at lunch, pricier à la carte in the evening. *First Class.*

Rogano's (Exchange Place, Glasgow) packs in Glaswegian business types at lunch, when there's a reasonably tabbed prix fixe of mostly British specialties. At dinner, this winning restaurant, with suggestions of Art Deco in its high-ceilinged quarters, takes on French overtones—and with success. Location is perfect—just off pedestrians-only Buchanan Street. *First Class.*

Carvery (Albany Hotel, Bothwell Street, Glasgow) is the less costly of this hotel's pair of restaurants and by far the better, in my experience. It's bright and cheerful and offers all you can eat of roast beef, lamb, or pork—chef-carved at the serving counter and served with potatoes and vegetables—preceded by an appetizer (which could be salads from a help-yourself bar, if you like) and concluded with cheese or a sweet and coffee. *First Class.*

Prince of Wales (Hospitality Inn, Cambridge Street, Glasgow): This most attractive of Hospitality Inn's public spaces serves up a tasty, reasonably tabbed prix-fixe lunch—which might be duck *pâté* or the day's soup to start, breast of chicken or lamb chops to follow, cheese or dessert, and coffee. *First Class.*

Willow Tea Rooms (above Henderson jewelry shop on Sauchiehall Street, Glasgow): The point about the Willow—upstairs over a core-of-town store—is not only that it's a delightful spot for a cup of coffee in the course of a shopping expedition, but that it was designed by the celebrated Glasgow architect Charles Rennie MacIntosh in 1904, and restored in recent years to its original Art Nouveau state—with spindly gray MacIntosh chairs at the tables and backed by walls inset with gray stained glass, again the work of the master, and not unlike the glass embellishing the building's windows. Special. *Moderate.*

Frasers (Buchanan Street, Glasgow): Waitress-service restaurants of leading British department stores are usually good choices for lunch. Frasers is an exception to the rule—with lovely ladies serving fare that is substandard college-dorm; better a sandwich or a salad at the adjacent self-service. Both are on the fourth floor. Restaurant is *First Class;* cafeteria, *Moderate.*

Copenhagen Room (Danish Food Centre, St. Vincent Street, Glasgow): I can't think of a Glasgow locale more festive, delicious, and attractive—with red and white, the Danish national colors, the basis of the contemporary decor. At lunch, there's a cold buffet along with *smørrebord*, the Danes' masterful open sandwiches. At night, dine à la carte—hearty soups, interesting seafood, pork and veal specialties, luscious sweets. *First Class.*

Trattoria Caruso (Hope Street, opposite Theatre Royal, Glasgow) is deliciously Italian; a dinner might comprise minestrone, followed by the house's own ravioli, with a green salad and a Sicilian wine accompanying, and cheese to conclude. Lunch, too. *First Class.*

Lewis's (Argyle Street, Glasgow) is a major department store. Choose the *Cafeteria* on five, and the *Soda Fountain* in the basement. *Moderate.*

Inversnaid Hotel (Inversnaid, Loch Lomond): You're lakeside-cum-view, and you can have a proper lunch or dinner or a more informal pick-me-up. *Moderate-First Class.*

Turnberry Hotel Restaurant (Turnberry, near Ayr): The chandeliered, seaview restaurant at the Turnberry makes a specialty of local treats like trout, salmon, Angus beef, and lobster; the lot can be ordered à la carte, prepared as you request. Or select the less pricey table d'hôte. Excellent cellar. *First Class-Luxury.*

Carle's (Burns Statue Square, Ayr) is heart of town, with excellent-value table d'hôte lunches and dinners upstairs; short orders, on the street floor. *Moderate.*

Laigh Houghton Mill (Kilmarnock, north of Ayr) makes for a diverting drive from the heart of the Burns Country. The mill has been deftly transformed into a restaurant evoking Old Scotland, serving up hearty lunches from the bar, as well as more formal dinners. *Moderate-First Class.*

AFTER DARK

Theatre Royal (Hope Street, Glasgow) is home to the Scottish Ballet, Scottish Opera, and plays, as well, in diverse array, including those of the Scottish Theatre Company. The Scottish Chamber Orchestra plays here, too. A handsome Victorian house.

City Hall (Candleriggs, Glasgow) is put to good use for Scottish National Orchestra, Glasgow Orchestral Society, and other symphonic ensembles. Impressive.

King's Theatre (Bath Street, Glasgow) has as diverse a schedule as any—rock groups, theater troupes, classical instrumentalists, and perhaps the Glasgow Grand Opera Company performing *Il Trovatore.*

Kelvin Hall (Argyle Street, Glasgow) is the site each spring of Prom Concerts on the order of those at London's Royal Albert Hall (the seats are all removed and you promenade about). Other concert events take place the year round.

Citizens Theatre (Gorbals, Glasgow) presents its own company in contemporary and classic plays, British and imported. *Note:* Ask your concierge for a free copy of *Leisure Glasgow*, published monthly.

SHOPPER'S GLASGOW

Scotland's largest city (and Britain's third largest), Glasgow is a shopping center to be reckoned with. Concentrate on pedestrians-only Buchanan Street, core of town, site of *Frasers* department store, the city's priciest, centered with a splendid atrium, with dazzling main-floor china department; and such shops as *Burberrys, Jaeger, Liberty, Scotch House*—all branches of chains you know from London (and, in some cases, from the U.S.); as well as such fine local stores as *Henry Burton* (one of the few Glasgow sources of cashmere sweaters, along with Frasers and Jaeger [above]) and *Lawrie's* (Scottish woolens, kilts). Stroll through the atmospheric *Argyll Arcade*; opened in 1827, it is lined with jewelry and watch shops and the site of venerable *Sloan's Restaurant*, a good *Moderate* lunch or afternoon tea stop. On Argyle Street, you'll find immense *Lewis's*, the No. 2 department store (with impressive Food Halls and a choice of eateries); *Arnott's*, still another long-established department store; a big outlet of bargain-laden *Marks & Spencer*; and *Miss Selfridge*, a women's clothing chain that's an offshoot of London's Selfridges department store. Also-mercantile Sauchiehall Street is the site of *Bremners* department store. *Stockwell China Bazaar*, with vast selections, is on Glassford Street. *Scottish Design Centre* (corner St. Vincent and Nile streets) is chock-filled with contemporary glass, textiles, pottery, and toys. For antiques and trendy boutiques, head over to the West End's *Byers Road*.

INCIDENTAL INTELLIGENCE

Glasgow has Britain's newest Underground, or subway; half a dozen lines extend into the city and suburbs from Queen Street and Central Railway Stations. Prestwick Airport, just south of the city, is Scotland's transatlantic airport, but Glasgow Airport, even closer, is used for domestic flights throughout Scotland, including Aberdeen and the Highlands, as well as points in England. British Airways operates a Glasgow-London shuttle. Rail service between Glasgow and London is, like that connecting Edinburgh and London, absolutely crack, day and sleeper. Trains leave Glasgow from Queen Street Station every half-hour on the half-hour, for Waverly Station, Edinburgh; running time: 45 minutes. *Further information:* Glasgow Tourist Information Centre, St. Vincent Place; Ayr Tourist Information Centre, Miller Road; Trossach Tourist Association, Leny Road, Callendar; Stirling Tourist Information Centre, Dumbarton Road.

26

The Highlands
Perth to Inverness and Skye

BACKGROUND BRIEFING
It is, surely, their altitude and their northerly isolation that have kept the Highlanders apart. In no other developed region of Europe, at least of which I am aware, do people cling more tenaciously to ancient tribal organization, proudly retaining clan names (the main clans total nearly seventy) and the traditional dress associated with a centuries-old culture. But Highlanders are more than proud. They are perhaps the most history-savvy of Britons, still punctiliously observing anniversaries having to do with the ultimate loss—in the eighteenth century—of the crown of Britain from the Scottish-founded Stuarts to the German-descended family still on the throne.

Isolated though their part of the world may be, it has not been left alone for a long time. Remnants still are to be seen of the prehistoric Highlands, and if Roman colonists in Britain did not settle that far north, early Christians made their presence known, with as celebrated a missionary as St. Patrick preaching in the Highlands in the fifth century.

Later centuries saw Christian Highlanders often the losers in raid after Viking raid. Ever on the defensive—as, indeed, it could be argued, they are to this day—Highlanders protected themselves and their clans from their fortified castles, while the Catholic Church became their religion (today, ruins of ancient abbeys and churches dot the region). By the time the Middle Ages evolved into the Renaissance, Scottish kings had long since expanded their realm into the north. By the time the Stuart dynasty began with Robert II in the late fourteenth century, Highlanders had become loyal Scottish subjects and remained so well into the sixteenth century (when Mary Queen of Scots' son, James VI, became James I of England), and through the eighteenth. That was a period of repeated, albeit abortive, attempts to restore Stuarts to the throne through battles like those led by Bonnie Prince Charlie, son of the "Old Pretender," himself the son of English King James II. The decisive battle was that at Culloden outside of Inverness in 1746. The Highlanders lost not only militarily but otherwise, as well. Clans' arms were confiscated, and the sound of bagpipes in the air was but a memory. (It became illegal to play them.) And, foulest of blows, wearing of the kilt was proscribed—at least until 1782, a date well in advance of the rise of Highland tourism in the latter part of the nineteenth century.

ON SCENE

Perth is pretty. It remains a small, conservative city, with nary a "must-see" monument. Which is just as well, given a situation that makes it ideal as an entry point for exploration of the Highlands to the north and west. Its ace-in-the-hole is scenic River Tay, flanking its eastern edge. Queen's Bridge leads from Tay Street—a riverside promenade—into the city center and High Street. This is an agreeable town in which to amble about, still with remnants of Georgian, Victorian, and, in the case of *St. John's Kirk* (just off South Street, near the river), a late Gothic work, splendidly vaulted, with a fine nave. *Perth Museum & Art Gallery* (Mill Street) is at its most impressive without—classic-style out of the last century, with Ionic columns supporting an elegant portico and dome. There is a fairish collection of paintings (Lely among the English, Cuyp among the Dutch, of which there are many) and a creditable collection of seventeenth- and eighteenth-century furniture—Chippendale, Adam, Sheraton, Queen Anne. *Fair Maid of Perth's House* (Northport), seventeenth-century and unpretentious, it's a venue for the sale of locally produced crafts; it takes its name from a similarly titled Sir Walter Scott novel whose heroine lived in the neighborhood. A final word on pronunciation: think of the fruit as you say *Pear*-th.

Scone Palace (two miles north of Perth): With a crenellated medieval facade—it is essentially early nineteenth-century within—this mansion is filled with facets of Scottish historical significance, not to mention French eighteenth-century furniture and paintings by Ramsay and Reynolds in a dozen treasure-filled state rooms, which the Earl of Mansfield opens to his guests. Restaurant.

Dunkeld (14 miles north of Perth) is a tiny town so jewel-like that its medieval houses are under the care of the National Trust for Scotland. Still, the real draw of this village that straddles the River Tay is *Dunkeld Cathedral*, at its prime an eclectic mix of Romanesque and Gothic and, as it stands today—a Church of Scotland parish church—part modern, part very old, indeed, part still roofless. A mile or two distant is another National Trust mini-property, the *Hermitage* —an eighteenth-century summer house, tiny but charming, perched at the edge of the River Braan, just above an even older stone bridge.

Glamis Castle (25 miles northeast of Perth): Everyone in Britain knows Glamis (pronounced *Glamss*) for two reasons: Queen Elizabeth the Queen Mother and her younger daughter, Princess Margaret, were born there. The Queen Mother returns upon occasion to visit the 17th Earl and Countess of Strathmore and Kinghorne, her niece and nephew and descendants of the earlier Lords Glamis who built the castle—still marvelously medieval, a symphony of towers and turrets and crenellated walls—in 1372. There have been alterations and embellishments over the centuries. But Glamis is a veritable Scottish history lesson and a spectacular one at that. (It is the same Glamis where Shakespeare set the murder of Duncan in *Macbeth*.) Down you go to a formidable stone-walled crypt, its walls hung with ancient armor. In you go to the drawing room, its arched ceiling surmounting portraits (one is a Clouet) of early Lords Glamis. The chapel is surfaced with seventeenth-century Dutch frescoes depicting the life of Christ. The billiard room's walls are hung with Mortlake tapestries. Among the bedrooms are those named for guests extending from Scotland's Malcolm II to Britain's George VI, with the bedroom still used on her visits by George's widow, the Queen Mother. Café. (With a National Trust for Scotland-operated *Folk Museum* occupying a row of seventeenth-century houses in the nearby village of Glamis.)

Pitlochry (27 miles north of Perth) is a small Highlands town, the site of an annual summer performing-arts festival and the open-to-visitors *Bells Distillery*. It's surrounded by perfectly beautiful countryside, verdant and mountainous, with *Loch Broom* due east and *Lochs Tummel* and *Rannoch* to the west.

Blair Castle (Blair Atholl, seven miles north of Pitlochry) is the home of the 10th Duke of Argyll—and seat of the only private army allowed by law in the United Kingdom. (Don't worry about being attacked; it's handpicked by the duke from among deserving locals, and it is notably peaceable.) The point of a visit to Blair—90 percent of which dates to the eighteenth century, even though the facade is medieval— is its incredible riches. A tour involves a trek through no less than 32 rooms, and I don't know of another private house in all the kingdom where you get so much for your entrance fee. Beginning with the high-ceilinged entrance hall—its paneled walls a veritable armory of swords and guns—you move along at your own pace through a series of chambers designed for sitting, sleeping, dining, taking tea, break-fasting, inspecting paintings, steeping in Scottish history, and danc-ing. The drawing room, its red damask walls hung with portraits by Hoppner and Zoffany, with a brilliant plasterwork ceiling—is the most spectacular, with the dining room, tapestry room, and red bed-room not far behind. Paintings throughout—Lely through Lawrence through Landseer—are exceptional. But so are the furniture, porce-lain, and objects of historical worth. Restaurant.

Inverness, self-styled "capital" of the Highlands, is a principal termi-nus of trains from the south, dotted with hotels, and convenient to the scenic splendor of the region. Walks through its center—along shop-lined High, Academy, and Church streets and along Ness Walk, flanking the River Ness—are by no means out of order. The *Inverness Museum & Art Gallery* (Castle Wynd) has the dubious distinction, along with its Fort William counterpart, of being closed Sundays, just when local people (not to mention visitors, heaven knows) might like to have a look at a collection having to do with Highlanders' eight-eenth-century attempts to reseat the Stuarts on the British throne. A miniature painting of a very young Bonnie Prince Charlie is among this Never-on-Sunday institution's treasures, which also run to early views of the city and exhibits relating to the region's archeology. *St. Andrew's Cathedral* (Ardross Street) is Scottish Episcopal, Victorian Gothic and—except for services—also closed on Sundays; likewise, *Abertarff House* (Church Street), a National Trust for Scotland proper-ty dating to the late sixteenth century. *Culloden Battlefield* (six miles east of town) is the site of the decisive battle lost by the Jacobite army led by Bonnie Prince Charlie in 1746. You can see the cottage around which the soldiers fought and a National Trust for Scotland Visitor Centre. *Cawdor Castle* (12 miles east of town) is the moated fortifica-tion inhabited by Earls of Cawdor these many centuries—Shake-speare's Macbeth, who murdered Duncan at Glamis Castle (above), was a thane of Cawdor—with interesting paintings in the drawing and other state rooms, central tower dating to 1454, and a superb facade. Restaurant.

Loch Ness: The River Ness, from which Inverness takes its name, flows into 23-mile-long Loch Ness to the south and, aside from its good looks and considerable size (22 square miles is a lot of water), you will also be attracted by the *Loch Ness Monster Exhibition* (at Drumnadrochit), an intelligently assembled documentation of the Loch Ness Monster controversy, which, according to the displays, is hardly new; reports began circulating as early as the seventh century of a "fearsome beastie" resident in the lake. Modern-day interest began, again according to the exhibition, in 1933, when the lakeside highway was completed and motorists began to report sightings, with the number, contemporarily, totaling something like 3,000. The exhibition's management believes, according to its literature, that "it is becoming increasingly likely that the myth will be replaced by the fact that there really is a colony of large, previously unknown, aquatic animals inhabiting the loch." Study the display and come to your own conclusion.

Eileen Donan Castle (near Dornie, east of Kyle of Lochalsh) is a fairy tale come true, a small, medieval château on its own peninsula protruding into the blue waters of mountain-backed Loch Duich. Access is over a triple-arched stone bridge as old as the thirteenth-century castle. A portcullis—one of those doorlike gratings made of iron bars that are raised to admit friends and lowered to keep out enemies— separates the exterior from the castle courtyard. Actually, getting there is more than half the fun; there are only two viewable rooms within, a stone-walled, beamed-ceiling banqueting hall the more interesting of the pair.

The Isle of Skye, so close to the northwest coast that it is accessible by car-ferry from four points (Kyle of Lochalsh on the mainland to Kyleakin and Maillag on the mainland to Armadale are the top two), is, understandably, the most visited of the Scottish islands. Fifty miles long and 30 miles at its widest, its terrain is at times verdant, to be sure, but the overall impression is of an eerie—at times bleak and lunar—beauty, with high cliffs and jagged peaks framing vast valleys, the lot encircled by a thousand miles of intricately indented coastline. The Skye life is a simple life. Tourism notwithstanding, standard of living remains low, hotel accommodation is mostly modest, good restaurants are minimal, and the only settlement of any substance is tiny *Portree*, on a pretty peninsula jutting into the Sound of Raasay on the island's east coast, north of the ferry terminal at Kyleakin. *Dunvegan Castle*, hugging the rugged northwest coast, is the island's showplace, smallish as British castles go, but venerable (it dates back seven centuries) and history-rich (it is the seat of the Chiefs of Mac-Leod—the current chief, John MacLeod of MacLeod, is a grandson of the late and celebrated Dame Flora MacLeod of MacLeod). It offers especially good eighteenth-century paintings by Ramsay, Zoffany, and Raeburn, superb views from its windows, and a restaurant opposite. The *Old Skye Crofter's House* (Luib) is a thatched cottage, furnished as it might have been at the turn of the century by a family that would have combined farming with weaving, as many Skye residents still do. (Skye tweeds—finer-weave than Harris—are lovely.) The *Skye Black House* (Colbost, near Dunvegan) is still another crofter's house-museum, albeit of the mid-nineteenth century. The *Talisker Distillery* (Loch Harprot) welcomes visitors, as does the *Edinbane Pottery* at Edinbane. Ponies may be hired for rides into the lonely hills from the *Strollamus Pony Trekking Centre*, four miles north of Broadford; and vessels chartered for deep-sea fishing and pleasure-cruising, from *Strollamus Boat Centre*, opposite the pony-trekking centre (above). Licenses for the sporty fishing—sea trout, brown trout, salmon—may be obtained through the *Portree Angling Association*, Masonic Buildings, Portree.

Fort William and Glencoe: A small Highland town with an agreeable, unexceptional core, Fort William's interest for the visitor centers on the *West Highland Museum* (Cameron Square). Like its counterpart in Inverness, it irritates with Sunday closing. But it is visit-worthy, as much for charming memorabilia—paintings, drawings, prints, maps—of the region going back some centuries as for exhibits dealing with Jacobite rebellions by the clans of the area, even a mock-up interior of a typical crofter's home of the last century. *Glencoe*, ten miles to the south, is one of Scotland's scenic spectaculars, but a historic spot as well: the scene of a massacre in 1692 when a party of anti-Jacobite Highlanders—of the Clan Campbell—massacred forty Jacobites, all MacDonalds. Scots still call Glencoe "The Glen of Weeping." But the drive through it—on the Fort William-Glasgow road—is one of Britain's most beautiful. The glen cuts through mountains to the right and mountains to the left, soaring to nearly 4,000 feet, with the waters of Loch Achtriochtan flowing from the River Coe, adding a lovely dimension to the scene. National Trust for Scotland operates a Visitor Centre (with details on hiking the area, among other things) just off the highway a few miles east of little Glencoe village, alongside Loch Leven. Its *Glencoe Folk Museum* is in a neatly restored thatched cottage.

SETTLING IN

Station Hotel (Leonard Street, Perth), at once friendly and attractive, is an elderly house—multigabled in the style of the Dutch Renaissance—that is nicely updated, with baths in most of its 53 rooms—some of them extra large—as well as a dining room offering good-value table d'hôte lunches and dinners. Cocktail lounge. *First Class.*

Stakis City Mills Hotel (West Mill Street, Perth) is an ancient city-center structure modernized to blend contemporary with antique—and very cleverly. You look through a glass area of the lobby floor to see the old mill's stream, below. All 40 rooms have showers in their baths. Handsome restaurant, bar-lounge. *First Class.*

Royal George Hotel (Tay Street, Perth) is scenically situated, a hop and skip from the River Tay. There are 43 neat rooms, a pair of restaurants (one specializes in beef), and as many bars. Trusthouse Forte. *First Class.*

County Hotel (County Place, Perth) has baths in more than half of its 19 rooms and makes a point of Scots specialties in its restaurant. Bar-lounge. Friendly. *Moderate.*

Gleneagles Hotel (Auchterarder, 15 miles west of Perth): Even in its last days as flagship of the now defunct British Transport Hotels, Gleneagles was spectacular. How could it be otherwise? Surrounded by the 700 acres of its own park, it was as eye-filling without—a sprawling Renaissance-style pile dating to the 1920s—as within, where its public spaces were high-ceilinged and generously proportioned. Still, a major renovation was called for; Gleneagles Hotels, the recent landlords, have spent $6 million. Thirty-nine junior suites, with four-poster beds, were added. The remaining 254 rooms were thoroughly refurbished. The Gleneagles Country Club—a glass roofed pavilion appended to the hotel—embraces a jumbo swimming pool, gym, squash courts, Jacuzzi baths, and its own café. There are, as well, a pair of restaurants in the main building, the very grand Strathearn—one of the great British resort dining rooms, and the à la carte Eagles Nest. The cocktail lounge is quite the most elegant in Scotland. There are five tennis courts, sporty trout-fishing and shooting surpassed nowhere in Scotland (it was on a Gleneagles-organized shoot that I bagged my first duck!), and the glory of Gleneagles: golf. By that, I mean three 18-hole courses, with an additional 18-hole mini-course, for good measure. Member, Leading Hotels of the World. *Luxury.*

Cromlix House (Dunblane, 18 miles southwest of Perth) makes for an agreeable overnight en route to or from the Highlands. You might well be putting up with the lord of a turn-of-century manor. Ancestors' likenesses are on public-room walls, the bar induces conversation, the quite grand restaurant does well by game and by beef, and there are just 10 good-size suites and rooms, antiques-accessorized. *First Class.*

Atholl Palace Hotel (Pitlochry): In its own hillside park of some 50 acres, high above Pitlochry, the Atholl Palace does indeed look more palace than hotel, with a meld of mansard-roofed towers and mock-medieval turrets out of the last century, when resort builders had romantic inclinations. This is a honey of a vacation headquarters, with smartly decorated lounges, restaurant, and bar, 92 super bedrooms—all of which will have showers when a current refurbishing program is concluded—and assorted fun-and-games facilities, cinema to billiard room—along with an outdoor pool on the lawn, half a dozen tennis courts, pitch-and-putt golf, and a nature trail with every species labeled. Trusthouse Forte. *First Class.*

Craigard Hotel (Strathview Terrace, Pitlochry) is attractive, heart-of-town, and full-facility, with baths in 51 of its 81 rooms. *Moderate.*

Station Hotel (Academy Street, Inverness) is adjacent to the Railway Station and was, when I last visited, in need of refurbishing of its architecturally handsome lobby area. Withal, most of the rooms have been brightened (more than 50 of the just over 60 have baths, some with showers), the restaurant is one of the best in Scotland, one of the bars serves Scots-accented lunches, and in no Highlands hotel that I know is there kinder or more professional service. *First Class.*

Kingsmills Hotel (Damfield Road, Inverness) is an away-from-the-center, originally eighteenth-century house with modern appendages, traditional-style decor, and more than half a hundred delightful rooms, a dozen of which are equipped with electric hair-dryers. Restaurant and a bar in which casual lunches are served. A Best Western hotel. *First Class.*

Glen Moor Hotel (Ness Bank, Inverness) began as a town house in the Victorian era and now sees service as a congenial hotel, good to look upon and enjoyable to live in, with baths in 25 of its 30 nice rooms, excellent-value restaurant, and bar-lounge. *Moderate.*

Royal Hotel (Academy Street, Inverness) is so attractive and so conveniently central that I wonder its Trusthouse Forte owners don't invest in the installation of baths in more than half of the nearly 50 rooms still without them. Nice restaurant, bar, and staff. *Moderate-First Class.*

Glenmoriston Hotel (Ness Bank, Inverness): Like the Royal, the Glenmoriston—so commendable otherwise—could do with more baths; only 9 of its 22 rooms have them. There's a nice lobby-lounge-bar and a very good restaurant. *Moderate.*

Dunain Park Hotel (Route A 82, a mile south of Inverness) is, to be sure, out of town. But it is special, a perfectly charming Victorian house that is at once a small hotel (six no-two-alike rooms, four of which have bath) and a restaurant of consequence. *First Class.*

Culloden House (Culloden Moor, two miles east of Inverness) is an eighteenth-century brick mansion embracing a central house to which are linked an elegant pair of lower pavilions. It is one of the better looking country houses in northern Scotland. It has been thoroughly refurbished in recent seasons by a management that turned it into a hotel of considerable charm, with a score of no-two-alike bedrooms (some with four-poster beds, some with curtain-framed beds. The reliable restaurant is Adam-style, the bar-lounge inviting. Member, Prestige Hotels. *Luxury.*

Lochalsh Hotel (Kyle of Lochalsh): You're a step or two from the car-ferry to the Isle of Skye. What's better yet, you have views of the island from public spaces and front bedrooms of this competently refurbished old house, 26 of whose 45 bright and crisp bedrooms have baths, some with showers. The restaurant serves well-priced and well-prepared dinners, and lunches come from the bar. But I anticipate a question. You wonder if you should headquarter here for Isle of Skye exploration or book on the island. My answer: You won't do any better across the water. An Orient Express hotel. *First Class.*

Skeabost House Hotel (Dunvegan Road, six miles from Portree, Isle of Skye): I don't know who built this isolated mansion a century or so back, but the two owner-couples—the McNabs and Stuarts—have retained the individuality of the place. You think you're in a private country house. Fourteen of the nearly 30 rooms—each distinctive, some bigger and nicer than others—have baths. Bar is convivial, lounge lovely, and restaurant one of the best on Skye—which, in all fairness I must add, is not the culinary capital of Scotland. *Moderate-First Class.*

Coolin Hills Hotel (Portree, Isle of Skye) straddles a hill, so that you have views from it of tiny Portree and its bay. This is an elderly, gabled house that has been modernized with a certain sense of style. Most of the 29 neat rooms have baths. Restaurant, bar-lounge. *Moderate-First Class.*

King's Haven Hotel (Portree, Isle of Skye): A personable and clever couple, Tony and Judith Vaughn-Sharp, have turned this Georgian house into a dilly of a six-room hotel (with shower-equipped baths in all but the sixth of the rooms). And what's more, the Vaughn-Sharps know food, as witness their inn's restaurant. *Moderate-First Class.*

Inverlochy Castle Hotel (two miles north of Fort William): Queen Victoria stayed at Inverlochy Castle in 1873—when it was still a private house—and wrote positively of it in her much-quoted diaries. As well she might. It still is absolutely super; along with Gleneagles (above), it is the most luxurious hotel in Scotland, occupying a mid-nineteenth-century country house designed to emulate baronial châteaux. The ceiling of the two-story-high great hall is frescoed and the furniture there and in the drawing room is mostly eighteenth-century, with paintings to match. There are just a baker's dozen rooms, each with attributes quite its own. And the restaurant is among the best north of the Tweed. Closed in winter. Member, Relais et Châteaux. *Luxury.*

Alexandra Hotel (The Parade, Fort William) is not unlike other century-old, granite-faced, gabled hotels you'll encounter in Scotland. Almost 70 of the 90-plus rooms have baths, and there are both restaurant and lunch-serving bar-lounge. *Moderate-First Class.*

Palace Hotel (Ness Walk, Fort William) welcomes with a bright red-and-gold lobby-lounge and pleases also with at least the better of its 82 rooms (of which 50 have baths). Restaurant. Bar. *Moderate.*

DAILY BREAD

Station House Restaurant (Leonard Street, Perth) is about as impressive a dining environment as Perth has to offer, with an even more important lure the sensibly priced, three-course-and-coffee table d'hôtes, with such entrées as filet of sole or local lamb roasted with rosemary. Nice sweets. *First Class.*

Penny Post (Tay Street, Perth) is more than a cutesy title; it was indeed an early post office, with reminders of its first function still at hand. Hot pies are good lunch buys; dinners are more elaborate. *Moderate-First Class.*

Lucky (South Methven Street, Perth): The adjective used as a noun makes sense. Lucky is Chinese and does a nice job with essentially Cantonese standbys. And he stays open late. *Moderate-First Class.*

Strathmore Arms (High Street, Glamis): A fine stop-for-lunch locale, the historic Strathmore Arms allows a choice: a proper meal, table d'hôte or à la carte, in its handsome dining room; or a casual libation in its pubby bar-lounge. *Moderate-First Class.*

Atholl Palace Hotel Restaurant (Pitlochry): Guest or simply passing through, I don't counsel missing the Atholl Palace. Lunch is served from a groaning buffet—with hot as well as cold dishes. Dinner is a three-course-and-coffee affair with Scottish specialties—lentil and oatmeal broth, roastit bubbly jock (turkey to you, pardner), cod with mustard sauce—always part of an extensive menu. À la carte, as well. *First Class.*

Station Hotel Restaurant (Academy Street, Inverness) is ballroom size; and, more to the point, it offers some of Scotland's best food— the chef's *pâté* served with Scottish oatcake or a hearty cock-a-leekie soup; roast beef no better anywhere in the kingdom and served in a variety of novel ways; other delicious entrées—mustard-flavored scampi, chops of local lamb, creative chicken preparations; and absolutely super sweets, pear butterscotch and peach Highland cream among them. With an excellent wine list. *First Class.*

Falcon Bar (Station Hotel, Academy Street, Inverness): Okay, you've finally worked up the courage to try haggis. Well, Falcon Bar is as good a place to get it as any, served traditionally, as "Haggis, Neeps (turnips) and Tatties (mashed potatoes)." Additional fare—Pub Grub, it's called—if you're weak of heart. *Moderate.*

Eden Court Theatre Restaurant (Bishop's Road, Inverness) is open for both lunch and dinner, regardless of the bill—or lack of one—in the auditorium. There's an appealing buffet lunch, with hot, as well as cold, choices, and dinner is both table d'hôte (recommended as good value) and with solid steaks among other à la carte victuals. *Moderate-First Class.*

Coach Inn (Nairn Road, Inverness) has a nice cottage-of-yore look, serves up the likes of steak and kidney pie at lunch, with dinner more varied. *Moderate-First Class.*

Royal Hotel Restaurant (Academy Street, Inverness) is an attractive, well-proportioned, chandeliered room up a flight from the lobby, with the lure three-course dinners (haggis is always one of the appetizers if you want a wee taste rather than a whole portion). Salmon steak and lamb chops are among the entrées. *First Class.*

Kingsmill Hotel Restaurant (Damfield Road, Inverness) advises, before you get into the nitty gritty of the menu, that "Robert Burns dined here Wednesday 5th September, 1787." Chances are he had a good meal. Seafood—sole, trout, scallops, scampi, salmon, lobster—is the specialty. But there's a tasty table d'hôte as well. Attractive. *First Class.*

Dunain Park Hotel Restaurant (Route A 82, a mile south of Inverness) is very small and good-looking in the best Victorian manner and offers delicious comestibles. Dinner might run to hare *pâté* or smoked trout, with carrot soup following, chicken with honey and ginger sauce, or pigeon in port among the entrées; chocolate mousse or orange caramel trifle are but two of the sweets choices. With cheese and biscuits, to conclude and coffee following in the hotel's charming drawing room. *First Class.*

Kintail Lodge (Glen Shiel, 15 miles east of Kyle of Lochalsh) serves nourishing lunches in its bar that are worth knowing about if you're motoring in the direction of—or from—the Isle of Skye. Arrive in the evening and dinner is served in the smart restaurant on red-and-white checked cloths. *Moderate-First Class.*

King's Haven Hotel Restaurant (Portree, Isle of Skye) comes up with delicious choices on its handwritten daily dinner menus—lentil soup or kipper *pâté*, to start; pork cutlets in cider, grilled steak, or fish of the day among the entrées; and splendid desserts with Scottish accents, Sligham mousse most especially. Lunch is more informal. *Moderate-First Class.*

Inverlochy Castle Hotel Restaurant (two miles north of Fort William) is about as close as one can come to a hotel meal that resembles an invitation to a private country estate. There is no written menu; the captain simply explains the chef's preparations for that evening—start with a salad or an unusual *pâté*, choose the fish of the day superbly sauced, with beef and lamb specialties invariably excellent. Pastries are delicious, but *soufflés* are even more interesting. Fine wines. Closed in winter. *Luxury.*

Crofter (High Street, Fort William) is indicated for a lunch or dinner that might be built around local lamb or salmon. *Moderate-First Class.*

Angus (High Street, Fort William) specializes, not surprisingly, in sound Scotch beef, but the local fish is tasty, too, with the table d'hôte lunches and dinners noteworthy. *Moderate-First Class.*

AFTER DARK

Perth Theatre (High Street, Perth) is scene of a variety of entertainment—plays, opera, and ballet, much of it by touring companies.

Perth City Hall (South Street, Perth) has an excellent auditorium with fine acoustics that are sympathetic to the sounds of symphonies. (It and the Perth Theatre [above] are the main venues for performances in the annual Perth Festival of the Arts every spring.)

Pitlochry Festival Theatre (Foss Road, Pitlochry) has been the scene, for more than thirty years—mid-May, usually, through mid-October—of an ambitious festival of the performing arts, with plays performed by its own well-regarded repertory company and other attractions, from, say, the Scottish Ballet, through Gilbert and Sullivan, to classical pianists and professional puppeteers.

Eden Court Theatre (Bishop's Road, Inverness) is a modern performing arts venue for plays and music.

Northern Meeting Park (Inverness) is the site, each evening mid-May through mid-September, of Highland entertainment adored by visitors—bagpipe bands, kilted dancers, and the like.

INCIDENTAL INTELLIGENCE

Perth is served by the airport at nearby Dundee, from where there are flights to and from Aberdeen to the north and Manchester to the south. Inverness is connected by air with island points to the north. British Rail trains cover most of the Highlands region, but it is perhaps worth noting the especially scenic Skyeways bus route linking Glasgow with Kyle of Lochalsh, via Loch Lomond, Glencoe, and Fort William. It departs from Glasgow at 9:00 A.M., and you reach Kyle at 2:00 P.M., May through September. *Further information:* Perth Tourist Information Centre, Round House, Marshall Place; Pitlochry Tourist Information Centre, Atholl Road; Inverness Tourist Information Centre, Church Street; Isle of Skye Tourist Information Centre, Meall House, Portree.

27

Aberdeen and the East

Shetland to St. Andrews

BACKGROUND BRIEFING
Look at a map of Europe, and you perceive immediately that Aberdeen is synonymous with North. Scotland's third city is Britain's northernmost city of consequence (population is about a quarter of a million) and is, as well, among Europe's northernmost communities, with capitals like Copenhagen and Moscow lying to the south.

Still, it is only since the mid-1970s that we began to hear about Aberdeen abroad, when it was transformed silently, and almost overnight, it would appear, into Europe's North Sea oil capital, as part of a development that happily left the city proper unspoiled, with rigs considerably out to sea and oil personnel headquartered in detached communities beyond town.

Its contemporary eminence as an entrepôt for precious fuel aside, Aberdeen over the centuries has evolved into the prime governmental, educational, industrial, shipping, and—not to be underestimated in connection with its interest for the visitor—cultural center of Britain's far north.

Its geography—no port in the United Kingdom is closer to Scandinavia—has been a boon and a bane, for Aberdeen was subject to Middle Ages raids by Viking marauders in about the same proportion as those by English troops from the south. Nor did it escape involvement in Baroque-era battles—often more associated with the Highlands to the west and the Lowlands to the south—that eventually resulted in Scotland's union with England (Aberdeen's main thoroughfare, Union Street, attests to this) through the Scottish Royal House of Stuart.

The Stuarts' successors continue to frequent the Aberdeen area; Balmoral Castle, nearby, is the Royal Family's summer retreat. And the region is chock-filled—surprisingly so, considering its northerly situation—with country houses of distinction and, for that matter, distilleries in which are manufactured the Scottish national beverage so beloved the world over. Go north, if you like, to the Shetlands, most distant of the UK's islands, and south to the university town of St. Andrews.

ON SCENE

Lay of the Land: No important British city is easier, geographically. Central, or New, Aberdeen, with its still-picturesque harbor to the Esplanade-lined east, bases itself on imposing Union Street, which bisects it in an east-to-west direction, with the historic Schoolhill area on its northern tip, ancient Market Cross and a clutch of major monuments at its eastern edge, and the Railway Station a step or two south.

But we haven't dealt with Old Aberdeen—a historic district, on no account to be overlooked, a few minutes' drive north along King Street, with the River Don at its northern edge.

Aberdeen Art Gallery (Schoolhill) is Great Britain's best-kept cultural secret. The building itself is a winner, neoclassic, originally built in 1885 around an arched, pool-centered courtyard, with its collection surrounding it on two capacious floors. The gallery owes its underappreciated eminence to a series of fortunate turn-of-century bequests—supplemented by municipal funding and later public contributions—that led to the opening in 1925 of the substantially enlarged present quarters by King George V.

But it's the paintings that attract. Eighteenth- and early nineteenth-century portraits—Scottish (Ramsay and Raeburn), as well as English (Hogarth, Reynolds, Rowlandson); later British masters—Blake, Turner, Bonington, Landseer, pre-Raphaelites like Rossetti; and—as interesting at Aberdeen as any provincial gallery in the kingdom—lesser-known, though gifted, painters, like, say, Aberdeen-born William Dyce, Sir William Quiller Richardson (don't miss his two-part *Mariage de Convenance!*), Sir Hubert Von Herkimer (don't miss his *Our Village 1890*), George Hitchcock (don't miss his *Maternité 1889*). There are more prominent Britons—Sir David Wilkie, Augustus John and Gwen John—on hand, too; along with modernists like Paul Nash, Ben Nicholson, Francis Bacon, and Sir Stanley Spencer; and great sculptors—Henry Moore, Dame Barbara Hepworth, Sir Jacob Epstein. French treats are a bonus—including Monet, Pissarro, Sisley, Signac, Toulouse-Lautrec, and Renoir among the Impressionists, Courbet and Daubigny among their predecessors, and Bonnard and Vuillard among their successors. Restaurant.

Provost Skene's House (Guestrow, off Broad Street) is a superb stone house built by the rich merchant whose name it still bears—he was later provost of the city—all the way back in the middle of the seventeenth century. The Aberdeen Art Gallery has restored the house and furnished it, room by room, and with panache. You want most to note the painted ceiling in the chapel, a range of beautifully furnished rooms of the house's initial period, and later chambers—Georgian dining and bedroom, Regency music room, and Victorian parlor.

Aberdeen Maritime Museum (Shiprow) occupies Provost Ross's House, a somber stone mansion dating to the eighteenth century, the era that saw the city develop its maritime prowess through shipbuilding, whaling in the Arctic, herring fisheries, passenger service to the northern islands, and the contemporary North Sea oil and gas boom. Through ship models, paintings, actual boats, and historic documents, along with an array of objects related to them, the museum relates Aberdeen's maritime history. It is operated by Aberdeen Art Gallery.

James Dun's House (Schoolhill) takes the name of the eighteenth-century merchant who inhabited it. It is today an Aberdeen Art Gallery-operated special exhibition center, with the themes invariably having to do with the city and its arts and its crafts. Go in.

University of Aberdeen Archeological Museum (Broad Street) is as good an excuse as any to have a look at Marischal College, the nineteenth/twentieth century addition to the university's initial sixteenth-century building. My goodness, there's a lot here: the fruits of assiduous collectors among Aberdonians sent, in Her Majesty's Service, to the colonies round the globe in the last century—tattooed heads and sculpted jade, boomerangs and blow-pipes, costumes and ceramics.

Kirk of St. Nicholas and the New Aberdeen cathedrals: St. Nicholas's (Union Street) is a two-building, part-Gothic complex—with the largest carillon of bells in the country—that serves as the principal Church of Scotland parish for central Aberdeen. Aberdeen is a three-cathedral city. Two are in the center—*St. Mary's* (Huntly Street; Catholic), mid-nineteenth-century Victorian Gothic; and somewhat older *St. Andrew's Scottish Episcopal* (the north-of-the-Tweed name of the Anglican Church), which is interesting to transatlantic visitors, what with a room of exhibits pertaining to Aberdeen-ordained Bishop Samuel Seabury, who became (in 1784) head of the Episcopal church in the American colonies.

St. Machar's Cathedral and Old Aberdeen represent the town at its mellowest—and most beautiful. Dating to the Middle Ages, this time-stood-still precinct waited until as recently as 1891 to amalgamate with the "new" part of town to constitute a united Aberdeen. The Cathedral (actually a Church of Scotland parish church) on the street called The Chanonry, is an enchanting, twin-spired structure with a short but eye-filling nave, surrounded by a stone wall punctuated with fifteenth-century Gothic arches. The wooden ceiling is embellished with nearly fifty coats-of-arms, Pope Leo X (from the period when St. Machar's was Catholic), through early Scottish and fellow-European kings, on to Highland earls and, not inappropriately, the Royal Burgh of Aberdeen.

Walk about, after a cathedral visit, to Old Aberdeen's *Old Town House* (High Street), a classy eighteenth-century mansion now a public library; U-shaped, low-slung *Mitchell's Hospital* (1801); and *King's College* (High Street), allowing time, later, for the King's College complex, a part of Aberdeen University in and about The Chanonry and High Street and including *Crown Tower* (you'll be reminded of the summit of Edinburgh's St. Giles's Cathedral) and the adjacent sixteenth-century chapel. End at that point of the River Don traversed since 1329 by the *Brig o' Balgownie*, its original Gothic-pointed stone arch still spanning the wooded shores.

Haddo House (11 miles north of Aberdeen): Visit one country house in northern Scotland, and it should be Haddo, the winner, hands down, of open-to-the-public mansions. William Adam, father of the renowned Robert and a distinguished architect in his own right, designed Haddo (he was the original architect, as well, for much more ambitious Hopetoun, outside of Edinburgh [Chapter 24]; like Hopetoun, Haddo had later embellishment). Earls of Aberdeen were Haddo's owners; one—the fourth—was a Victorian prime minister (Victoria was a house guest), and the wife of a successor, late in the last century, remodeled the house in the original Adam style—and with success of a kind unusual in that era. There are paintings by the likes of Van Dyck, Murillo, and Lorrain, and each room is more sumptuous than the one before—the high-ceilinged dining room most spectacularly. Café. National Trust for Scotland.

Crathes Castle (seven miles southwest of Aberdeen) is that oddity among medieval châteaux: a veritable skyscraper, six stories, plus attics under the turrets and gables. The stone-walled salons do not disappoint, but the room to remember is the oak-paneled long gallery. Unless you prefer haunted spaces: In Crathes' Green Lady's Room, the presumed ghost is a long-ago resident with a baby in her arms. Restaurant. National Trust for Scotland.

Craigevar Castle (12 miles west of Aberdeen) is nothing if not sublimely Scottish, with its severe seventeenth-century facade; arched, stucco-decorated great hall, plaid-carpeted and plaid-upholstered; paneled Queen's Room, rich with Raeburn portraits; and what is perhaps the castle's most endearing feature: an early resident-family's coat of arms on the stone stairwell, with the admonition: *Doe not Vaiken Sleiping Dogs.* National Trust for Scotland.

Balmoral Castle (45 miles west of Aberdeen, and nicely combined with Craigevar Castle, above) is, as almost any newspaper reader knows, the Royal Family's northern retreat. Architecturally astute Prince Albert, Queen Victoria's consort, masterminded its design, as he had that of Osborne House, on the Isle of Wight (Chapter 20), except that Osborne, a mock-Italian villa, comes off more interestingly than Scottish Baronial-style Balmoral. But the point is academic, because—with the exception of an exhibition about Balmoral's history that is sometimes—not always—viewable in the nearly 70-foot-long ballroom—the castle is closed to visitors. Only its grounds are open to the public, and these when there are no Royal residents within. Still, you might want to observe the crests of Prince Albert's family, half a dozen odd, on a Balmoral wall and pay a visit to adjacent *Crathie Church*—with memorabilia on view of Royal worshipers from Victoria and Albert's time to this very day.

Shetland, as any wearer of the shaggy sweaters bearing its name knows, is the appellation for a cluster of islands considerably to the northeast of Scotland's northern shores. Far enough so as to make John o'Groats—at the northeast tip of Scotland and traditionally considered its northernmost point—almost southerly. (John o'Groats is near the Village of Canisbay, whose churchyard contains the grave of John o'Groat; John's house at the site named for him has long since been razed.) If Shetland is not a something-for-everybody destination, it is grist for the conversation mill at cocktail parties easily stretching over several seasons. You are bound to be the first on your block if you sail (overnight) from Aberdeen, or—more conveniently—fly up to *Lerwick*, Britain's northernmost town, and the friendly and unpretentious little capital on the principal Shetland island conveniently called—everything being relative in this remote part of the world—Mainland. The town is a symphony in stone; brown, somber, and in pleasing contrast to the blue waters of the harbor—invariably filled with fishing boats, pleasure craft, larger freighters. Lerwick revolves around its main thoroughfare, aptly titled Commercial Street, with its emporia ranging from, say, A. L. Laing, the intown branch of an outlet at exurban Freefield that is "the most northerly pharmacy in Great Britain," to Solotti's Tea Room ("Tea, Coffee, Lemonades, Confectionary and Tobacco Always Available") and Shetland Silvercraft, as well as Hjaltasteyn Stone Polishing Workshop, for locally made silver souvenirs. There are any number of outlets for the sweaters—bargain-tabbed on the island of origin—that are knit on hand-operated machines in homes of Shetlanders, who work for manufacturers and distributors and usually farm, as well; best buys are probably to be made at the establishment known simply as "The Factory" near the Shetland Hotel. The *Shetland County Museum* is a heart-of-town landmark that tells the anything but prosaic story of these windswept, treeless islands, Viking long before they were British—and still with close ties to not-far-distant Norway. Exhibits run from third-century sandstone discs, through Norse silver brooches, on to contemporary fishing boats. The nearby *Town Hall* is graced with stained glass windows that depict the Shetlands' history, including a pair portraying Danish Princess Margaret and Scottish James II, by whose marriage the islands became part of Scotland in 1469. And you want to consider ferry excursions for bird-watching—a major Shetland visitor-pastime—on the satellite islands of Noss and Bressay, perhaps lunching at Maryfield House, on Bressay.

St. Andrew's is to the southern flank of the east coast what Aberdeen is to the north. Still small but perky, it is an unlikely but successful blend of a university—Scotland's oldest and most prestigious—with the golf courses that fans of the game cross oceans to wait their turn to play upon. South Street is shop-lined, cutting through from the western edge of town to the harbor and the Cathedral precincts, with the university to the south and the golf links to the west. *St. Andrew's Cathedral* (Castle Street) is, alas, no more—as a full-fledged building, at any rate. Not since the destructive days of the Reformation four centuries back. But with its brilliant seaside situation, it just has to be Britain's most spectacular ruin, and from what remains—including the landmark tower—it is not difficult to perceive that—at 357 feet—it was the longest of the Scottish cathedrals, a Romanesque-Gothic mix, wherein—among much else—Mary Queen of Scots' mother, Mary of Guise, married Scotland's King James V. Take in the *Cathedral Museum's* fragments, before walking north along the bay to *St. Andrew's Castle*, not unlike the cathedral (whose bishops used it as their palace), a seaside ruin, its grassy ramparts evocative of not a few great moments of Scottish history. *St. Andrew's University* is scattered about town, nothing like as grand and on a much less monumental scale than either Oxford or Cambridge. Which is hardly to say that you want to ignore it. *St. Mary's College* (South Street) surrounds a lovely quadrangle, one of whose buildings, the onetime University Library, was home to the Parliament of Scotland in 1645. *St. Salvator's College* embraces, in its quad, a sublimely handsome chapel, circa 1450, with fine stained glass. *St. Leonard's Chapel*, part of another old college, was recently refurbished (it had lacked a roof for two centuries). Visit St. Andrew's in term-time and it's a blaze of scarlet; students in their academic robes, using their favorite form of transport: the bicycle. *Golf courses:* If St. Andrew's University is ancient (it dates to 1410 and is Scotland's oldest), so is golf in this town where it was born, so the locals have it, at the still-in-use, still-imposing, classic-style *Royal and Ancient Clubhouse*, whose members formulated the rules of the game in 1754. Now, then, golfers, you don't just amble over and tee off; too many fellow-golfers want to play. In order to try your skill on the most celebrated of the town's links, the *Old Course* (adjacent to whose 18th green is the Royal and Ancient Clubhouse), you are wise to book in advance—a couple of months is not too early—by communicating with the Links Management Committee, Golf Place, St. Andrew's (telephone 0334-75757). Arriving on the scene without having done so should not deter you, however, so long as you allow at least a day prior to play for signing up on the "ballot," as it is called, with an official called the Starter. Bear in mind, too, that there are three other St. Andrew's courses—*New, Eden,* and *Jubilee*—as well as nearly a dozen in the immediate vicinity of the town.

Falkland Palace (10 miles west of St. Andrew's) dates to the sixteenth century, when it went up as a royal retreat, with Mary Queen of Scots among the occasional revelers. Double-turreted and still impressive from without, it is, within, the most disappointing historic site that I know of in Britain. You get about on a self-guided tour, walking around in circles, before finally finding the exit (sign-posting is poor), and there is precious little to see in what is, you learn too late, a mostly nineteenth-century restoration. National Trust for Scotland.

SETTLING IN
Huntly Hotel (Huntly Street, Aberdeen) has everything going for it: smart, traditional-style ambience, professional staff, showers in the baths of all rooms, a super main restaurant, and a bar-lounge wherein are served tasty, casual meals. In a nutshell: one of the best—and best-looking—hotels in Scotland. *Luxury.*

Caledonian Thistle Hotel (Union Terrace, Aberdeen) occupies a still-handsome Victorian building, tastefully updated but with its old-school look still dominant in the spacious public areas. Forty of the 77 rooms and suites have baths, and a dozen more have showers replacing tubs. Pair of handsome restaurants and a cocktail lounge that serves informal lunches. Charming. *First Class.*

Station Hotel (Guild Street, Aberdeen) has the Railway Station as a near neighbor. Rooms have been modernized in this old house, to the point where most of the 50-odd have baths. Restaurant, pair of bars, one where casual lunches are served. *First Class.*

Victoria Hotel (Market Street, Aberdeen) is attractive, friendly, and nicely equipped—with a convenient restaurant and bar-lounge and 80 full-facility rooms. *First Class.*

Imperial Hotel (Guild Street, Aberdeen) has the advantage of baths, if not showers, in all of its hundred rooms. Elderly. Restaurant, two bars, one of which serves lunch. *Moderate.*

Skean Dhu Airport Hotel (Argyll Road, Aberdeen) attracts oil-industry executives and has nearly 150 generous-size rooms, the lot with showers in their baths; a couple of luxurious suites; attractive restaurant, coffee shop, bar-lounge. *First Class.*

Holiday Inn Aberdeen (Oldmeldrum Road, Bucksburn, Aberdeen) is more interestingly designed than the town's other Holiday Inn (adjacent to the airport). This one is a white-stucco mock-château with a tile-floored lobby that comes off rather well; just 99 capacious rooms with showers in all their baths, restaurant, pub-lounge that serves bar lunches, indoor pool. Neither central nor at the airport, which is not, however, far away. *First Class.*

Shetland Hotel (Holmsgarth Road, Lerwick, Shetland), a 10-minute walk from the center, is hardly felicitous in look, at least from without. But this sleekly contemporary house has 57 well-equipped rooms, pair of good restaurants (try local salmon in the main dining room—packed with locals for Sunday lunch), leisure center (with pool, sauna solarium, and gym) and welcoming bar-lounge. *First Class.*

Lerwick Thistle Hotel (South Road, Lerwick, Shetland) is modern and has, moreover, baths in most of its 60 rooms; restaurant, pair of bars. *First Class.*

Queen's Hotel (Lerwick, Shetland) is old and, to understate, inelegant. But it overlooks Lerwick Harbor; its bar is the logical place to meet Shetlanders. There's a restaurant, too. *Moderate.*

Old Course Hotel (Old Station Road, St. Andrew's): You might expect a traditional-style house of yore, given the name of this hotel. Quite the reverse: this most likable 72-room house has the distinction of being 100 percent contemporary with well-equipped, really comfortably designed rooms with shower in every one of its baths. There are two smart restaurants and as many bars, including one—Jigger Inn—in a converted onetime stationmaster's house. St. Andrew's most famous links are just out front, with the sea beyond. *Luxury.*

Rusacks Marine Hotel (Links Road, St. Andrew's) is everything that the Old Course Hotel (above) is not: venerable (a superb granite mock-Renaissance stone palace) and quietly traditional, with a repeat clientele—mostly mature—that likes serenity. There are just 50 thoughtfully equipped rooms, views of the links and the sea from the sun lounge, and a gracious restaurant and cocktail bar. Lovely. *Luxury.*

Scores Hotel (The Scores, St. Andrew's) scores. Views from the front rooms—all 30 have showers in their baths—are of the Old Course and, from the back, of a flower-filled garden; with decor essentially contemporary. A Best Western hotel. *First Class.*

St. Andrew's Hotel (The Scores, St. Andrew's) occupies a clutch of houses out of the last century, with views of the sea and the Old Course and 25 functional rooms. *Moderate.*

Star Hotel (Market Street, St. Andrew's) retains a good bit of the charm of an early nineteenth-century coaching inn, which was its original function. With its central situation, it draws university and local clientele, as well as visitors—a nice mix. Twenty-five rooms, restaurant, popular bar. *Moderate.*

DAILY BREAD
Gerard's (Chapel Street, Aberdeen): The Frenchman of the title is boss and operates a no-nonsense French restaurant in attractive surroundings (it's fun to have a premeal drink in his plant-and-rattan Garden Room). Order with confidence interesting appetizers and hearty soups, solid beef, veal, and—not to be overlooked in this seaport city—seafood, simply grilled or properly sauced, if you prefer. Good-value table d'hôte lunches. *First Class-Luxury.*

Simpson's (Schoolhill, Aberdeen): This is a handsome spot, with a diverting mix of chairs, late eighteenth-century through Victorian, surrounding the tables in a room of golds and beiges. Menu is conventional—roasts, chops, daily specials—with super sweets. Table d'hôte lunches and dinners are buys. *Moderate-First Class.*

Pinnocchio (Justice Mille Lane, Aberdeen): Pick a pasta to start, following with scampi the Italian way or a veal dish: well-priced table d'hôte lunches. Italian wines. *Moderate-First Class.*

Atlantis (Crown Street, Aberdeen): This seafood house builds its menu around the local North Sea lobster, served half a dozen ways. Local scallops and sole, too. *First Class.*

Beau Brummell (Caledonian Thistle Hotel, Union Terrace, Aberdeen): There's no better table d'hôte at dinner than Beau's with deviled whitebait or soup of the day to start; grilled lamb chops or roast chicken with fresh vegetables among a typical day's entrées; banana brandy snaps or, from the trolley, cakes or a board laden with cheeses, to conclude. *First Class.*

Peking (John Street, Aberdeen): Stick to Cantonese specialties— wonton soup, sweet and sour pork, egg foo yung—and you'll be happy. *Moderate-First Class.*

Chapel House (Chapel Street, Lerwick, Shetland), a desanctified chapel turned restaurant—No. 1 in Lerwick—is indicated for a steak or seafood dinner. *First Class.*

St. Magnus Hotel Restaurant (Hillswick, Shetland)—Victorian Nordic in look—makes for a worthy stop, in the course of a round-island excursion, for lunch in its carvery-style restaurant (all you can eat of roast beef, lamb, and pork) or for a hearty afternoon tea. *Moderate.*

Road Hole (Old Course Hotel, St. Andrew's): The Old Course's principal dining room is sleekly understated in look—not unlike the rest of this contemporary hotel—and creditable, as regards fare (ask for Scottish specialties, cock-a-leekie soup through Scotch beef, local game, and North Sea sole). And the same hotel's budget-category *Fife and Forfar* is good, too. Good wines. *Moderate-First Class.*

Niblick (Golf Place, St. Andrew's): If there were not already a restaurant with this name in this golf mecca, someone would surely create one. As it is, the Niblick, with its amusing golf motif, is a source of tasty seafood. *First Class.*

Pepita's (Creil's Lane, St. Andrew's) fills the bill for nourishing sustenance—salads, daily hot specials, and omelets at lunch, treats for tea, and more formal dinners—by candlelight. *Moderate-First Class.*

Pancake Place (South Street, St. Andrew's) emphasizes pancakes, starters through sweets. But you may vary your order with salads and sandwiches. *Moderate.*

AFTER DARK

His Majesty's Theatre (Schoolhill, Aberdeen) is a traditional setting for drama.

Arts Centre (King Street, Aberdeen) is the venue for a variety of entertainments, plays through dance.

St. Nicholas House (Broad Street, Aberdeen) and *Music Hall* (Broad Street) present orchestral groups.

Byre Theatre (Byre Wynd Court, St. Andrew's) is the *wunderkind* of the Scottish east coast, with its repertory company presenting plays by talented Scots, celebrated non-Scottish Britons, and acclaimed playwrights from abroad. *Note:* In Aberdeen, ask your hotel concierge for a free copy of *What's On In Aberdeen*, published monthly.

INCIDENTAL INTELLIGENCE

Passenger ships link Aberdeen with Lerwick in the Shetland Islands, the Faroe Islands (Danish-related and in the North Sea), Denmark, and Norway. From Aberdeen Airport, six miles northwest of the city, British Airways flights connect Aberdeen with other British points and Scandinavian and continental European cities. *Further information:* Aberdeen Tourist Centre, St. Nicholas House, Broad Street; Lerwick Tourist Information Centre, Alexandra Wharf; St. Andrew's Tourist Information Centre, South Street.

28

Wales

Cardiff to the Castles

BACKGROUND BRIEFING

The wonder of Wales is that even with the publicity value inherent in the heir to the British crown taking its name, it remains terra incognita, at least to the non-Welsh-descended visitor from across the Atlantic, which flanks its magnificent western shore. Singers and poets though they are, the Welsh have been nothing like as successful as the Scots and Irish in calling attention to the special qualities of their land—small, but as rich in natural splendor as its mountains are high—and of their culture, based on a still-taught, still-spoken, indeed, tenaciously retained language of their own.

This hiding of their light under a bushel is anomalous for the proud—and, to be sure, articulate—Welsh, whose goal over long centuries has been to preserve their identity at all costs. And there have been many costs. The Romans learned, nearly two thousand years ago, that Wales would not be as easy to colonize as England. And it wasn't. Later, Welsh warriors resisted forces of the Anglo-Saxon kingdom of Wessex, taking on aggressive Vikings as well.

The Welsh-born saint, David, and his fellow monks, had converted the land to Christianity as early as the sixth century (Wales's St. David's Cathedral celebrated the 800th anniversary of the construction of its current—not the first—building in 1981), and by the tenth century disparate tribes had united under a king who promulgated a nationwide code of laws. By that time—a thousand years ago—the Welsh were expressing themselves as musicians, poets, and teachers.

William the Conqueror's victory over the English was one thing; over the Welsh, another. To deal with them, in the eleventh century, he established a ring of militarily strong earldoms along the English side of the frontier—the region became known as the Marches and is, still. The idea was to discourage Welsh invasion, but both countries were aggressive over a two-century period. Under two national leaders, each named Llewelyn, Wales had become politically united, the while flowering culturally.

But England's King Edward I—immortal as a consequence of the extraordinary, still-to-be-visited castles he built to overawe the Welsh—vanquished the enemy in 1282, and by the terms of the Statute of Rhuddlan two years later the English became Wales's rulers. Edward I, to placate his new subjects, designated his son Prince of Wales, beginning a tradition that ever since has dictated that the monarch's male heir be so named. (Caernarvon Castle, where Edward II was born, has been the site of the investitures of two modern Princes of Wales, the late Edward VIII in 1911 and in 1969 the current heir, Prince Charles, who—with his then-recent bride, the first Princess of Wales since Mary, consort of George V, became queen in 1910—revisited the castle in 1981.)

Still, the Welsh did not accept English hegemony. They revolted in force in the fifteenth century and in that same century achieved some satisfaction when Henry VII, first of the Tudor dynasty and Welsh-descended, took the crown, inaugurating a period during which Wales—and its people—became more assimilated into the English scheme of things, at least the more powerful upper classes. Your everyday Welshman—in the coal mines, on the land, in the towns (1536 Act of Union with England notwithstanding)—has always resisted Anglicization and employed religion in this regard. Though it supported Charles I over Cromwell in the seventeenth century Civil War, Wales, in the eighteenth century, began to turn from the Church of England to less ritualistic Methodism, with worship in unadorned chapels as opposed to art-filled churches of the Anglicans. (Though with several cathedrals in Wales, the Anglicans are a minority church, called The Church in Wales.)

The last century saw Wales transformed—especially in the south—by the Industrial Revolution. A whole generation of Americans' sole identification with it is through Richard Llewelyn's novel, *How Green Was My Valley*—and a Hollywood film based upon it—depicting life in the coal-mining company towns. Modern Wales has given Britain a prime minister (David Lloyd George) and a beloved poet (Dylan Thomas), and its fortunes have, in many respects, been not unlike those of the rest of Britain. But make no mistake, Wales is very Welsh (the Welsh Nationalist party voted in 1981 to seek a Welsh Socialist state independent of Britain, discarding its previous goal of self-government within the United Kingdom), unpretentious and egalitarian (there are virtually no luxury hotels or exceptional restaurants), and not a little xenophobic (it welcomes visitors but can be wary of them). And even though the Welsh are, of course, English-speaking, the continued use of their own language is a kind of barrier setting them apart. In a word, Wales is Britain at its most exotic.

ON SCENE
Lay of the Land: Land's End in England's Cornwall (Chapter 18) extends more westerly. But St. David's in Wales comes very close. This western peninsula of Great Britain is relatively compact: 160 miles at its longest, 60 miles at its widest. White farmhouses and their stone barns are tucked into crevices of the north's magnificent mountains (Mt. Snowden, at 3,650 feet, is the highest peak of England or Wales). The center is a lovely mix of sheep farms in verdant valleys, and half-timbered houses are everywhere; the south is lower, albeit hilly. The long coastline is one of wide beaches and tall cliffs, with three national parks: Snowdonia in the north; Pembrokeshire Coast, in the west and south; and Brecon Beacons, in the southeast. There are some two and three quarter-million Welsh; more than half a million speak Welsh, which you'll hear a lot of in the north and west. Don't let signs you'll see everywhere, in Welsh, throw you; an English translation invariably follows. Which is just as well, for the languages have little in common. For example: "Welsh Office" (the organ of the British government that deals with Welsh affairs) comes out in Welsh as "Y Swyddfa Gymreig." You get the idea?

CARDIFF AND THE SOUTH

Cardiff, the capital, is requisite to an understanding of Wales, contemporarily and with respect to the past, as well. It's all here, in this medium-size, easy-to-negotiate city, ancient castle through to the newest Welsh-created play or painting. The River Taff flows along the west side of town, and the Central Railway Station delineates its southern edge. From the station, one may walk St. Mary Street north, passing Howell's, the leading department store, and its competitors, and on into High Street, which terminates after a block or two at a thoroughfare with three names—Castle Street, Duke Street, and—when it becomes pedestrians-only—Queen Street. On its northern side is a major landmark. Cardiff Castle, while an easy walk to the northwest, along Museum Avenue, is the classic-style Civic Centre, with the Welsh Office—the regional government administration—and the City Hall at its core.

National Museum of Wales (Museum Avenue, in the Civic Centre) is easily the best show in town. King George V journeyed from London to open this elegantly domed and colonnaded pavilion in 1927; it has been the Principality's principal cultural treasure house ever since. The archeology sections, especially as they pertain to Wales—carved monuments from early Christian Wales and prehistoric Welsh objects, bowls to bracelets—are fascinating. So is the display of regalia worn by Prince Charles and his great uncle, the late Edward VIII, when they were invested as Princes of Wales at Caernarvon Castle. Move along, learning about Welsh botany, Welsh geography, Welsh industry.

Until you come to the paintings. Why hadn't anyone told you of Old Masters on display here, by the likes of Fra Angelico, Piero de Cosimo, and Murillo to Boucher, Reynolds, and Gainsborough? French Impressionists and post-Impressionists are represented by Renoir (a lovely lady in blue), Van Gogh, Derain, and Cézanne—to name but a quartet. And there are modern Britons' works, including—appropriately for this of all museums—a portrait of young a Dylan Thomas by Augustus John. Restaurant.

Welsh Folk Museum (St. Fagan's) is a quarter-hour's drive from the center and requires a lot of footwork once you've arrived. But don't let the word *folk* in the title—I know it can imply dullness—keep you away. The Welsh have done the kind of thing undertaken in the United States, Canada, and Scandinavia—and done it with a sense of style. Representative buildings from all over Wales have been moved to an 18-acre site on the grounds of a superb Elizabethan castle—St. Fagan's by name. You begin, though, in a proper museum, with exhibits portraying Welsh culture, furniture, farm implements, clothes, and guns. Wander to and through the complex, then visit the seventeenth-century farmhouse, eighteenth-century pigsty, nineteenth-century barn, gypsy caravan, and country chapel. Finally, saving the best for last, examine the opulent interiors—among the best of any open-to-public country houses in Wales—of St. Fagan's Castle, including paneled parlor, tapestry-hung drawing room, four-poster bedroom, and a long gallery hung with portraits of early resident Earls and Countesses of Plymouth. Restaurants.

Llandaff Cathedral (Llandaff) is a near-neighbor to the Welsh Folk Museum (above) and, ideally, is visited in connection with it. Not much remains of the eleventh-century structure erected by the first Norman bishop in the area. Today's Llandaff, seat of an Anglican—or to use the term used in Wales, Church in Wales—bishop, is essentially Early English and Decorated Gothic, rebuilt first after Cromwellian forces destroyed much of it in the seventeenth century and again after Nazi bombers did likewise in the twentieth. The refurbishing includes a daringly contemporary sculpture by Sir Jacob Epstein, framed by a bold arch surmounting the nave and dividing it from the choir.

You may well consider the Epstein a jarring note. (I do.) But you want to see it—and the ancient graveyard encircling the cathedral, as well, in this pleasant Cardiff suburb.

Cardiff Castle (Castle Street) was at first Roman and later Norman. It has seen many battles—Romans vs. Welsh, Normans vs. Welsh, Welsh vs. Cromwell's Parliamentarians. In the mid-nineteenth century, it was acquired by the locally eminent Marquess of Bute, who, with the best of intentions, hired an architect-designer named William Burges to restore it. You either love or loathe Burges's work. I fall into the latter category—an admirer of many Victorian interiors throughout Britain, but not this one, which falls somewhere between the Bavarian castles of Mad King Ludwig and Disneyland, albeit lacking the artisanship and skill of the former and the fun of the latter. The Burges state rooms—banqueting hall, dining room, library, "Arab," and smoking rooms—are shown regularly on guided tours. Regardless of how you react to them, you're bound to like the derring-do exteriors of the castle complex, especially its walls on which Burges—at his best—superimposed, at intervals, sculpted animals (lions, tigers, and the like) in the process of climbing over, onto the street.

St. John's Church (Working Street) is Cardiff at its most charming: a neighbor to Cardiff Castle (above) and, in its early centuries, parish church for the Castle's occupants. Now preponderantly Gothic—the nave is in the Perpendicular species of that style, lined by slender columns—it has nineteenth-century embellishments and a chapel of historic worth, called Herbert after the two brothers whom it memorializes, one a secretary to both Queen Elizabeth I and King James I and VI, and the other a seventeenth-century Keeper of Cardiff Castle.

Tintern Abbey (30 miles east of Cardiff, near Chepstow) ranks, in my view at least, as one of the most evocative of British ruins: a roofless and windowless, but otherwise remarkably intact, Early English church, whose Wye Valley setting is positively idyllic, with parts of the one-time Cistercian monastery—cloister, visitors' parlor, refectory—remaining, along with a detached building sheltering a visitor center.

Caerphilly Castle (five miles north of Cardiff): You enter by a water-filled moat. There's a leaning tower, Pisa-like, albeit nearly destroyed by Cromwell; an imposing keep; and formidable fortifications. Caerphilly dates to the thirteenth century, and history-knowledgeable Welsh can reel off the battles it has known.

Carmarthen, a small town in the interior as one heads west from Cardiff, is stopover territory, if only to see midtown, twin-towered remains of its once proud castle. Edward I restored this twelfth-century work two centuries after it went up. Have a look at the town's *Roman amphitheater* and the onetime *Bishop's Palace* (the chapel still is to be seen) now housing a museum of regional lore and history.

Tenby, a small southwestern port, has two monuments. The National Trust operates its *Tudor Merchant's House* on Quay Hill. Narrow, stone-walled, single-gabled, it dates to the fifteenth century and is nicely furnished in period. *Tenby Castle*, alas, is in ruins, but what remains—its five-arched west gate particularly—stands out in silhouette high on a hill backing the pretty harbor.

Pembroke Castle (Pembroke) is dominated by its 80-foot-high keep, beloved for its romantic, water-flanked setting, which impresses at least as much as the largely ruined interior where, it is worth noting, Harri Tudur (to use the Welsh spelling)—who grew up as Henry VII, first of Britain's Tudor dynasty—was born.

Haverfordwest, not unlike Carmarthen (above), is graced by a mid-town ruined castle, built in the twelfth century. Beyond town in *Picton Castle*, a private residence, is a mini-museum whose subject matter is the work of the contemporary English painter, Graham Sutherland, gifts from him in appreciation of the inspiration afforded by the area, where he worked over the years.

St. David's is the eye-filling little town overlooking a bay at Wales's westernmost point, a stretch of coast that is the Principality at its comeliest. But hold, there's more: *St. David's Cathedral*, built into an unusual hollow, is one of Britain's most beautiful, named for the locally born saint—Dewi Sant, in Welsh—who, as a bishop-abbot, founded a dozen monasteries in the sixth century and was sainted because of his zeal in promoting Christianity. He is, to this day, Wales's patron saint and national hero. (St. David's Day—March 1—is celebrated as the Welsh national festival, not only in Wales, but by Welsh communities the world over.)

William the Conqueror himself prayed at the original St. David's in 1081, but the current cathedral was begun in the following century. Although it is now essentially early Gothic, original Romanesque arches lining the nave still are to be seen. Look up as you walk about at the meticulously carved oak ceiling, the asymmetrical choir screen, the amusing themes of the misericords (carved-wood folding seats of the choir), and the royal stall, reserved for sovereigns but used only by two: Edward I in 1284 and Elizabeth II exactly 671 years later, with a still-in-place needlepoint cushion to mark the occasion. Take your time in the St. David's area, strolling the town (the main square is picture-book) and the area—scenic *Solva; Fishguard*, with John Cleal's Artists' Workshop; and *Newport*, with its Georgian houses and antique shops.

THE CENTER AND THE NORTH

Aberystwyth is the coastal town noted as the site of the Principality's most prestigious university; ruined *Aberystwyth Castle*, overlooking the town (go up if only for the views along the coast); the *National Library of Wales*, doubling as a museum with exhibits not only of manuscripts and other historic documents, but of special treasures, including a set of 50 Thomas Rowlandson drawings executed by the cartoonist in the course of a late eighteenth-century Wales tour; Aberystwyth University's *Art Centre Gallery*, with displays both temporary and from its permanent collection; *Aberystwyth Cliff Railway*, for cable-car journeys up Constitution Hill; and *Nanteos*, an eighteenth-century house two miles southeast of town, furnished with Georgian and Victorian objects.

Harlech: Wales's principal castle towns have a nice perk to them, none more so than Harlech. Go first to *Harlech Castle*, majestic on its own rocky eminence commanding the town. Tremadog Bay, as well as Mount Snowdon and neighboring peaks of Snowdonia National Park. One of Edward I's most important castles, Harlech warrants exploration. Each of the four circular towers punctuating its high wall had a distinct function; today you may visit what had been a prison and chapel among this quartet, making your rounds, as did troops over the centuries, on walkways atop the walls.

It's fun to amble about the compact town directly beneath the castle and to swim from its white-sand beach. Allot time for a look around *Snowdonia National Park*, via foot (following park-created walking tours), horse, pony, car, or bus, making use of the tips and literature from the *Snowdonia National Park Visitor Centre*, which you're bound to pass as you explore the High Street. Two good hotel-towns are nearby: *Dolgellau*, about 20 miles southeast, and *Portmeirion*, about 10 miles north.

Caernarvon: With its continuing royal associations and functions, it should come as no surprise that *Caernarvon Castle* is the most impressive—and, I might add, the costliest to enter—of the Welsh fortifications. Its location—a point at the edge of a tourist-trod (and tourist-trappy) town taking its name, with the Seiont Estuary and Menai Strait (leading to the Irish Sea) framing it—is at once strategic and scenic. And its design is ingenious: two gargantuan courts that conne'ct, near the moated main entrance, with no less than nine octagonal towers and a pair of double gatehouses inserted into massive walls. *Queen's Gate* is where the sovereign introduces the Prince of Wales to the people, upon investiture. A museum, with photos of the investitures, is in the North East Tower. Take in, as well, the chapel in the Gate Tower, *Caernarvon Historical Museum* in the Eagle Tower, and the *Royal Robing Room* in the Chamberlin Tower. Pause, then, in a café on Bridge Street, leading from Castle Square, just outside, before visiting the town, whose monuments include Gothic *St. Mary's Church*, with a long castle association; the waterfront Promenade adjacent to St. Mary's; and *Segontium Fort and Museum* (Constantine Road), which was the westernmost outpost of the Roman Empire. You're ready, then, for a ride—allow a half day—to the top of Mount Snowdon, Wales's highest peak (3,560 feet), aboard the *Snowdon Mountain Railway* at Llanberis. Unless you would rather explore the Snowdon foothills on the back of a pony or horse—most gentle enough for novice equestrians—from *Snowdonia Riding Stables*, at nearby Waunfawr.

Plas Newydd (a mile southwest of Llanfairpwll) is, for me at least, the most beautifully situated of the Welsh country houses—on an eminence above Menai Strait, with views, as well, of Snowdonia peaks. Essentially the work of eighteenth-century architect James Wyatt, it is Gothic Revival without, partially Georgian inside, with the Music Room its grandest interior, a sumptuous main hall-cum-staircase, and half a dozen additional principal rooms on two floors, the lot of them hung with paintings by artists including Ramsay (George III and Queen Charlotte), Lawrence (Marquess of Anglesey, and early owner), Hoppner, and Laguerre. Café. National Trust.

Bangor's in-town treat is little—and little-known—two-tower *Bangor Cathedral* (High Street), interesting as much for its modest proportions as for the mix of architecture; originally Norman, with Gothic and mock-Gothic embellishments. A mile east is *Penrhyn Castle*, among the rare species of architecture dubbed neo-Norman—an early nineteenth-century variation of Romanesque. It's a fairy-tale castle, with a towering keep (actually a bedroom wing), archers' towers, and crenellated battlements. State rooms are of heroic proportions—great hall, drawing room, dining room, and, most curious, the depressing ebony room—which, in gray and black, was expressly designed for family funerals. Queen Victoria slept in the gargantuan oak bed of the state bedroom; her son, Edward VII, when Prince of Wales, slept in a nearby chamber. Café. National Trust.

Conwy (also spelled Conway) is the town bearing the name of the last of the network of Edward I's thirteenth-century fortresses. *Conwy Castle* hugs the shore, with yachts and motorboats bobbing in the waters of the town's bay. The castle's 125-foot-long great hall was headquarters for its constable. There are a pair of towers and, in the inner court, the suite that had been a Conwy home away from home for Edward I and his consort. Conwy town is special: Don't fail to notice its walls; they've a score-plus towers and are unique in Britain. On High Street, pay a visit to *Aberconwy House*, only a century younger than the castle and now an absorbing National Trust-operated historical museum.

Chirk Castle (10 miles east of Llangollen and 30 miles south of Ruthin—two agreeable towns suitable for headquartering in the northeast) is a medieval fortress from without, a mostly Georgian mansion within. Indeed, of the Welsh country houses, only Powis Castle (below) is grander. Originally an Edward I castle, Chirk eventually passed to Sir Thomas Seymour, who married Queen Catherine Parr, widow of Henry VIII. Later, Elizabeth I gave it to her adored courtier, the Earl of Leicester. Later still, it became the property of the Myddleton family, still resident. The saloon—coffered ceiling, Mortlake tapestries vying with a portrait of Queen Anne by Kneller, and eighteenth-century furniture—is the finest room. But the drawing room with Kneller and Romney portraits and the long gallery (with an ebony cabinet given by King Charles II to a seventeenth-century Myddleton) are important, too. And there's a bed in which Charles II's father, Charles I, slept.

Powis Castle (just south of Welshpool and about 30 miles south of Llangollen) ranks, with Chirk, as the premier Welsh country residence. It looks like a Gothic castle when seen from its exquisitely terraced gardens. But it is essentially seventeenth-century. Powis's seigneurs, the Marquesses—now Earls—of Powis, became linked through marriage with the eighteenth-century hero of India, Lord Clive, many of whose treasures grace the castle. You want time for the formal Orangery and garden and, inside, the dining room with elegant plasterwork, Chippendale furniture, and paintings by Romney, Reynolds, and Nathaniel Dance; frescoed library; and state bedroom, in whose bed slept George V and Queen Mary on one occasion, and their son, Edward VIII, on another. Café. National Trust.

Erddig (18 miles southeast of Ruthin and 12 miles northeast of Llangollen): There are more beautiful eighteenth-century houses than Erddig (not that the quality of the furniture in its state rooms—canopied bed in the state bedroom, Queen Anne chairs in the tapestry room, Regency chairs in the dining room—is not superior). But the special quality of this house is its servants' quarters. In no other British country house that I know is it possible to get better insight into the "downstairs" segment of the country-house life than here, with paintings of ten eighteenth- and nineteenth-century servants in the servants' hall, housekeeper's room furnished as it was a century back, agent's office, blacksmith's shop, sawmill, laundry and bakehouse. Worth noting, with respect to the staff portraits: Various generations of the owning Yorke family painted them, appending tributes to the subject of each—in verse. Restaurant. National Trust.

St. Asaph Cathedral (in the little town taking its name, not far inland from the north coast) is the smallest such in Britain. First built in the sixth century and seat of a bishop of The Church in Wales (which is what the Anglican denomination is called in the Principality), it is named for an early local saint, straddles its own hill, and is cruciform in shape, partly medieval, and largely a mid-nineteenth-century restoration by the celebrated church architect of that period, Sir George Gilbert Scott. Note the remaining fifteenth-century stalls, ascend to the tower for a valley view, and take in the cathedral's unusual museum of ancient artifacts. On your way down the hill, pop into atmospheric, originally fifteenth-century *St. Asaph Parish Church.*

SETTLING IN

Angel Hotel (Castle Street, Cardiff) is Cardiff's *grande dame*—and likable from the moment you enter the lobby, Waterford-chandeliered and with a knock-'em-dead grand stairway, pair of lovely lounges—for coffee in the morning, tea in the afternoon—adjacent Louis XVI-style restaurant, contemporary grill, and two filled-with-locals bars. Just over 80 of the 100 comfortable rooms have baths. *First Class.*

Park Hotel (Park Place, Cardiff) is a long-on-scene house that has been stylishly refurbished, with the motif traditional and showers in all 108 rooms' baths. Two attractive restaurants, dark-paneled bar-lounge. A Best Western hotel. *First Class.*

Cardiff Centre Hotel (Westgate Street, Cardiff) is more functional than beautiful; all of the 160 compact rooms have showers in their baths, and there are a restaurant and a pair of bars, one of which serves casual meals. *Moderate-First Class.*

Sandringham Hotel (St. Mary's Street, Cardiff): You must not expect anything like the royal residence, similarly named, in East Anglia. But the Sandringham has the virtue of a central situation, well-equipped rooms (just under 30), restaurant and bar. *Moderate.*

Ivy Bush Royal Hotel (Spilman Street, Carmarthen) is convenient as a stopover spot in the course of southern exploration. It's low-slung and modern and has baths in 81 of its 104 neat rooms; restaurant, bars. Trusthouse Forte. *First Class.*

Royal Lion Hotel (High Street, Tenby) occupies a nicely modernized house of yore, central, with baths in most of the 21 rooms and views of the harbor from front ones. Restaurant, bar. *Moderate.*

Robeston House Hotel (Robeston Wathen, near Narberth, which is near Haverfordwest): Complex address, to be sure, but this gracious country house—though small in capacity, with but six rooms, only three of which have bath—is a find. I wish Grahame and Pamela Barrett would install facilities in the three bathless rooms, but their hotel's lounges and top-notch restaurant are among the most attractive I know in the Principality. And they sell jars of their own marmalade! *First Class.*

Mariners Hotel (Mariners Square, Haverfordwest) dates to the eighteenth century; the facade lures you in. More than half the bedrooms have baths. Restaurant, bars. *Moderate.*

Warpool Court Hotel (St. David's) occupies a multigabled stone structure in its own capacious compound at the edge of town and has the virtue of showers in the baths of 9 of its 25 rooms, whose mattresses, however, tend to be soft. Restaurant, bar, swimming pool. *Moderate-First Class.*

St. Non's Hotel (Catherine Street, St. David's) is at once well equipped, close to the cathedral, and friendly, with 20 functional rooms; attractive, good-value restaurant; pair of bars. *Moderate.*

Golden Lion Hotel (Lion Street, Dolgellau): A dozen of the 30 charming, comfortable rooms in this venerable, twin-gabled stone house have baths. The restaurant is super, the bar delightfully Victorian. Lovely. *Moderate-First Class.*

Royal Ship Hotel (Queen's Square, Dolgellau) went up as a coaching inn in the early years of the last century and retains the charm and ambience that come with age. Only 5 of the 28 rooms have bath. Inviting restaurant and bar. *Moderate.*

Bontddu Hall Hotel (just outside Bontddu, a hamlet that is just outside of Dolgellau): Elegance is not often come across in Wales—to understate the case. Bontddu Hall is a major exception—a century-old country house in a sumptuous, parklike garden overlooking an estuary, flanked by mountains, and flowing into the sea. The interiors fairly bristle with style, melding the contemporary with the antique. No two of the 26 rooms, 4 of which are suites, are quite alike, although most have ravishing views. Lounges are a delight for tea or a drink. Exceptional restaurant. *Luxury.*

George III Hotel (Penmaenpool, just outside Dolgellau) is an agreeable resting spot in the course of neighborhood exploration, with a dozen nice rooms in two low-slung pavilions; the half in the newer building all have baths with hand-shower attachments. Restaurant, bar. Pretty setting. *Moderate-First Class.*

St. David's Hotel (Promenade, Harlech) has a super, over-the-sea setting, just below the core of town, with an 18-hole golf course and a heated swimming pool adjacent. Many of the 80 rooms have baths. Restaurant, bar. *Moderate-First Class.*

Portmeirion Hotel (Penrhyndeudraeth, near Harlech) dates to the 1920s, when it became part of a curious fantasy-village that preceded Disneyland by a few decades and continues as a mass-appeal visitor attraction. The complex is too spread out for my taste, and I don't care for the amusement-park flavor of the "village." You, of course, may feel otherwise. At any rate, there are 50 no-two-alike rooms in the vividly decorated main hotel building and surrounding cottages; not all have baths. Restaurant, bar. *First Class.*

Royal Goat Hotel (Beddgelert, in Snowdonia National Park) is indicated for an overnight stay in this scenic region. Almost all of the 18 functional rooms have bath. Restaurant, bars. *Moderate.*

Royal Hotel (North Road, Caernarvon), originally a coaching inn with a still-pleasing facade, has a central situation and baths in all but 4 of its 72 rooms. Restaurant, bar. *Moderate.*

Stables Hotel (Llanwnda, Caernarvon) has the disadvantage of being three miles south of town, but the virtues of modernity—all 12 motel-style rooms have showers in their baths—and a good restaurant. Bar-lounge, outdoor pool. *Moderate.*

Castle Hotel (High Street, Conwy) is elderly but updated, with baths in 20 of its 22 well-equipped rooms, a restaurant with good-value table d'hôte menus, and a bar where casual lunches are served. Trusthouse Forte. *Moderate.*

Ruthin Castle Hotel (Corwen Road, Ruthin): This hotel—in a beautiful 30-acre park edging one of North Wales's more attractive old towns—is a genuine medieval castle, crenellated tower and all, with interiors that blend Victorian with contemporary, not always with esthetic grace. But no matter. Rooms are comfortable, and the restaurant is, by Welsh standards, exceptional. *First Class.*

Castle Hotel (St. Peter's Square, Ruthin) goes back to the eighteenth and sixteenth centuries in its two contiguous buildings on Ruthin's main square. Bedrooms vary—ask for an older one—but most have baths; there are 30, all told. It has a restaurant and two bars. Charming. *Moderate.*

Royal Hotel (Bridge Street, Llangollen) is a lovely old house on the banks of the River Dee, near the landmark medieval bridge of this atmospheric old town. There have been considerable guests since the house took its present name after Queen Victoria—still a princess—visited with her Mum, the Duchess of Kent, in 1832. The 32 rooms are all functional, but you want one with a view. Restaurant, bars. Trusthouse Forte. *First Class.*

Hand Hotel (Bridge Street, Llangollen) is quite as felicitously situated as the Royal (above), with attractive public areas, including an interesting bar and restaurant, as well as nearly three-score pleasant rooms. A Best Western hotel. *First Class.*

Trelydan Hall (a mile and a half north of Welshpool): Iona Trevor-Jones, a modern-day Renaissance Woman, at once TV horticulturist, folklorist, historian, international good-will promoter of the Principality, and—more to the point, here—winner of the Prince of Wales Award for the skilled refurbishing of the half-gabled Tudor manor house that she shares with the public on guided tours and as a guest house. There are just half a dozen rooms—each immense, antiques-furnished and with its own bath—in this lovely mansion, the main-floor rooms of which are furnished in Tudor style. You dine with Mrs. Trevor-Jones and her personable husband, John, in the candlelit family dining room. And breakfasts are among Britain's most special. Vive Iona! *First Class.*

Bodysgallen Hall Hotel (just outside the resort of Llandudno on the North Coast) is a remarkable seventeenth-century manor house set in a seven-acre garden. It has been skillfully converted into Wales's premier hostelry. Public spaces are striking—oak-paneled entrance hall; drawing room up a flight, with a pair of fireplaces and dramatically tall mullioned windows; restaurant embracing two elegant salons (menus have a Welsh-Anglo-French twist, and wines are distinguished); comfortable bar where guests get to know each other; and just under 20 antiques-accented rooms, with 9 cottage suites, to boot. Same skilled management as York's Middlethorpe Hall Hotel. Member, Prestige Hotels. *Luxury.*

DAILY BREAD

Gibson's (Romilly Crescent, Cardiff) is a five-minute drive from the center but rewarding, for, though it's Welsh-operated, the fare is authentic—and delicious—French. Owner Irene Canning alternates with evenings devoted to the specialties of various provinces—Provence, Normandy, Alsace, Burgundy, the Loire. Unpretentious, welcoming. *First Class.*

Harvester's (Pontcana Street, Cardiff) is owned by a Welsh-speaking Italian who is a talented chef, as well as a linguist, as witness his Welsh lamb roasted with rosemary and honey; other Welsh specialties like leek and potato soup, as well. *First Class.*

Nino's (St. Mary's Street, Cardiff) is conveniently central and the source of satisfying Italian standbys—minestrone soup, well-sauced pasta, veal entrées. *First Class.*

Ye Olde Wine Shoppe (Wyndham Arcade, St. Mary's Street, Cardiff): Count on a tasty meal—a daily hot special, reliable soups, steaks, salads. With a glass or two of the house wine. *Moderate.*

Howell's (St. Mary's Street, Cardiff) is a department store that obliges with its *Coffee Bar* for snacks and *Circles*, a licensed waitress-service restaurant, with table d'hôte lunches. *Moderate.*

Plymouth Arms (St. Fagan's, Cardiff) is a relaxing locale for a pub lunch in connection with a visit to the nearby Welsh Folk Museum. The steak pie is good, accompanied by a glass of lager. *Moderate.*

Queensway (Queen Street, Carmarthen): The upstairs wine bar of this two-story eatery is indicated for invariably reliable roast beef. *Moderate-First Class.*

Richmond (Castle Terrace, Pembroke) operates out of a delightfully atmospheric old house just below the castle; soups, salads, sandwiches, and very tasty sweets. *Moderate.*

Robeston House (Robeston Wathen, near Haverfordwest) is as much country hotel (above) as restaurant. Go for deliciously cooked, smartly presented dinners—*taramosalata* or avocado with Stilton sauce to start; roast duck, beef Stroganoff, or roast pigeon with cider and herbs as an entrée; Belgian chocolate biscuit cake or raspberry hazelnut crunch to conclude. *First Class.*

Cartref (Cross Square, St. David's) is pleasant for lunch or a snack in the garden, during the day, or a more formal dinner—à la carte only—that might be created around roast beef with Yorkshire pudding or grilled trout. *First Class.*

Harbormaster Hotel (High Street, Aberaeron), in a town of attractive Georgian houses, up the coast from St. David's, is a restaurant-pub rather than a hotel, with fried chicken and hamburgers big draws at lunch, lobster salad along with game and chicken pies the lures at dinner. Congenial. *Moderate-First Class.*

Bontddu Hall Hotel (Bontddu, near Dolgellau): Go for lunch on a fine day, and you'll be served at a white, wrought-iron table on the terrace overlooking Mawddach Estuary; have the table d'hôte or a salad. Candlelit evenings in the handsome restaurant are more formal, with a wide-ranging à la carte, including game, oysters, salmon, crayfish of the area, as well as beef and veal—and a set menu as well. Fine wines. *First Class-Luxury.*

Hwyrno's (Sospan, Dolgellau) is fun every evening, with what it terms its Farmhouse Feast—vegetable soup, roast honeyed leg of lamb that you carve at table, dessert, and wine—with harp music and Welsh folk songs as a bonus. Setting is the upper floor of an aged stone house. *First Class.*

La Petite Auberge (Smithfield Street, Dolgellau): A French bistro, of the kind you remember in, say, a village along the coast of Normandy: *coq au vin, entrecôte et frites,* other tasty standbys. *Moderate-First Class.*

Plas Bowman (High Street, Caernarvon) is in quarters that are but a century younger than the nearby castle. Your best bet is the table d'hôte, midday or evening, with local salmon among the entrées. Very pleasant. *Moderate-First Class.*

Shades of Green (Wellifield Court, Bangor): You've worked up an appetite inspecting the nearby cathedral or Penrhyn Castle. Well, have the daily special or a soup and salad lunch—or dinner, for that matter—in this wine bar. *Moderate.*

Celtic (Bangor Road, Conwy) satisfies with unpretentious lunches, more substantial dinners; local fish, simply but deliciously prepared, is good; meat entrées, too. *Moderate.*

Gale's (Bridge Street, Llangollen): The house *pâté* is super in this wine bar; so are daily specials. And so, I should add, are wines, of which there are an exceptional number. *Moderate.*

AFTER DARK
New Theatre (Park Place, Cardiff) is home base for the widely traveled Welsh National Opera, whose repertoire extends from Janacek's *The Makropoulous Case* and Offenbach's *The Song of Fortunio* to Verdi's *Il Trovatore*, Rossini's *The Barber of Seville*, and Mozart's *The Marriage of Figaro*; voices, in this country of singers, are beautiful; productions, likewise. The New has a theater company, too, and hosts visiting troupes.

Sherman Theatre (Senghenydd Road, Cardiff) is a two-auditorium house operated by the University College of South Wales, with presentations of university drama and music groups, as well as touring professional troupes.

Theatr y Werin (Pehglais, Aberystwyth) is the University College of Aberystwyth's venue for theater, opera, concerts, and ballet.

INCIDENTAL INTELLIGENCE
There are two annual music festivals of note. The Principality's major cultural event is the *Royal National Eisteddfod*, held on alternate years in towns of North Wales and South Wales, with choir competitions and concerts, over a week-long period, usually in August. The town of Llangollen is the fixed site, for one July week each year, of the *International Musical Eisteddfod*, when some 12,000 members of choirs and folk-song groups from as many as 30 countries sing, sing, sing— day and evening the week long. The Principality's international airport is at Cardiff, ten miles from the city center; flights to Paris, Amsterdam, and Dublin, as well as to English and Scottish points. *Further information:* Wales Tourist Information Centre, Castle Street (opposite the castle), Cardiff, and local information centers in towns throughout the Principality.

Acknowledgments

I suspect this book took shape several decades back when, as a student at Southampton University, I trotted into the Hampshire countryside on field trips with Professor Alexander Farquarharson and his wife, Dorothea. It was under the Farquarharsons' tutelage that I began taking notes as I traveled, and it was when Lady Wood, wife of Sir Robert Wood, late principal of the university, gave me a farewell gift of a picture album of neighboring Winchester, that the seeds of the present volume were planted. I acknowledge my debt to them and, in the course of repeated Britain-wide visits over the years, to other valued British friends and colleagues.

In the case of this project—researching and writing a book about a country that's actually three countries, as fascinating and complex as Britain—I have been fortunate, indeed, with support received from the British Tourist Authority, from the start. In New York, Lewis Robert, skilled and personable Director of Marketing for North America; Bedford Pace, razor-sharp Director of Public Relations; Bedford's colleagues, press officer Robin Prestage and Ann Onishi; and Robert Titley, Director of Information have been generous in their cooperation—I am more grateful to them than I can say. And I am equally grateful to their colleagues at British Tourist Authority's London headquarters, old friends with whom I have worked on many assignments, knowledgeable Press Facilities Officer Peter ffrench-Hodges and his astute associate, Catherine Althaus; no two Britons know Britain better!

Max Drechsler, research editor for my books, and a longtime Anglophile like me, has been of immeasurable help; so has still another Anglophile, my agent—and a frequent traveler in the United Kingdom—Anita Diamant. I'm appreciative, too, of the support of the Big Three at National Textbook/Passport Books—S. William Pattis, Leonard I. Fiddle, and Mark R. Pattis; and my skilled and sympathetic Passport editor, Michael Ross.

I want also to thank, alphabetically, the following friends and colleagues in England, Scotland, and Wales and on the western shore of the Atlantic, as well, for their personal kindness and professional cooperation: Malcolm M. A. Aitken, Brian J. Anderton, J. K. S. Bannatyne, Adam Barker, Douglas Barrington, O. B. E., Patricia Bascom, Peter Bates, Georgia Beach, Mary Berkett, Polly Booth, Doreen Boulding, Amanda J. Bowers, Ian Brett, David M. Brockett, Ian Brown, Isobel Bryant, Tony Byrne, Gordon Campbell-Gray, Donald Carr, Denis Carter, P. V. Christensen, Lord Crathorne, Judith Dagworthy, Richard Davis, The Duchess of Devonshire, Paul F. D. Duffie, Gavin Elwes, Humphrey M. Evans III, John Fanelli, Margaret Fotheringham, Eddie Friel, Linda Gallagher, Donald Gillies, Richard Grant, Maisie Grant, Paul G. Grunder, Mary Gunther, Linda Gwinn, Maureen Hamilton, Nicola Hancock, Tim and Stefa Hart, The Marquess of Hartington, The Marquess of Hertford, Alexander Hidalgo, Robert Heim, Judy Hoade, Mary Homi, Wendy Hopper, Tiffany Hunt, Judith James, Graham K. L. Jeffrey, Joy Johnson, Avril Jones, Virginia Kelly, Cherry Kennet, Barry J. Kirman, John W. Lampl, Molly Leigh, Nigel Le Noury, Michael Leonard, D. W. Lester, Tom Letham, Cecilie Lloyd, Al Madocs, D. S. McDermid, R. C. MacGilchrist, J. F. McGuire, Irene Mann, The Duke of Marlborough, Keith A. Martel, Julian A. Martyr, Peter Maxwell Stuart, Jayne P. Mitchell, Antonia Palmer, Sue Peter, Gillian Pope, David Prior, Paul Reynolds, Kirk Ritchie, Glyn Alban Roberts, Mr. and Mrs. David Robins, Robin Rue, A. R. Rushton, Peter Salmon, Simon Salter, The Viscount Scarsdale, Bob Schaeffer, Rachel Semlyen, Morris Silver, Paul Simons, Martin Skan, Sue Smith, Anna Span, The Countess Spencer, Michael S. Stoddart, Joan Stokoe, Kenneth Stradling, Christopher N. R. Strange, The Countess of Strathmore and Kinghorne, Neil Stumbles, Nick Tarayan, Patricia B. Titley, John J. Tovey, Mr. and Mrs. John Trevor-Jones, Graeme Tully, Peter H. Turner, Christine Tustin, David Twist, F. Paul Weiss, Sir Hamilton Westrow, Bart., Robert White, Teddie Whitley, D. D. Wilson, Jill Wiseman, and Mr. and Mrs. David P. S. Wrench.

R.S.K.

Index

ABOUT THE AUTHOR

Robert S. Kane's initial writing stint was as editor of the [Boy Scout] *Troop Two Bugle* in his native Albany, New York. After graduation from Syracuse University's noted journalism school, he did graduate work at England's Southampton University, first making notes as he explored, in the course of class field trips through the Hampshire countryside. Back in the United States, he worked, successively, for the *Great Bend* (Kansas) *Daily Tribune, Staten Island Advance, New York Herald Tribune,* and *New York World-Telegram & Sun* before becoming travel editor first, of *Playbill,* later of *Cue* and *50 Plus* magazines; he writes regularly for *Travel & Leisure* and leading American and Canadian newspapers, and frequently discusses travel on TV and radio talk shows. *Africa A to Z* was the progenitor of his acclaimed 14-volume A to Z series, which in turn led to creation of the current World at Its Best Travel Guides. A past president of both the Society of American Travel Writers and the New York Travel Writers' Association, Kane makes his home on the Upper East Side of Manhattan.